THE MIRROR OF TRUE WOMANHOOD

A Book of Instruction for Women in the World

BY

Rev. BERNARD O'REILLY, L. D.
(LAVAL.)

Published by Left of Brain Books

ISBN 978-1-396-31871-9

First Edition

Table of Contents

TO

THE MEMORY OF

MY MOTHER,

TAKEN FROM ME IN MY CHILDHOOD:

AN IRREPARABLE LOSS,

AND A LIFE-LONG REGRET.

IMPRIMATUR.

JOHN CARDINAL McCLOSKY,
ARCHBISHOP OF NEW YORK.

New York, Nov. 10th, 1877.

ARCHIEPISCOPAL RESIDENCE, QUEBEC, November 16, 1877.

REV. B. O'REILLY, New York.

REVEREND AND DEAR SIR:—I received in good time your letter of the 6th instant, with the first 256 pages of your last work, "The Mirror of True Womanhood."

Before sending you an answer I wished to read a few chapters of this book, and now I can but congratulate and thank you for it. It would be desirable to have this work translated into French, and circulated among our Canadian people, who, I am quite certain, would read it with interest and benefit to themselves.

Pray accept once more my congratulation and thanks, and believe me your devoted servant.

E. A., ARCHBISHOP OF QUEBEC.

CINCINNATI, November 12, 1877.

REVEREND AND DEAR SIR:—Thanks for your beautiful new book, "The Mirror of True Womanhood." Like St. Francis de Sales' "Devout Life," written, I think, at the suggestion of the Bon Henri (Henry IV. of France), it shows that, if we should look for the perfect religious in convents, perfection is also attainable in the world.

May God grant you the *multos annos* to write more books!

Yours sincerely,

J. B. PURCELL, ARCHBP. CINCINNATI.

278 OHIO ST., CHICAGO, November 12, 1877.

REV. DR. O'REILLY.

DEAR REV. SIR:—Your very kind letter reached me this morning, and it was followed in a few hours by the superb copy of your "Life of Pius IX." I am rejoiced to hear that your publisher has been compelled to commence a seventh edition.

The new work of which I have received the advance sheets to-day, "The Mirror of True Womanhood," is a work fitted to the times. It will be of vast service to many mothers and daughters in the Church, by showing them how they may practically conform their lives to the bright pictures of womanly virtue you have so felicitously portrayed. And if others outside the Church may be induced to look into your pages, how many may be saved who are eager to do good and live virtuously, and have no one to teach them! There is a vast multitude of women in this country marching toward a precipice of ruin, and it is a mystery to know what to do to arrest their downward progress. Many of them have no religion, and, though a man without religion is dangerous to society, a woman who is destitute of it is prone to be a monster.

I shall welcome your complete work with the highest satisfaction.

Gratefully your servant,

THOMAS FOLEY,
BISHOP ADM. CHICAGO.

The Author's Preface.

It is not without diffidence that this book is sent forth to take its place in the literature of Christian households. The form in which its teachings are imparted is novel, and may appear to many strange. But a word of explanation from the author may suffice to the fair-minded reader.

Ascetic works we have in superabundance; but these would not reach the class of readers for whom these chapters are destined, nor would they be taken up and perused in the hours which might be given to a work which is not professedly one of devotion. Perhaps, too, there may be found in the following pages instructions which will prove more attractive and profitable to its readers than the more arid lessons of the ascetic or the didactic writer.

The chief object which the author had in view in undertaking to write this book was to help, so far as his abilities permitted, in withstanding the spread of the prevailing naturalism, which is daily invading more and more our homes, the minds and lives of parents as well as of children.

If we can preserve the Home from its influence, by making of every mother a supernatural woman, living a life of faith, loving above all things self-denial and self-sacrifice, fondly attached to the heroic ways and virtues of our ancestors,—the Home, in our midst, will bring forth supernatural men and women, unselfish, pure, truth-loving, trustworthy, and devoted to the best interests of country and religion.

What is attempted here may encourage others to pursue the same theme with far better prospects of success. This holy emulation would in itself reward the labor bestowed on this book; and who knows but, imperfect as it is, it may bring happiness to more than one hearth, light to more than one mind, and nobler aims to more than one life hitherto wasted? It is not only the ripe fruits which Autumn pours into our homes that are treasured by young and old alike; the very last withered leaves which the storms of this dreary November weather whirl along the roadside, or through the forest wastes, may serve as a welcome couch to the benighted wayfarer or the homeless outcast.

And, dear reader, do not quarrel with the writer's method. A book written for pleasant recreation, as well as for solid instruction, cannot be like the broad surface of a royal river over which the largest and the smallest craft can move together without hindrance or interruption. Our path, in these chapters, lies along a shallow stream amid sylvan scenery: we can rest in the noonday heat beneath the shadow of some wooded overhanging crag, stretching our limbs on the green sward, inhaling the fragrant air, and soothed by the noisy river beneath as it frets and foams among the rocks, discoursing the while on the Home we have left, and on the busy world toward which we are journeying. Or, as we wend our way later along shady banks where the stream glides, noiseless and unruffled, as if it also reposed after a toilsome passage, we can discuss together the difficulties of life's road, examine the grounds of our hopes and our fears, propose in turn our ideals and aims; and thus beguiling the length of the way, forget the sultry weather, and the flight of time, till, with the declining sun, we descry afar the streamlet joining the broad river, where the river itself skirts the vast and crowded city, and mingles with the golden expanse of the vast ocean beyond.

Enjoy the shady and restful nooks you will find as you proceed from chapter to chapter; open your eyes to the prospects they here and there afford; and if they prompt you, in looking on the pleasant earth around, or in gazing up into the blue heavens overhead,—in picking up the simple flower that springs by the wayside, or listening to the sweet songsters of thicket and grove, to bless the Great Giver of all that is good and beautiful,—you will be grateful to your guide ere your journey's end.

As it will be apparent to the reader, frequent quotations have been borrowed from the works of Kenelm Digby, which have ever been especial favorites with the author. Nor can he abstain from expressing his thanks to the spirited publisher, who spared no expense in securing the very highest typographical excellence in the establishment of J.J. Little & Co., of this city, and in Mr. J. S. King, an engraver whose artistic skill will be admired in the exquisite plate which forms the frontispiece to our MIRROR OF TRUE WOMANHOOD.

NEW YORK, November the 25th, 1877.

CHAPTER I.

INTRODUCTORY.

Omnis honos, omnis admiratio, omne studium ad virtutem et ad eas actiones quœ virtuti sunt consentaneœ refertur.

All honor, admiration, and zealous endeavor is referred to virtue and to the actions which are conformable to it.

CICERO.

It is said of one of the most celebrated men of the last century, that, when a mere babe, he was made to love flowers and all beautiful things in nature. His father, a distinguished naturalist, would take the child with him into the garden, and while he was busied watering the plants and examining how it fared with each of them, he would place in the child's hands and on his lap bunches of the most lovely flowers. Whether or not it was an inbred disposition in the child, he would—so the story of his life relates—amuse himself with the bright and fragrant things, admiring and studying them more and more as he grew up, till this pursuit became an irresistible fascination; and thus, from botany to other departments of natural science, the student progressed, revealing to his fellow-men the wonders that he had discovered, and leaving behind him an immortal name.[1]

Even so is it possible to place in the hands and keep before the eyes of childhood some of the loveliest and most fragrant flowers of goodness, purity, and heroism which bloom innumerable in the Church of God, and thereby awaken in the innocent soul the sense of moral beauty, till the study and pursuit of all that is ennobling and elevating becomes an absorbing passion.

And talking of flowers, we are reminded of the story of that demented youth preserved among the graceful fictions of ancient Greece. He was a simple child, and would wander away into the neighboring woods and along

---

[1] Linnæus, or Carl von Linné, born in 1707, died in 1778.

the pleasant banks of streams. One day as he stooped down to drink from the deep, smooth current of one of them, he beheld his own face in the crystal mirror, and forthwith became enamored of the fair apparition, which he mistook for an inhabitant of the waters. And his passion and his madness grew apace, vainly appealing to the image which gazed up into his eyes, for words of love in answer to his own, till he pined away and died; and from him the beautiful flower Narcissus derives its name.

But in the deep, pure, and never-deceiving mirror formed by that bright, broad river of holiness of life, which springs in Paradise from beneath the throne of Christ, and flows down through the ages to us,—glorious figures appear with which it will be no madness to fall in love. For, to love them, to study their beauty, to imitate their loveliness, to become like to them in thought and feeling and word and deed,—is to become most truly the children of God.

In the Eternal Son of God become for our sakes the Son of the Virgin Mary, we have the Author of our nature living on earth, and displaying in His life the virtues which can make every child born of woman most like to Himself, who is at one and the same time our adorable model and our judge. Generosity, devotedness, self-sacrifice are the characteristic virtues of woman: in Him they shine forth with surpassing splendor; and, next to Him, the Blessed Mother,—so near and dear to Him,—is the most perfect mirror of womanly perfection. She is the "Woman clothed with the Sun."[2] She gave him the sacred body in which He practiced the sweet human virtues befitting childhood, boyhood, and manhood,—the deeds which graced the lowly home of Joseph and Mary at Nazareth, and those which adorned the three years of his public life, till His work was consummated on the cross. Enlightened and warmed by this close and continual union with Him, who is the true Sun of Holiness, during the thirty years of intimacy at Nazareth,—this Mother, blessed among women, could not help reflecting more perfectly than any other human being the thoughts, the aims, the sentiments,—the humility and the self-sacrificing charity of her divine Son. Thus her life was invested from this most privileged intimacy, with such a light of supernatural holiness, that it vividly pictured the life of Jesus. She had been closest, nearest, and dearest

---

[2] Apocalypse xii. 1.

to Him, had studied Him most attentively and lovingly, had followed faithfully in His footsteps from the manger to the cross, and was, when He ascended to heaven, the living image of her crucified love to all who believed in His Name.

We are all the children of these great parents, and are therefore bound to become like to them in mind and heart and conduct. None can attain to the eternal glory of the children of God in the life to come, but such as will have acquired this living likeness by generosity in imitating God's incarnate Son.[3]

It is precisely because women are, by the noble instincts which God has given to their nature, prone to all that is most heroic, that this book has been written for them. It aims at setting before their eyes such admirable examples of every virtue most suited to their sex in every age and condition of life, that they have only to open its pages in order to learn at a glance, what graces and excellences render girlhood as bright and fragrant as the Garden of God in its unfading bloom, and ripe womanhood as glorious and peerless in its loveliness and power, as the May moon in her perfect fullness, when she reigns alone over the starry heavens.

Nor is it for women secluded in the cloister, or consecrated by religious vows to the pursuit of perfection and the sole love of Christ and His poor, that our teachings are intended. It is for home-life—the home-life of the artisan and the lowliest laborer, much more than that of the lordly and wealthy—that this little book is calculated to bear sweet fruits of manifold blessedness and utility.

Religious Communities are so favored, in return for their generous devotion to the Divine Majesty, by graces so lavish and so extraordinary and by so exceptional a culture, that they resemble those royal gardens in which bloom the whole year round all the rarest plants, and most exquisite flowers of every clime. But it is the wife or daughter of the man of toil, crushed beneath her load of care and fatigue, or cooped up by night between the narrow walls of an unsavory dwelling in a crowded neighborhood,—that we would fain teach how to rear in the little garden of her soul those flowers of paradise, which will make her a spectacle to angels and to men.

---

[3] Romans viii. 29.

Among the latest heroines of sanctity those women who shine at long intervals of hundreds of years, throwing into the shade the brightness of very many of their contemporaries—like stars of surpassing brilliancy in some beautiful cluster in the firmament—is a poor little peasant-girl, St. Germaine Cousin, canonized with such extraordinary solemnity on June 29th, 1867. Farther on, we shall examine more leisurely the figure of this little French shepherdess, whose life, amid the mountain solitudes of Southern France, was made so bitter by a stepmother's cruelty, but whose soul soared above the hardships of her condition, to heights of holiness unknown to the great, the rich, the learned in her own day.

How many souls will look into these pages, who have it in their power, with His aid who yearns to help us toward the acquisition of all goodness and the most blessed fruits of all spiritual joy, to rise to these same heights of true womanly greatness, to that near resemblance to Christ and to her who is the Queen of all saints? We cannot say. But much is certain—that the living lessons reflected from reading must enable every heart which tries to understand them, to be better, stronger, braver, truer, even from looking, for a few moments, on the angelic features of any one of the heroic women reflected in our MIRROR.

CHAPTER II.

THE TRUE WOMAN'S KINGDOM—THE HOME.

> Who is not struck with beholding your lively faith; your piety full of sweetness and modesty; your generous hospitality; the holiness which reigns within your families; the serenity and innocence of your conversation?
>
> ST. CLEMENT, Pope and Martyr, *First Epistle to the Corinthians.*

We are about to describe the sacred sphere within which God has appointed that true women should exercise their sway, that most blessed kingdom which it is in their power to create, and over which the Author of every most perfect gift will enable them to reign with an influence as undisputed as it may be boundless for all good. The home of the Christian family, such as the Creator wills it to be, and such as every true woman can make it,—is not only the home of the wealthy and the powerful, but more especially still that of the poor and the lowly. For, these constitute the immense majority of mankind, and must ever be the chief object of his care who is Father and Lord over all. From him spring the laws which regulate all the sweet duties of family life, and the graces which enable the members of a household to make of their abode a paradise.

Hence it is, that when the Author of our nature deigned to become man and to subject himself to these same laws and duties, he chose not a palace for his abode, nor a life of wealthy ease, while upon earth, but the poor home of an artisan, and the life of toil and hardship which is the lot of the multitude. It was a most blissful design, worthy of the infinite wisdom and goodness. The human parents he chose were of royal blood, that the highest on earth might learn from Joseph and Mary how holiness can exalt princes to nearness to God, and how the most spotless purity can be the parent of a regenerated world. And he made all his human virtues bloom in the carpenter's home at Nazareth, in order that the poorest laborer might know that there is not one sweet virtue practiced by the God-Man, Jesus, which the last and hardest driven of the sons and daughters of toil may not cultivate in their own homes, though never so poor, so naked, or so narrow.

So, dear reader, standing on the shore of the calm and beautiful Lake of Galilee, near which our Lord was reared, let us see his humble home and his home-life reflected therein, as in a most beautiful mirror; and with that divine image compare our own home, and the life with which we study to adorn it.

There is nothing here below more sacred in the eyes of that good God who governs all things, and will judge all men in due time, than

The Family Home.

All the institutions and ordinances which God has created in civil society or bestowed upon his Church, have for their main purpose to secure the existence, the honor, and the happiness of every home in the community, from that of the sovereign or supreme magistrate to that of the most obscure individual who labors to rear a family. There is nothing on earth which the Creator and Lord of all things holds more dear than this home, in which a father's ever-watchful care, untiring labor, and enlightened love aim at creating for his children a little Eden, in which they may grow up to the true perfection of children of God; in which a mother's unfailing and all-embracing tenderness will be, like the light and warmth of the sun in the heavens, the source of life and joy and strength and all goodness to her dear ones, as well as to all who come within the reach of her influence.

The most learned men of modern times agree in saying, that the sun's light and warmth are, in the order established by the Creator, the sources of all vegetable and animal life on the surface of our globe. They regulate the succession of seasons, the growth of all the wonderful varieties of tree and shrub and flower and grass that make of the surface of the earth an image of Paradise. They give health and vigor to the myriads of animals of every kind that live in the air or in the waters or on the dry land, and to which, in turn, the vegetable world furnishes food and sustenance. The very motion given to the rain in falling, to the rivers in their course, to the oceans and their currents, comes from that sun-force,—as well as the clouds which sail above our heads in the firmament and the lovely colors which paint them. Nay, there is not a single beauty in the million-million shades which embellish the flowers of grove or garden or field, or clothe, at dawn or noontide or sunset, the face of earth and heaven, which is not a creation of glorious light, the visible image of His divine countenance in whom is the source of all splendor and life and beauty.

Even so, O woman, within that world which is your home and kingdom, your face is to light up and brighten and beautify all things, and your heart is to be the source of that vital fire and strength without which the father can be no true father, the brother no true brother, the sister no true sister,—since all have to learn from you how to love, how to labor lovingly, how to be forgetful of self, and mindful only of the welfare of others.

The natural affection by which the Creator of our souls draws to each other husband and wife, and which, in turn, they pour out on their children and receive back from these in filial regard and reverence, is the very source of domestic happiness. We cannot estimate too highly this holy mutual love which knits together the hearts of parents and children. It is as necessary to the peace, the comfort, the prosperity, and the bliss of every home, as the dew and the rain and the streams of running water are necessary to the husbandman for the fertility of the land he cultivates and the growth of the harvest on which depend both his subsistence and his wealth.

Let the dew and rain of heaven cease to fall on the fairest valley, let the springs of living water be dried up all over its bosom, and the rivers which brighten and fertilize it cease to flow but for a few seasons, and it will be like the vale of death, forsaken of every living thing.

Do you wish, O reader, to learn how the springs of true life, of true love and joy, may flow, unfailing and eternal, within the little paradise of your home? Then weigh well the words of the great Martyr-Pope placed at the head of this chapter. These point out the virtues and qualities which should adorn every household in which Christ is worshiped:—a lively faith, a piety full of sweetness and modesty, a generous hospitality; holiness of life, serenity and innocence of conversation. Let us examine together how much there is in every one of these. We need not send to a great distance for one of those men famed for their skill in discovering hidden and plentiful springs of water beneath the surface of the ground. Their mysterious knowledge and the use of their magic wand are useless here. For, here we have seven pure and exhaustless wells of living water, created for our home by the Maker of all things, and placed ready to our hand for every need.

And, first of all, is a lively faith. We Christians are given that eye of the soul which enables us to see the invisible world, as if the vail which hides it were withdrawn. God becomes to us an ever-present, most sweet and most comforting reality. The great patriarch, Abraham, was bidden, in his long exile, and as a sure means of bearing up against his manifold trials, to walk before God,—that is, to have God ever present before the eye of his soul. This sense of the Divine Majesty as a vision always accompanying us in our every occupation, in labor as well as repose—just as the pillar of cloud went with the Israelites in their journeyings toward the Promised Land—gives wonderful light to us in our darkness and difficulties, cheers us marvelously in distress and adversity, lightens the hardest labor and the most intolerable burden, imparts a divine strength in the hour of temptation;—for, what can we not undertake and accomplish, what enemy can we not resist and put to flight, when we feel that His eye is on us, that we have him there face to face, that his arm is ever stretched out to support and to shield us, and that all the love of his fatherly heart sweetens the bitterness of our struggle, and rewards our generosity in overcoming all for his sake?

Joseph and Mary at Nazareth were privileged above all human beings to behold that Wisdom which created the world living and laboring daily beneath their humble roof, and growing up into the successive perfection of holy infancy, boyhood, and manhood, while concealing his quality from the surrounding multitude, and revealing only to a few like themselves his Godhead and his mission. It is certain, that he practiced all the virtues and fulfilled all the duties of his age and station in the way best fitted to glorify his Father: he was enlightening the world, sanctifying himself, and marking out the path of life as truly for every one of us, during these long and obscure years of his abode in Nazareth, as when his teaching and his miracles drew around him all Galilee and Judæa.

And what an eloquent lesson was there, exemplifying that "life of faith," without which the existence of the Christian man or woman is barren of all supernatural merit! Christ, in the helpless years of his infancy and boyhood, when his life was one of entire dependence and submission, glorified and pleased his Father by solely seeking his good will and pleasure in obeying those appointed his earthly parents, and in accomplishing the obscure duties of his age. This lesson Mary and Joseph were not slow to learn and to practice. They read in the rapt charity with which their worshiped Charge offered to the Divine Majesty every day and hour and moment of these golden years of humility and toil,—this all-important law of life for the children of God: 'That the value of what we do does not depend on the greatness or publicity of the work accomplished; but on the spirit of love toward the Father with which it is undertaken and carried out; and that the pure purpose and offering of the heart is what God prizes above all else.'

It has been the constant belief and teaching of Christian ages that the lives of Joseph and Mary consumed in the voluntary poverty, lowliness, and toil of their condition, were ennobled, elevated, sanctified, and made most precious before God by being—after the example of the Divine Model before them—devoted to God alone, and animated by the one sole thought and purpose of pleasing and glorifying him by perfect conformity to his holy will.

The Mother who ruled in this most blessed home, beheld in the Divine Babe confided to her, the Incarnate Son of God walking before her in the true way of holiness, and, like him, she applied herself to set the Eternal Father constantly before her eyes, studying to make every thought and aim and word and action most pleasing to that Infinite Perfection.

When Christ had begun his public life, when the home at Nazareth was broken up, and Mary had taken up her abode with her kinsfolk at Capharnaum, the light of the Father's countenance, in which she had learned to live, accompanied her, and the grace of her Son's example continued to surround her like a living atmosphere. After the terrible scenes of Calvary and the glories of the ascension, she brought with her to the home which St. John and his mother, Mary Salome, so lovingly offered her, the image of her Crucified Love, as the one great mirror in which she could behold the new heights of sanctity and self-sacrifice which she was called on to tread with him.

Since her day who was Mother of our Head, Mother of the Church which she labored to beget and to form, and Mother of us all—since she quitted her home on earth for heaven—the image of the Crucified God has ever been the chief ornament, the principal light, and the great Book of Life in every true Christian home.

Not one saintly mother among the millions who have trained sons and daughters, ay, and husbands and dependents, to be the true followers of Christ, his apostles and his martyrs, when need was—but always his faithful servants and imitators;—who did not read in the ever open page of her crucifix, how she might best lead a life of self-sacrifice, and best induce her dear ones to be "crucified to the world."

But let no one fancy that, in placing before her this holy model-home of the ever-blessed Mother of God, it is the intention of the writer to urge any one who chances to read these pages to expect to equal in self-sacrifice either herself or her Divine Son. No: the aim of the instruction here given is to encourage all who look into this mirror to adorn their homes with some of the heavenly flowers which bloomed in Nazareth, to bring to the performance of their daily duties in their own appointed sphere, that lofty spirit of unselfish devotion to God which will make every thing they do most precious in his sight, transform the poorest, narrowest, most cheerless home into a bright temple filled with the light of God's presence, blessed and protected by God's visiting angels, and fragrant with the odor of paradise. It is merely sought to open to the darkened eyes visions of a world which will enable the burdened soul to bear patiently and joyously the load of present ills; to fire the spirit of the careworn and the despairing with an energy which will enable them to take up the inevitable cross and follow Mary and her Son up to heights where rest is certain and the promised glory unfading.

No—you shall not be asked to quit your home, or exchange your occupations, or add one single particle to the burden of your toil, your care, or your suffering; but she who is the dear Mother of us all will teach you by the silent voice of her example, how to bring the light of heaven down into your home, the generosity of the children of God into the discharge of your every occupation, and the sweet spirit of Christ to ennoble your toil, to brighten your care and your suffering.

Travelers among the loftiest mountains often chance upon calm, bright lakes within whose crystal depths are mirrored not only the blue heavens into which the eagle alone can soar, and the cold, ice-covered summits which only the feet of the most daring few have trodden, but the low and fertile hills around the shore covered with the green woods, the healthful pastures, and frequented by the shepherds and their flocks. It is to these lovely, safe, and accessible heights of virtue that this little book would guide the footsteps of mother and maiden alike.

And of such easy access is the height of purity of intention and living faith which should be the constant light of your home. It is characteristic of the depth and constancy of womanly affection that the thought of the loved one, during the longest and most painful absence, will suffice to sustain them and to brighten a life which otherwise would appear cheerless. Thus it is said of that truest of wives,

St. Elizabeth of Hungary

that during her young husband's long spells of absence at court or in the wars, she was wont to animate herself and her large household by the thought of how much he would be pleased, on his return, that they had endeavored to do every thing as they knew he would wish them. Elizabeth, before her marriage, had received from him, in a moment of bitter trial to her, a small pocket-mirror which gentlemen in those days usually carried with them. It was of polished silver, with the reverse adorned with a crucifix set in gems. She never parted with this dear pledge of his truth, often taking it out of her satchel to kiss it. During her cruel widowhood and when driven ruthlessly forth from her palace with her helpless orphans, she would continually hold this mirror in her hand, kissing the image of her crucified Lord and recommending unceasingly to his mercy the soul of her husband. Nor was this perpetual remembrance of him a source of prayerful resignation only; it also stirred her up to vindicate the rights of his plundered children. As she pleaded their cause before the Thuringian nobles, she would hold the well-known mirror in her hand, kiss it frequently, and press it to her heart, as if to warm herself to greater energy and eloquence. Nor were her nobles insensible to the spectacle of their young mistress's fidelity and truth to her earthly love.

In like manner, if the thought of God and the remembrance of his incomparable love have any influence on our lives, they will be the soul of all our actions, inspiring, directing, cheering, and sustaining us in all that we plan and undertake and suffer day after day.

St. Clement next praises in the Corinthians a "piety full of sweetness and modesty." Piety is a word of Latin origin, and, among the old Romans who first used it, meant that spirit of dutiful and generous love with which children do the will and seek the interests of their parents. This sense of free, generous, disinterested, and unselfish devotion to the happiness, honor, and interests of one's parents, is always contrasted with the selfish, mercenary, or compulsory service of a slave or a servant in a family. True-hearted children make their happiness to consist in seeking how they can best please and honor father and mother: what they do is not dictated by the fear of punishment or the hope of reward or the prospect of gain or self-gratification. The hope or certainty of delighting or pleasing or helping the dear authors of their being, such is the thought which prompts the labors or obedience of a loving child.

Not so the mercenary: his motive is to gain his wages. He bargains to do so much in return for such a wage. The happiness of the family, the interest or honor of his employers, their satisfaction or the praise which they may bestow, do not, most likely, enter into the thoughts or calculations of venal souls.

You have known, perhaps, in many families, daughters so noble-minded, that they were content to labor untiringly for their parents, placing their whole delight in doing all they could to lighten the burden of father and mother, or to make the home bright and pleasant for brothers and sisters, without seeking or expecting one word of praise and acknowledgment. This is the best description of filial piety.

Only transfer to God's service that same unselfish and generous disposition,—asking yourself only how much you can do to please him, to glorify him, to make yourself worthy of him, to make him known and have him loved and served by others,—and you have an idea of what piety toward God is.

Thus faith gives to the soul that "purity of intention," which not only makes the thought of God habitual, but enables one to lift one's eye toward the Divine Majesty in every thing that one does,—in labor as well as in repose,—in suffering as well as in enjoyment, at home and abroad, in company and conversation, as well as in solitude and silence. It kindles in the heart that flame of love which makes one burn with the absorbing desire of pleasing Him supremely. It is thus the foundation of piety, the motive power of every good work,—just as fire is the generating force of steam, and steam itself is the mighty force which annihilates distance on sea and land and transforms all the industries of the modern world.

The soul accustomed to keep God before her eyes in all her ways, cannot help being pious in the truest sense: nothing can prevent her from seeking in all that she does the Divine pleasure, and of esteeming all that she can do and suffer too little for so great a majesty and such incomparable goodness.

This piety—working ever beneath that all-seeing Eye—must be both sweet and modest: sweet, in the calmness and gentleness with which every thing is undertaken and accomplished; modest, in that no seeking of self and no consciousness of evil can disturb or overcast the limpid purity of a soul which reflects only the light and serenity of Heaven, and is divinely sheltered from every blast of earthly passion.

When we remember who these early Christians were whose sweet and virginal piety was praised by St. Clement, we are filled with astonishment at the total and sudden transformation which the truth of the gospel—the knowledge and imitation of Christ and his Virgin Mother—effected in the most ill-famed city of the pagan world and the most abandoned population known to history. The very name of Corinth was odious to the ancient Romans of the true republican era,—and when she fell beneath the Roman arms, she was utterly blotted out, lest the simplicity and austerity of the conquering race should become corrupt by contact with the voluptuous city. A Roman colony was afterward planted there, and Corinth arose once more from her ruins on that enchanted shore, shorn indeed of her greatness and power, but scarcely less infamous than her former self. It was like the alkali plains of our Western territories, where nothing seems able to grow but the sagebrush which saddens the eye. No sooner had St. Paul preached there, practicing all that he preached, than piety, purity, and modesty—all the gentle virtues of Mary's home at Nazareth—spread with the faith from house to house in Corinth, till the infant church there resembled a society of angelic men and women.

In soil deemed hitherto incapable of producing a single fruit of heavenly modesty, the cross of Christ had been planted; the curse of centuries was removed, and the land began to be fair with flowers of supernatural promise. What was the part of woman in this extraordinary renovation? Three women are mentioned in the New Testament as having been associated with the apostles in the work of planting and fostering the Christian faith in the beautiful city and its dependencies,—Prisca or Priscilla, Chloe, and Phebe, revered as saints from the apostolic times by the churches of the East and West alike. It was in the house of Prisca that St. Paul took up his abode when he first arrived at Corinth. Her husband, Aquila, was, like Paul himself, a tent-maker; for it was the admirable custom, even of the highest and most wealthy Jewish families, to teach every one of their sons some trade or handicraft, which might place them above want, and thereby secure their independence, when persecution or adverse fortune deprived them of country and riches. Aquila had been expelled from Rome by the Emperor Claudius just before Paul's arrival on the Isthmus of Corinth, and was working at his craft of tent-maker, weaving for that purpose the hair of the Phrygian goat into a much esteemed and water-proof cloth. Their common craft was a first bond of intimacy between the great apostle and this household; the Christian faith drew them still closer together. At any rate, though Priscilla and her husband opened their home and their hearts to the apostle and the divine message which he bore, we know from Paul himself that he would be beholden to no one for his support and that of his fellow-laborers in the gospel. Still that laborious and well-ordered household became the cradle of Christianity in Western Greece, the first sanctuary in Corinth where the Divine Mysteries were celebrated, and the word of God explained to the highest and lowest among the proud, cultivated, and pleasure-loving population. Not unlike Priscilla was Chloe, in all probability also a married woman, while Phebe, the female apostle of Cenchreæ, the eastern suburb and seaport of Corinth, was unmarried, a deaconess, and the first fruits, on that long-polluted land, of the Virgin-Life destined to be so fruitful of holiness in Christian Europe.

Priscilla and her husband followed Paul to Ephesus in Asia, a city scarcely less ill-famed than Corinth, where the devoted and energetic wife shared the mortal dangers which beset the apostle, and instructed in the Christian faith the accomplished and eloquent Apollos, who was sent to Corinth to continue there the good work so gloriously begun. When Paul was sent in chains to Rome, the noble woman and her worthy husband forsook every thing, risked even life itself to be near him, and to share his labors and perils. Priscilla's house in Rome became a church, a center of Christian activity and charity, and Chloe and Phebe's names are associated with hers in the heartfelt commendations of the imprisoned apostle, and the undying gratitude and veneration of every succeeding age.

Most blessed, therefore, of God and man was the sweet and gentle piety as well as the unbounded hospitality of these early Christian homes. But pass we not lightly over this great home-virtue of hospitality: this, and the two other precious virtues mentioned by St. Clement, we must reserve to the next chapter.

CHAPTER III.

The Home Virtues (continued)—Hospitality, Holiness, and Innocence of Conversation.

Let each one inquire in the Church for the poor and the stranger; and when he meets them, let him invite them to his house; for with the poor man Christ will enter it. He who entertains a stranger, entertains Christ. The glory of a Christian is to receive strangers and pilgrims, and to have at his table the poor, the widow and the orphan.

St. Ephrem, *De Amore Pauperum.*

Hospitality.

The Christian religion, beside inheriting all the divine legislation of preceding ages, and consecrating all that was ennobling and purifying in public and private life, perfected every virtue practiced by Jew and Gentile by assigning to each a supernatural motive and by assisting the weakness of nature with most powerful graces.

Doubtless in the most ancient times, men, wherever they chanced to live, were not altogether unmindful of their being sprung from the same parents, and the first impulse of nature urged them to open their house to the stranger as to a brother, one who was their own flesh and blood. In the patriarchal ages we find a higher motive superadded to that of common brotherhood: that to receive the stranger, was to discharge a debt due to God himself—that to shut him out was, possibly, to close one's door against the Deity in disguise. Abraham and his nephew Lot gave hospitality to angels disguised in human form, and were rewarded, the former by the birth of Isaac, the latter by being saved with his family from the terrible destruction in which Sodom and the neighboring cities were involved.

Not dissimilar was the reward divinely granted to the poor pagan widow of Sarephta who harbored and fed the famished and fugitive prophet Elias, and to the wealthy lady of Sunam who sheltered Elisæus. Their generous hospitality was rewarded by the restoring to life of the only son of each.

But in the gospel, Martha and Mary made their home the resting-place of the Incarnate God, and their hospitality was accompanied by a public and unhesitating confession of their Guest's divinity,—and that, too, at a time when he was most opposed and persecuted by the leading men of the nation. Not only were they, also, rewarded by the restoration to life of their dead brother, but they had the further recompense of becoming the apostles of the Divine Master.

This was, moreover, the return made by Him to his Mother's cousin, Mary Salome, mother of St. James the Elder and St. John the Apostle, for the hospitality so generously bestowed on Mary, after the breaking up of her own home at Nazareth. The same may be said of that other Mary, the sister of the apostle St. Barnabas, and the mother of another apostle, John-Mark. It is the common tradition that her house was that in which our Lord celebrated the Last Supper, in which the Blessed Virgin found a refuge during the interval between the Crucifixion and the Resurrection, and in which the apostles and disciples were wont to assemble till the Holy Ghost came down on them.

Certain it is that there the faithful were wont to meet with Peter and the other apostles till after the martyrdom of St. Stephen and St. James, the imprisonment and miraculous liberation of St. Peter, and the visit made to him by St. Paul after the latter's conversion. Her home was the common home of the infant church of Jerusalem, and, as tradition affirms, the first Christian church in that city. This generous mother's hospitality was rewarded by seeing both her brother and her son called to the glorious labors and perils of the apostleship.

Thenceforward, the bestowing hospitality was for the mistress of a Christian household to receive Christ himself, the God of Charity, in the person of every guest who crossed her threshold, be he rich or poor, kinsman or stranger, friend or foe, sick or loathsome, the holiest of men or the most abandoned of sinners.

But we must reserve for another place the rules of hospitality to be observed by the mistress of the home and all her dependents. We are at present only pointing out the distinctive character and the ideal of Christian hospitality.

Holiness.

A holy house is one in which God is truly King; in which he reigns supreme over the minds and hearts of the inmates; in which every word and act honors his name. One feels on entering such a house, nay, even on approaching it, that the very atmosphere within and without is laden with holy and heavenly influences. Modern authors have written elegantly and eloquently about the home life which was the source of all domestic virtues and all public greatness in the powerful nations of antiquity. They describe, in every household, in the poor man's cabin as well as in the palace, that altar set apart for family worship, on which the sacred fire was scrupulously watched and kept alive night and day. No one ever went forth from the house without first kneeling at that altar and paying reverence to the divinity of the place, and no one, on returning, ever saluted his dearest ones before doing homage there. There, too, at night the household met for prayer and adoration, and there again with the dawn they knelt together to beg on the labors of the day before them the blessing of the deity worshiped by their fathers.

This altar and this undying fire were regarded as a something so holy that only the most precious wood and the purest material was employed to feed the flame. Nothing filthy or defiled was permitted to approach the spot; and every indecent word uttered or act committed near it was deemed a sacrilege. This hearth-altar, or hearth-fire, as it was called, was symbolical of the fate of the family. If it was neglected and allowed to die out, this was deemed an irreparable calamity foreboding the ruin of the home and the extinction of the race.

In the Christian home it is the flame of piety, ardent love for God, and charity toward the neighbor, which constitutes the hearth-fire that should ever burn bright. Old Catholic homes—how many of our readers will remember it?—were wont to have the cross placed outside as a symbol of the love for the Crucified which ruled all hearts within; and in the interior his name, as well as his image could be seen on almost every wall, informing the stranger-guest that he was in the house of the common Parent, and in the midst of dear brethren.

And how many of us may also remember the poor but cleanly cottage of the laborer, or the narrow room of city families, on whose bare but white walls there was no ornament but the crucifix, and no glory but that of the Holy Name written there as a seal of predestination?

Where the fire of divine love is fed as carefully, and the mother and her daughters watch as jealously as the Roman matrons and maidens of old that its flame shall never be extinguished, there is little fear that any conversation but what is "innocent" shall prevail. Purity and charity are the twin-lights of every home deserving of God's best blessing and man's heartfelt veneration.

What the Home Ought Not to Be.

The Spaniards say, "Shut the door and the Devil passes by;" the true woman who has read the preceding pages and understood the teaching conveyed therein, will know how to preserve her home-sanctuary from evil. It is, comparatively, an easy task to cultivate and cherish in one's own life and in the souls of those nearest and dearest to one, all the sweet virtues and holy habits indicated above, or connected with true piety. But how hard it is, when once evil habits have been formed, to resist or reform them! There are certain horrible skin diseases to which persons of the purest blood and most refined nature are most liable. And the terrible poison, sometimes caught by a breath or a touch of the hand, once deposited in blood hitherto untainted, will spread instantaneously, and commit the most fearful ravages.

So is it with souls highly privileged: a single voluntary act of sin may be followed by such a state of spiritual leprosy, that all their former beauty and glory appear changed into hideous deformity and seemingly incurable corruption.

Be careful to keep evil far away from the hearts of your dear ones; and close and bar the door of your home at all times, when you know that wickedness is abroad in the street or on the highway. Keep out the fatal influences which might weaken or destroy the precious boon of Christian faith in your household; bar and bolt your door against uncharitableness, immodesty, and that odious spirit of irreverance toward age, authority, and all that our fathers have taught us to respect and love.

And, O women who read this, learn here how to make your home, though never so poor and bare, lovely to your dear ones and an object of respect and envy to all who know you. This you shall be taught in the next chapter.

CHAPTER IV.

HOW THE HOME CAN BE MADE A PARADISE.

Malcolm (IV.), King of Scotland... shone like a star in the heavens; for, being prevented [supplied beforehand] by God in the benediction of sweetness from his tender years, he had a fervent love for God, and was of such pure conscience and gentleness of manners, that when amongst persons of the world he seemed like a monk, and, indeed, an earthly angel.

WILLIAM OF NEWBURY, *Rerum Anglicarum,* lib. i. 25.

How Saint Margaret, Queen of Scotland, Made Her Home Lovely and Her Kingdom a Paradise—How Every True Woman Can Imitate Margaret, and Make Her Little Home-Kingdom Sweet and Attractive.

This Malcolm was the grandson of St. David, and the great-grandson of St. Margaret, the blessed scion of a line of heroic kings. Let us see how the gentle Margaret transformed, by the irresistible ascendency of her womanly virtues, her rude, worldly-minded, and warlike husband into a saint, and all Scotland into a school of gentleness and piety. Her example will teach most eloquently how every truehearted woman can make all hearts yield to the influence of her goodness, and her own life be like a reservoir of living waters in a thirsty land for many a generation after her day.

Margaret, born in exile, reared in Buda in Hungary beneath the eyes of its apostolic king, St. Stephen (997-1038), returned to England in her early girlhood only to become an orphan, and to have to fly for dear life with her sister and brother across the seas. A storm providentially cast them on the shore of Scotland, where they found a refuge in the court of Malcolm III., or Malcolm Canmore (Greathead). Malcolm had himself tasted the bitterness of exile, having seven years before been obliged to fly to England after the murder of his father by Macbeth. St. Edward the Confessor, Margaret's grand-uncle, had warmly befriended the fugitive and enabled him to recover his own. So the generous Malcolm was but too happy to repay to the helpless descendants of Alfred the Great the debt of gratitude thus contracted.

Margaret was then in her twenty-fourth year, and had been during their long orphanhood a second mother to her sister, Christina, and her brother, the chivalrous Edgar Atheling. Her wonderful beauty and her angelic modesty, much more than her royal birth and the accomplishments due to the careful education she had received, drew on her the admiration of the untutored Scottish nobles and their warlike king. He was attracted by the manifold graces of the royal maiden; for hers were the supernatural virtues which he had learned to worship in Edward the Confessor, and which shone with a softened and gentler charm in the lovely exile. She became, a few months after her arrival in the court of Dunfermline, its mistress and the queen of all Scotland, to the unbounded delight of every class in the community.

It was a rude age, in a country which a long series of invasions by the Northmen, frequent wars with England, and perpetual feuds between the native clans, had kept half-uncivilized in spite of its Christianity. Providence had reserved for a woman, for this young queen, whose soul had been so chastened and tempered by a whole life of trial, to complete the work begun by St. Columba and his brethren five centuries before that.

Let a woman's hand trace the first outlines of the glorious picture of piety, charity, and patriotism offered in this queenly life of twenty-three years on the throne.

"Margaret was a true daughter of Alfred, and the traditions of the Alfred of Hungary (St. Stephen) were fresh upon her, and, instead of sitting down to cower alarmed amid the turmoils round her, she set herself to conquer the evils in her own feminine way, by the performance of her queenly duties. She was happy in her husband: Malcolm revered her saintly purity even more than he loved her sweet, sunny, cheerful manner, or admired her surpassing loveliness of person."

"He looked on her as something too precious and tender for his wild, rugged court, and attended to her slightest bidding with reverence, kissing her holy books, which he could not read, and interpreting her Saxon-spoken advice to his rude Celts."

"She even made him help her to wash the feet of the poor, and aid her in disgusting offices to the diseased, and his royal treasury was open to her to take all that she desired for alms. Sometimes she would pretend to take it by stealth, and Malcolm would catch her by her wrists and carry her to her confessor to ask if she was not a little thief who deserved to be well punished. In his turn he would steal away her books, and bring them back after a time gilt and adorned with beautiful illuminations."[4]

We have not, in order to form an estimate of the incredible amount of good done by this extraordinary woman, to depend upon legends or disjointed historical fragments. Her confessor himself, a monk of Durham called Theodoric or Thierry, composed a history of this most admirable and most imitable life.

The Scottish chieftains who were least inclined to reform their lives or refine their manners in emulation of Malcolm Canmore, could not resist the influence which drew them to Dunfermline, were it only to enjoy the privilege of looking upon a beauty which appeared to them unearthly, of being addressed by their royal mistress with a grace that borrowed more of its charm from piety than from courtesy, and of bearing with them to their homes some trifling present, which borrowed infinite value in their eyes from the angelic goodness of the giver.

She effected in the thoughts, the sentiments, the manners, and the morals of these hitherto untamed and unruly nobles, not a little of the same change which had taken place in the mind and heart and conduct of the king; and thus the blessed influence of her virtue and gentleness spread from above downward, through every class, till the lowliest peasants and the remotest Highland glens were made to feel the refining and elevating effects of Margaret's rule and motherly solicitude.

The court of Malcolm—from the boisterous meeting-place of turbulent and intemperate warriors that it had been for centuries—became the image of the court of Buda, where St. Stephen made Grecian culture and Magyar magnificence to reign side by side, blended and sanctified by the cross. "Not one of them (her nobles) ventured to use a profane word or make an unseemly jest before her. They had a rude, ungodly practice of starting away from table without waiting for grace, and this the gentle queen reformed by sending, as an especial gift from herself, a cup of wine to all who remained.

---

[4] Charlotte Mary Yonge, "Cameos from English History," vol. i., p. 98.

In after times, the last cup was called, after her, St. Margaret's cup, or the grace-cup."

"To improve the manners of the ladies, she gathered round her a number of young girls, whom she brought up under her own eye, and she used to sit in the midst of them, embroidering rich vestments for the service of the Church, and permitting cheerful talk with the nobles whom she admitted, all men of whose character she had a good opinion."[5]

From these young ladies she exacted that their homes should, in turn, become so many centers of zeal for the good of others; and thus every home in Scotland was benefited by the examples and teachings of the queen. But above all her other qualities shone her tender love for the poor and the sick. She founded hospitals and asylums for them; and among her nobles, her most especial friends and favorites were such as distinguished themselves by their active charities.

Fully aware that true religion is the parent and nurse of that great chief virtue, she bent herself, from the first year of her reign, to the task of making it flourish wherever the misfortunes of the times had caused it to languish, and to plant it by serious missionary labors wherever the missionaries had not penetrated or had only had an imperfect success.

She caused councils to be convened, encouraged the bishops and abbots to enact the most salutary decrees, supporting them with the whole force of the royal authority; obtained the erection of new episcopal sees, did away with every abuse condemned by the Supreme Pontiff, insisted on cordial and unqualified submission to his teaching; repaired churches and monasteries in decay, and built new ones in every place where they were most needed or promised to be most useful, and, above all, spared no effort and no expense to give to Scotland a thoroughly educated, exemplary, and devoted clergy.

While thus proving herself to be a true mother to her adopted people, she was not unmindful of her English origin or of the sufferings and needs of her countrymen. The wars between the two kingdoms which she was powerless to prevent, left many English captives in Scottish prisons. But her generosity and her influence found means to alleviate their condition and to hasten their ransom. She founded an hospital for sick and infirm prisoners, where they

---

[5] Miss Yonge, *ibidem*.

were tenderly cared for till they obtained their freedom; and for this purpose, she spared not her own purse, nor warm appeals to the generosity of the Scottish captors and the affection of the prisoners' English relatives.

Thus the veneration and love felt for Margaret in Scotland spread beyond its borders to every part of England; and from the nearest counties emigrants flocked across the boundary to settle in the Lowlands, and enjoy there the security and other manifold blessings bestowed on their subjects by Malcolm Canmore and his angelic queen.

There are other inestimable benefits for which Scotland has always acknowledged herself indebted to St. Margaret: the foundation of her great schools of learning, the establishment of a large and flourishing commerce with continental Europe, the encouragement of the liberal and the industrial arts, and the enactment of wise and enlightened laws protecting the liberties and fostering the best interests of the people.

Of the nine children with whom her union was blessed, one, Ethelred, died in infancy, the eldest, Edward, was slain with his father before Alnwick Castle in 1093; of the others, three sons, Edmund, Edgar, and David, reigned successively on the throne of Scotland, continuing the Golden Age inaugurated by their parents: of her two daughters, Matilda or Maud became the wife of Henry I. of England, and was her mother's living image, and Edith was married to Eustace, Count of Boulogne, becoming in her turn the mother of her people.

Surely it was a beautiful life, this of the tempest-tossed royal child, born in exile far away from the land of her fathers, and then cast by the storm on the Scottish coast, like a treasure beyond all price to be cherished by king and people, and to live in the hearts of all succeeding generations.

With the mirror of this most admirable life before us, let us see how every woman can in like manner make of her home a paradise, and be the loved and worshiped queen of the little kingdom which no one can take from her.

How the Poor Man's Home Can Be Made Rich and Bright and Delightful by a True Woman's Industry.

Lest persons who are not of princely station or noble birth should fancy that the lessons of St. Margaret's life do not concern them, we shall devote this section to showing how easy and necessary it is for the mistress of a poor and lowly home to imitate the sainted Scottish queen: women of wealth and rank will find practical instruction for themselves in the succeeding sections.

As it was to a poor and lowly home that the Son of God came, when he began the work of our redemption, as it was in the home of a poor mother that he lived so contentedly during thirty years, so, ever since, his followers have looked upon the dwellings of the poor with inexpressible love and tenderness. Ah! he is no true lover of Christ who is not drawn to the home of poverty and labor; and the spirit of Christ dwells not in the heart whose sympathies do not go forth to the trials and distresses of those who are, above all others, the friends of Jesus Christ.

But our concern is now with the wife, the daughter, the sister of the laboring man and the poor man; we wish them to understand what royalty of spirit can and ought to be theirs, in order to be the true imitators and true children of that great Mother, who knew how to make the poor home of Joseph so rich, so bright, so blissful, so lovely in the eyes of men and angels.

She, too, was of right royal blood who was the mistress of that little home where Joseph toiled and the Divine Child grew up in all grace and sweetness, like the lily of the valley on its humble stem beneath the shadow of the sheltering oak.

It was the lessons of Mary's life at Nazareth that Margaret had learned from her royal kinsfolk at the court of Buda, and had practiced so industriously through girlhood and early womanhood, till she became mistress of a court and a kingdom. One lesson above all others she was trained to practice from childhood—*to be forgetful of self, and mindful only of making every one around her happy.*

Woman's entire existence, in order to be a source of happiness to others as well as to herself, must be one of self-sacrifice. The first step in this royal pathway to all goodness and greatness, is to forget self. Self with its miserable little cares and affections is the root of all the wretchedness we cause to others, and all the misery we endure ourselves. Every effort we make to forget self, to leave self behind us, and to devote ourselves to the labor of making every person with whom we are bound to live, happy, is rewarded by interior satisfaction and joy. The supreme effort of goodness is,—not alone to do good to others; that is its first and lower effect,—but to *make* others good. So with unselfishness: the first step is to forget one's own comfort in order to seek that of others; the next is to forget one's own pains and suffering, in order to alleviate those of others, or even to discharge toward others the duties of sisterly or neighborly kindness.

We have known such great-souled women among the log-cabins of the forest settlements of Canada, in the crowded tenement houses and most ill-favored quarters of London and Liverpool and New York, as well as in the hard-worked manufacturing population of the New-England towns and the poor slaves of Maryland: women animated, enlightened, and moved in all their actions by the Spirit of God,—the Spirit who filled Mary at Nazareth, Elizabeth in her mountain home, and Margaret of Scotland amid the manifold cares and duties of a kingdom.

What our country,—indeed, what every Christian country under the sun,—needs most, are these great-souled wives, mothers, and sisters in the dwellings of our over-burdened laborers; women for whom the roof above them and the four walls which inclose their dear ones are the only world they care to know, the little paradise which they set their hearts on making pleasant, sunny, and fragrant for the husband who is out in the hot sun or the bitter cold, beneath the pelting of the rain or the snow or the sleet,—who, poorly clad and shod, with his scanty fare of hard bread and cold tea, is working away for the little home and the wife and babes,—and who is singing in his heart as he bethinks him of the warm welcome that awaits him when the long day is over,—of the bright smile and the loving words that will be sure to greet him when he crosses the threshold of his own little Eden,—of the cheerful fire in winter and the humble meal made so delicious by the love that prepares it and the sweet words that season it,—of the rest and the security and the peace which force the overflowing heart of the husband and father and brother to think and to say that there is no spot of earth so dear and so blessed as the little sanctuary built up and adorned and made full of song by a true woman's heart.

O woman, woman! if you only knew how much you have it in your power to do,—with His assistance who can never fail us when we do our best,—to make true men of the husband of your choice, of the sons whom God has given you as his most precious treasures; true women, in their turn, of the little girls who are growing up at your knee,—to be, when you are gone to your reward, mothers blessed and praised by all who know them!

We have just spoken of the Divine assistance which never fails the soul striving earnestly to fulfill important duties and to do all the good she can. Think of the contract God entered into with you, when you entered into the married state and received at the hands of the Church the nuptial blessing. You were told that the matrimonial union had its model in the union of Christ with his Church, that his great love for her, which brought him to the Cross and binds him to be present on our altars to the end of time,—is the type of the great and self-devoting love which husband and wife should ever have for each other. Did you ever reflect, that when you put your hand in your husband's hand before the Church, giving him your heart and your life thenceforward,—that God, who is ever by the side of those who believe and trust in him, promised you a mighty wealth of grace to be all your own till death, enabling you to love your husband more and more daily, with a deeper and a holier love, to make your own life like that of the Church toward her Crucified Love, one perpetual act of devotion and self-sacrifice, giving him in his every need your own strong love to sustain and comfort and strengthen him, taking up his cross courageously, and cheering him to labor and to suffer, because you both know, or ought to know, *that God is ever with you?*

Were your lot cast and your home built in a treeless plain amid a dry and barren country, how you would thank the man who would dig for you at your very door a well so deep and so unfailing that its cool and sweet waters would ever flow forth, winter and summer, for yourself and your dear ones! And yet the great graces attached by Christ to the worthy reception of the divine sacrament of matrimony, form within your home, wherever you chance to be, a well of water for the soul's health and strength so divinely prepared, that no length of time can exhaust it. Why do you not drink of the waters of your own well?

We have just said how much the true woman has it in her power to do,—no matter how poor her home or hard her husband's lot,—if she only knew both the extent of her power to cheer his lot and the sacredness of the obligation which binds her to do it.

We now appeal to the experience and generosity of the wife, mother, and sister of the laboring man. There was a rapid sketch above of the comforts and delights of the poor hard-working man's home, when love and devotion were toiling to prepare a sweet rest for him when the day's work was ended.

Dark and Cheerless Homes.

But have we seriously thought of the number of homes made dark and cheerless and desolate and hateful to the husband, the brother, the son, and the daughter too, by the absence of that bright spirit of love, which works at home from dawn till sunset, to have every thing warm and pleasant and restful for the weary ones coming back after their eight and ten hours of labor?

If the devoted, God-fearing, sweet-tempered woman is rewarded by seeing her dear ones unhappy when kept away from the bright home she makes for them, and most happy when seated near the warm hearth and charmed with her smile and her voice, it is no less certain that the selfish, untidy, ill-tempered, and bitter-tongued woman succeeds in making home unbearable for every one who is dependent on her.

Why is it that so many men,—thrifty, hard-working, made to be and disposed to be devoted husbands and most exemplary fathers,—are driven, at the end of their day of toil, to find—not rest, indeed, nor recreation—in the neighbor's house,—but some distraction from the thought of their own comfortless home, some rest from the din and lash of the ceaseless tongue which is their torment? Why are so many, at length, driven to the tavern to seek forgetfulness in intoxication? Is it not because woman forgets to be loving and devoted and ingenious in the sweet arts of making her fire burn brighter on the hearth, and her own person more attractive to her dear ones by some little ornament put on to welcome the laborers at evening, and her humble meal made more appetizing by some of the many cheap seasonings that the poorest can buy, and her whole house shining with cleanliness and filled with the sweet music of her own delighted tones? Ah! love has stores from which can be borrowed without stint and at little cost kind words and warm smiles and a thousand other things which go straight to the heart thirsting for the endearments, the joys, and the repose of home. Why will you not be a queen in your own little kingdom, O wife, O mother, O sister, and make all hearts subject to you by this ascendency of your goodness and devotion?

There are worse consequences still,—especially in cities and manufacturing towns,—which are caused by the want of the wifely and motherly qualities described above.

Young people of both sexes who are forced,—perhaps from early boyhood and girlhood,—to seek for employment outside of their home, feel an imperative need of the rest and comfort and love of their own fireside, when the end of their long day of toil has come. Blessed is the mother who knows how to make their home bright and warm for them! But what shall we say of her who cares not to do so? or who makes her home intolerable to her dear ones?

This much is certain, that in our over-crowded cities, if not elsewhere, thousands upon thousands of hard-working young people are driven into dangerous company and corrupting amusements because they have no home to love, to be proud of, in which to find the repose of heart and body so needful for their age especially. There is in this a mine of suggestion for parents, for pastors, as well as for all persons to whom Providence has given the means and the will to prevent the ruin of our youth.

But far better than all explanations or dissertations may be the bright examples quoted in the next chapter. Before we come to these, however, let us complete the present subject-matter by showing

How the Selfishness and Folly of a Fashionable Woman Can Make the Most Magnificent Home Intolerable.

We wish the reader to understand the term "fashionable woman" in the odious or objectionable sense in which it is taken by the sound judgment of people of the world. With "fashions" in so far as they are unobjectionable and mark the changes in dress to which even the best and least worldly persons in society—men as well as women—have to conform, we do not mean to find fault; this would be foreign to our present purpose and serve only to distract the reader unprofitably. It will be seen by a glance at what we have to say, that our censure addresses itself to an exceptional class of wealthy women, whose number, unhappily, is increasing daily.

The home of the wealthiest, we take it, no matter how splendid outwardly or how magnificent and luxurious within, can be at best but splendid misery, where unselfish and devoted love does not preside over the household, provide for the comfort of every person there, and minister to their happiness by the bright cheerfulness without which the most gorgeous furniture has no luster, and the electric warmth of affection, without which courtly manners are but a lifeless show.

Here is a man who has fought a hard battle with fortune, but has won it at last. Like true soldiers on every field, he has not cared during his long struggle for many comforts,—luxury was beyond his reach. But now that fortune lavishes her favors on him, he wishes to enjoy life in a home that shall be, he hopes, a paradise. Would that many of our most thrifty and fortunate men, though never so upright and honorable, would remember the old pagan superstition about exposing one's bliss to the eyes of the gods or flaunting one's prosperity in the sunlight! The "loudest" wealth is never likely to yield unmixed or lasting felicity; this is better secured by quiet tastes, and the repose enjoyed in the shade and with the select few.

But our fortunate man has built and furnished a home so comfortable that only a companion who can be devoted to him is wanting to complete it. He has been attracted by a handsome face and a name without reproach. Perhaps, on his part, there has been none of that romantic feeling to which the superficial world gives the name of love; but there is in his choice the hearty purpose of finding one who will love him truly, and to whose happiness he wishes to devote his fortune and himself.

She is a woman, young, indeed, and stainless, but selfish and vain; fond of dress, of admiration, of display, and who is anxious to wed a fortune large enough to permit her to gratify all her frivolous tastes. Her husband had the ambition to succeed in business,—that ambition is now gratified; but he had other and nobler aims which he had to forego in the hard striving after wealth, and which now possess his soul. He would fain cultivate his mind, he would indulge his taste for such of the fine arts as make home beautiful and home enjoyments more delightful. In the wife's family were several persons noted for their culture and scientific attainments; indeed, an accidental acquaintance with one of these had led to a first introduction to the woman whom he had made his bride, and in whom he hoped to find a perfect sympathy for the intellectual aspirations which served to brighten the future before him.

But the literary tastes and scientific pursuits of her relatives had been this woman's aversion from girlhood; and her husband was not slow in discovering that there was not one particle of intellectuality in her composition. Her honeymoon, instead of being spent in traveling, was taken up with an unbroken round of receptions and parties. Her powers of endurance, when the ball-room or the theater were concerned, seemed to be unlimited; but, once in her privacy, she seemed never to think that her husband wished to enjoy her companionship, or that she was expected to converse with him, to play or sing for him, or to make a single effort at being his companion for a single hour. The afternoons were spent in the park, when her equipage had to outshine the richest, and her toilet was made to eclipse the most fashionable. The evenings, for the most part, were consumed in interminable sittings with her French maid, who decked her mistress out with incomparable art for the ball or the theater. The bridegroom had hoped that this thirst for display and dissipation would be quenched by the unlimited indulgence of the first year of married life, and that after this necessary infliction he should have the quiet of his home and the sweet company of his young wife. Besides, his health could not stand the serious disturbance caused in his regular habits by late hours and this unnatural changing of day into night and night into day.

The second and third years of his matrimonial life found him disappointed, dispirited, and utterly miserable, with the certainty, moreover, of having bound himself for life to a woman who never could be a companion to him, who had neither head nor heart, nothing, in fine, to recommend her but a pretty face, like a painted mask covering an empty skull.

His beautiful home became intolerable to him; and there is no knowing what desperate or downward course the heart-broken man might have pursued, if he had not been asked by one of his wife's relatives to accompany him on a scientific expedition to our Western territories. This offer kindled once more his purest ambition; and, after limiting to a very generous amount the monthly expenditure of his young wife, he was glad to escape from his home and to seek knowledge and fame in the field of science.

She, meanwhile, had but one purpose in life, *to dress*. At the death of a distinguished fellow-citizen she literally spent three whole days and nights visiting the most fashionable warehouses and closeted with the most reputed milliners, to find out what style of hat and what dress she might wear at the funeral, so as to throw the whole of "Vanity Fair" into the shade.

When the springtide of that heartless beauty had passed away, it was already autumn for her. The complexion which was her only charm had been early ruined by the reckless and needless use of cosmetics, much more even than by her feverish life of enjoyment. No splendor of dress could conceal the fatal decay, and no depth of paint could mask it. And with the consciousness of this premature decline, her fretfulness and peevishness made her intercourse intolerable, unrelieved as its dullness was by a single mental accomplishment, or a solitary conversational grace.

There are showy trees in our American forests whose brilliant flowers attract the eye in spring; but the flowers themselves are of an offensive odor, and they bear no wholesome fruit, while the wood itself is unfit for any useful purpose.

The husband, on his return from the West, sought relief from the dreariness of his home-life in the speculations of the stock-exchange, heeding little, if at all, the remonstrances of a wife he heartily despised. When last heard of, his name was mentioned as one of many ruined by some sudden fall in railroad stocks. His house and furniture passed out of his possession, and he was left alone with poverty, obscurity, and a wife without head or heart or even beauty.

CHAPTER V.

FURTHER ILLUSTRATIONS OF SELFISHNESS AND UNSELFISHNESS.

I have seen on earth angelic and heavenly manners, admirable beauties in this world, insomuch that the remembrance charms and afflicts me; for all that I now behold seem but dreams, shadows, and smoke. Love, wisdom, merit, sensibility, and grief, formed, in weeping, a sweeter concert than any other ever heard on earth, and the hearers were so attentive to this harmony, that not a leaf trembled on the branches, such was the sweetness which pervaded all the air around.

PETRARCH.

It is strange and amazing that those very women who are so delicate that the mere humming of a bee is sufficient to chase them from the most delightful garden of the world, should have the courage to introduce discord into their houses.

LE MOIN, *La Dévotion Aisée.*

How Husband and Wife Together Make a Happy Home.

In one of the exquisite books written by a contemporary author,[6] many examples and extracts are given, all tending to show how blissful is the condition of every family in which the principles of the Catholic religion are sedulously practiced by parents and children. In the house of Count St. Elzear—the son of a saint and the husband of another, the tutor of a king, the governor and savior of his kingdom; the gentle knight, the great-souled statesman, and skillful general, who died at twenty-eight, the idol and model of two nations—we have the perfect mirror of domestic government. It is not

[6] We mean Kenelm Digby. We here borrow from his *Compitum*, or the "Meeting of the Ways at the Catholic Church," book i., chapter iv.

easy to say, whether his wife, St. Delphine, and her saintly husband, are more to be admired for the supernatural virtues which shone in their lives, or for the practical common-sense which dictated the rules they established over their household and over their princely domains.

But, though Elzear had been reared as a saint from infancy, and had scarcely emerged from boyhood when they were affianced and married,—Delphine, who was by two years his elder (though only fifteen), became thenceforward the guiding and controlling spirit. Although intrusted, at so unripe an age, with the government of large estates in France and the kingdom of Naples, and finding himself at the head of so numerous a household, it was affirmed by the unanimous testimony of his servants, retainers, and subjects that not a sign of ill-temper or impatience ever betrayed a disposition naturally passionate and fierce.

His wife, who studied him so closely, wondered at this extraordinary mastery over self, and said to him one day: "What kind of a man are you, never to show anger or emotion when treated with insolence or seriously wronged?... Are you incapable of feeling resentment? What harm could it do to the wicked men who occasionally do you foul wrong, if you manifested a little indignation at their conduct?" "Why should I betray temper or give way to indignation, my dear Delphine?" was the reply. "Anger never serves any good purpose. Nevertheless, I shall let you into a little secret of mine. Know, then, that often enough, when wronged in word or deed, I do feel my anger swell up within me. But I never fail to recall how our dear Lord was treated in his passion; and say to myself, 'Even if thy servants did buffet thee and pluck thy beard, how much more outrageously was he treated!'" He died in 1323.

The Wrathful Husband Transformed by Patience.

In 1355, lived at Sienna, in Italy, a nobleman, Giovanni (John) Colombino, who was quite the opposite of St. Elzear. He was extremely irritable, and took no pains to master his temper. Coming home one day at his dinner hour, and finding that the meal was not ready, he flew into a furious passion, and began to upset and break the furniture in the dining-room. His wife—a holy woman—endeavored to pacify him, and, while urging the servants to hurry forward their preparations, she argued sweetly with her husband on the unseemliness of such displays of anger, and begged him to read a book, while she would go to aid the cook. He flung the book away from him, and stalked back and forth in his rage, while the lady hastened to the kitchen.

Presently, however, he began to cool down and to feel heartily ashamed of his weakness. So, picking up the book, he began to read it. It was the Lives of the Saints,—and in the mirror of their conduct he beheld the horrible deformity of his own life. From that hour there was a total change in Giovanni Colombino;—he became the wonder of Sienna, died in odor of sanctity, and added one more name to the long roll of Christian heroes, who owed, under Providence, their greatness and heroism to the irresistible influence of a saintly woman.

What an Angelic Daughter and Sister Did.

In the year 186—, a family, composed of father and mother, with three children, came from afar to live in a quiet suburb of one of our great Eastern cities. The father, Mr. S—, had been the heir to a considerable fortune, which he had first impaired by mismanagement, and then completely lost by involving it all in unwise ventures. He had been induced to come to the East by the offer of employment as bookkeeper or accountant in a large shipping firm. He took possession of his modest little suburban house under peculiarly distressing circumstances. His wife, a woman of uncommon beauty and goodness, was in the last stage of consumption, and the fatal termination of the malady was hastened by the fatigues of a long journey, the bitter cold of an unusually severe autumn, and the material discomforts of her new home. The cottage which the family had rented was old, damp, had been for some years untenanted, and was but scantily furnished and insufficiently warmed.

"I trust in you, Nora,"—gasped the dying mother, as she held the hand of the kneeling girl in one of her own, and with the other touched the bent golden head half in blessing and half caressingly,—"and I know God will help you." The priest, who had just brought to that death-bed the Divine Pledge of the eternal possession, was standing near, deeply moved by all that he had seen of these interesting strangers. The simple, enlightened faith and exalted piety of the mother, the angelic grace of the eldest daughter, and the helpless, hopeless expression of the poor father, as he supported the younger child,—fragile, fair-haired, and dazzlingly beautiful, but with consumption written on her wan cheek and wasted form,—all that went to his heart and kept him there till the divine messenger, Death, had performed his errand. An only son, a lad of eighteen, apprenticed to a civil engineer, was absent, and could only reach the house of mourning as they were about to set out for the church and the cemetery.

When the priest, with moist eyes, summoned courage to say to the remaining parent and his offspring, that all was over, and that one more saintly soul had gone to her rest and reward,—Nora, startled by an exclamation from her father, turned round to see her sister apparently lifeless in his arms. "O my darling, my darling!" she said as she raised the rigid form and covered its face with her tears and kisses; "you must not leave me now! Oh! God will not take you from me!"

The priest, with a few earnest words of sympathy in the father's ear, hastened away, when the fainting girl revived, promising to return soon and obtain for these afflicted ones all the aid they needed in their bereavement.

A few weeks deepened immeasurably the gloom which had fallen on that now motherless household. Mr. S—, naturally irritable, had become intolerably peevish in consequence of his many disappointments. His temper had sorely tried his sick wife; and after her death it proved a source of continual suffering to her children. The boy, William, was seldom at home, and so escaped these domestic discomforts; but poor Nora and her little suffering Fanny were made to feel their bitterness daily and almost hourly.

For, to add to the pinching poverty they were enduring, their father lost his place of accountant. His haughty manner, which misfortune had not softened, his censorious and prying disposition, which a certain scrupulosity had only made more troublesome and intolerable to others, gave offense to every subordinate in the office. He also took it on himself to lecture his employers on certain transactions with the custom-house which excited his suspicion. Just as December was beginning to tax to the utmost Nora's resources in housekeeping, her father was dismissed.

This was terrible news for the poor child of fifteen, who knew not where to look for the means of keeping a roof above them in a season rendered exceptionally severe by intense cold and the great dearth of all things. She was a stranger, too, in the city and their immediate neighborhood,—and to no human being, not even to her confessor, had she breathed a word of the utter destitution which had fallen on them.

With the tidings of her father's dismissal a new enemy to her peace appeared. She had,—strange as it may seem,—never known by any experience of hers what drunkenness was, had never seen an intoxicated person. What was her horror and dismay to behold her dear parent in that condition! Hitherto she only had eyes for his virtues; in the light of her perfect innocence and sinlessness his imperfections had been overlooked or viewed only as the shadows inseparable from the bright sides of his character.

It was a fearful revelation to the care-burdened girl. But her womanly instinct and true nobleness of nature impelled her, even when this first manifestation of infirmity was renewed again and again, only to treat him whom she loved and reverenced so singularly, with the tenderness, the respect, the delicacy due to a sick and helpless father. She hid him away from every eye, even from those of her young sister, who was encouraged to believe that the change she could not but remark was due to grief and exhaustion. Nora spent hours of the night in prayer, when all was still in her cottage, bedewing with her tears her mother's crucifix, and conversing with the Court of Heaven as if the vail had been withdrawn, and she were permitted to plead for her dear ones at the Mercy Seat, and face to face with the Divine Majesty.

From that Presence she always arose overflowing with comfort, with peace and light and strength; and the morning ever found her armed with increased courage for the struggle before her. It had been the invariable custom of her parents to perform together their night and morning devotions. Nora, by a happy inspiration, took her mother's place by his side from the beginning of his bereavement, and to his unspeakable satisfaction. Even when half stupefied by drink, he would be persuaded to kneel with her and lift his soul to God: the morning never failed to find him humiliated, conscience-stricken, and self-accusing, but irritable and despondent. She never uttered one word of reproach or so much as hinted, in their conversation, at the growing habit which filled her with undefinable terror and foreboding.

One night he returned late,—she knew not whence,—and unable as he was to say his night-prayers, had lain down half-undressed on his bed,—his angel-daughter watching wearily near the half-opened door of his chamber. On awaking, he was struck to the heart with sorrow, and when his pale and hollow-eyed child made her appearance, he cast himself on her neck in a mute agony of tears. She kissed him, soothed him, lavished on him words of love and comfort such as God puts on the lips of the pure and brave-hearted. At length—"O Nora," he said, "this must be no more!" and kneeling by her side they both prayed in silence. God heard their united prayers. That trial was thenceforth spared to Nora.

Another blessing, a few days afterward, rewarded her filial piety. She wrote to her father's late employers, soliciting an interview, and received a favorable answer. Recommending, as was her wont in every serious undertaking, the success of her visit to the Father of the orphan and afflicted, she presented herself at the office, surprised and charmed the chief partner with her beauty, her artless simplicity, the rare culture in one so young displayed during the interview, and especially by the eloquence with which she pleaded and won her father's case. Mr. S—was given an occupation more suitable to his years and antecedents, and the daughter was delicately told of his former unpopularity and its causes.

These, with all a woman's tact, Nora set about correcting; and, wonderful to relate, in good time she succeeded in effecting a great change in her father's temper, his bearing toward his associates in business hours, and his disposition to fault-finding. The humiliation which the old gentleman felt at his late weakness made him as docile as a child to his daughter's training. And so Nora was left free to devote herself to her sick sister, and to a long and earnest correspondence with her brother, whose duties compelled him to long absences, and whose health as well as conduct began to cause her watchful heart no little alarm.

Fanny's constitutional debility had suffered much from the long journey the family had recently made to their new abode, as well as from her mother's death, and the loss of many luxuries and comforts the child had till then been accustomed to. About Christmas-tide the physician pronounced her case one of chronic spine disease, but the sweet sufferer was not allowed to know of it. She seemed, however, to brighten, revive, and gain strength under the warm sunlight of her sister's love, and the tender nursing of that gentle and cunning hand. But just then Mr. S—caught cold, and the illness soon assumed the form of violent pleurisy, leaving but little hopes of recovery, as the New Year dawned on them.

When the priest was summoned hurriedly on the evening of the great feast of Christmas, his impression on entering the cottage was,—as he afterward declared,—one of reverential awe; for a something heavenly seemed to pervade the atmosphere which filled it. The door was opened by Fanny, looking, in her simple dress of black, and with her dazzling complexion, like an angel just descended to tarry a brief space with the mourners. The whole house was decorated with evergreens and artificial flowers, but a refined taste had presided at the decoration, and was evident in the few simple ornaments of the mantel-piece, in the exquisite neatness of the sick-chamber, and in the preparation of the temporary altar for the sacrament. The patient was in a deep slumber when the priest entered: Nora was kneeling by his side, her hand held in her parent's with so tight a grasp that she could not or dared not withdraw it without interrupting the repose which powerful narcotics had procured him.

As she turned her head to greet the priest, he was struck with the rapt look of gratitude for his coming and of adoration for the Gift of which he was the bearer. The poor slumberer soon awoke, and his spirit was prepared for the reception of the divine and awful graces ordained for the Christian's death-struggle by Him who is the Author and Finisher of our faith. Nora moved about the sick-room like some one of the virgin train who evermore accompany the Lamb; and her sister knelt at the foot of the bed, silently pouring forth her tears and prayers. When Holy Viaticum had been administered and the last benediction given, the elder spoke to the priest with an air of quiet but preternatural fortitude. She knew what was coming, and trusted in the Comforter for strength to sustain her.

Both on quitting and entering the cottage the priest had remarked that there was only fire in the sick-room; his previous inquiries about the circumstances of the family had elicited from the neighbors information enough to make him feel certain that Nora had to contend with great distress. From herself he could obtain no answer to his timid and indirect questions. But it so happened that Mr. S—'s employer, hearing of his serious illness, called, with his eldest son, on the priest, and begged the latter to accompany them to the cottage. It was a timely visit—a glance satisfied the merchant of the urgent want of relief. The cottage was his property; he resolved at once on making it most comfortable; and besides begged Nora to draw at once her father's full year's salary, which was trebled without her knowledge. The most skillful medical aid was also secured, and a lively interest was created by the good priest's frequent praise of these afflicted strangers.

William hastened to his father's sick-bed, traveling night and day from the upper Mississippi, where he and his patron were superintending the building of a bridge. Whether he had inherited his mother's constitutional weakness, or his frame was not proof against the fatigue of so long a journey, and the discomforts and privations from which his very slender purse could not purchase an exemption, he reached the house of death only to be prostrated with fever. His father died a few hours after his son's arrival, and the good priest who had been the former's consoler in his last hours was called in to minister to the latter before his parent had been borne to the cemetery and laid beside his wife.

Nora, with a woman's fortitude, bore up against this new trial, and God, who has stored up in woman's heart such treasures of love and enduring devotion, enabled this tender girl, exhausted as she was by the grief and labors of all these weary months, to be for her brother all she had been for both her parents. There were no Sisters of Charity at hand; but the merchant's wife, a Protestant lady of rare goodness, had visited Nora under her new affliction, and insisted on remaining with her for a few days. The principal Catholic ladies, also, touched by what they heard, came to sympathize and to admire; and to see the lovely orphans was to become attached to them. But Nora would devolve on no one her duties toward her sick brother, on whom both she and Fanny now centered their entire affection.

Their brother was saved. And now, why delay the reader? William's convalescence was a long and painful one. He had inherited his father's peevishness, and had apparently lost in his somewhat wandering life as a civil engineer every trace of the early piety inculcated by his mother. People wondered that such an unamiable and God-abandoned youth could have come of the same parentage as the two angelic beings whom he called sisters.

Nora, while he was slowly recovering his strength, had been casting about for some occupation which might enable her to maintain the two now entirely thrown on her care. The merchant's wife continued to be devoted to the orphans, and had occasionally brought her son to visit William during the latter's convalescence. When able to bear exercise in the open air, the young men drove out together, and so an intimacy gradually sprang up between the two families. It was remarked, not without wonder, that under Nora's influence William became gradually transformed into another man. But few traces of his petulance and irritability remained. Indeed, after the first weeks of his recovery, the frequent oaths which startled the echoes of that pious abode were heard no more, and the old habit of night and morning prayer was resumed, William from his bed or his arm-chair heartily joining in his sisters' devotions. A new moral sense seemed to be growing up in him, refining not only his language but his very features, so that before spring had passed into summer the neighbors, who at first could see but a slight resemblance between the sisters and their coarse and burly brother, were struck with the remarkable likeness he bore them in features and expression.

It was not all: the merchant's son had seen too much of Nora not to have been charmed with her beauty of soul much more even than with her graces of person. His mother shared his admiration of such extraordinary worth, nor was his father indifferent to the virtues which he had himself more than once warmly eulogized. Nora, after imploring the divine guidance and consulting the priest who had been her counselor and benefactor, listened favorably to the young merchant's suit, and accepted gratefully his mother for her own. When the days of mourning were ended, just as another spring was spreading her fairest charms over earth and sky, she became the wife of this lover, having her sweet Fanny with her as the angel of her home. They are both, at this day, the models of Christian mothers and maidens in another land, whither the young husband's extensive business forced him to transfer his residence; they are the idols of the young and the worshiped benefactresses of the poor and suffering, blessed in hundreds of homes to which they bring light and comfort, prized in their own above all earthly treasures, and more and more reverenced daily by those who daily and hourly witness their goodness and humility.

How Woman's Selfishness Ruins the Home.

It may be that many of the class we are most anxious to benefit by the suggestions herein conveyed, the over-burdened with toil and care and poverty, will think and say that these lessons point not to the improvement of such a miserable lot as theirs. If they only knew how many a poor home is a paradise of heroism, of spotless purity, of truth and honor and contentedness! It is especially with the homes of the laborer, the mechanic, the struggling parents with a numerous family and scanty sustenance, that the writer of these pages has been all his life familiar. For one man of wealth, or high birth, or distinguished social position with whom he may have been acquainted, there are hundreds of the hard toilers, of the over-burdened and the hard driven, whose hand he has grasped, whose brave true hearts he has read, and whose humble homes he has found adorned with virtues and merits a prince might envy in vain.

It is to this loved class of readers that he would bring light and comfort by the perusal of such examples as are here set forth.

Eugene F—was the seventh son of a stone-mason, who had begun his married life with a sum of five dollars over and above all the expenses of his wedding. But he had what was more to him than five thousand, a soul which was incapable of wronging God or the neighbor willfully and knowingly, a pair of strong arms, a brave and trustful heart, a firm determination to improve himself in his craft and to conquer independence for himself and his wife—and, more than all that, he had in that young wife a soul as spotless as his own, and a treasure of devotion, sound sense, and unalterable sweetness, which made his life one long bridal day of unclouded joy and unmixed bliss. Thirteen children blessed the home of this laborious couple, six of whom were girls, and all of whom, inheriting the untainted blood and robust constitution of their parents, survived them, and were worthy of them.

In the home in which Eugene was born, there was indeed independence, comfort, abundance for all the need of the large nestful,—but never affluence. Eugene had been early apprenticed to a worker in brass, had mastered his craft with singular ease, and at the age of twenty had several thousand dollars,—his own earning,—placed to his account in the savings bank.

Three of his brothers were happily married. They had not only taken every precaution which their religious training suggested in choosing their companions, but had been guided by the wise counsels and the judgment of their admirable mother. Not so Eugene: he had been attracted by the fair face and lively manners of the only daughter of a neighboring family, and had set his heart on marrying her, without much consulting his parents in the matter. This was the very point where he failed in his duty, and in which a prudent mother's judgment and advice would have saved his life and happiness from utter shipwreck.

Henrietta B—, being an only daughter among six children, had been allowed her own way from infancy. She had been a sickly child, and her natural peevishness and hatred of all restraint had been at first tolerated on account of her many ailments. When she arrived at girlhood she became the pet of the whole family. Innocent, openhearted, impetuous, her sallies and outbursts of temper were laughed at by her brothers, and overlooked by the too fond and indulgent mother, in the hope that her real goodness and piety would shake off these imperfections as the girl grew into the woman, just as the heated metal in the furnace purges off its dross at a high temperature.

Unfortunately, the pure gold of her nature was subjected by her unwise parents to no sort of tempering or chastening of any kind, and the dross remained there to give, in due course of time, its coloring and quality to the gold which it was sure to overlie and conceal.

Eugene's mother had detected this want of training in her future daughter-in-law, and warned her son in the mildest and most affectionate manner, that she feared his happiness would not be safe in the keeping of a woman who was not sweet-tempered, and who was also, she suspected, selfish and vain in no common degree.

Passion is blind and deaf and headlong. The mother's warning was mistaken for prejudice and resented as a foul wrong done to the loved object. It only served to impel Eugene to hire and furnish a comfortable residence, and to hasten his marriage with Henrietta, without any regard to his father or his mother's advice to weigh well the question. There was added to this want of filial reverence a total neglect of the duties which piety toward God imposes on Catholics in the reception of the august sacrament of matrimony. It was treated by the bridegroom and the parents of the bride as a ceremony on which religion does indeed bestow a blessing, but which, after all, is, in too common estimation, but a joyous family festivity.

Still, not without admonition from his venerable father, from the admirable mother who had taught him his duties well, and from his married brothers, did Eugene fail to implore on his own nuptials the blessing of that

God and Lord without whose aid they "labor in vain" who set about building up the house of their own prosperity and happiness. The honeymoon was soon ended; but before the end Eugene had discovered that the woman of his choice was but little like his own mother—from whose lips, amid all her cares and unceasing activity, he had never heard one loud word; whose sweet features, even when under bodily or mental pain, he had never seen clouded for a moment with anger or passion of any kind. To him, to all his brothers, as to her doting husband, that dear mother of his had ever been a true companion, sharing, from infancy upward, his every joy and hope and fear, receiving his unbounded confidence, as if his whole soul had been laid bare to her motherly eye. And she was more than companion: she was a friend, a counselor, directing his studies, encouraging his ambition, and guiding his labors.

But his pretty wife, though loving him as well as she knew how, expected him to devote himself to her every caprice, while she had never been taught to devote herself to any one, or to seek any other's happiness at the expense of her own comfort. In his mother's home, which resembled a beehive where every inmate worked from early dawn till sunset, amid the most perfect order and the pleasant hum of happy voices,—Eugene had been accustomed, at his return from each day's toil, to find the bright faces of mother and sisters all aglow with the welcome of true affection. His room, like those of his brothers, was the picture of restful comfort; and a sisterly hand, the whole year round, would daily place a tiny vase of fresh flowers beneath the picture of the Virgin Mother over his mantel. The supper or dinner table was, in the truest sense, a feast of soul much more even than a repast for the body, to all the members of the household. Labor gave to each a keen appetite for the delightful meal, and a hearty relish for the warmth, the joyousness, and the deep repose of that most blessed fireside. So much so, that the young men as they grew up could not bear to be away from that family board at which true love presided.

Eugene expected, most naturally, that the woman he had chosen from among all women would hold toward him the place of mother and sister, just as he resolved to be for his young bride the tenderest and most devoted of husbands, compensating, by the thousand devices of his affection, for the loss to her of her parents, home, and kinsfolk.

The first week of their home-life had not passed, ere Eugene discovered, to his dismay, that not only there was no companionship between them, but that Henrietta was totally careless of her husband's comfort, totally untrained to the management of a household, and averse to every thing relating to domestic cares.

Her husband's business was a thriving one; he loved it, and was now more than ever ambitious to push his way to the foremost rank as a mechanician. His past economies had been nearly exhausted by the furnishing of his little home and the lavish expenditure of his month of honeymoon. He had returned to his workshop with a new zest for exertion, and bent himself to the task before him with all the more ardor that he hoped to find praise and encouragement from her to whom he had given his life.

As he came back from his work on the very first day after resuming it, his hands and face covered with the honorable dust and stains of his toil,—his heart was chilled by the greeting, "Oh! dear! how dirty you are! Do go and wash and change before any one sees you!" Nor did she accompany him as he hastened, with a strange sensation at his heart, to comply with his wife's desire. Not so had he been ever treated in the old home by the noble woman he called mother, to whom his begrimed face and soiled hands had always been a motive for a warmer and more loving welcome home. When he had put on his wonted home-clothes he found his wife surrounded with a bevy of young female friends. They had dined, without waiting for him, nor did Henrietta so much as offer to accompany her husband to his cold and solitary meal.

When the evening was over, the young mistress of the home complained of a headache, complained of the intolerable length of the day, without having her husband to converse with her and amuse her, and ended by declaring that she thought the lot of a mechanic's wife a hard one. There was not the slightest attempt at cheering him after his long day of unusual exertion, brightened, too, by the thought of the sweet rest he looked forward to at its close.

The days and weeks which followed only served to dispel one illusion after another. True love is founded on esteem, as esteem rests on respect; when respect fails, there is no ground for love. Poor Eugene was soon doomed to discover that his young wife was utterly UNTRUSTFUL, and had not the slightest scruple in deceiving him, even where deception was unnecessary. What would he not have given to open his heart to his mother and take counsel with her on the terrible difficulty which beset his path in life at the beginning! But he knew that one of the rules inculcated by his parents on all their married children was never to allow their domestic trials to be made known outside their own roof; and especially, not to have the families of husband or wife made acquainted with secret troubles, which the young people must themselves learn to settle between them and beneath the eye of God.

Eugene's mother had studied Henrietta's disposition carefully, and read clearly in her son's sad and thoughtful face how it fared with him and his wife. In her first visits to her daughter-in-law she discovered the whole truth; but with admirable tact she not only concealed the grief she felt, but forced herself to praise every thing she saw in Henrietta's management, feigning to see in the single servant's handiwork the result of the mistress's housewifery. She feigned to believe that the latter superintended in person her kitchen, pantry, and laundry, and would go to help Henrietta there, forcing the other thereby to see how every detail of domestic economy should be managed; she had the choicest and most fragrant flowers brought from her own house to Eugene's, and made his favorite sister, Margaret, plan and dispose them where they should best thrive and be most ornamental, culling a little bouquet of the most delicate for Henrietta's own room, and another for the dinner table, as if it were a matter of course. Music was Henrietta's sole accomplishment, and Eugene, himself a proficient on the violin, was gifted with a voice of uncommon power and sweetness. His fond mother purchased his favorite songs, and wished to hear the young people play and sing together on the very first evening she and her husband spent with them. But Henrietta pretended a headache, and would neither sing nor play. Nor, for months after their union, could she be coaxed to sit at her piano. The other pious industries of her mother-in-law were equally unavailing; she never set her foot in her kitchen, though not born far above her cook, nor ever busied herself with any one of the household duties. Her one servant had to do every thing or to let it alone.

More than that: she hated Eugene's mother and his sisters for their very virtues, and took the very first opportunity of telling her husband that she hoped his mother would stay at home and keep her daughters there, as she did not intend to allow any one to teach her what she had to do in her own house.

And so the clouds gathered and grew darker above that little home, which had been unhallowed by the blessing of Him who should ever be first and middlemost and last in the thoughts and designs and affections of those who call themselves his children. The gulf which had been opened by the young wife's utter selfishness between her husband and herself grew wider day by day. His spirit drooped, his business was neglected; his first babe was born in his father-in-law's house, whither his wife persisted in going some weeks before her illness. To her husband's home she never returned! In his turn, Eugene found its solitude intolerable, and sought solace and distraction elsewhere. Happy had it been for him if he had betaken himself in his darkest hour to the light and warmth of his mother's hearth! He yielded to far different attractions; and soon the house to which he had taken his bride was closed, and, like a forsaken dwelling in a valley inundated, it was swept away with all his substance by the ill fortune which ever follows fast on the heels of ill conduct. The wretched young man migrated to California, where he soon perished, broken in heart and energy; while his wife continued in her parents' home to nurse her idle regrets, and to accuse the dead of the ruin and the misery which were of her own making.

CHAPTER VI.

THE WIFE IN THE CHRISTIAN HOME.

Man first enters on the forest of life from the paternal house, where, if the will of God were done on earth as it is in heaven, the divine commandments would be known and dear and familiar to all; for the precept was thus given; *Thou shalt tell them to thy children, and thou shalt meditate upon them sitting in thy house, and walking on thy journey, sleeping and rising. And thou shalt bind them as a sign on thy hand, and they shall be and shall move between thy eyes. And thou shalt write them in the entry and on the doors of thy house.* Such is the ideal of the Catholic home; and wherever this type is realized, it is evident that its members are even already in possession of the truth and of the blessed life which constitute the pledge of the supreme good of man.

KENELM DIGBY, *Compitum.*

The Church, among her solemn benedictions, had one for every dwelling-house, being the same for that of the poorest man and for that of the wealthiest, for the lowliest cottier on his little plot of ground, as well as for the royal palace. Just as she lovingly blessed and guarded near her temples the bodies of her children without distinction of rank, even so she was desirous of hallowing by her prayers every spot in city or in country where her dear ones were born and reared, and where she would have God's angels live with them as their unseen guardians, companions, and helpers.

"We send up our supplication to Thee, O God the Almighty Father (one form of blessing begins) in behalf of this dwelling, of all who live therein, and of all things within it; praying that thou do bless and sanctify it, and fill it with all good things. Grant them, O Lord, plenty from out the dew of heaven, the sustenance of life from out the fat of the earth, and fulfill their desires in thy mercy. On our entering this house, therefore, do thou deign to bless and sanctify this abode as thou didst vouchsafe to bless the house of Abraham,

Isaac, and Jacob: and within these walls let the angels who behold thy light abide, to guard this home and its inmates."

Another ancient benediction added: "Abide ye in peace in your home: may the Lord grant you rest and peace and comfort from all your enemies round about! May he bless you from his throne on high, as you rest or walk, sleeping and waking; and may your family flourish to the third and fourth generation!" Elsewhere the Roman Ritual says in another form of blessing: "Bless, O Lord, God Almighty, this house, that in it may abide health, chastity, victory, fortitude, humility, goodness and meekness, the fullness of the law, and thanksgiving toward God the Father, and the Son, and the Holy Ghost."

In the design of God's fatherly providence, as well as in the intention of the Church, the Christian family-home is a place "blessed and sanctified," over which, with its inmates, angels keep watch and ward. This divine protection and angelic watchfulness secure "peace," and safety from all surrounding dangers; the blessing is fruitful in "health" of body and soul, in that purity of life which renders the inhabitants of the home worthy of being the fellow-servants and citizens of the angels, in victory over self, in that fortitude which ever strengthens man to bear and to forbear, in that humility which keeps us like little children in presence of the Divine Majesty, in "goodness and meekness," in the loving accomplishment of the law which is only the expression of his will, and in devout gratitude toward that Trinity of Persons whose blissful society in the life to come is to be the completion and reward of the home-life sanctified and made most happy by every duty fulfilled.

In thus setting forth the sanctity of the Christian home, and the exalted nature of the duties and the virtues which should adorn it, we are only endeavoring to recall men's minds to the venerable ideals so dear to our fathers, and to those "ancient paths" from which modern free-thinking would lead the young generation to stray.

Angels Guard the Catholic Home.

It is for every father, who is by the divine law of nature, king in his own family, to consider well the truth here presented to him, and to conceive of his own little kingdom the pure and lofty notion, which is that of the divine mind as well as the mind of the Church. When a father, though never so poor, firmly believes that his little home and his hearth-stone are a thing so precious and so holy that God will have "his angel keep, cherish, protect, visit, and defend it, and all who dwell therein," he, too, will lift up his eyes and his heart to that Father over all and most loving Master, and exhort himself daily and hourly "to walk before Him and be perfect."

But it is to his companion,—the queen of that little kingdom, the wife,—that it is most necessary to have high and holy thoughts about the sacredness of her charge, the obligations incumbent on her, the incalculable good which she can do, and the many powerful helps toward its accomplishment that the All-Wise and Ever-Present is sure to multiply under her hand.

To every true man and woman now living there is no being on earth looked up to with so pure, so deep, so grateful, so lasting a love, as a mother. Let us look at our mother, then, in that dear and holy relation of wife which she bears to him who was for us in childhood the representative of the God "of whom all paternity in heaven and earth is named."

Woman's Duties as Wife.

The first duty of the wife is to study to be in every way she can the companion, the help, and the friend of her husband. Indeed on her capacity to be all this, and her earnest fulfillment of this threefold function depends all the happiness of both their lives, as well as the well-being of the whole family. Hence the obligation which is incumbent on parents providing for the establishment of their children,—to see to it, so far as is possible, that the person chosen to be a wife in the new home should be a true companion for their son, a true helpmate in all his toil, and a faithful friend through all the changes of fortune.

She Ought to Be a Companion to Her Husband.

One half of the unhappiness of married life comes from the fact that the wife is either unfitted or unwilling to be a true companion to her husband. This companionship requires that she should be suited by her qualities of mind and heart and temper to enter into her husband's thoughts and tastes and amusements, so as to make him find in her company and conversation a perfect contentment and delight.

Persons who are perfectly companionable never weary of each other,—indeed, they are never perfectly happy while away from each other;—they enter into each other's thoughts, reflect (and increase by the reflection) the light in each other's mind; cultivate the same tastes, pursue the same ideals, and complete each other in the interchange of original or acquired knowledge.

But there is more than that in the companionship of the true wife. She studies to make herself agreeable, delightful, and even indispensable to him who is her choice among all men. If true love be in her heart, it will suggest to her, day by day, a thousand new devices for charming the leisure of her husband.

Woman has been endowed by the Creator with a marvelous fertility of resource in this respect: it is an unlimited power, productive of infinite good when used for a holy purpose and within her own kingdom; but productive of infinite evil when employed in opposition to the design of the Giver, or allowed to lie idle when it should be used to promote the sacred ends of domestic felicity.

There are wives who will study certain languages, sciences, arts, or accomplishments, in order to make themselves the companions of the men they love, and thus be able to converse with them on the things they love most, or to charm the hours of home repose by music and song. The writer of these lines remembers, that, while a young priest in Quebec, upward of thirty years ago, he was much struck by seeing a young lady of one of the best families there, applying herself assiduously to study the sign-language of the deaf-mutes in order to converse easily with her husband—a wealthy young merchant, thoroughly trained himself in the admirable Deaf and Dumb Institution of his native city. They were devoted to each other, and the young wife's earnestness in making herself companionable to her husband, must have brought many a blessing on the home in which the writer beheld them so wrapt in each other, so virtuous, and so full of bright hope!

It must not be concluded from this, that a woman who applies herself to acquire knowledge for the purpose of being more of a companion to her husband, should thoroughly master either a language, a science, or an art... In the case of the young wife just mentioned, a thorough familiarity with the language of signs was indispensable as a means of easy conversation with her husband. But this is evidently an exceptional case;—and is only mentioned to show what difficulties love will overcome to be helpful or agreeable to its companion.

The word helpful, just used, will furnish to every wife the true measure of the knowledge she may be prompted to acquire. Her husband has to know perfectly whatever he knows, because his success as a professional man or a business man depends on this thorough knowledge, whereas his wife only acquires to please and to help her companion.

But there are other things beside this scientific, literary, or artistic knowledge, which may be more needful to a wife, if she would make herself of all earthly beings the most delightful and necessary companion to her husband. She must study him,—his needs, his moods, his weak as well as his strong points,—and know how to make him forget himself when he is moody and selfish, and bring out every joyous side of his nature when he is prone to sadness. God, who has made the soul both of man and of woman, and who has united them in the duties and burdens of home-life, wills that they should complete each other. Man has bodily strength, because it is his duty to labor for the home and protect it; he has also certain mental and moral qualities which woman does not need, and which fit him for the battle of life and his continual struggle with the crowd. But she has, on her part, far more of fortitude, of that power to bear and to forbear, to suffer silently and uncomplainingly herself while ministering with aching heart and head to the comfort, the cheerfulness, the happiness of all around her.

At any rate, she has by nature the power, the art, and the disposition to please, to soothe, to charm, and to captivate. It is a wonderful power; and we see daily women exerting it in a wonderful way and for purposes that God cannot bless, and that every right conscience must condemn. Why will not women who are truly good, or who sincerely strive to be so, not make it the chief study of their lives to find out and acquire the sovereign art of making their influence as healthful, as cheering, as blissful as the sunlight and the warmth are to their homes?

Let us give an example of what is meant here—and this illustration will suggest, of itself, many other applications. We all know—a mother more than any one else—what a potent spell praise is in making children master whatever they are learning, and, what is far more difficult, acquire a mastery over themselves, both in repressing wrong inclinations and in gaining the habits of the noblest virtues. A word of praise from a mother will stir the heart of every well-born child—and few children are ill-born, that is, with radically bad dispositions—to the most extraordinary exertions, and fill the whole soul with delight, when that word is sweetly spoken of successful efforts made. We say nothing here of the stimulus which praise from the queen of the home gives to the zeal and conscientious labors of servants.

We are concerned with the master of the home. Do you not know that all men, even old men, even the proudest and coldest men, are only great children, who thirst for praise from a wife, a mother, or a sister's lips? There are men—and they are the noblest, the most high-souled—who care but little, if anything, for the praise or censure of the crowd, even of the learned or titled crowd; but their heart is stirred through all its depths by one sweet word from the lips of mother, sister, or wife. Why, O women, are you so niggard of a money which you can bestow without making yourselves the poorer, and which your dear ones prize above gold and gems?

Give generously, but discerningly, what is held so dear as coming from you, and which will only encourage those you love above all the world to strive to-morrow for still higher excellence, and look forward to still sweeter praise.

The Philosopher Husband.

Without unlocking the door of a home dear to the hearts of American Catholics, and on whose hearthstone the fire is now quenched forever—we can say here that the most illustrious of our Catholic publicists was ever prompt to attribute to his wife much of the success of his writings. She was in truth,—so say those who were admitted to the intimacy of the great philosopher,—in her gentleness and simplicity by the side of his sturdy and robust nature, like the vine wedded to the elm; apparently all weakness and dependence, drawing her life from the strong man on whom she leant. But she gave more life than she received; she imparted to her companion confidence in his own judgments, firmness and constancy of purpose through all the vicissitudes of his trying existence.

He was a proud man;—but, like all who have been most buffeted by public opinion, he was easily and deeply touched by the praise of those whose judgment he valued and whose sincerity he had no reason to distrust.

He would often say that he was never sure or perfectly satisfied with what he was preparing for the press, till he had submitted it to his little wife and obtained her approbation. Her admirable common sense had been one of the qualities which won his esteem when he first knew her,—and that sure sense continued to be through life his chief guide and stay. A word of hearty praise from her would inspire him with a youthful enthusiasm, give fresh vigor to his thought and eloquence to his pen, even when past his sixtieth year. The praise, and not unfrequently the admiration of two worlds, were not half so sweet to him, as the simple words of that devoted wife and mother. "My dear Doctor, that is very good!" Nor would he hesitate to cast aside or tear up the pages which had cost him most labor, when she told him that she thought what he had written was dull, or not to the point, or exaggerated.

From his early mental struggles, all through the phases of his long and not inglorious battle with error and ill-fortune, she was the angel ever by his side, consoling, encouraging, enlightening, strengthening, and guiding him. The soul of his genius seemed to have departed with her; and, though he made a brave battle in his last years in favor of the Church to which he had given his faith, and against the triumphant errors of the day, he felt that half his strength and half his heart were in the grave with his loved wife.

The reader can offset this example by calling to mind wives who, though wedded to men of the purest virtue, the most heroic temper, and the most undoubted talent, became a life-long torture to their husbands, by the absolute absence of all the amiable qualities which make a woman the companion, the helper, the friend and counselor of her husband. We have known men who rose to a proud preeminence from the lowliest beginnings without ever finding in the heart of their wives one pulsation of sympathy for their aims, their struggles, their defeat or success; who, while suffering most bitterly from the inconstancy or injustice of the popular voice, turned vainly to their own home for rest, or to the mother of their children for one word of sweet comfort. We have seen men on both sides of the Atlantic at whose feet a whole people were willing to lay down the highest offices and honors in their gift, and who feared to go from the triumph and intoxication of the senate-hall or the public meeting to the coldness, the neglect, the misery which awaited them at home.

Surely such women,—women who turn to ashes and bitterness the fairest and sweetest fruits of hard-won success,—who turn a home that could and should be a paradise into a purgatory,—surely they must expect a severe judgment hereafter. But even here they are severely judged, and have their punishment in the censure of their own household and the condemnation of all right-minded persons.

We shall find other and more touching examples taken from the laboring classes and the poor, when we shall have concluded what is to be said of the wife's office as friend and counselor. Let us resume what we have been saying about companionship. All these arts and industries which make a woman's companionship so dear, so useful, so exalting are only a part of her nature, of her true self, as the Creator intends her to be in order that she may shine in the home of her husband, and whose price is from "far, and from the uttermost coasts."

"Ah, wasteful woman!—she who may
 On her sweet self set her own price,
Knowing he cannot choose but pay—
 How has she cheapened Paradise!
How given for naught her priceless gift,
 How spoiled the bread and spilled the wine,
Which, spent with due, respective thrift,
 Had made brutes men, and men divine!"[7]

The Wife as Helpmate in the Home.

In the earthly paradise of the true Christian home, the wife is a helpmate, the equal of her husband, neither his inferior nor his servant. It is not in such homes that our modern theories or discussions about "Woman's Rights," or "the Sphere of Woman," have originated. No woman animated by the Spirit of her Baptism, filled with the humility and generosity which are the soul of that self-sacrificing love indispensable to husband and wife in the performance of their undivided life-labor,—ever fancied that she had or could have any other sphere of duty or activity than that home which is her domain, her garden, her paradise, her world. There, if she is truly a wife, all are subject to her, even her husband. There never existed a true-souled Christian man

[7] Coventry Patmore.

who did not believe himself and demean himself from his bridal hour till his dying day like a willing and loving servant of his wife inside his own home.

This is true especially of the home of the wealthy and the great, where reigns and should ever reign the infinite respect and reverence of man for woman, in whom Christian faith bids us see the majesty and purity of her who is Mother of Christ. There is no excuse for the high-born and the wealthy, when they fail to honor themselves, by doing service inside their homes to mother, wife, and sister. The difficulty will here be with the poor man, the laboring man, coming home at evening worn out by the toil of the day, faint with hunger too, and fearful it may be of the morrow. Has he not to be served rather than serve?

The answer is an easy one, and easily understood, where minds are enlightened and hearts are upright. If the poor man's wife has done her duty throughout the day, she will have found in her home-work enough to weary. The very labor of preparing for her husband and her sons, perhaps, the meal which is to restore their strength, and the care required to brighten up that home so as to make it look a paradise of repose for them,—is the task of her who is the natural helper in the household—and whose blessed help consists precisely in making the home what it ought to be, man's heart-rest from all outside cares.

But that is enough about the fundamental notion of equality between husband and wife, the father and the mother in the Christian family. Both are necessary to each other, they ought to have but one heart and one mind in the pursuit of the one great purpose of their lives,—the happiness of their home and the rearing to the practice of all goodness the children whom God sends them. Understanding this, their only true position toward each other, the husband never can entertain any notion of domineering over his wife, nor the wife feel any sense of servile inferiority toward her husband.

But the love which binds her to him is an enlightened love which makes her view their respective labors as only two distinct parts of one task. Beside all that she accomplishes in ordering, brightening, and warming the home,—there are a thousand ways in which she can be a helpmate to her husband, beyond what is required for mere companionship.

For it is one thing to be delightful company to a person one is traveling with, by being able to converse with him in his own language, or to discuss with him every favorite topic, or to enter into his recreations and amusements with zest, and thus to lighten the weariness of the road and charm away its dullness; and another to be a helper. One's companion may fail in strength, or be beset with dangers and difficulties:—and then it is that the office of the helper begins.

It is precisely when man's heart fails him, and his courage yields to disappointment or difficulty, that woman comes to his aid. And if this help is most sweet and welcome and above all price in moments of professional weariness, of business difficulties, or when all seems dark and bleak and hopeless to the stoutest heart,—how much more valuable is it in matters which concern the soul's welfare, in troubles of the heart, in the dark and stormy hours of temptation!

But we must not trench on the next and dearest function of wifely love,—that of being the truest and most faithful of friends.

The Wife as Her Husband's Friend.

A story very apposite to our purpose is told by a writer of the middle ages. A man who wished to make a visit to Cologne, famed at that time as a pilgrimage, possessing as it did the tomb of the Three Wise Kings. He was a wealthy man, but not a wise one. He had an admirable wife, whose worth he knew not, and whose company he neglected for that of two neighbors, who played friends with him because he was rich and lavish of his money. As he was setting out on his pilgrimage, he asked his friends what he should bring them from Cologne: one answered that he would like a rich cloak, and the other begged him to buy a tunic of rare stuff. He next asked his wife what he should get for her, and she besought him to bring back sense and wisdom which might enable him to see and correct the evil of his ways.

After having paid his devotions at the shrine of the Three Kings, he went among the merchants, bought the cloak and the tunic, but sought in vain for some one who would sell him sense and wisdom. They were not to be found in the market. As he returned crestfallen to his inn, the host inquired why he seemed downcast, and, learning the cause, advised him on his return home to pretend to his friends that he had lost all his money and could give them neither cloak nor tunic. He followed this piece of advice, and both of the false friends turned him out of doors, abusing him as a fool and a vagabond.

Not so his wife, however: he told her the story of his loss; but she, seeing that he was weary from the road and filled with sorrow and indignation because of this ill treatment, tenderly embraced him, consoled and refreshed him, assured him that God would send him heavenly treasures for the money he had lost. So his eyes were opened to know what wealth he possessed in her true love and faithful friendship; and thus did he "find sense and wisdom from having visited the City of the Three Kings."[8]

"What is friendship?" asks Alcuin, and he answers forthwith, "A similitude of souls." Where the wife labors conscientiously to be a true companion to her husband, there is little fear but she will also become a true, faithful, and constant friend. For the successful effort made to establish perfect companionship must end in effecting that "similitude of souls," which constitutes the essence and ground of friendship.

The reasons which will urge every right-minded and truehearted woman to be the most delightful and constant of companions and the most devoted of helpmates, must also inspire her with the resolution of being the most cherished of friends. She must not be jealous of the men for whom her husband entertains feelings of real friendship. On the contrary, it were wise to vie with him in showing them every mark of regard, as if she were thereby the interpreter of his dearest wishes. Nothing pleases a man more than to see his old and true friends warmly acknowledged and treated with all honor and affection by the persons most dear to him.

This, however, is only a passing admonition to which every woman who is careful of her home-duties will do well to attend. It is not only virtue but good policy in a wife to have the sincere good-will and respect of all who consider themselves to be her husband's friends. Not only will they contribute much to the pleasantness of the home in which they are always welcome and honored guests, but they will not fail to spread far and wide the fame of its hospitality and the good name of its mistress.

It happens but too often that women will take it into their heads to regard the friends of their husband as persons who steal away a heart which should

---

[8] Joannes, *Magnum Speculum*, 12.

exclusively belong to themselves, and through an unwise and narrow jealousy make themselves odious and their homes intolerable to men whom they ought to conciliate and to bind to themselves. More than one wife has lost for ever the heart of her husband and destroyed the peace of her fireside by such insane conduct.

Let the young and the wise take warning therefrom, and learn betimes how a true wife can be the counselor, the guide, as well as the sanctifier and savior of her husband. And here let a practical example dispense us from pursuing the subject further.

The Carpenter's Wife a True Wife.

John and Eliza H—were both natives of England, and came, with their infant son, to settle in one of our thrifty manufacturing towns in 1849. He had learned the trade of a house carpenter, had had remunerative employment in London, but, being ambitious to rise to something higher, had come to America with the hope of improving his knowledge and becoming in time an architect. His education, unfortunately for his design, had never gone beyond that of an ordinary common school, while his wife, who had studied in one of the excellent normal schools taught in England by the Sisters of Notre Dame de Namur, had graduated there with the highest honors, and had further improved her opportunities by perfecting herself in drawing and other branches taught gratuitously in the government schools. The young people had known each other from childhood, and their union was one of deep and pure affection. They were also most exemplary in the fulfillment of all their religious duties. The husband was too proud of his young wife, and too sincerely devoted to her to consent to her accepting even the most advantageous position as school-teacher. He had set his heart on rising in the world, and would be the sole provider for his family and the sole artificer of their fortunes.

During the first ten months of their stay in America every thing went well with them, and John's emoluments far exceeded his household expenses—exceeded, indeed, anything which he could have looked forward to at home. He found, however, that men of his craft in America had received an education superior to his, and that his inferiority in this respect was a serious bar to his advancement. At this point began the incomparable services rendered to him by his wife. She proposed to devote a few hours daily, after his return from work, to teaching him all that she knew herself. It was a loving offer, lovingly accepted, and love seemed to quicken the intellect both of teacher and pupil, the progress made by John being marvelously rapid. God also blessed these studies, for the two never began or ended a lesson without kneeling to implore the divine light. It was a habit acquired in school and kept up through life by both the one and the other.

Six months had not elapsed since the beginning of these lessons, when John's expertness as a draughtsman astonished his companions and employers and obtained him promotion. But he did not relax his home studies. Not a little of his spare money was used to purchase the best works on architecture, and the young man applied himself many months with enthusiasm to mastering every detail of that great science,—especially all that pertains to design and construction. His wife, who now left him to himself, was nevertheless made the companion of all this preparatory labor. He could not bear to have her out of his sight while he was making a plan, or calculating the strength of such and such building materials. A second child came to gladden the pair, while thus toiling together beneath the eye of God. And almost simultaneously with the birth of their babe a new blessing was sent to them. It was proposed to build a new church in a remote part of the State, and John, after visiting the locality, had sent in a plan so well conceived, and an estimate of costs with specifications so carefully drawn up, that the construction of the church was awarded to him.

This was John's first triumph; it called forth his utmost gratitude, but it did not make him proud. He referred his success to the Divine Author of every blessing, to whom both he and his wife had most humbly and earnestly recommended it; and, after God, he thanked his dear helper and mistress, whose teachings and encouragement and bright affection had given him both the light to know how to do his new work, and the unfailing courage to undertake and accomplish it. She had a little oratory in her bedroom, with a water-color painting of one of Fra Bartolomeo's sweetest Madonnas executed by herself, hangings of exquisite embroidery the work of her own hands, a lamp of beautiful design fed with the purest olive oil, and rare fragrant flowers which she cultivated in honor of her dear Mother. The little framework with its carving and illuminations was the work of John's chisel. There they offered up together their night and morning devotions; and there John knelt when he received the tidings of his success, reciting with overflowing heart the *Te Deum*, while his little wife made the responses from her sick-bed.

With the first triumph came also their first trial—their first separation. For the building of the church required that the architect should be often on the spot; and beside his being charged with the construction, he was most anxious that this, his first building, should be perfect; so far as his skill and care could make it. It was a terrible trial for these young hearts. The clergyman for whom John was building, though not of his own faith, was much interested in him. He was shocked not a little at first to hear of John's going on Sundays to the far-off little Catholic mission-chapel, and his trustees murmured at having a Romanist to superintend the building of their beautiful and costly church. But the gentleness of the young man, his constant attendance at the works, his perfect control over the workmen, the exceeding beauty of his own designs as well as of the carpenter's work, which he began to have executed in advance for the interior of the edifice, and, above all, the comparative cheapness of all that he did, soon silenced the murmurers.

What most touched the clergyman, however, was the yearning which the architect felt for his home, and the emotion he could not conceal when speaking of his wife. The enterprise was happily brought to a close, and a handsome donation in money, with a vote of thanks from the parishioners, was added to the price originally stipulated. There was more than that: during the progress of the works the name of the architect was mentioned so favorably in clerical circles, and the quality of his work elicited such genuine admiration, that he was asked for designs for two other churches.

His enforced absence from home now seemed to the husband and father so painful a sacrifice, so great a loss of all that a true man holds most dear, that he began to repent him of the ambition which had impelled him to soar above his carpenter's craft: the reputation he had already acquired and the brilliant fortune which smiled upon him seemed too poor a compensation, he thought, for the loss of that dear companionship of his wife, his friend, his instructress; for the caresses of his babes, and all the bliss of the peaceful and sunny home for which his soul thirsted continually.

Still, when he mentioned his regrets to his wife, she would not—though her heart was oppressed by the prospect of these long and frequent separations—allow him to repine or draw back from the career on which he was but entering. Without giving up their home, rendered doubly dear to both by their first struggles and John's apprenticeship for his present profession, Eliza resolved to be with him as much as possible during the fine season. She wrote to him daily, sometimes twice a day, cheering him and encouraging him especially to be more than ever faithful to those solid and soul-nourishing practices of piety, which maintain the union of our spirit with the Spirit Creator, and give us the confidence to undertake and the power to accomplish every thing planned for his glory and in accordance with the duties of our avocation.

You are impatient to know the end, gentle reader. It shall soon be told. Just as John was carrying out the most important of all his constructions, an accident in his workshop (for he would persist in designing himself all decorations in woodwork, and in carving what was most difficult and delicate) maimed his right hand for life. Thenceforward he could never handle the chisel or the pencil. And hitherto he had not had any assistants or cared to form pupils.

The blow was a heavy one to him, and all his prospects seemed to him blighted forever. His wife was soon by his side, however, to comfort and reassure him. She could draw, she said, if he could not, and he could direct her in filling up any design demanded of him. As his studies in architecture had been carried on in her company and with her guidance and co-operation, she was more competent than he thought in all that pertained to his profession; indeed it was to her sure and excellent taste that he owed, without being aware of it, the originality and purity of his architectural designs.

So the young wife and mother, acting under the inspiration of her love, and responding to his unbounded belief in her capacity, not only studied architectural drawing under her husband's eye, but induced him to advertise for assistants and apprentices, and soon found herself with no less than six remarkable young men studying her husband's noble profession in his house and under their joint superintendence.

Alas, the season of unhoped-for prosperity which ensued was but of too brief a duration. Eliza had been, at the time to which our narrative has brought us, twelve years in America—twelve years of unmixed happiness springing from a love which increased with each successive year, because each year revealed in the wife some new perfection her husband had not discovered, some treasure of goodness more precious than any possessed till then. Five children surrounded the board of the proud fond mother; and every one of them she was herself educating. After the birth of her sixth child her health failed; no scientific skill availed to stay the progress of the insidious disease which had declared itself.

Her death was indeed a spectacle for angels and men to admire. To the last she would have her husband by her side, comforting him, instructing and strengthening him with a sweet and glowing eloquence which borrowed its light and warmth from the near vision of eternity.

He was not crushed, because she seemed to have breathed into him in dying her own heavenly spirit of resignation. He understood that he must now take up her work, and be to his six orphans both father and mother. He was rich enough to give up his profession; and devoted himself entirely to the education of his dear ones.

There was one service—greater than all the others—for which the widowed husband never ceased to thank her who had been to him companion, helpmate, and friend; she had saved him from his own weakness. During his frequent absences he had by degrees contracted convivial habits, which filled her with unspeakable alarm. She eventually proved his savior; but it is only consummate tact and a love full of tender and most patient reverence for the diseased soul that can render the intemperate *willing to be saved*. Eliza's ascendency over the heart which had never known any other love than hers, was that of the mother over a sick babe, which yields itself absolutely to the loved voice, the tender hand, and the encircling arms.

Would that every wife who reads this book may thus learn to be to her husband a friend and a savior! She would thus be most truly the Angel of the Home, keeping the steps of all within it from straying to the right or the left, and guiding them through life toward the blissful goal of their pilgrimage. Speaking, as we do throughout this book, not of the monastic life of spiritual perfection, self-crucifixion, and apostolic labor, but of the home-life which is the nursery of true men and women, both for the common paths of worldly toil and duty, and for that other higher and more perfect road, we can safely say of the results of a Christian wife or mother's training: "No man ever lived a right life who had not been chastened by woman's love, strengthened by her courage, and guided by her discretion."

Looking to the influence for all good and honor and greatness that a wife, in God's design, is capable of exercising over her husband, and to the implicit obedience that every true-hearted husband yields through life to her he has made queen of his home,—we cannot but place here the beautiful words of a living author:[9] "Chivalry, to the original purity and power of which we owe the defense alike of faith, of law, and of love,...assumes that in this rapturous obedience (of the husband) to the single love of his youth, is the sanctification of all man's strength, and the continuance of all his purposes."

"You cannot think that the buckling on of the knight's armor by his lady's hand was a mere caprice of romantic fashion. It is the type of an eternal truth—that the soul's armor is never well set to the heart unless a woman's hand has braced it; and it is only when she braces it loosely that the honor of manhood fails."

The poor man and the rich man, the man destined to labor all his life as well as the man fitted to fill every public trust, needs more than at any period in the past to have his wife arm him for the daily battle against temptation; against the terrible corruption and dishonesty which rule over every class of public men; against the contempt cast by modern public opinion on all that the Past held sacred, reverence for the home, for the church; faith in God and in all that is most capable to make man God-like; against Christianity itself, and the civilization and manifold sanctities it created. Let every true wife daily brace more and more tightly round her husband's heart the armor of the old principles which made our fathers invincible in their long battle against error and wrong.

Thus "the honor of manhood" will not fail among us, so long as every wife and mother aims at being the Angel of the Home.

---

[9] Ruskin.

CHAPTER VII.

Duties of the Wife as the Dispenser of the Home Treasures.

> Who shall find a valiant (brave-hearted) woman?... The heart of her husband trusteth in her... She hath sought wool and flax, and hath wrought by the counsel of her hands... She hath tasted and seen that her traffic is good: her lamp shall not be put out in the night... She hath opened her hand to the needy, and stretched out her hands to the poor. She shall not fear for her house in the cold of snow.
>
> *Proverbs* xxxi.

Nothing so animates the head of a family to honorable exertion as the certainty, that his wife bestows her utmost care in providing for the comfort of his home, in dispensing wisely the store which he places at her disposal; making it her rule to be just to him by never exceeding his means when she cannot increase them by her industry, in being just to her children by supplying them with becoming raiment, food, and instruction, just to her servants, whom she treats with a motherly tenderness which never condescends to familiarity;—and just to God's poor, whose claims she holds to be most sacred.

But let us proceed understandingly. The first care of the wife is to establish discipline and order;—discipline, without which there may be much noise and agitation, but no work done;—and order, because where there is confusion every thing is out of place, or done out of its proper time. To have discipline,—where there are children and servants,—the mistress must have authority, and she must assert and establish her authority by being both firm and calm, and giving every one to understand that she means what she says, and that what she says must be done.

Order means that every work must be done in its proper time, and every thing in the house be put in its proper place. Order means economy both of time and of labor. For where every occupation has its own appointed time, the household duties are sure to be attended to and to be fulfilled with singular ease and pleasure.

If this order and economy of time are necessary in large households, it is still more so in the home of the poor man, where every thing has to be done single-handed by the wife. There are poor households,—those of the daily laborer, the poor tradesman,—where the wife, with a large family of children to care for, will quietly get through an amount of work of different kinds that would seem to require the joint energy of several persons. Go into these bright and orderly homes, where the housewife rests not from early dawn till long after sunset of the longest day, and see the cleanliness, the tidiness, the calm and the contentment that fill the place like an atmosphere!

Of course there will be comfort for all where there is such order. For there can be comfort with poverty, or at least with little, though never with want. There will be comfort for the husband when he returns to that bright, warm, pleasant hearth, where the deep love of his companion fills the house with a spiritual fragrance more pleasant than all the flowers of spring; there will be comfort at the simple meal set on the board shining with cleanliness; and there will be comfort in the sweet conversation in which the outside world is forgotten, in the joy of being all in all to each other; and there will be bliss in the night's rest won by hard and hearty toil, and undisturbed by peevish ambition or by the dreams of a spirit at war with God or the neighbor.

There will be loveliness, too, in the home where true love causes order and comfort to reign. For the poorest room can be made lovely by a woman's cunning hand. She can have flowers at her window, and flowers on her mantel and her table. And the curtains of windows and beds may be beautified by some simple ornament devised by a woman's taste and executed in spare moments by the hand of even the busiest.

There is not one among the readers of this book but has seen such homes—albeit lowly, narrow, and poor in the literal sense—in which this order, comfort, and loveliness gave the beholder the evidence of a womanly spirit that might have graced a palace. This remark, however, is only preliminary to what pertains to the wife's stewardship in her home.

Man, in Every Condition, Responsible for His Stewardship.

We must not, especially in an age which tends daily more and more to deny that man owes any account to God for the use of the wealth he chances to possess—whether that be inherited from his ancestors, or obtained by his own thrift and industry—be carried away by the torrent of error. No matter whence derived, all that man has as well as all that he is belongs to God—his Creator and Lord and Judge; and to Him must he return to give an account of the use which he will have made of his being, his life, his time, his property. Reason, even without the light of supernatural revelation, teaches this truth as fundamental and unquestionable.

The great and the rich will have to account for their stewardship,—for the uses to which they have put their time, their riches, their power, their influence, their opportunities, just as the laboring poor will have to account for their thrift, and the awful uses to which one may see, day by day, our hard-working heads of families put their earnings in drunkenness, gambling, and all manner of vice.

But, as we have said, it is the province of the housewife to be at home a wise steward in the use of her husband's means, while his chief business is, outside of the home, to procure these means by honorable industry. Both are responsible to God. The wife's immediate responsibility however is toward her husband. She is his minister, his eye, his hand, his head and heart, in applying his wealth or the produce of his industry to the ends for which God wills it to be employed.

The Stewardship of the Wealthy Wife.

Of persons of royal, princely, or noble rank, we do not think it necessary to treat in this place. We speak of wealth wheresoever it exists, and of the duties and responsibilities of the wife in its home-uses.

Hers should be a wise economy. Wisdom consists in a clear perception of the ends or uses for which money is to serve, and in the careful adaptation of one's means to one's expenditure. You have so much and no more to spend each week, or each month, or each year; you have so many wants to provide for: let your wisdom be proved by always restraining your outlay so as to have a little balance left in your favor.

We know of a wife,—a young wife too,—who after her bridals was made the mistress of a luxurious home, in which her fond husband allowed her unlimited control. They were more than wealthy, and his business relations and prospects were such as to promise certain and steady increase for the future. Still the young wife did not allow herself to be lavish or extravagant. She provided generously for the comforts of her home, for the happiness of her servants, for the duties of a generous hospitality; she had an open hand for all charities and good works. But she was also, young as she was, mindful of the future; and this wise forethought is eminently the characteristic of women. Without ever whispering a word of her purpose to her husband, she resolved from the beginning of their housekeeping that she would lay by in a safe bank her weekly economies. The husband, in all likelihood, would have deemed this saving an ill omen, pointing to future calamity. It was, however, only the prophetic instinct of the wise woman, who, in the heat of summer and the overflowing plenty of autumn, looked forward to "the cold of snow," and made store for the need and warmth and comfort of her household.

The "calamity" came after a good many years; it came by a fatal chain of circumstances in which the misfortunes or dishonesty of others brought ruin on the upright and prudent and undeserving. One day the husband came home with heavy heart, and tried in vain to hide his care from the penetrating eyes of love. He had to break to his wife the dreadful news of their utter ruin. She listened unmoved to his story: "All is not lost, my dear husband," she said; "I have been long preparing for this. If you will go to such a bank, you will find enough laid up there to secure us either against want or poverty."

In order to secure this wise and provident economy, even in the midst of wealth, two extremes must be avoided, parsimony, which destroys domestic comfort and makes the mistress of the proudest house despicable in the eyes of her cook, her butcher, and her grocer,—and waste or extravagance, which is ruinous to the largest fortunes and most criminal in the sight of God. "Waste not—want not," used to be inscribed on the huge bread-platters of our fathers, both in the servants' hall and the family dining-room. "Waste not—want not," ought to be the rule of every housewife in all departments of household economy. Waste is always a sin against God, against your husband

and children, as well as against the poor, who have a right to what is thus thrown away: and, forget it not,—waste never fails to lead to want, as surely as stripping a tree of its bark is followed by its pining away and withering.

Another rule, which a wise woman will never violate, is to tell her husband when she exceeds her means or allowance. It is fatal concealment to allow debts to accumulate without one's husband's knowledge; it tempts the woman weak enough to do so to have recourse to most unworthy and most dangerous expedients, which are sure to be known in the end, and to lower the culprit or ruin her for ever in her husband's esteem. The equivocations and the downright falsehoods which are often used as means of concealment, cannot but be considered by every right-minded man as a greater calamity than the accumulation of the largest debt or the loss of an entire fortune.

In this respect, as indeed in every other, no concealment will be found to be the wife's only true policy; and to secure this policy of no concealment let her make it the study of her life to have nothing to conceal.

The Wife the Dispenser of Hospitality.

To the wife's stewardship belongs also the discharge of a most important, not to say most sacred duty—that of hospitality. It is one of the chief functions of the divine virtue of charity. Of its nature, its necessity, and its importance we do not wish to discourse here. Few are the homes and the hearts to which hospitality is a stranger. Those to which this book may reach will easily understand what the word means without either definition or description. We can, therefore, convey our instruction by the simplest method.

Whoever is received into your home as a guest—precisely because he is your guest—forget every thing else to make his stay delightful. It matters little whether persons thus hospitably received may or may not appreciate your generosity, your cordiality, and that true warmth of a welcome like yours, inspired by Christian motives much more than by worldly reasons; it matters much for you that none should ever enter your home without finding it a true Christian home, or should leave it without taking away with them the pleasant memory of their stay and a grateful recollection of you and yours. Doubtless some will be found whom no courtesy, no kindness, no warmth of hospitality can change from what they are,—little-minded, narrow-hearted, selfish, cold, and unable to judge the conduct of others by any other standard than their own low thoughts and sentiments. They are only like bats entering a banquet-hall by one window and passing out at the opposite, after having fluttered blindly about the lights, or clung for a few instants to the walls or the ceiling. Let them come and let them go. The social and spiritual atmosphere of the place is not for them.

Nor must you complain of the number. It is wonderful how much place a large-hearted woman can find for her company, even in a very small house! A hospitable spirit can do wonders in its way: it can make the water on the board more delicious than the wines of Portugal, Spain, or France or Italy; it can make the bread which it places before stranger or friend as sweet as the food of the gods; it can multiply its own scanty stores—as the Master did with the loaves in the wilderness. For God's blessing is with the hospitable soul to increase, to multiply, and to sweeten; to fill all who sit at her board with plenty, with joy, with thanksgiving.

"There is," says Digby, "a castle on the Loire held by a lady of ascetic piety and of noble fame, in the latest pages of French heroic annals. There one of my friends, received to hospitality, finding many guests, supposed himself surrounded by men of illustrious condition, till he was informed that they were all persons reduced to poverty, whose title to familiarity under that roof was founded precisely on their indigence and misfortunes."[10]

Ah, noble France, how many other homes along the Loire, the Mayenne, the Sarthe, and the Somme do we not know which are always open to the stranger and the pilgrim from other lands, while their generous masters and mistresses deem every sacrifice a blessing, because performed for Christ present in the guest of one day, or one week, or one month!

Léon Du Coudray's Widowed Mother.

More than one eye will read this page and share the feelings of the writer in recalling that hospitable home near Laval, where the widowed mother of an only son gave, yearly, hospitality for two whole weeks to fifty or more of the

[10] *Compitum*, book i., chapter vi., p. 177.

student-sons of St. Ignatius—young men from Canada and the United States and New Granada, as well as from Spain and Italy, from Great Britain and Ireland, from France and Germany—nay, even from Russia's old Moscovite capital. How the son—not a priest yet, but one who had renounced a brilliant career in the world for the poverty and humility of a Jesuit's life—would daily invent new forms of amusement and recreation with which to make the mother's lavish hospitality the more graceful and the more charming! How each evening found that band of apostolic youths (reminding one of the "Schools of the Prophets" in the days of old) engaged in some new pastime on the green sward, blending needful recreation after hard study with some beautiful literary enjoyment! We still hear the glorious tenor voice of that thrice-blessed son, Léon du Coudray, rising above the loud chorus of song and hymn; we remember the pleasant open countenance, the ever sweet smile, the gracious words of heartfelt affection, as natural to the true-hearted youth as its native notes are to the nightingale. And then we bethink us, as we just read the latest accounts of his heroic death,[11] of this young man, become the Superior of the noblest Christian school in France, seized with several of his brethren as a hostage by the Commune, and turning to them as they were led to prison through the streets of Paris amid curses and insults, and saying aloud in the old joyous tones: "*Ibant gaudentes*... 'They went,...rejoicing that they were accounted worthy to suffer'—is it not so?" He went as joyously to prison, that only son of the widowed mother, as ever bridegroom to his bridals; and when the fatal 24th of May, 1871, had come, it was on his strong arm that the Archbishop of Paris leaned, as they were hurried forth to be obscurely butchered; it was by his side that the prelate stood facing their bloodthirsty executioners; and when the first volley had been fired, only wounding the archbishop, who fell to the ground, and leaving his companion almost unhurt, it was Léon du Coudray's strong arm that lifted him up, and on his brave heart that his sinking head was laid, when a second volley mingled their blood and freed both their souls at once. Ah, brave heart, true heart! Was the widowed mother still living to learn of her martyr's death, and to receive in the bittersweet of that so glorious ending the reward of her profuse hospitality and of all her Christian virtues? With Léon perished and was

---

[11] See Maxime du Camp, *Prisons de Paris sous la Commune*, in the *Revue des Deux Mondes*, 1st September, 1877.

buried another young priest dear to the writer of these lines, Father Alexis Clercq, once a navy officer, and, at the time of his arrestation, a professor in the College S. Geneviève, *Rue des Postes*. The writer had prepared him for his first mass, and assisted him at the altar during its celebration. May they both from near the throne of the Lamb beseech a blessing on these pages, and obtain for every mother who reads them the grace of being not all unlike that hospitable widow, and of rearing, like her, sons ready to sacrifice life itself rather than betray Christ and the faith of their baptism!

There are, however, examples nearer home, which if not connected with such tragic scenes as this, have also their touching record of heroic devotion crowned by the death of the saints.

How a Noble Husband Was Sustained by a Devoted Wife While Passing Through Financial Difficulties.

One family in particular will help to teach the reader that womanly excellence is no rare or recent flower on the soil of the New World. A young wife, born among our Western valleys, and wedded to the man of her choice, had encouraged him in a chivalrous literary enterprise which promised precious and plentiful fruit for the highest purposes of patriotism as well as religion. Their home had been blessed by six beautiful children, reared by the accomplished mother with inconceivable tenderness and care. It had been the delight of the grandparents to fill that home with every article of furniture and object of art which could make it what it was in reality—a paradise for its inmates as well as for a large and devoted circle of friends.

But the mind, the heart, and the hand of the happy young wife it was which gave to that home its bright look of refinement, of goodness, of perfect happiness.

One day, while she and her eldest daughter were wreathing some flowers round the frame of a favorite picture, the husband and father came in, and received from both the usual rapturous welcome. "Look, my dear," the proud little housewife exclaimed, after the first greeting, "look and see if any thing can be more beautiful than this room! Had we our choice from the richest stores and the rarest collections of art, what could we add to all this! What dear object could we part with for a better?" The fond husband's eyes glanced rapidly round the room; but they did not shine with the enthusiasm which fired his companion's. A cloud of a sudden settled on his brow as if the question caused a pang in spite of the strong effort he made to repress his emotion. To his wife's enthusiastic queries he only answered by bending over her and kissing her in silence.

She divined that some misfortune had befallen or was impending. And he, who had ever, since their wedding-day, found in her a trusty friend and most wise counselor,—now told her that the enterprise which had promised to be a most profitable as well as a most beneficial investment, had proved a most ruinous failure!

His friends, he said, had generously offered to come to his assistance and lend him all the money needed to meet his engagements. To cumber himself with this debt or to sell his home and its costly furniture, was the only alternative left to them. He had not had courage to mention to her till the last moment the strait to which he was reduced; for he feared, and their friends feared, lest the parting with her beautiful home and the loss of so many precious things should crush her.

"You cannot hesitate, dearest," was the quick reply;—"we must part with every thing rather than become dependent on others by being their debtors. You shall see how easy it will be to me to part with these treasures, provided I have a little home for you and your darlings, into which no creditor may intrude or pry. Am I not too rich and too happy with the wealth of love you and my children bring to me?"

There was not a moment lost; a little cottage was rented in another part of the city, and only the most needful articles of furniture were provided for parents, children, and servants; the busy hands of the young wife were never idle for several days beautifying the new home for the dear ones, who were kept, as well as friends and neighbors, in ignorance of the approaching change; and the little ones soon found themselves all of a sudden transported to the new nest!

Then, to the astonishment of all in the neighborhood, and the regret of many, the auctioneer came, and piece after piece of the beautiful furniture—some of it made by the best upholsterers from the timber grown on the paternal estates far away—the objects of art and *virtù*, with which the young mother was wont to illustrate her lessons on the beautiful given to the oldest children, and the dear piano—the gift of a fond mother—all were unhesitatingly sacrificed.

But what was the astonishment of friends and relatives, when, after a few days of pity or wonderment, they called on the brave little woman in her new home, to find it so fair, so bright, so beautiful! The carpets were plain, it is true, and the furniture was of the commonest kind; but chairs and sofas and ottomans had been covered with a chintz so pretty that no one stopped to inquire what was beneath the covering. There were white curtains to the windows, looped up with garlands of artificial flowers, and there were fragrant flowers on mantels and tables; and the little mistress was there with her face all aglow with happiness, with her sunny smile and merry laugh, and the warm hospitable welcome for every friend and acquaintance;—and there, too, were the rosy children, as unconscious of any change of fortune as the happy guests of Aladdin's fairy palaces, who found in one suite of apartments objects so ravishing that they quite forgot what they had seen before. The little ones saw no change around them, save that the light of their mother's smile was even more sunny than ever, that she loaded their dear father with fonder caresses and called forth from his big heart louder bursts of joy and mirth,—and that she had been busier than ever with her active hands and restless needle in transforming and beautifying the face of things in every room with the smallest possible expense.

The change of residence, as well as the circumstances which occasioned it, only served to raise both husband and wife in the esteem of the community and to inspire their intimate friends with a warm admiration for their magnanimity. And so the happy nestful increased, and the husband rose higher in public confidence and in his noble profession,—while his wife bestowed her whole care on the lovely children, whom she educated herself in every branch of learning and in every accomplishment necessary or suitable to their position. It was no small labor; but she found it light,—such was the order which she had established in her household, so sure was she of the devoted zeal of every one of her servants, and so delightful did she know how to make to her worshiping pupils every step in the most arid pathways of learning.

And yet the house was ever full of visitors. The numerous relatives belonging to both families were always expected to make their home with these good young people while in town; and there were friends who could not resist the attraction they felt for a family which seemed to them the ideal of human felicity. Limited as was their income, neither the husband nor the wife ever bestowed a thought on the expenditure consequent upon such an unbounded and uninterrupted hospitality. The little wife managed to have a bountiful table at all times, never an extravagant one; and thus she never once allowed her household expenses to go beyond her means. What made her table, her drawing-room, the whole atmosphere of her home so full of an undefinable charm, was the love, the innocence, the paradisaical purity and charity which parents and children shed around them.

The dinners were true feasts of love and joyousness, and the evenings in the drawing-room were festivals of song, in which mother and children had the chief part, but in which all guests who could play or sing were impelled to join by some powerful spell.

Those who had been privileged to share once or twice in this genuine hospitality, or who had been during one or two evenings under the charm of that blissful family circle, would yearn to return.

And now, it will be asked, does this blessed home still exist? Alas, no! The nest is empty, cold, and songless. Like many a sainted mother in the past, the brave-hearted little woman could truly sing:

"I pray you, what is the nest to me,
My empty nest?
And what is the shore where I stood to see
My boat sail down to the west?
Can I call that home where I anchor yet,
Though my good man has sailed?
Can I call that home where my nest was set,
Now all its hope hath failed?
Nay, but the port where my sailor went,
And the land where my nestlings be:
There is the home where my thoughts are sent,
The only home for me—
Ah me!"[12]

[12] Jean Ingelow, "Songs of Seven."

The Wife as the Friend of the Poor.

We should have told how dear to the hearts of the poor, to the hearts indeed of all who were acquainted with misfortune and suffering in any shape, was the home into whose privacy we have been just glancing,—for every heart and every hand within it were ever open to the needy. We may intersperse through these pages many gracious acts of goodness and true charity originating with the queen of that blessed home,—just as the silversmiths of old would detach pearls and other gems from an over-rich crown to adorn the vesture of royalty or religion. So pass we now to that dear function of home-life in the good old Catholic times.

And connecting here hospitality toward the poor with almsgiving, let us see what was in that respect the spirit of the ages of faith. "Padua," Digby informs us, "had forty-five houses for the entertainment of poor strangers; in Venice all comers were entertained by many Doges; and, above all, say the old Italians, Vicenza was distinguished for its munificence toward needy strangers. At Venice, the senators who presided over the public administration were so hospitable that the whole city resembled a hotel for guests, and a common home for all strangers coming to it. At Cesena every one used to dispute for the honor of receiving the stranger, till, to obviate such quarrels, the pillar was erected, having a ring for each noble family, so that to whichever the stranger on arriving fastened his horse, to that family was he to repair. '*Receive kindly whoever comes,*' says St. Francis in his rule,—the spirit of which ruled many castles as well as cloisters—'*all, whether friend or foe, thief or robber.*' We read, indeed, of one proud castle standing near the road, over the portal of which the knight who built it, through the sole motive of vanity, caused lines to be inscribed...intending to signify that no one should be received but knights, philosophers, or clerks, or noble ladies. But the ancient legend states that by a terrible vision this knight was converted, and so delivered from his former error that he resolved thenceforth to entertain rather the poor, effacing that inscription and substituting for it words which signified that the naked and poor, the sick and infirm, and the exile and the pilgrim, would be thenceforth his guests."[13]

---

[13] *Compitum*, b. i., c. vi.

In Brittany a most beautiful custom still exists, in spite of modern legislation, which tends to forbid almsgiving of every kind, and to prevent the poor, even when they have a hovel of their own, from leaving it and making their dire need known to their neighbors. The day following marriage is "the day of the poor." They troop from every side to the door of the happy pair, and find tables spread for them in the vast hall of the nobleman, when the bridegroom is such, or on the greensward when he is of inferior degree. The tables for the men are set on one side, those for the women on the other, the bridegroom waiting on the former, and the bride attending to the comfort of those of her own sex. When they have had their fill, all dance together, and then take their leave, pouring blessings on their kind entertainers. Surely such blessings and the heartfelt wishes and prayers of the poor must be more profitable to young people entering on the married state and its doubtful fortunes, than the idle congratulations of a fashionable throng, and the selfish modern custom of hastening from the foot of the altar to the railway train or steamboat, in order to escape from the irksome duty of receiving friends or feasting the poor.

If from Brittany you cross in imagination the broad expanse of sea which separates the westernmost shores of France from Spain, you will find among another proud and ancient race, the Basques, with a faith by no means less deep than that of the Bretons, Catholic notions about poverty and almsgiving which are full of eloquent meaning. Land at any point of that rock-bound shore, in any one of the fishing towns and villages so famous all through Christian history, and you will see how the few native poor, in a country where nobody is ever seen idle, are treated with a sovereign respect and tenderness. A recent traveler[14] landing at the little town of Elanchove—which clings with its one street to the almost perpendicular face of a mountain two thousand feet high—saw, as he toiled up that ladderlike street, "a poor old woman all bent double with age standing at a door and asking for alms. A charming young married woman, her mouth all wreathed with smiles, hastened to come out. I saw her take from her pocket a small brass coin, kiss it, and then give it to the old woman. The latter took the alms, made with it very devoutly the sign of the cross on herself, and then kissed it in her turn. Such is the custom

[14] L. Louis-Lande, *Trois Mois de voyage dans le Pays Basque.*

throughout the Basque country, and does it not add a touching grace to charity?"

Such noble and touching customs as this are not, however, confined to Biscay or to Northern Spain; they are everywhere characteristic of the Spanish Catholic. The lofty spirit of self-respect which is the soul of the Spaniard, is shown in the reverence with which he treats the poor, whom word or look of his will never humble; but as his faith teaches him to consider Christ himself present in the person of the beggar or of the sick man, his respect for them becomes downright and heartfelt veneration.

It will cheer and enlighten us to gather some of these choice pearls of Spanish custom to deck our own crown of merit withal. "Cheating and extortion seem incompatible with the Spanish character. Even the poorest peasant who has shown us our way, and who has walked a considerable distance to do so, has invariably refused to receive any thing for his services; yet all are most willing and anxious to help strangers. The same liberal spirit seems to breathe through every thing, and was equally shown at our little posada (inn) at Elche,...where a number of maimed, blind, and halt collected daily to receive the broken viands from the table-d'hôte, which the mistress distributed to them, and in the delicate blacksmith's wife opposite, who keeps two lamps burning nightly at her own expense before the little shrine of 'Our Lady of the Unprotected' in her balcony. The temporal works of mercy—to give bread to the hungry, and drink to the thirsty, to take care of the sick, to visit prisoners, and to bury the dead, these are the common duties which none shrink from."

"As I write, a handsome, dark-eyed brown boy in rags, who looks as if he had stepped out of one of Murillo's pictures, is leaning against the opposite wall in the moonlight, watching a shrine of the Virgin. It is a picture typical of Spain, ruined and superstitious, but still most beautiful—and so is the cry of the watchman which is ringing through the silent air, '*Ave, Maria Santissima!* it is a quarter to twelve o'clock!'"[15]

Ah, give us back this superstition,—this living faith rather, which built up Spain and Portugal till they were the wonder of Christendom. The ruin of the Peninsula is coeval, step by step, with the decline of that glorious spirit of

[15] Hare, "Wanderings in Spain," v., pp. 83, 84.

"superstition." But we can pardon this perversion of judgment in a Protestant who has the eye to see and the heart to appreciate so much that is beautiful in Catholic customs.

It is well known that from time immemorial the sovereigns of Spain visit the hospitals nearest to the royal residence once at least every year. The rule is to go there with the entire court. On entering the sick ward royalty at once goes to the nearest bed and humbly kisses the hand of the poor patient. Then sovereigns and courtiers wait on the sick, performing in their behalf the most menial services, and addressing the sufferers with as much reverence as if they beheld the God of Calvary or the Divine Babe of Bethlehem visibly present in every sick-bed.

The Leprous Infant Cared for by Elizabeth of Hungary.

Is not this the significance of a most beautiful legend from the life of St. Elizabeth of Hungary? Her mother-in-law, Sophia, was, at the time of the occurrence about to be related, bitterly prejudiced against the saintly wife. "She neither shared nor approved Elizabeth's charities and merciful ministrations. In her son, however, she found no sympathy. Yet one account shows how even his kind heart was overtasked. One day a child afflicted with leprosy was brought to the hospital in the Wartburg; but his state was such that even the most courageous attendants in the institution would neither touch him nor admit him. Elizabeth, coming at her usual hour, no sooner beheld the little sufferer lying helpless and forsaken at the gate, than she took him up in her arms, carried him to the castle, and placed him in her own bed."

"Sophia, indignant, flew to the landgrave. 'My son,' she burst forth, 'come with me instantly, and see with whom your wife shares your bed;' and she led him to his chamber, relating in exaggerated language the extraordinary occurrence that seemed to crown all the mad acts of his wife's charity. The landgrave, though he said not one word, could scarcely conceal his irritation and loathing. He snatched the coverlet from the bed, *and lo! instead of the leper, there lay an infant, surrounded with a halo of light, and bearing the features of the new-born babe of Bethlehem*!"[16]

---

[16] "Heroic Women of the Bible and the Church," c. xxxiii., pp. 349, 350.

This example is, however, more admirable than imitable. It is a rare thing to have to perform heroic acts of any virtue,—even that of charity. Where a miracle occurs, as here, Providence means to inculcate a lesson. The teaching, to the Catholic mind, is a plain one: it is only the repetition, under a different form, of the Master's doctrine, that he is represented by the persons of the poor and the suffering.

So, with this conviction firmly seated in the soul of the Christian mistress of a household, it will be easy for her to see with what reverence and generosity she must treat the poor. We say "reverence." For if her womanly heart has schooled itself to behold Christ present in every one of the needy who come to her door, she will not have to be reminded to show to all, without exception, kindness. Kindness is something far beneath reverence; yet let us insist upon the absolute necessity of kind looks and kind words. No one better than a woman knows how far kindness goes, or how much and how long a kind word or a look of tender sympathy will be treasured up by those on whom they are bestowed. If you have nothing else to give,—if your purse is empty, and your bread has failed,—open the spring of kindness in your heart and let it pour out on the hearts of the poor sweet words of compassion, often more needed and more rarely bestowed than food on the famishing or cold water on the faint and weary.

Follow the rule of the great St. Francis, therefore: *Be invariably and unfailingly kind to the poor.* And this precious quality in the temper and bearing of man or woman can only be secured by the habitual practice of that "reverence" just mentioned. It is more needful than ever that in every Catholic home mothers should cultivate that ancient respect for husband and children which was inspired by a lively faith, and made every member of the Christian community view in his fellow-Christians the children of God, the person of Christ himself. This feeling inspired the father of the great Origen,—a father found soon afterward worthy to die the death of the martyrs,—with a reverence for his infant son so deep and so sincere, that he was wont as he passed his cradle to uncover the child's breast and to kiss it, kneeling,—knowing, as he said, that the babe was the living temple of the Holy Ghost.

Surely Catholic fathers and mothers ought to find an exquisite pleasure in such elevating thoughts and sentiments as this; surely they should so consider each other and respect each other as if they too were chosen vessels, vessels of grace, bearing about in their bosoms the Creator Spirit; and most surely ought it to be the mother's chief delight to reverence in every child of hers a something far more holy, more precious than the chalice used in the Holy Sacrifice, or the sacred vessel shut up in the Tabernacle and inclosing Christ's divinest gift to our souls.

Can we school and accustom ourselves so to reverence the poor as to see in them the Person of Him who is represented as evermore standing in the night, wet by the dew or the rainstorm, at the door of every one of us, and gently knocking for admission to the light and warmth of our fireside?

This said, it is not our design to say either to the wealthy or to the needy housewife what measure she is to follow in relieving the wants of the poor.

Let our spirit be the royal spirit of the ancient Catholic charity of our fathers. To the rich let this suffice. "A modern author relates that a merchant in Spain once said to him: *A rich Spanish tradesman would laugh at you if you talked to him of keeping his carriage; but ask him for alms, and he will think nothing of giving you a hundred, five hundred, or a thousand dollars.*"[17]

The Charitable Peasant-Girl.

In our own days we find in Catholic countries most illustrious examples of unbounded charity among the poorest classes of laborers. At St. Etienne-la-Varenne, in the south-east of France, lived a country girl named Magdalen Saulnier. "Pious from her cradle, she used to distribute every day to the neighboring poor part of the provision that she received for herself to take into the fields; though of a weak constitution, she used to walk long distances to visit other poor and give them alms, which she had begged from the rich. During fifteen years she supported in this manner a poor blind man and his idiot daughter, daily visiting them, though they lived a league and a half from her home. A poor woman afflicted with leprosy in the hamlet of Grandes-Bruyères had no one, during eighteen months, to come near her but Magdalen, in whose arms she breathed her last. In 1840, during the inundations of the Rhone, she narrowly escaped being drowned while conveying her daily provision to another poor woman in the Grange-Macon;

[17] *Compitum*, b. iii., c. vii.

and, when reproached for her imprudence, she replied, 'Why, what would you have me to do? I had not seen her the day before.' In the depth of winter, in 1835, she had discovered a poor woman, named Mancel, living far away in a hut, more like a wild beast's den than a human habitation. This poor creature was ill, and Magdalen would not leave her alone. Toward the close of a long night, a thick snow covering the ground, she lighted some sticks, which caused so great a smoke that she opened the door to let in fresh air, when a wolf stood ready to dispute with Death its prey. It required all her efforts, aided only with a large stone, to keep the door closed against the furious animal, which howled and struggled for entrance till the dawn. Some hours after, the woman expired. Then Magdalen, fearing that the wolf would return, took up the body on her shoulders, and carried it to the house of the nearest peasant, who received it till the burial took place."[18]

What an example is here—in this poor girl whose whole life was consumed in the incredible hardships of a field-laborer—for the wives and daughters of our laboring classes in town and country. There is not a narrow street, crowded with tenement-houses, in any one of our large cities,—nor a manufacturing population in any of our great industrial centers,—in which every woman who reads these pages cannot find some poor mother burdened with a family who is always busied in doing good around her to those poorer and more burdened than herself; some factory-girl, sparely clad and poorly fed, who is an angel of good counsel, comfort, and all manner of help to her companions. Travelers over a sandy and treeless waste often chance upon green and shady spots rising like islands of the blessed in the midst of an ocean of death and desolation. When they come to examine what has made these fairy spots so beautiful, they find a spring of living water gushing up from the bosom of the earth, overflowing its native spot, causing the grass to grow, and the shrub to flower, and the tree to take root and thrive, and thus the green carpet spreads round about that cool spring, and bird and beast and man himself hasten gratefully to enjoy the shade, the refreshing waters, the loveliness and repose of the spot. Examine well, in these moral wastes so frequent and so hideous amid our civilization and our Christianity, what is the source of the sweet and sanctifying influences you discover in certain

[18] *Ibidem*, pp. 265, 266.

neighborhoods: you will be sure to trace it to some womanly heart, in the poorest of hovels frequently, and not seldom in the coldest and most naked of garrets.

French-Canadian Women and the Irish Orphans of 1847.

But let us point out, nearer home, some heroic examples, which we may hold up as a mirror to American womanhood.

And first must be recorded here, by one who was an eyewitness of what he relates, and before the generation which beheld it has passed away, one of the sublimest instances of Christian charity known to ancient or modern times. New York and Quebec have not yet forgotten the Irish famine of 1846-47 and its terrible consequences. But 'tis with the latter city in particular that this narrative has to deal. Fearful as had been all through the fall and winter of 1846 the tidings borne to America about the privations endured by a whole famishing people, and the mortality caused by fever and other attendant diseases, but little apprehension was felt in Canada when navigation opened with the early spring. Consequently nothing like adequate preparation was made by the local authorities either at the quarantine station below Quebec, or at any of the usual landing-places along the St. Lawrence.

The result of this want of forethought was terrible both for the thousands of wretched immigrants cast all of a sudden on our shores, and for the populations among whom the poor fevered victims carried, whithersoever they went, the seeds of pestilence. The quarantine station on Grosse Isle, below Quebec, became a hot-bed of the most virulent typhus fever, and almost all the priests who were called in turn to minister to the spiritual wants of the crowded sick on ship and shore, caught the disease, many of them dying, and the others carrying disease, death, and dismay back with them to their parishes. In the city of Quebec itself but comparatively few ravages were committed by this dreaded "ship fever:" the steamers which conveyed the healthier immigrants to Montreal and the upper St. Lawrence not being permitted to land. In Montreal, however, and in Kingston and Toronto their arrival and passage were marked by a fearful mortality. In the first-named city Bishop Bourget, his coadjutor, Bishop Prince, his vicar-general, and some thirty priests were stricken down by the plague. The seminary of St. Sulpice alone lost eight of its members. Bishop Power of Toronto fell a victim to it, and its ravages were such, during the early summer, that they far outstripped those of the cholera.

Of course thousands upon thousands of orphans were left behind, and that, too, at a time when to give them a refuge in any home in town and country, appeared to be bringing certain death into the family. Yet,—and this is what must redound to the eternal honor of the French Canadian population of the present province of Quebec,—not only was there no hesitation manifested in adopting these little castaways, but at the voice of their bishops and priests the people of the country parishes vied with each other in their zeal to share their homes with them.

The author remembers returning from quarantine, in the second week of July, with the Rev. John Harper, rector of St. Grégoire, opposite Three Rivers. They had spent a fortnight among the fever-sheds, and had, at the urgent request of their parishioners, brought home with them a large number of orphans. The parishioners of St. Grégoire (the descendants of the noble Acadians eulogized by the author of "Evangeline") had chartered a little steamer to convey us and our orphans across the river. We had been delayed perforce on our way upward, and on our arrival about midnight at Three Rivers, we found a crowd of eager and excited women, mothers of families all of them, waiting and watching for us. Mr. Harper was among his parishioners, and on the spot these noble mothers were allowed to satisfy the yearning of their Christian hearts, and to take each her little orphan to her embrace. It was a spectacle worthy of the admiration of angels, which was beheld on that wharf at that sultry midnight in July, these farmers' wives, weeping every one of them with that holy emotion which sweetest charity creates, pressing around their pastor and choosing, when they could, in the uncertain light, the child that pleased them best, or accepting joyously and folding in a motherly embrace the little orphan allotted to them. The ladies of Three Rivers were also there, jealous of the happiness of their sisters and neighbors, and employing in the darkness some pious stratagem to decoy to their homes some of the weary, wasted, or fevered little creatures.

The author was a hundred miles distant from his own parish of Sherbrooke, and had only dared to select a few orphans to take with him all the way. So, after an hour of confusion and excitement we were all content to rest till the approaching daylight. When the dawn came, and we left our resting-places for the ferry, all Three Rivers and its neighborhood were abroad to see the priests, their orphans, and the happy mothers to whom God had given the prize of an orphan, wending their way in a procession to the steamer and the ferry-boat. The heat of the preceding days, and the sultry night with its excitement, had told on more than one of the bewildered little strangers: there were several cases of declared fever. But no one seemed to mind. The charity of Jesus Christ was abroad, like a river overflowing its banks. Two children who had fallen to the author's charge were especially ill; one, a little boy, clung to his cassock as we set out from the hotel; the other, a little girl of four, he had to carry in his arms, as she was too sick to walk.

The scene has remained indelibly impressed upon heart and memory. We were wending our way through the crowd of weeping or pitying spectators, when the wife of a distinguished lawyer of Three Rivers, childless herself, as we were told, approached the author to caress the little motherless one who clung to him in apparent insensibility. As she kissed the child again and again, addressing it in the sweetest tones of womanly tenderness, the little sufferer looked into those appealing, tearful eyes, and stretched out her arms to that hungry heart which would not be refused. They were only separated by death thereafter.

But when we reached the other shore we found the Rev. J. C. Marquis, with the entire population of St. Grégoire, and every available mode of conveyance waiting for us; and so we proceeded some two or three miles to the beautiful parish church, where priests and people knelt in devout thanksgiving,—the priests grateful for their preservation from the plague, the people thanking God for the precious boon charity had bestowed on them. They did not rest contented with this, however: hundreds of other orphans were sought after subsequently and added to the happiness, and—let us hope—the prosperity of this excellent people. Not one of these stranger-children but became in every sense the child of the home into which it was received.

All through the remaining months of summer, the autumn, and the early winter, this generous flame of charity spread and burned among the French Canadian parishes along both shores of the St. Lawrence; and, strange to say, the good souls who thus vied with each other in opening their homes and hearts to the orphans of Ireland's exiles, were wont to say that while the plague spared the families into which the strangers were admitted, it swept away pitilessly such as gave them a passing or a mercenary refuge. Ah, generous people of New France, may the Saints of Ireland obtain for you length of days, with the richest blessings of true freedom, a constant increase in the noblest gifts of soul, and all the rewards of true piety!

The Wife of a Ship-Carpenter a Ministering Angel of Mercy.

One crowning instance must be selected, ere we close this chapter, to demonstrate what womanly hearts can and will effect for the suffering and the needy. It is November in Quebec, in that same memorable year 1847, and November had set in with unusual severity. The country parishes all round had each received its colony of Irish orphans or young girls, who were adopted by the excellent farmers, Still the temporary asylums in Quebec attached to St. Patrick's church remained overcrowded; no provision had been made for their sustenance during the long winter which was setting in so fiercely; and local charity, it was feared, had been exhausted by the extraordinary drain of the preceding six months.

At a meeting of ladies it was resolved that the most zealous would go by sub-committees of twos and threes into all the neighboring parishes, and knock at every door to exhort every family to adopt one of the many hundreds of homeless waifs left behind by the retiring tide of disease and wretchedness. Women's tongues are eloquent when fired by such a cause; they were welcomed everywhere, and a day was fixed when the orphans should be brought to St. Patrick's church, and all who wished to add one more stranger to their family circle were to go there and make their choice.

So, on the day appointed, the ferries from Point Levi and the Island of Orleans were early crowded with farmers' wives and daughters, while along the roads from St. Foye and Beauport, Charlebourg and Lorette, the vehicles of the country people streamed into the city as to some great public festival.

It was near noon, and in the house of a French Canadian ship-carpenter, out near the banks of the St. Charles River, at the extremity of the St. Roch suburb, the cheerful, active mother of six children was just concluding her morning's labor, sending off her oldest girl with the father's dinner to the shipyard, leaving her infant nursling with a kind neighbor, and then hurrying away,—a distance of full two miles, to Patrick's church. She had been delayed in spite of her utmost exertions, and her only feeling, as she almost ran along the road, was one of fear lest she should be too late at the church and miss the prize which she had promised her husband to bring home to himself and their dear ones.

The silent empty streets through which she passed on nearing the church made her heart sink within her; and as she entered St. Patrick's there was no one there but a few good old souls telling their beads before the altar, and some soldiers of the garrison performing "the Way of the Cross." The tears filled her eyes as she knelt a moment in adoration; and then she hastened to explore the two large sacristies behind the church. They were empty! As she passed through the lower one, what she deemed a stifled sob struck her ear; but the distant corner whence it seemed to issue was very dark, and her eyes were still half-blinded by the brilliant sun outside and the glare of the snow. So, in her excitement, she heeded not the sound, but crossed the courtyard to the rectory and knocked timidly at the door. The servant, on opening, saw this good woman in tears, and scarcely able to articulate one word. At length she gasped out, "The orphans?"—"The orphans, ma'am?" replied the other; "there are none here!"—"Where are they?"—"All gone—all taken away by the ladies."—"Have you kept none that you might let me have?"—"No, indeed," was the answer; and with this the poor woman turned away with a heavy heart. As she re-entered the lower sacristy on her way to the church, her ear was again struck with the sound of sobbing, and coming, this time, more audibly from the distant dark corner. She was there in a moment; and bending, or rather kneeling down, she distinguished a female child, with its head between its hands, sobbing and moaning piteously.

It was a little girl, some five years old, who on the voyage out had lost father and mother, brothers, sisters—all! The little thing, naturally a very beautiful child, had had in succession fever, dysentery, and small-pox; and beneath this complication she had almost sunk. She had partially lost the use of her lower limbs, and had been frightfully disfigured. In the church, whither she had been brought early in the morning with the other orphans, the charitable women had invariably passed her by, choosing, as was natural, the most comely children for their adopted ones,—and the sensitive slighted little thing sobbed so piteously that she was taken to the sacristy in order not to disturb the proceedings in the church. There she had sat in the corner, sobbing herself to sleep, and had been forgotten when the crowd left the church. So, as the opening of the sacristy door, a moment ago, had roused the forlorn one from her somnolency, she had looked up at the stranger coming in with a revival of hope, and a sob escaped her as the latter passed out by the opposite door. Once more hiding her face in her hands, she wept and sobbed with increased bitterness, as if the little wounded heart within would burst her chest.

And thus the good carpenter's wife found her, as she knelt in the gloom by her side. "What is the matter, dear child?" she said, with infinite tenderness in her tone. "Who has left you here?—Speak to me, my dear!" she went on, as she removed the hands from her face. The child looked up through her scalding tears at the sweet sound of that motherly voice, and all was plain to the speaker. The face thus revealed was so disfigured that the woman drew back involuntarily. But recovering herself instantly, and,—as she expressed it,—indignant at her own cowardice, she extended both arms lovingly to the weeper: "Kiss me, darling," she said, as her own tears flowed fast, "kiss me, come to my heart; don't be afraid, I am your mother now." And she folded her in her embrace, covering her face and head with tears and kisses. The ship-carpenter's family possessed a blessed treasure that night.

No, this is not extraordinary charity: great hearts, like that of that noble woman, abound everywhere among our laboring people. O women, who read these lines, remember, that your charity, your generosity will find in your every-day ordinary life rich opportunities for their exercise. Never neglect any occasion God sends you of doing the good you can. Great charity, like every other great virtue, does not consist in doing extraordinary things, or waiting for extraordinary circumstances; it depends on our doing with all our heart the good we have the chance of doing at every moment within our own homes and outside of them.

"I have known a word hang starlike
    O'er a dreary waste of years,
And it only shone the brighter
    Looked at through a mist of tears;
While a weary wanderer gathered
    Hope and heart on Life's dark way,

By its faithful promise, shining
    Clearer day by day.

I have known a word more gentle
    Than the breath of summer air;
In a listening heart it nestled,
    And it lived forever there.
Not the beating of its prison
    Stirred it ever night or day;
Only with the heart's last throbbing
    Could it fade away."[19]

[19] Adelaide Anne Procter.

CHAPTER VIII.

THE WIFE'S CROWNING DUTY—FIDELITY.

Ut nos junxit amor, nostro sic parta labore
Unanimes animos operit una domus.

As us love joined, so by our toil acquired,
One-minded souls one mansion covereth.

Ancient inscription on a French house.

Do you know where you are? Do you know that this is the house of a man rich in virtue?... Do you know that these marbles, these stones, these paternal ceilings, represent the ancient honor and the venerated virtue of the family? The house of my father is the center of loyalty, and the sanctuary of honor.

ALARION.

The home is the nursery of the nation, and the deep and sacred love that binds into one existence the hearts and lives of husband and wife, is the soul of the home life. Every thing which tends to lessen, to divide, to sully that sacred union of hearts, strikes at the very life of the family and aims at upsetting the foundations of the moral world.

The sacred virtue, the immaculate honor of every family, is inseparable from the purity and perpetuity of the love pledged to each other by both parents; more especially, in universal estimation, is the family honor dependent on the inviolable fidelity of the mother toward him to whom she gave her early love.

Hence the deep significance of the prayer of the church in the solemn ceremony of marriage. She who had proposed to the imitation of all wives the undivided and unalterable love which she ever bears to Christ, her Spouse,—who gives them in her inviolable and eternal fidelity to him, to his honor and interests, the model of the true woman's unwavering, sustained, and devoted fidelity to her husband,—makes of this notion the central point in her magnificent marriage ritual.

Throughout all ages known to history, the most refined peoples have looked upon the ring as the symbol of eternity—as the proper emblem, therefore, of the union of souls underlying the matrimonial contract.

The Ring Symbolic of Eternal Fidelity.

When the Church has witnessed and sanctioned by her blessing the mutual and solemn pledge given by bride and bridegroom, she proceeds to bless a ring, which is given to the bride as a symbol and seal of the union into which she has entered, and of the enduring fidelity with which she is to feed the sacred fire of mutual affection and to watch over the honor of her hearth-stone.

"Bless, O Lord, this ring," such is the prayer, "which we bless in thy name, in order that she who wears it, by preserving unbroken fidelity to her husband, may continue in peace and the accomplishment of thy will, and also ever live in mutual charity."

Where the beautiful ceremonial is carried out in its intended fullness, the nuptial benediction is followed by the offering of the adorable sacrifice. Christ comes down on the altar, who so loved the Church, his Bride, that he "delivered himself up for it, that he might sanctify it, cleansing it by the laver of water in the word of life, that he might present it to himself a glorious Church, not having spot, or wrinkle, or any such thing, but that it should be holy and without blemish."

There, at that altar and in that presence, kneel the two for whom the Saviour God comes down, his hands filled with blessing for these his children beginning life together, and his heart overflowing with untold treasures of grace,—so needful to them on their pathway of pain and labor.

But there is more than this; the Church breaks in on the most solemn portion of the liturgy,—that between the consecration and communion,—to pronounce a further blessing on the bride. Turning toward the newly-married, the priest, as if his hands were laden with the blessings brought from on high, and his lips touched with the hallowed fire to prophesy good things to the suppliants prostrate there, thus prays:

"O God, who by thy might didst create all things out of nothingness; who, having ordered the first stages of this universe, and made man to the image of God, didst make man's substance the principle of woman's being, that she should thus be his inseparable companion, teaching us thereby that a union originating in such unity may never be broken without crime; O God, who didst hallow this conjugal union by so surpassing a grace as to make the primitive nuptial alliance the prophetic figure of the mysterious union of Christ with the Church; God, by whom woman is thus united to man, and the primordial society thus formed is endowed with a blessing which alone survived the punishment of original sin and the judgment executed through the deluge; look down propitiously on this thy handmaiden, who, about to begin her companionship with her husband, beseeches Thee to grant her Thy protection: in her may the yoke of love and peace ever abide; faithful and chaste, may she wed in Christ, and be evermore the imitator of holy women: may she prove lovely to her husband, like Rachel; wise, like Rebecca; long-lived and faithful, like Sara; may the fell Author of (Eve's) prevarication find no trace in her of the actions which he counsels; may she be immovably attached to thy faith and law: the spouse of one man, may no other love ever touch her; may she school and shield her own weakness by home-discipline: may she be modest and dignified, chaste and venerable, enlightened by wisdom from on high;...may she win approval by her stainless life, and thus attain to the rest of the blessed and the heavenly kingdom."[20]

The Wife's Honor the Fount of All Honor.

Pagans, in ancient times, were wont to attribute the origin of each mighty river to a peculiar deity; so they built a temple at its head-waters, and there offered frequent sacrifice in order that the stream throughout its course to the ocean might be pure and healthful, and fraught with all manner of blessings to the lands it watered.

This, like many other customs, was only the perversion of a deep religious truth. God has committed this earth and all therein that is most beneficial to man to the custody of those blessed spirits, who, destined to be in eternity the

[20] The Roman Missal in the "Nuptial Mass."

fellow-citizens of men made perfect in glory, take delight in watching over their welfare and being their companions in this life of trial.

But if a perverse sentiment induced the heathen of old to consider as a something holy and divine the well-spring of mighty rivers, what must not a Religion which comes from the true God think of the home which he destines to be the source of a race of men and women designed to be his own adopted children? What solemnity must the Church not employ to hallow that union, on the permanence and sacredness of which depend the honor, the unspotted name, the greatness and happiness of a family throughout all succeeding generations?

Hence the inconceivable care with which the Church has, ever since the days of Christ,—the second and truest Parent of mankind,—watched over the unity and sacredness of that bond which makes of father and mother the one, sole, loving and beloved well-spring of the family existence, pride, and honor.

How the Church Has Guarded the Honor of Families.

During nineteen centuries, as the history of Christendom attests, the Church has endured, in the East as well as in the West, many bitter persecutions at the hand of emperors, kings, and other sovereign princes, because she would not permit them to put away their lawful wives, become distasteful to them, or sanction their unhallowed union with others, while the former were still living. Thus did she, who is here below the mother of the true life and of beautiful and chaste love, protect the weakness of the woman and wife against the unholy passions of all-powerful husbands; surely, being such as she is, she has a right, as she has a charge, to save woman sometimes from the tyranny of her own headlong inclinations.

At no period in Christian history, however, has there existed such a blind and general conspiracy of governments and peoples to ruin the sacred institution of matrimony as in the present age. So long as Christendom was governed in things spiritual by the judicial decisions of the Roman Pontiff, no State dared pass a law contrary to the unity and indissolubility of the marriage tie; no individual, whether sovereign or subject, prince or peasant, could violate with impunity the law which guarded the honor of every family. The sword of excommunication was as sure to reach the transgressor,—whether he sat on the throne, or lived in a palace, or dwelt in a shepherd's cot,—as when Paul first drew it against the incestuous Corinthian in the first days of Christianity.

Modern Legislation Destructive of the Family Honor.

Now States, legislatures, sovereigns, and governments, abetted or unresisted by their respective peoples, have dechristianized and unhallowed the marriage contract and all its solemnities, and made it a civil act, deriving its value, sanction, and binding power from the civil authority. Non-Catholic sects and ministers have neither the power, nor, seemingly, the will to assert the sacredness of Christ's institution. Luther,—as he set out on his downward path as a reformer,—declared against the unity of the marriage tie, and further desecrated the solemn rite of matrimony by taking to wife a nun, both being previously bound by solemn vow never to marry, and thereby incapacitated from contracting valid nuptials. The Mormons of Utah have only pushed to its legitimate limits the liberty of Biblical interpretation invoked by Luther and the Reformation; and European governments and legislatures, like the several States of the American Union, are only consistent with the universal teaching of Protestantism,—denying to marriage among Christians any sacramental or supernatural character.

Christian families still find in the teaching of the Catholic Church and the far-reaching authority of her Pontiffs, the only divine safeguard on earth against the invasion of their homes and their honor by Mormonism or State secularism.

It is that same teaching, that same fatherly voice which, while protecting you, O wives and mothers, against the passions that would sanction the unfaithfulness of your husbands, ever bids and exhorts you to unwearied devotion and fidelity above reproach or suspicion.

In What the Wife's Fidelity Consists.

In the two preceding chapters we have insisted much on the qualities which enable a wife to be, in the fullest sense, the most delightful companion, the most efficient helpmate, the most trusted friend and confidante of her husband. All this she cannot be, without being at the same time most truly devoted to him in thought and affection,—so that he alone, after God, fills her mind and her heart.

We have touching examples of this inviolable fidelity,—springing, in the first instance, from that single-hearted and absorbing love of a good husband which leaves no thought of any other love being possible; and, in the second, from a wife's own high principle and fear of God, which keeps her true to the love she pledged, even when its object has become most unworthy, or, possibly, most hateful.

Fidelity Illustrated.

In the patriarchal ages before Abraham,—in the age of Noe and those preceding the flood,—there was no question among the families of the blessed line of Seth of admitting a second wife into the family. That was characteristic of the evil brood of Cain,—his son, Lamech, being mentioned as the first who had departed from the unity of the institution of marriage as it came from the hands of the Creator. But Seth himself, and every one of the blessed descendants who kept alive on earth the primitive faith in Jehovah and the belief in the promised Redeemer, also maintained in their households the faith they had pledged to the wife of their youth. Though these men lived five hundred, six hundred, or even nine hundred years and more, their hearts were content with the love, and their lives filled with the fidelity, of that one woman: it was a sacred fire in these august patriarchal homes, burning undimmed century after century on the hearth-stone,—an example, even at this distance of time, deserving of the wonder and veneration of their degenerate descendants.

Rebecca's Fidelity Prefigures that of the Church.

The violation of that unity by Abraham, even at the solicitation of his faithful Sara, was a manifest imperfection in him, who should have known better, and a want of faith and error of judgment in her, who had been brought up among the licentiousness of the Mesopotamian idolatry. But Abraham's son and successor, Isaac, and his bride, Rebecca, departed not from the great primitive law. For Isaac, who bore the wood of his sacrifice up the mountainside was the figure of Christ; just like Isaac's early and only love, Rebecca, brought to him so wondrously from afar, was the type of the Church.

It is the love of both Rebecca and the Church that forms a model and a rule for every Christian wife.

Judith's Example.

We have nearer to us in the Old Testament history other touching examples of fidelity in wives to the husband of their youth. Judith the Deliverer, "the Joy of Israel," the glory and honor of her people, was widowed young, and, though surpassingly beautiful, and most wealthy, she remained true to the memory of her husband, inviolably faithful to the love she had plighted to him. The sudden inspiration which came to her to offer herself to the admiring eyes of the Assyrian general, was no deviation from the law of fidelity which she had so scrupulously followed till then. She trusted to God's angel to keep her honor safe in the Assyrian camp, and, as she afterward declared, he had watched over her coming and going till she had struck the blow which freed her country. The victory once won, and the national thanksgiving over, she put off her rich robes, resumed her sober widow's weeds, buried herself once more in the solitude of her own house, and gave up the half-century of life which remained to her to prayer, fasting, alms-deeds, and the cherished worship of her husband's memory.

Anna the Prophetess.

So is it with that remarkable woman whom we meet with in the temple at our Lord's presentation therein,—Anna the Prophetess. She, too, had been left a widow after seven years of companionship with her husband; and "she was a widow till fourscore and four years; who departed not from the temple, by fasting and prayers, serving night and day."

She was rewarded by beholding in the flesh the Redeemer promised to Adam and Eve in the garden, and whose glory, like the first fires of sunrise above the eastern hills, patriarchs and prophets had only looked on "from afar." She was also privileged to see in the temple the Mother most blessed who was prefigured by Eve as well as by Judith.

These are only landmarks on the glorious pathway of true womanhood, pointing out in the inspired writings the honor paid to fidelity and the reward bestowed on it even in this life.

Ideal Unity and Eternity of Conjugal Love.

They teach this lesson, at all events: That the purest and greatest of women considered the love which they had given to the husband of their youth as a something so sacred, a gift so divine, that they could allow no other love to intrude upon it; they had meant it to last for all time and for all eternity, and as such they cherished it, even when their loved companion had been taken early away from them.

There is no doubt that this ideal eternity and unity of conjugal love is that upheld and blessed by the Church.

But what is of the deepest practical importance, is

Fidelity to the Living.

Of this we have most touching examples all through the pages of Christian history. Nor is it necessary to insist at length upon this, where matrimonial unions are well assorted, and where, on both sides, there is the fear of God, a love blessed of Him, and all the charities of the home-life ever fed by the reception of the sacraments. It is where a union is ill-assorted, unhappy, and where, particularly, the husband happens to be any thing or every thing save what the wife in her innocent dreams of goodness and manliness conceived as the real character of her lover.

It is in the home where these dreams have been succeeded by a sad awakening, where the ideal sought after and loved turns out to be a hideous specter, and where the idol the bride worshiped so sincerely has been dashed to pieces on the hearth-stone,—that the young wife needs to look up to God, to call on his Name, to seek for his grace in order to be true to him and to herself,—in spite of the terrible deception of which she is the victim.

Let us give, first, a few pregnant rules, which may serve for all, whether happy or otherwise;—we shall afterward point out to the unhappy and sorely tried the only road on which they can find salvation.

Rules.

A cardinal principle in home-life is, never to allow one's self to suspect or to distrust one's dear ones, save only when the evidence of guilt or unworthiness is irresistible. Even then, the terrible truth must be kept secret from every living soul; it is only when absolutely necessary and in an extremity that a wife should mention it,—though never so guardedly,—to an experienced and holy guide. From one's relatives on both sides,—from father or mother, brother or sister,—the secret should be strictly and sacredly kept, so long as the reformation and salvation of the guilty one or the protection of one's children, or some such weighty consideration, does not compel one to speak so much of the truth as is needful.

Keep Your Family Troubles to Yourself.

It is impossible for a wife to be too reserved on this point: it would be fatal to seek confidants even in one's nearest and dearest. Where conscience is concerned extreme care should be taken both in choosing the person to be consulted and in the manner in which the communication is to be made. Even a father, if he be a man of wisdom, experience, and high principle, will rarely encourage a married daughter to make him her confidant in her secret troubles. If he has been a good husband, blessed with a good wife, his own heart will have taught him how jealous a husband is of seeing any man made his wife's confidant.

There must be extreme necessity, then, to justify a wife in revealing her troubles to priest or to father,—even with all the reservations made above. To make a confidant even of a brother, is most unwise under any but very extraordinary circumstances; but to go with one's troubles to a stranger, be he what he may, is to court danger, and to go more than halfway to meet ruin.

If confidence given to persons of the opposite sex is fraught with such certain peril, how much more so is friendship?

The Friendships Baneful to Fidelity.

Lady friends and lady confidantes unwisely chosen, and kept in spite of a husband's remonstrances, have destroyed the peace of many a home where there was, otherwise, every element of happiness,—sincere mutual affection, companionship, and faith in each other's virtue. But gentlemen friends—where a wife is so bereft of sense, of discernment, of womanly tact, as to permit such a monstrosity to come into her life—*gentlemen friends* are the worst enemies of her honor, her home, and the happiness of all belonging to her.

If a wife be already happy in possessing a husband who fulfills her ideal of manliness, who is all in all to her, she does him the foulest wrong and her own honor irreparable injury in transferring to any man living any part of her affections. If, as we suppose, she loves her husband with her whole heart, how jealous would she feel of any woman on whom her husband would bestow any thing like friendship! Would she not resent it—and most justly—as a grievous wrong done to herself? But she is not to forget, that, in a family, a husband's friendships do not tend to bring dishonor on the children, like the aberrations of a mother's heart.

We cannot affirm it too strongly, the honor of families depends chiefly on a father's reputation and achievements; the dishonor of families on the unhallowed friendships of mothers.

When Danger Begins.

The greatest danger for the heart of the wife, till then blameless, unconscious, and unsuspicious of evil, arises in those seasons of deep domestic trouble, discord, and unhappiness. It is in these seasons of trial that a wife should go to the heart of the Crucified for sympathy, light, and strength. Oh! if women whose hearts are sore and whose troubled spirit yearns for consolation and counsel, only knew what light and sweetness and energy of soul can be found in one quarter of an hour's secret converse with the Crucifix,—that most eloquent of books and most enlightened of all counselors and consolers! If they could turn aside from the hollow and dangerous sympathies of human friendship—even when least perilous—and betake them to the Divine Comforter, who evermore dwells on our altars, what a heart they would find there! And how they would rise from before the Vail and the Mercy-Seat refreshed, strengthened, and resolved to take up their cross and follow Him!

How many of our purest, bravest, best cannot put away from them the cross which is to be a life-long burden! Bear it they must. If they refuse to carry it, the weight crushes them; if they take it up willingly, joyously, as He did, it bears them forward, imparting to them an energy all divine, and heavenly joys amid all the bitterness of earthly trials!

Carry Your Cross and It Will Carry You.

We know such mourners,—whose young lives have been blighted by a union with guilt, secret vice, and falsehood; but who have taken up the cross with unflinching courage, determined to make of the ever-recurring trials and humiliations of each day a mine of merit with which to purchase the eternal joys. The pleasant and loved companionship about which their maiden dreams had been busy, had turned out, when viewed with carnal eyes and judged in the light of this world's wisdom, naught else but being hopelessly tied to a loathsome leper. The love of suffering, to which, under the divine inspiration, the wife, on awakening from her dream, opened every avenue of her soul, is a divine companionship,—it is treading with our thorn-crowned King the bitter but glorious road of crucifixion.

The Christian Woman Is Bound to Be Supernatural.

This lesson addresses itself to Christian wives,—to women bound to be *Supernatural*,—who are supposed to have entered on their matrimonial engagements with supernatural motives (and the not doing so is the source of untold and inconceivable miseries), who profess to lead a supernatural life amid all the joys, the cares, the trials, and disappointments of their subsequent condition. Woe to them, if they are not supernatural and lovers of the cross and the Crucified, when the fair and fond visions of earthly love requited vanish from their early path like the golden clouds of morning!

There is one book out of which every young wife, from her bridal day, would do well to read a daily chapter to her companion—"The Imitation of

Christ:" it is brimful of the Spirit of God. Would that the wife on whose life the shadow of the dreadful heart-trials hinted at here falls for the first time, would take up this almost divine book, and read such passages as the following:

"O Lord God, holy Father, be thou now and forever blessed! For, as Thou wilt, even so hath it been done to me; and what Thou dost is good.

"Let thy servant take joy in Thee, not in herself nor in any other being. For, Thou alone art true joy,—Thou art my hope and my crown,—Thou, O Lord, art my bliss and my honor!

"O Father, just, holy, and ever to be praised, the hour of trial is come for thy servant.

"Father ever to be loved, it is right that in this hour thy servant should suffer somewhat for thy sake.

"Father to be perpetually reverenced, the hour hath come which from all eternity Thou didst foresee as about to be sent to me;—that thy servant should be outwardly borne down, but should, interiorly, still live unto Thee; that she should be for a little time held of no account, humiliated, and disappear from the sight of man,—that she should be crushed beneath the weight of suffering and helplessness; in order that so she may rise as from the grave in the dawn of a new light, and be glorified in Heaven.

"Holy Father, so Thou hast appointed, and so willed, and this hath come to pass which Thou hast ordained.

"For this is a favor to Thy friend, that she should suffer and be afflicted in this world for the love of Thee, how often soever, by whom soever, and in what manner soever Thou permittest it to befall her."[21]

The Crucifix and "The Imitation of Christ."

What soul will not rise from the foot of the crucifix, after such a prayer as this, with the consciousness, the deep-seated conviction, that God with her and in her will enable her to face and overcome the trials before her?

It is time that in every Christian household mothers should inculcate the lesson—morning, noon, and night—that their children—both sons and

[21] "The Imitation of Christ," b. iii., c. 50.

daughters—never will be or can be any thing, unless they study before and above all things else to be Supernatural men and women.

They must be that, or they will become worse than pagans.

But let us look into the mirror of a life tried by humiliations and sufferings such as no one of our readers (we may safely predict it) will ever be called on to endure;—and we shall see therein how a brave womanly heart can find courage to be the light and benefactress of a whole country, while that same heart is riven by the most terrible domestic griefs.

Glorious Examples of Fidelity—The Child-Wife.

We shall not give the names of the persons or the countries till our glorious tale be told, and the lesson hath sunk deep into the mind of the attentive reader.

A child of thirteen, reared with the most extraordinary care, and responding by every excellence and grace of mind and heart to this most careful culture, our heroine was given in marriage to one much her elder, and who to extraordinary qualities added passions and vices which threatened to make him the scourge of all who depended on him.

In his heart, sullied and wasted by lawless affections, there was no room for any thing like pure and true love for the beautiful, innocent, and artless child which policy had made his wife; nor could an intellect dulled and clouded by unbridled sensuality even begin to understand a soul which was as unconscious of evil in herself or in others as the babe newly born.

So this child-wife was allowed to indulge amid her servants, in the beautiful home to which she had been brought far away from her native country, all her tastes for piety and beneficence under every form,—while her husband spent, during months and years, the leisure which should have been devoted to her in the most scandalous indulgence and the most unworthy companionship.

The light only dawned on the forsaken and outraged one by degrees. Hers was a most loving nature; for a pure love is the deepest of all. But, as she had been reared in childhood under the especial care of a grandfather, whom three kingdoms venerated as a living saint, she had been made to look upon offenses toward the Divine Majesty as the supreme of evils, and the hideousness of sin as a something surpassingly loathsome.

How the Child-Wife Bore Her Trial.

Though the knowledge of her husband's infidelity inflicted a wound so deep that her life was feared for, she never allowed one word of complaint or blame to escape her lips; but she moaned unceasingly over the outrage done to God and the scandal given to the people. She undertook, with the thought of turning away the divine anger from him and from those subject to him, to expiate his guilt by protracted prayer, by austerities which her counselors could not prevail on her to mitigate, and by all manner of alms-deeds and works of mercy.

The hoary sinners who had encouraged or tolerated her husband's early wickedness, at first laughed at the young wife's innocence, simplicity, and evident ignorance of all moral evil. But they were touched by the greatness of soul which knew not how to utter one word in blame of the guilt that dishonored her home and her husband; and they were awed into veneration and love by the courage which resented so openly the injury done to the Divine honor, and the splendid munificence that sought to make of the poor and the suffering intercessors between her offended God and her offending husband.

Patience and Saintliness of Life All-Powerful to Win back a Heart.

He, too, was touched by the sweet and uncomplaining sorrow of the injured wife. The sense of wrong had suddenly transformed her, and, in a day, she passed from the guilelessness of the child to the majesty of a woman sensible to her wrongs. Yet, not a word or a look betrayed the terrible grief which was gnawing away her heart's core.

The peerless flower of beauty and spotless purity which had been laid upon his bosom was drooping before his eyes; the atmosphere of evil which surrounded him had blighted its freshness. He was conscience-stricken, and filled with reverence, if not yet with love, for the angelic creature of whom he deemed himself unworthy.

His remorse gave her the hope that his heart was not dead. With the instinct of the true woman and the saint, which she was, she resolved to win that soul to God by patience, and by the irresistible power of prayer and charity. Of winning his love to herself she thought not. Thenceforward no opportunity was lost of doing on every side all the good she could in favor of the sick, the poor, and the erring. The false friends and companions who pandered to her husband's vices and shared in his criminal pleasures, were to her but a portion of the great host of the Evil One leagued together to destroy men's souls and blight all that was fairest on earth: she was fain to enlist all she could under the banners of Goodness, which delighteth not so much in doing good as in making others good. And she was blessed.

The Armies of the Poor and Sick Lifting up Their Hands in Prayer.

The hosts of the poor, the suffering, and the reclaimed who daily and nightly lifted up their prayers in union with hers, prevailed with heaven; and heaven's grace, aided by the growing splendor of the young wife's spiritual beauty, at length won the husband's heart. The conquest was, however, only a slow one. The habits of evil had cast roots too deep and too wide into that rich nature to permit them to be plucked up in a day, or to prevent their often cropping out at the surface in spite of the prudent wife's constant though gentle culture, and despite his own generous efforts at thorough amendment. The supernatural wisdom which sanctity bestowed on one so young as she was, taught her a patient husbandry both in eradicating inveterate evil and in waiting for the growth of virtuous fruits. This, she knew, was the law in the natural world around her, and she also knew that a similar law regulated the supernatural life of souls.

The Husband's Heart Won to God and His Wife.

The day came, ere she had passed out of her early womanhood, when she was blessed with the certainty that her husband's heart was all God's and her own. From that hour her happiness was unspeakable, and her gratitude to the Author of all heavenly gifts showed itself in her increased fervor and joyousness, and in her unmeasured generosity toward the poor. From that hour also her husband lost no opportunity of proving to the world that he had determined to be in God's hand a docile and faithful instrument for every blessed purpose which his own conscience and the wisdom of his wife might counsel.

Of all the men who ever wielded power in that ancient Catholic land, none achieved what he and his angel-wife thenceforward planned and accomplished. He died with the title of "Father of his Country," given to him by the gratitude of his contemporaries and confirmed by the admiration of after-ages. And she, his savior, his better self, the prompter of every heroic and patriotic enterprise? She needed not to be called the mother of her country; she became its patron-saint and protectress, and the memory of her perfect life still helps to keep alive the light of faith and the flame of charity among the sad ruins of national greatness.

The Wife's Heart Tried by Calumny.

Sorely tried as had been the fidelity of that young heart, it was not spared,—even when happier days had begun to dawn for her,—the most cruel pain that a faithful and sorely tried wife can endure. She was calumniated by her servants, and rashly suspected by her husband, but too prone to see the motives and actions of others in the light of his own guilty conscience. One most painful trial, in particular, is recorded by historians. A page,—perhaps a relative, or the young son of some most noble family, who had commended himself to his mistress by uncommon piety and tenderness toward the sick and poor,—was frequently employed on errands of mercy. This excited the envy or the malignity of some of his companions, men accustomed, in all likelihood, to serve their master's worst vices, and who felt themselves ill at ease in the chaste atmosphere that surrounded his lady.

The Calumniator Miraculously Punished.

However the calumny was insinuated, it was but too readily believed, and the instant death of the supposed culprit was resolved upon. It was an age of violence,—when might made law. But Providence interfered to save the innocent and punish the guilty. The calumniator perished by the hand of the assassin, and through the very device invented to take the life of his victim. The hand of God was visible. Other and more touching instances of miraculous interposition are also recorded of the long period of heart-trial through which the young wife had to pass. One and the same truth shines forth from all: she had placed her trust in God, and God is bound not to deceive those who trust in him.

The Moral Conclusion.

And thus we come back to the moral purpose of our illustration. Let the wife whose eyes rest on these words, if Providence should ever permit her soul to be thus tried in the furnace, take well to heart these other words from the divine book already quoted:

A Divine Prayer.

"Without Thy counsel and providence, and without cause, nothing happeneth on earth. *It is good for me, O Lord, that thou hast humbled me; that I may learn thy Justifications* (Ps. cxviii. 71); that I may cast away all pride of heart and presumption. It is for my profit that shame hath covered my face, that I may take Thee for my consoler rather than men... There is not one among all who are beneath the heavens that is able to console me but thyself, O Lord God, the heavenly physician of souls, who strikest and healest, 'who bringest down to Hell and leadest back again.' *Thy discipline is upon me, and thy rod itself shall instruct me*" (Ps. xvii. 36)...

"Behold, O beloved Father, I am in thy hands; I bow myself down under the rod of thy correction... Myself and all that are mine I commit to thee for chastening; it is better to be chastised here than hereafter... Grant me, O Lord, to know what I ought to know; to love what I ought to love; to praise that which is most pleasing to thee, to esteem that highly which to thee is precious; and to reject and despise what thou deemest vile and worthless."[22]

Such sentiments as these are like the fragrant air of the heavenly hills to one who has just passed through the valley of the shadow of death, like the sudden brightness and warmth of sunlight to one long imprisoned amid the snows and darkness of an arctic region. But He, who guided the pen and warmed the heart

[22] "Imitation of Christ," iii., c. 1.

of the man who wrote them, will know, when you come to him in your sore need, how to whisper far sweeter words than man can write,—for he made the heart, and knoweth where lie the springs of its weakness as well as of its power.

Love Tried in the Flame.

But if glowing words from the well-tried heart of the sweetest of Catholic singers in our tongue have virtue to warm and comfort, then read:

"Let thy gold be cast in the furnace,
  Thy red gold, precious and bright,
Do not fear the hungry fire,
  With its caverns of burning light:
And thy gold shall return more precious,
  Free from every spot and stain;
For gold must be tried by fire,
  As a heart must be tried by pain!

"I shall know by the gleam and glitter
  Of the golden chain you wear,
By your heart's calm strength in loving,
  Of the fire they have had to bear.
Beat on, true heart, forever;
  Shine bright, strong golden chain,
And bless the cleansing fire,
  And the furnace of living pain!"[23]

The Vanity Which Leads to Dishonor.

Would it not be a most ungracious act to darken these pages with a description, though never so brief and lightly shaded, of the home, whether of rich or poor, ruined or made desolate by infidelity? Better far, so our readers will think with us, to paint the heroic constancy and preternatural joys of the faithful wife,—faithful even while "the hungry fire with its caverns of burning light" was trying and searching every corner of her heart.

---

[23] Adelaide Anne Procter, "Legends and Lyrics."

Only let a priestly hand add, before concluding this most important chapter; a brief warning and as brief an exhortation.

If it be most true, and the voice of experience attests that it is, that the danger for the womanly heart tried to its utmost by marital unworthiness, lies in the need of sympathy; so, in happy homes, where there exists perfect love and neither unsuitability nor disappointment, ruin comes from vanity and from the appetite for display and enjoyment.

The Home-Pleasures Which Are a Safeguard to Honor.

Against this vanity there is no remedy, apart always from the grace of the sacraments and these aids which God may vouchsafe to some souls; there is no remedy, we say, but in a wife's never seeking to please any other eye than that of her husband, or valuing any praise on dress, personal appearance, and accomplishment of any kind, but what falls from his dear lips, or caring for any amusement that is not shared by him, or in wishing to have any theater for the display of any gift natural or acquired, how transcendent soever, save the bosom of one's own family.

We have heard of women, most gifted and most accomplished, who, blessed with a large family, and burdened with the care of a numerous household, made it a point of conscience to dress every day of their lives, even in extreme old age, with the greatest care, in order to please their husbands, and give them thereby an outward proof of undiminished love; and to please their children, by ever setting them an example worthy of imitation. With these admirable wives and mothers it had been a life-long study how to make their own gifts and accomplishments contribute daily to the delight of the family circle. Intellectual and artistic culture, music and song, and the charming illusions of private dramatic entertainments, all was made to serve the one great purpose of rendering home the sweetest, brightest, dearest spot of earth.

The Love of Display Which Knows Not Peril.

One need not fear to display to the utmost within the home sanctuary and for the delights of one's own dearest, every best gift of God; the praise which comes from these dear lips is not that which intoxicates dangerously; the vanity which such praise may create is not that which is to be dreaded by mother or by daughter; and the delicious satisfaction enjoyed both by the delight a wife and mother gives, and by that which she receives in return, is not one which the good angels may look on with displeasure.

On the contrary, the love of praise and display, which is so common and so natural in a certain measure, will find its lawful and most healthful satisfaction in these home-pleasures and celebrations; in these lie the antidote or preservative against the vanity fraught with peril.

Home-life, home-pleasures, home-virtues, in this respect, as in so many others, are the great means Providence employs, and religion counsels, to prevent or to counteract the tendencies toward finding one's only or chief distractions and enjoyments outside of home and the family circle. There are men who only sleep at home, and spend the remainder of their time outside of it. They cannot be said to have a home, or to have any conception of what a home is or could be. If they are blessed with wives able and anxious to make their homes a paradise for them, what shall we say of their folly or their guilt? And who will pity them, if the home thus forsaken and absolutely neglected by its appointed guardian should become a prey to the Tempter?

But of the women who only make their homes a brief breathing or resting-place in their unbroken and eternal round of vanity and dissipation, we need only say what every body sees,—that the curse is upon them, and that shame is ever flitting round their homes,—like these legendary evil spirits that haunt the precincts of families doomed to perdition.

To the nobility of true womanly natures we need not recommend to be watchful over the sanctity of the homes in which they are the priestesses of the family religion, the jealous guardians and loving teachers of the Ancestral Faith, and the custodians of that treasure,—dearer and more precious to every home where God is feared and men's good opinion is valued than royal power or fabulous wealth,—the peerless jewel, Honor.

Honor, the Tree of Life of the Home Paradise.

When our first parents were thrust forth from Paradise, they might have seen, as they turned to have one last look at what they had lost forever,—

cherubim set there to guard its entrance, "and a flaming sword, turning every way, to keep the way of the tree of life." To you, O faithful women, who read this, be this truth welcome: Your Paradise is your home, the tree of life is your honor, and from beneath its shade, from the sweet and safe center of your bliss you can look to the gate of your Eden, and see with the eyes of faith, as certainly as you see your own right hand, God's angels set to guard your home, and the "flaming sword, turning every way" to defend you and yours from evil.

So, when evil, overleaping the walls of your sanctuary, would threaten to desecrate its holiness and steal away its priceless treasures, remember the noble rebuke of the Spanish maiden to the invaders of her father's home: "Do you know where you are? Do you know that this is the house of a man rich in virtue?... The house of my father is the center of loyalty and the sanctuary of honor!"

CHAPTER IX.

THE MOTHER.

> When at some holy festival or eve the church at nightfall begins to be filled with confused steps and lighted tapers; when, amidst the chant of men and children and women, a figure can be distinguished among all these, in a far recess, half obscured, having grouped around her near the sombre wall four young heads, on which she casts at times a look more sweet than solemn,—oh! whoever you may be, bless her! It is she—the sister, visible to the eyes of my immortal soul: my pride, my hope, my shelter; the joy of my young years: the hoped-for treasure of my age;—it is she—the wife who has no joy but my happiness; who, if my children or myself ever seem to totter on the brink, without a severe word or a reproachful look supports them with the hand, and me with the heart; she to whom I have said always, and who has said to me: "THROUGH ALL!" It is she, in a word, a flower of beauty, which goodness has perfumed: the flower is of earth, and the fragrancy of Heaven.
>
> Quoted by DIGBY in *Compitum.*

The above poetic picture presents the true woman in the twofold aspect of wife and mother,—young still and in the active discharge of her duties as such,—and hence this quotation serves as an apt transition to the all-important subject which now solicits our deepest interest. The faithful love which clings to husband, home, and honor, "through all," through the storm, the flame, and the sea of bitterness, will not be apt to omit one sweet duty of motherhood. Even when all her womanly virtues are powerless to exorcise the demon of evil from her household, there remains to her, in the discharge of her maternal office, an unfailing source of deepest consolation as well as of merit before God and man.

And here it is, most especially, that it behooves woman to be supernatural, so that the result of her motherly labors shall be to make of her dear ones men and women truly deserving the name of children of God.

Meaning of the Term "Supernatural," as Applied Here.

When the word supernatural is used, the entire non-Catholic world, as well as a great many Catholics—even educated Catholics—are but too apt to entirely misapprehend its meaning. There is in the modern mind, particularly where the masses are not Catholic, a disposition to look upon whatever is supernatural as contrary to nature, and therefore absurd, or as miraculous, and therefore outside of the common laws of action and beyond our ordinary reach.

There is a general tendency to reject the supernatural order altogether, and to admit nothing as existing or possible but what is strictly in accordance with nature.

This is not the place for a philosophical or theological disquisition. But every mother will be glad to find here clear and simple notions enabling her to seize at a glance what the supernatural order is, and so to convey the light in her own mind to that of her children all through her training.

Looking upon the human race as one great family composed of the descendants of the one father and the one mother, and considering them in their relation to God's government over them in this life and the life to come,—we conceive that He who created them, could reward them after death in accordance with their degree of fidelity to the law of nature written equally on the heart of the savage and on that of the civilized man. This would be the "natural order" in which God would impose upon men no duties beyond those of love, obedience, reverence and worship to Himself,—of the reciprocal obligations and duties which bind together husband and wife, parents and children,—family to family, and toward the authorities lawfully acknowledged in civil society. The virtues of truthfulness, honor, honesty, and of the general brotherly charity which should make every man look upon all other men as his brothers,—the reverence for justice in all one's dealings,—and so many other virtues that need not be named, belong to the "natural order," and are, inseparable from man's condition under God's providence.

But the supernatural order, without doing away with a single one of these natural virtues, obligations, duties, and charities, considers man as belonging to a higher condition, to which, with all his natural powers and virtues and duties, he has been raised by the gratuitous love of his Creator. Man never could, in any supposition, have been created without being bound to his Maker by service in this life, by charity and justice toward his fellow-men, and by the retribution of the immortality following after such service and fellowship. But God was not content to leave man in this essential condition of mere natural service, fellowship, and charity;—He raised him to the rank of His own adopted child, imparted to his mind a distinct knowledge of this glorious destiny, to his heart sentiments and energies enabling him to live up to it, added to man's natural duties, obligations, and virtues, new aims, new obligations, a higher charity,—a new ideal of goodness and greatness, and generosity, all looking forward to an eternal fellowship with God in his own inner life in the world to come.

Thus the supernatural order is that in which God stands in the relation of Father to us, in which we hold the rank of his real adopted children, with all the sentiments, obligations, rights, honors, and graces attendant on this sublime elevation, all tending to the possession of that glory of the life to come,—the beatific vision, the seeing God face to face, the being taken into society with the Three Infinite Persons of the Godhead, and into fellow-citizenship with his angels.

This adoption, this divine rank, these graces given in this life to mind and heart, and this unspeakably glorious and blissful fellowship of eternity, is a something so far above nature, so undue to it, so entirely beyond its requirements and capacities, that it is deservedly called "supernatural," that is—above and beyond nature.

How the Child Must Be Made Acquainted with the Supernatural Order.

To inculcate on her children, as soon as their reason begins to dawn, that God is not only their Maker as he is that of the heavens above them and the earth around them, but also to them a true Father, who cares for them and gives them a right to the most magnificent of all inheritances, must be one of the Christian mother's early cares. Her own sense of piety, her womanly wit and instinctive knowledge of child-nature will teach her the best methods to be employed in order to let in by degrees, and one after the other, the beautiful and divine realities of the supernatural order,—of that kingdom of God, whose sovereign is true Father to us,—of that glorious world in which Christ and his Blessed Mother are central figures.

There are few households so poor but they can afford to have one or two sweet prints representing the mysteries of our Lord's infancy and childhood, as well as a handsome crucifix, or, at least, a good print of the crucifixion. It is well to reject the abominable daubs published in our large cities and "misrepresenting" every subject they profess to set before the devout mind. The sweet pictures of the Blessed Mother and her Babe by Luini, or Fra Bartolomeo, and Crucifixions by such religious painters as Velasquez, cannot fail to produce a powerful impression. There are good engravings of them, for which it would be well to pay a little more;—good chromos, like those published in London by the Arundel Society, are, unfortunately, beyond the reach of poor families. Would that we had both in city and country parishes some sodality interested in seeing that the homes of the laboring classes were provided with such objects of religious art as would inspire reverence and piety in the beholder. Nor must mothers forget to have a little statue or a print of the Angel Guardian; he is a friend to be known and loved early.

It must be the part of the judicious mother to explain in due time to her little ones, when they are able to inquire about that heavenly Woman and her Babe, what relation they both bear to us. Some mothers, we know, have in their nurseries "The Flight into Egypt" or the "Adoration of the Magi," subjects which will naturally oblige the children to inquire about the birth of the Divine Babe, and the whole story of his birth.

When, precisely, parents can draw the affection of the child-mind to the story of the Passion, and the Crucifix, they alone can determine. Some are averse to doing so before children are a little more advanced in years. Certain it is that they should be made acquainted with the sufferings of our Divine Benefactor before they emerge from childhood. This point of time being left to the judgment of mothers, let us be firmly convinced that of all the vehicles of supernatural instruction and solid piety there is no one more efficacious than

The Crucifix.

The Crucifix in Catholic households is not only the most eloquent and instructive of books for youth and old age; but it can also be made to speak divinely to the sense of childhood. Children are all athirst for knowledge once they begin to speak and to be capable of instruction by word of mouth. Their mind and imagination are forcibly impressed by the figure of the Man of Sorrows nailed to the bitter tree. They are quick to seize the reverence, the love, the worship with which a mother or a nurse looks upon this pregnant story of Love Crucified. Who is He? What brought Him there? What He is to us; what we owe Him, hope, and fear from Him, are lessons which a child may soon learn,—for they are questions which arise in his own mind, and to which he is impelled to seek an answer by a Prompter within him.

For Christian mothers should not forget that in the infant soul dwells the Divine Spirit, communicated in baptism, and never expelled thence save by voluntary mortal sin. In the soul of every mother, too, who is in a state of grace, dwells the same Divine Instructor, prompting her to do her duty by her child, and pledged to aid her in her work.

The Divine Spirit's Share in the Work of Education.

Surely it must be a consolation and an encouragement to the mother to know that in this laborious but sweet work of forming each mind and heart under her care, she is doing God's own most blessed work, in which she has a right to count on his most effective and continual co-operation.

In imparting instruction, in forming the minds and hearts of her dear ones, the mother only does one part of God's work; He takes on himself to do the other and the most important part. This she must rely on with undoubting certainty; but this, unhappily, is what so many Christian mothers never think of.

Let them,—such, at least, as are desirous of profiting by the directions here given,—only look at the work of the husbandman. He clears away the ground in which he purposes to grow his crop; plows it, prepares and examines his seed, casts it in the furrows, and covers it over. The rest is the work of all-bountiful nature,—of Him, rather, who is the all-wise and provident author of nature. He gives the warmth, the rain, and the dew. His hand unfolds the rich germ in the soil, till it grows up and fructifies and ripens for the harvest.

So is it with your culture, O mothers: the precious seeds of truth which you cast into the minds of your children, just when the spring-tide of their souls begins to dawn, are far more the care of God than the crops of the husbandman,—dear as these surely are to His fatherly providence. Fear not then but his Holy Spirit dwelling in the dear souls you are cultivating, will shed on the germs you deposit the warmth of his sunlight, the late and the early rain. Do your best,—and trust to the Divine Husbandman for the certain increase and the rich harvest in his own good season.

The Cross Is the Alphabet of Spiritual Knowledge.

The all-important thing for you is, that, above and before all things, your children should understand that they are "children of God," that Christ is their Elder Brother, who has purchased them with his blood the right to co-heirship with him. The mystery of the Cross and the Crucified, once understood by them, will be a central light in which they can read all history before and after his death.

It is impossible for children to get a true knowledge of that great love, without feeling their hearts overflowing with love for Him, as well as for that dear Mother who stood in sorrow beneath the tree on which her adored One hung in the death agony. Friendships formed in childhood, in the lovely years of innocence and youth, are friendships that last forever. Make your dear ones love that Friend well, and He will take care that no lapse of time or change of mind and heart, that no perversity of men, or experience of false-heartedness through life, shall disturb the image of that august and early affection in the soul's inmost sanctuary.

Make the Crucified and the Mother of Sorrows the first friends of every child of yours; and fear not but they will befriend them in life and death.

What has just been said will suggest how a true mother's teaching and formation may be supernatural in all other respects. Particular stress has been laid here on early devotion to our crucified Lord, both because it is the foundation of all the rest, and because in our eagerness to read all the trash daily poured forth by the modern press, we seem not to bestow one thought on that Book of books—the Crucifix.

Early Love of Children for the Crucified.

Even Catholics, nowadays, read with astonishment or half-incredulity what is related of the early love for our dear Lord and his Blessed Mother of

St. Stanislas, St. Aloysius, St. Rose of Lima, or St. Teresa and her little brother Rodrigo,—without mentioning instances taken from the writers of the middle ages. Children, almost before the ordinary dawn of reason, become enamored of Him whose unspeakable love is sculptured in such divine characters in that ever open and most simple book of the Crucifix. A sacred thirst of voluntary suffering takes such possession of their souls that they long to suffer martyrdom,—as we read of Teresa and her favorite brother. St. Francis Borgia, when quite a child lost his mother, the Princess Joanna, of Aragon; but her teaching and example had so familiarized the child with the supernatural love of suffering, that, after her death, he could not be prevented from fasting for her and inflicting pain on himself.

There can be no mystery, no cause for wonder in this when we remember that the domestic piety of our fathers was grounded on an intimate knowledge of our Lord and his mysteries. The birth in the stable, the sudden flight across the wilderness to Egypt, the hidden and laborious life at Nazareth, and, above all, the history of his passion, were to childhood itself living realities,—so was the divine story with all its impressive circumstances brought home to them by what they heard and what they saw! They could not enter one of the beautiful churches of olden time, without finding these scenes of suffering appealing to their young souls from the sculptured doors and porticoes outside and from the painted walls and windows within;—while in that great book of the Lamb,—such as every Christian church aimed at being,—they saw, grouped around Christ and his Mother the apostles and saints who had most closely imitated them by their suffering life and death.

Faith was the very principle and breath of life in the old Catholic homes,—and the great central mystery of faith, the Crucifixion, and its memorial sacrifice, the Eucharist and the Mass, were to the youngest children, as to their parents, teachings brought home to mind and heart, not for mere sterile admiration, but for practical gratitude and imitation.

From this living spring of faith in the young heart flowed the piety which gave a color to the entire after-life. And to this we beg the earnest attention of the mothers who read our pages. With this supernatural tendency imparted to thoughts and aims and actions from the very beginning of childhood, the fundamental natural virtues which we shall enumerate further on are sure to be practiced with the supernatural view of pleasing the Divine Master and Model.

Other Qualities in the Mother's Character and Government.

This supernatural spirit animating both a mother's life and her teaching, will only be successful in its purpose and labors when she shows herself careful to cultivate the qualities without which piety would be barren or be mistaken for unreasoning superstition or absurd inconsistency.

Every mother must be consistent in her maxims and rules of government. Let her, in her moments of leisure and solitude, weigh well what rules she is to lay down for her children,—so that in her government of them she may not be exposed to either promulgate a law rashly and then have to withdraw it, or to contradict at night what she has said in the morning with all seriousness, or to undo to-morrow what she is doing to-day.

Children,—very young children especially,—are exceedingly serious-minded. They mean exactly what they say,—and they think, of course, that their elders, superiors, and, above all, their parents, mean what they say. You shake their confidence in you when they discover—which they do with amazing quickness—that you did not mean what you said. This discovery is most fatal in another respect;—it lays the foundation for the child's untruthfulness.

Perfect truthfulness is not only truth in our words when they are the exact expression of our knowledge and meaning, giving to our hearers a perfect picture of our mind; it is also consistency in our actions when these are in literal conformity with our professions and our promises. A child's mind is perfectly and pitilessly logical; its open, candid, watchful eye has the virtue of Ithuriel's spear to unmask falsehood and deception. And, as children are imitative, naturally disposed to copy the example of their parents, if they find these untruthful, or equivocating, or artful,—they will acquire their vices as speedily as they would their virtues.

Hence a mother must be cautious and deliberate,

Consistent and Truthful.

It is on this latter quality alone that we insist here. The whole career of a child, its fortune or misfortune, its honor, happiness, misery, or disgrace,—all will depend largely, perhaps mainly, perhaps altogether, on this one great moral virtue of *Truthfulness.*

It is absolutely necessary to this (ordinarily speaking), that a mother should never, in any one instance, be known to utter an untruth. Hence the horror which she ought to have herself of every species of falsehood, if she would inspire her dear ones with a like horror, and fill them with a sincere love of the truth.

We know, at this moment, a man placed at the head of one of the most flourishing and widely-trusted establishments in America, who owes his rise from the most extreme poverty to his present eminent position to the strict love of truth inculcated by his mother,—a poor washerwoman. As virtues, like vices, always travel in companies,—the boy's truthfulness was only one of the many noble qualities which adorned him from childhood upward. His open, ingenuous, handsome face, when attending Sunday school and preparing for his first communion, struck the priest who taught him. His threadbare and patched, but strictly neat garments, told their own tale of home-struggles and of a poor mother's careful training. His companions all respected him, although by no means the eldest among them. A visit to the mother's home, where an asthmatic husband and four young children, beside our little hero, depended on her labor, enlisted in their favor the sympathies of the Christian Doctrine Society attached to the parish church. The family were provided with work which both parents could attend to at home,—for the mother's anger was roused at the very thought of aid from charity. The oldest, after his first communion, was sent to an excellent commercial school, where he soon outstripped all his companions, but won the esteem of all by his manliness and inflexible truthfulness and honesty.

From an humble position as errand-boy in a merchant's office he became clerk, and rose steadily in the confidence of his employer till he became his partner and right-hand man. During all this time every penny he earned was brought to his mother, every hour he could spare from business was spent with her and the family. She rose with him to comfort and then to affluence, and to this day he will have it said, although surrounded by a large family of his own, "that he is living with his mother." Her daughter-in-law has long learned to revere the true nobility of soul of the modest, quiet, unassuming little woman, who, at the age of seventy, is still, without seeming to be so, the teacher and idol of her grandchildren, no one of whom has ever been known to tell an untruth.

The True Mother Must Be Just, Kind, and Gentle.

A quality akin to this sterling quality of truthfulness, is justice in the mother. Not only must she never exaggerate the faults or imperfections of her children, but she must also impress them with the conviction that she is absolutely impartial, never preferring one to the other,—at least she must so control herself that neither by word or action must she manifest any unjust preference, or, indeed, any preference at all.

There is only one kind of preference tolerated in families, and that is in favor of the suffering or infirm. It will be the duty of the good mother to teach herself and every one of her dear ones to lavish on the sick, the suffering, the infirm, their most constant, affectionate, and delicate attentions. This is one of the "true charities" of home-life.

But what is destructive of all the "home charities," of peace and concord and happiness in every home cursed with such preferences, are the unenviable beings known as "Father's Pet" and "Mother's Pet."

Justice in Rewarding and Punishing.

Let the mother be also just in rewarding and punishing, as well as kind and gentle when she has to reprove and correct. It is wonderful how some women can magnetize children, command their attention and submission, make them listen, obey, work, and do most willingly things apparently the most opposite to their inclinations.

We have seen a room full of children in the wildest uproar, defying the authority and combined efforts of mother and nursery-maids, hushed suddenly into silence, order, and quiet work, by the appearance of "Grandmama,"—the very rustle of her garments seeming to quell the noise, while the bright, pleasant look, and a few words in a subdued tone, would still the tempest as if by some magic spell.

What is the spell? Firmness, gentleness, kindness,—all combining to form that wonderful thing in man or woman which we call AUTHORITY. We do not mean, of course, thereby authority of place or office,—but that authority which attaches to "character." And into this character—so irresistible in governing children or grown-up people, a household, a nursery, a school-room, or a multitude—the above qualities must enter. Add another,—self-control,—and you have a perfect mother and mistress of a household.

Self-Control—How Indispensable.

We do not mean by this term that social self-possession or that perfect command of the muscles of one's countenance which our savages have learned to perfection. The self-control which is here recommended is only one degree,—and that an inferior one,—of the Christian virtue of meekness beatified by our Lord. It is the result, in persons naturally hot-tempered and passionate, of habitual victory over self and of habitual watchfulness to secure the fruits of victory. This victory must be impressed on the tender minds of youth as most meritorious in the sight of God,—as one of the many characteristics which make the Christian man or woman most like to Christ himself.

But it will be in vain for a mother to preach it to her children if she is not herself in possession of it. Besides,—and this is the important point,—no mother ever yet controlled her children, or taught them successfully the practice of self-control, who did not know how to control herself; no mistress of a household ever governed children and servants, so as to maintain order, discipline, obedience, and industry,—who did not show that she could govern her own words and temper,—who was not perfect mistress in the house of her own soul.

It is God's will and wish that every mother should study this self-control, which is only the outward manifestation of that meekness and gentleness of spirit, so lovely in the sight of God and angels. Ay, and most lovely is it also in the sight of men, in the estimation, particularly, of children and servants, and all persons dependent on us. And most blessed is it, as well as the source of manifold blessedness to all around us!

Children and servants never ought to see their mother and mistress angry, or with the slightest sign of anger or impatience. We once heard servants at the death of an honored master affirm, with tears in their eyes, that they had never heard from his lips an angry or a loud word. This was also the unanimous testimony of his children. But on this admirable parent and master, what was the influence of his wife? He was by nature hot and fiery, proud and imperious and resentful. And so was by native disposition his young wife, whom he wedded while yet in her teens. But she had been trained in a model home, and by the hand of a mother to whom gentleness was the fruit of many an early struggle with self.

The young wife, all enthusiasm and fire in her own disposition, was yet so gentle in her every word and act, so thoroughly devoted to her husband, that she soon made him as gentle as herself; and after a union of more than thirty years, when death separated them, it was attested by servants, relatives, and acquaintances,—by the numberless visitors who loved to partake of the hospitalities of that home,—that not one angry word was ever heard from parents to children, or from one child to another.

This was the fruit of self-control,—the blessing bestowed on gentleness and meekness.

Gentleness Need Not Be Weakness.

There is a natural softness which is often mistaken for the gentleness we have been describing. The former is the flexibility of lead, which permits itself to be bent in any direction you please; the latter is the elasticity of steel which has passed again and again through the furnace, and has been beaten beneath the hammer till it unites a proper degree of flexibility with its well-known firmness.

There are weak persons who persuade themselves that firmness consists in unbending stiffness, in a cold, harsh, cruel inflexibility, which never knows how to yield. But this is not what we mean, when we say that the mother ought in her dealings with her children, in admonishing, correcting, or punishing them, to be at once firm and gentle.

We shall never forget the passionate tears of a young mother, when she detected her boy in a first falsehood. "Oh! my child, what have you done?" she gasped out, with the tears streaming down her cheeks. "Told me a lie! And don't you know I *must* punish you?" The punishment was inflicted by the gentle-hearted mother, who wept the while; and it was firmly and severely administered. And then the boy, worthy of such a mother, seeing her inconsolable, flew to her arms, forgetful of his own pain, to weep on her neck, as he said: "Oh, mama, I am only sorry I pained you! Don't cry, dear mama, and I promise never to do so again." And the promise was kept.

Never Correct or Punish in a Passion.

One golden rule should be ever kept in mind by mothers,—indeed by all persons charged with the training or correction of others,—never to administer reproof, correction, or punishment when under the influence of passion or emotion.

If you would not lose the respect of your children, your authority and influence over them,—wait till you are perfectly calm to speak to them or to chastise them. Of course, the heartfelt grief of the young mother just mentioned went still further, and made a far deeper impression on her child.

Win the Hearts of Your Children.

It is a capital mistake made by parents,—and a fatal mistake, when one looks at its dreadful consequences,—to think that they can rely on the natural affection which their children bear them, and thus make no effort and use no industry to win their love.

To be sure, nature has laid up in the heart of the child a deep store of affection, gratitude, and reverence for the dear authors of its earthly being. And it may take many years of neglect, or harshness, or even downright cruelty, to exhaust that store, to kill that deep and strong root of filial love in the soul. But experience daily shows that the store is not exhaustless, and that the most robust root of love and reverence can be killed.

There are mothers to whom their children are a burden, who bestow on them only a few rare moments of the time they devote to vanity or dissipation, who grudge them the few crumbs of affection with which they fondly imagine they can feed the hungry hearts of their babes, who leave the little unfortunates to the chance tenderness of strangers; and yet these mothers will expect love from their grown-up sons and daughters! These are unnatural mothers, however, who are a curse to their children, and to whom, in turn, by an inevitable retribution, their children will prove a curse. It is not with them we are concerned: they will not be taught or reformed; so, they will go down the steep and slippery slope on which the heartless move to perdition! We are addressing ourselves to parents who think they love their offspring, or who do really love them, but who err most fatally in their way of showing it, and who may be still open to instruction.

There are parents,—all too numerous in every class of society,—who never seem to think that they need gentleness, kindness, loving words and ways, in dealing with children. It is not only fathers among the laboring and hard-worked classes, who usually address both girls and boys with loud and angry words, with a curse, or an oath, or a vile epithet, or a blow; this is but two frequently the treatment which mothers have recourse to.

Can such unchristian parents expect either affection or reverence from these boys and girls, even before they have grown up to manhood and womanhood? We touch here upon one of the inveterate sores of domestic education among our laboring population, and would fain say more on the visible fruits of such training. But, for the present at least, we must content us with sketching the portrait of a motherly love indefatigable in its endeavors and admirable in its methods of securing and increasing continually the grateful love of children.

Of the importance and necessity of binding her children to herself by the ties of the strongest affection, surely every true mother must be convinced. Not only her own happiness through life, but the temporal and eternal welfare of her children, depends chiefly, generally, not to say almost universally, on the influence which a noble mother can wield over the mind and heart and the whole conduct of her dear ones. And there is not one woman who reads this page, but can and ought to be such a noble mother!

It is her duty and her interest. But how is this to be done? Women can teach themselves these methods far better than any man can teach them. They know how contagious love is,—how resistless it is where it is ardently and constantly shown to those who may and ought to return it. The wisest and strongest are made foolish and weak by the show of a sincere, ardent, but unlawful affection. But, where God commands us to love, and to love tenderly, constantly, and unweariedly, and where—as we have seen above—He co-operates with us in our labor of love, how can we not make sure of a certain and a rich return? Your love, O mothers, is as natural, as necessary, to the life of your children's souls, and to the health of their lives, as the sun's light and warmth are to the growth of the grass on the meadow or to the ripening of the corn in the field. And your children are as certain to grow and ripen in perfect and lasting love for you,—the dearest and best objects ever given man to love,—as the grass and the corn to prosper in the sunlight and the warm air.

You have flowers in your garden, in your greenhouse, or in your room. There are among them some favorites which you wish no hand but your own to tend. You have studied their nature, their habits, what can help them or what can hurt and kill them. You know the kind of soil which suits them, and the quantity of moisture and warmth each needs. There is a sort of love in the care which one bestows on beautiful plants and flowers. And to this care, this intelligent and loving culture, these beautiful creatures respond by healthful growth and a more brilliant bloom.

Would that many mothers would bestow on cultivating the hearts of their dear ones the care, the study, the intelligence, the tenderness,—we had almost said the love, which they devoted to the favorites of greenhouse or garden! A mother's loving eye is, daily and hourly, more to the growth and health of the noblest affections in the dear souls committed to her, than the great sun in the heavens is to the life of forest or field; her sweet words of praise, of encouragement, of correction, descend, like the rain and the dew, into the inmost sources of life in the heart, stirring up therein and fostering into bloom the germs of every manly virtue and noble womanly affection. See how each tree in the great virgin forest will send its trunk straight upward toward the sunlight and the warmth, and how its branches stretch upward toward the sky to catch the raindrops by day and the dews of night!

Are you not, in the midst of your dear ones, the sunlight and warmth of their home and their souls? And do not these souls continually open their bosoms and reach out to you with unceasing hunger and thirst for the rain of your instruction and the cool, refreshing dew of your love? Why are you so sparing of what does not impoverish you, and what is sure to bring you a harvest of immortal gratitude and happiness?

But, leave we to the next chapter the many other most interesting things which yet remain to be said about the mother's duties, as well as the magnificent examples which illustrate woman's husbandry in cultivating the souls of her children.

CHAPTER X.

THE MOTHER'S OFFICE TOWARD CHILDHOOD.

Oh! the joy
Of young ideas, painted upon the mind
In the warm glowing colors fancy spreads
On objects not yet known; when all is new
And all is lovely: he looks around, and lo!
As if returned to Eden bowers, every thing
Is very good.

You know the manners of boys, the characteristics of children—that these are innocence, simplicity, purity, truth, and humility. They have no passion they need blush for, no ambition, no care for riches, no anxious solicitudes, neither malice, nor fraud, nor suspicion, nor hatred... All is pure, so that the very word boy, or *puer* (in Latin), is derived from purity. O happy state of boys! O golden age of children! Add intelligence, and what will be wanting to make them angels? For in both are the same beauty, the same countenance, the same native joyousness. O how often, when I see them passing by, do I wish that they might grow in intelligence and not in stature! Truly it would be good for them to continue thus until Christ shall come.

ST. THOMAS VILLANOVA.

Assuredly if Christian mothers make it the chief purpose of their life to be supernatural in their own interior, and in all their motives, actions, and methods,—they will only have to labor with the divine assistance, "to add intelligence" to all the treasures of mind and heart bestowed upon their babes by nature, increased and hallowed in such a wondrous way by Baptism,—and nothing "will be wanting to make them angels." Nay, if they cultivate in them the "gifts of the Holy Ghost," bestowed in an inferior degree in Baptism and in their fullness in Confirmation, they will grow in that understanding which is all divine in its objects and the light it pours on all things, without ceasing to grow "in stature." Such mothers, by the careful and loving culture of the pure souls confided to them, will omit nothing that is "wanting to make them angels;" and as the result of such training many will continue angels "until Christ shall come."

We have some of these angelic men and women before our mind's eye now,—watched over in childhood, as if they were incarnate spirits intrusted to the mother's care, to be trained in all the perfection of manhood and womanhood while preserving all the glorious characteristics of their angel-nature; they grew up in the spiritual beauty and spotless innocence of their baptism, unfolding in mind and heart these priceless "gifts" of the Holy Spirit, just as they developed all the exterior graces and loveliness of their human character; and so they continued till Christ came to summon them away,—all too early, the world thought, from the society which so much needed the light of their examples.

The Divine Reality in Childhood.

Once more, let us see in the baptized babe of the Christian mother what God sees in it: let the same sublime conception of the child's position and destinies which is in the Divine Mind be also in the mind of the parent. Just as a savage, ignorant of the value of gems or the precious metals, will prefer brilliant-colored glass beads to the diamonds of Brazil, the emeralds of New Grenada, or the pearls of Coromandel, even so will it be with the mother who forgets or ignores what is the divine destiny of her babe, what price Christ has paid on the cross to lift it up to his own level, and what capacities are in that young soul for the most godlike virtues and goodness.

In the child brought back from the baptismal font to the mother's arms, there is the human being with the fallen nature inherited from Adam, but redeemed and restored in Christ, and there is also the godlike being created anew in baptism in the likeness of its Divine Parent. In spite of the sacrament of the second birth and the grace of elevation with all its attendant gifts and aids,—there remains in the child the wound left by the primeval transgression: our inclinations are downward, and they have to be resisted, to be overcome, mortified and deadened, if we would rise to the glorious heights of Christian heroism and godliness, which belong to the angelic and heavenly nature we have put on in Christ.

Thus, the mother has to watch over the manifestation of the evil dispositions which early peep out in the child, and tend to drag it down, because they are the inclinations of flesh and blood, and are of earth, earthly. These have to be combated, counteracted, immediately and unceasingly, from their first appearance in infancy and childhood, if the mother would not see them shoot up in boyhood and girlhood, overtopping and choking the growth of every supernatural, or even natural, virtue.

It would be a fatal neglect,—one, in all likelihood, irreparable,—to allow the babe to have its own way in every thing. Wise mothers are careful to check the temper of their youngest infants, and they do succeed in making them acquire even then habits which ever after grow with their growth.

Even pagans looked upon the soul of the child as a something so mysterious, so deep, and so holy,—as if a divine being tenanted the little helpless body,—that they would have their babes treated with infinite reverence. We Christians know clearly what mighty spirit dwells within that regenerated soul; and we may divine somewhat of the workings and promptings of the Paraclete in His living tabernacle. Who of us, who has roamed in boyhood or early manhood through the solitudes of our great virgin forests, but has come unexpectedly upon a lovely little lake,—the parent spring of some lordly river,—nestling in a secluded valley, with the great trees along its margin sending their roots down to drink of the pure waters, that margin itself fringed all around with wild flowers,—while the calm mirror-like bosom reflected the blue skies above, with their white or golden clouds, and the mighty hills which stood sentinels around to protect from intrusion or profanation all the sanctities of the place?

It is not a mere reflection of the heavens, or an image of the eternal hills that the attentive and wondering mind can see within the pure passionless depths of the soul of infancy or childhood. We know that the God of that great temple we call the universe, the Spirit Creator and Sanctifier, is there himself in person. What is the nature of his working within these mysterious depths of the child-soul? What foundations of mighty things to come is his hand laying beneath the untroubled surface of that life in its well-spring?

Mothers,—the educated, the wealthy, the God-fearing,—would do wisely to ask themselves such questions as these,—when they gaze into the upturned face of their babe, and look down into these deep and fearless eyes, through which a glimpse is had of the mysterious infant world of thought and feeling within.

"Children in their tabernacle know the secrets, not of cities, not of human society, not of history, but of God—their fair eyes are full of infinite sweetness—their little hands, joyous and blessed, have not committed evil—their young feet have never touched our defilement—their sacred heads wear an aureole of light—their smile, their voice, proclaim their twofold purity. O the paradisaical ignorance, coveted, perhaps, by angels, of all the errors which heresy has sown in later times! What cruelty to intercept the view of children by suffering their feet to get entangled in such briers, and their minds to be thus cankered, as is the bud bit with an envious worm, ere he can spread his sweet leaves to the air, or dedicate his beauty to the sun! Later they will not thank you; far happier had it sufficed them to have known good by itself, and evil not at all! As terns and other birds from arctic solitudes, when found flapping their long, silver, tapering wings over our rivers that wind through woodlands and rich yellow meadows, show no fear of man, but keep close hovering over the clowns who with stones and staves assail them, so these innocent souls, coming first amid the crowded haunts of life, are ignorant of evil, and of all dangers unsuspicious."[24]

The Mind of Childhood.

What seeds of salutary truth should the mother sow in this virgin soil, in order that its first vital vigor be given to the growth of immortal and divine fruits? What was said, in the preceding chapter, to illustrate the supernatural teaching of a Christian parent, has, in a great measure, anticipated our answer to this question. Here, however, we have to descend to particulars.

"I remember," says Marina de Escobar, "that when I was a little girl, and did not know what was meant by mental prayer, I used to consider with great emotion the mysteries of the life of Christ."

---

[24] *Compitum*, b. i., c. 2, p. 31.

A young mother—we have the story from her own lips, of the blessed result of her early husbandry, others as well have been the witnesses—a very young mother, reared in her own honored home in the paradisaical innocence described above, once reasoned with herself as she looked down on the face of her infant daughter, her first child, lying on the rapt parent's knees: "Here I have in this sweet soul more than a precious piece of marble to fashion into some glorious shape. What form can I give it now, which shall last for all time? With what sentiments can I imbue my darling which can best insure her happiness and everlasting worth? What should I have wished my mother to implant in my own soul as the principle of a goodness and a felicity superior to all that mind can think of or heart desire?" And like a sudden flash of lightning amid the darkness, or a distinctly audible voice in a vast solitude, an interior answer came, *The Love of God!* Convinced that this was the response to the deepest wish of her heart, the young mother thenceforward set about watching for every sign of dawning intelligence in her babe, in order to make the notion of him the first light which should enter there, and his name the first word uttered by the infant lips. Thus, from the first month after the birth of that heaven-sent child, its fond parent would hang over it murmuring into its ears the fond wish that God should be first and last in its mind and heart, and that his love should be the light of its life evermore.

The Adorable Name, so far as mother's skill could effect it, was indeed stamped upon the child's soul. She was taught to thank Him for the motherly love which surrounded her with an enchanted world, as well as for the father's doting fondness and all the comforts of home. There was not a beautiful thing,—and the child's home was filled with such,—in house, or in garden and field, that she was not made to look upon as a gift from that Love which never wearies in giving, but whose lavish hand ever makes of the treasures poured out to-day the sure pledge of tomorrow's surpassing magnificence.

And thus was implanted in her little heart the early idea of

Generosity.

For childhood is open to the notion of a Goodness which only measures its own gifts on the gratitude with which the receiver acknowledges them, and the generosity with which the fitting return is made. And so the generous love of the Divine Benefactor waxed stronger and stronger in the child, in the girl, in the accomplished maiden who was the soul of every great and good work gotten up around her in favor of the poor and the suffering, till the close of her brief life of unsparing and self-sacrificing goodness.

At the age of three, necessity compelled a temporary separation from her mother and her home. But so firmly had the little heart been molded to generous self-control and abnegation even then, that she feigned joyousness as she bade farewell to father and mother on the deck of the steamer, and once they were out of sight burst into an agony of tears. To her uncle's remonstrances the child could only reply, "Oh! I did not want to distress dear mama!" It was the same generosity which impelled her, when a wife and mother, to tear herself away from her worshiped parents, and cast her lot with her husband in a Godforsaken land. Though her young heart was breaking, she would cheer all her dear ones as they clung around her at parting. In her new home, she felt called on to stir up in every soul brought within reach of her influence the zeal for God's name dishonored and for religion betrayed and desecrated and trampled upon,—filling every home far and wide with the piety which burned so brightly in her own. And, crushed down by the death of her father, and prostrate on a bed of sickness, she no sooner learned that yellow fever had attacked her servants, than she found strength to rise and tend herself the plague-stricken,—giving her life to the God of charity, and commending with her dying breath to his fatherly care her babes, her disconsolate husband, and the doting and thrice-afflicted mother thousands of miles away.

While the public was praising all the nobleness of a life thus sacrificed, the poor mother at home bethought her suddenly of the early inspiration to fill that soul with the love of God and to make of the existence of her child one continuous act of generosity. In looking back upon the past she saw clearly the divine purpose,—and like the Mother of Sorrows on Calvary, she sought comfort and strength in taking to her heart the Crucified.

And so was fulfilled in one near our doors what a noble Spanish author said of himself long ago when commenting the following text of Proverbs: *I love them that love me: and they that in the morning early watch for me shall find me.* (Proverbs viii. 17.) "In the house of all other princes," Guevara says, "it is the custom never to open to early visitors, but persons must come after noon; whereas this passage shows us that those who would transact business with Christ, should repair to him at the dawn of their existence, and seek him from their birth. O my God, my God, I confess it is true. 'I do not watch for thee from the dawn;' but on the other hand, Lord, thou wilt not deny that I have been from my birth a Christian, and that ever since I have had any memory, I have named myself always thine."[25]

Yes,—we all love what is freshest and earliest in nature; we love the first flowers of the spring and the first tender bloom of spring itself as it spreads over forest and field; and there are those,—the souls most sensitive to what is lovely and beautiful,—who are filled with rapture by the first glories of dawn, the awakening of the great heart of nature to renewed life and joy at the approach of the glorious sun, and the first fragrance of the dewy meads and gardens as they scent the air with their first fresh odors, and the first voices of the grove as they burst into a full concert when Light, God's great representative in the firmaments, begins to shine above the eastern hills. Pious souls love to give to God the first and freshest of all things, the first hours of the day, as well as the first dawn of their affections.

And does He, who made the human soul, set no store on what is most lovely and precious in our own existence, the first thoughts of the infant mind at its dawn, the first love of the sweet and innocent heart of childhood? O mothers! make sure that these are consecrated to Him, and be certain, on your part, that what God can bestow of choicest graces shall be given you and yours in return.

We only pray that every mother who, while she reads these lines, has such a little daughter as the one dedicated so early to divine love, may teach her child to emulate herself in the early paths of piety and generosity. How sweet will it be to be able to say in after life:

> "She was all I had
> To love in human life—this playmate sweet,
> This child of seven years old—so she was made
> My sole associate, and her willing feet
> Wandered with mine."

[25] Antonio de Guevara, *Epist.*, l. ii.

Joyousness and Love of Enjoyment.

Most important is it not to check in childhood the manifestations of its joyous spirit which is ever ready to break forth as naturally as the brook runs sparkling in the sunlight and singing down its pebbly bed. This joyousness comes from the unconsciousness of wrong, the freedom from all care, and the perfect delight the little innocents find in all that is good and beautiful around them. To their sinless eyes all is bright and sunny, all is new and lovely, and as the garden of Paradise appeared to Adam and Eve innocent, so to these "every thing is very good."

Even when a little boisterous, it is well to let the current flow. Do not restrain it or dam it up so near its source. Alas, the sweet years through which it lasts will have passed away all too soon. We have only to look back to the interval between our own happy and headlong childhood, and the cares and sorrows which settled so darkly on our early youth, and we shall be convinced that our too brief early happiness or joyousness of spirit was but too like the crystal stream from the sierra, rushing down from its source in the uplands, with the early dawn, filling its bed with the clear, bounding waters, and becoming at noontide a fillet of sluggish, muddy water amid a waste of barren sand.

Encourage this bright spirit in your child; let its soul sing with all its strength while it may. Even the song of the nightingale ends long before the summer; and there will be a long, long season when not one note of love or praise will resound through the joyless grove and forest.

The keen zest for enjoyment must also be encouraged and directed. Children only see what is good, beautiful, and lovely in God's blessed world,—that is, the children who are not cooped up between narrow and dark walls, and compelled to experience no necessities or no pleasures, but those of satisfying the craving for food, warmth, and sleep. They are the disinherited in God's rich and pleasant world; and it would be in vain to dwell at length here on the means of giving light and air and nourishment to these poor little starved buds of humanity.

We are speaking of children within whose reach are the usual sources of enjoyment. It is a blessed privilege for the mother to minister in every way she can to the delight and amusement of her dear ones. And one of the most beneficial industries of motherhood is to provide all manner of sport and recreation for her children at home, and to see to it that they feast their senses on garden and field and park and forest as often as possible.

We are not of those who are enamored with the modern methods of placing primers of natural history in the hands of children as soon as they are able to read words of one or two syllables. The love of nature and of all its exhaustless stores of beauty and grandeur and sublimity does not come to the human soul in this way. And, besides, we know that the new-fangled science which would make nature first and middlemost and last, is not the science that cares to set God before the mind of youth, either last or first or middlemost.

But you who believe that, without God, life would be a bitter road, ending nowhere, and this world a mad-house with a drunken manager, and man himself the most terrible of wild beasts,—you will know how to make the spirit of your children joyous by teaching them that the life of heaven is joy without end, and that all the beautiful things with which their Maker has surrounded them in the firmament above and all over this wondrous earth,—are only faint images of the beauties with which the infinite magnificence has decked out his and our eternal home.

Most true is it,—and how the grateful soul swells in dwelling on it!—that this visible universe, and this most beautiful earth in the midst of it, are, with all their untold and incomprehensible splendors, but the tent set up by the emigrant to shelter himself and his dear ones for the night on their homeward way. There may be in its furniture a few ornaments, one or two beautiful things, faint souvenirs of home; but they are at best but reminders of the wealth and glory of the resting-place and permanent abode to which the travelers are journeying.

So beware of these new teachers and the bitter fruit of science which they would give you and yours. Teach these early to find all joy and delight in thinking of Him who is the measureless ocean of perfection and beauty and blessedness. The old Catholic feeling is expressed by St. Francis of Assisi in his canticles of divine love:

> "Heaven and earth with one accord
> Are ever crying out to me:
> 'With all thy heart, oh love the Lord,
> For he created us that we
> Might draw thy spirit heavenward,

To love Him who hath so loved thee.'
Lo! what abundant beams
Of goodness all benign
Flow from that light Divine
In never-failing streams!"[26]

Or, if you would like a sweet singer nearer to your home and times, the following sentiment will find an echo in many a soul grown old with care and burdened with the regret of graces lost and opportunities thrown away:

"My mother's voice! how often creep
Its accents on my lonely hours,
Like healing sent on wings of sleep,
Or dew to the unconcious flowers!
I can forget her melting prayer
While leaping pulses madly fly,
But in the still unbroken air
Her gentle tones come stealing by.
And years and sin and folly flee,
And leave me at my mother's knee.

The evening hours, the birds, the flowers,
The starlight, moonlight,—all that's meet
For heaven in this lost world of ours,—
Remind me of her teachings sweet.
My heart is harder, and perhaps
My thoughtlessness hath drunk up tears;
And there's a mildew in the lapse
Of a few swift and checkered years—
But Nature's book is, even yet,
With all a mother's lessons writ."

Be not afraid of the book of nature, so long as you have your Catholic faith to enable you to read it aright, nor of the voice of poetry, so long as it sings to such a true tone as this.

[26] Translation from "The Month and Catholic Review" for October, 1877.

But, O mother,—whether you live in a palace or in a hovel,—if your chief care be to have God ever live in your heart, his light within you will shed such unearthly beauty on all things that you will make your little ones see a fairy palace in this world, in spite of your own poverty and your life of hard labor. So, keep that light ever full in your child's soul; you both will need to believe in the bright world in which God dwells with his saints and angels, in order to forget the sights you have to behold in this. But even the dingy, dusty, noisome world of a crowded street, or the close workroom, or the long day in the factory, will appear clothed with unearthly charms when you remember the presence of angels with you there, and the splendors visible to the eye of faith, which are ever streaming down on this vale of toil and tears from between the opened gates of our Eternal Home.

Feed your own soul with joy, therefore,—just as the bee gathers honey and treasures it up,—that you may pour it out on your little angels, and keep them angels as long as you can,—joyous, bright-eyed, bright-faced, and bright-tempered. Provided that you firmly believe in the angel-world, and in the presence of guardian angels in your own home, little harm will come of your children reading or learning fairy tales. It will be easy for you to explain to them how the popular fancy wove these graceful stories out of the true history of man's fellowship with these angelic spirits from the beginning,—and of the nearness to him of these other fallen spirits who are ever lying in wait for his ruin.

The chief aim in your sharing all joys and amusements with your dear ones should be to make them feel that your presence, your love is for them the source of all present happiness, and that they can come to your arms, to your heart at all hours,—just as the weary laborers breaking stories along the highways of France, can turn aside in their thirst at any moment to the nearest cool spring.

Never Repel Your Children.

when they approach you. They are drawn to you at first by the whole weight and bent of their nature; increase that attraction more and more by proving to them, through unruffled patience and a kindness which never varies, that your love, under God, is of all things the most needful to them, the most sweet, and the most unfailing. Child-nature must have been thwarted in some of its holiest inclinations when children fear to come to their mother with their every joy and grief and doubt and care.

This sweet trust in a mother's unbounded and unwearied love is a wise and most necessary provision of nature. See how that great nurse of all visible things (or, rather the all-wise Creator through her) lays up in the acorn the provision for the bud of the young oak during the first stage of its growth, and in the cocoa-nut the sweet and abundant nourishment for the young palm-tree, or in the egg the plentiful food of the young bird till it bursts its shell and can provide for itself or be fed for a time by its parents. But man has to depend through infancy, childhood, and youth on the love and fostering care of a mother's heart; and hence is it that God has filled the mother's heart with a living spring of tenderness and wisdom, which is to be the main reliance of the child, the young man or the young woman,—not through all childhood and youth only, but so long as lasts a mother's life.

And corresponding to this is the need every child has of the incomparable treasure of a mother's heart, and the powerful attraction which draws one to a mother's bosom in one's manifold doubts, trials, and temptations.

A mother violates one of the Creator's most beautiful dispensations, when she repels her child from her and does not make all her dear ones grow up in the blessed experience that their mother's heart belongs at all times as wholly to each of them as if she lived for that one alone.

The Mystery of Baptismal Innocence Preserved in So Many.

There are families, even in the midst of the most populous cities, and surrounded by an atmosphere of political and moral corruption, whose sons and daughters grow up to manhood and womanhood in absolute unconsciousness of the nature of moral evil, while mixing the while with the world of their own level, and possessing all the talents and accomplishments that can adorn the sphere in which they move. This is no vague or unfounded assertion, thank God! And we believe, moreover, that there are very many more such families and such beautiful souls than good people themselves are aware of.

Now, it may be laid down as a rule that in every such family the mother has been brought up herself in like sinlessness, and that she has been through life the trusted confidante of every one of her boys and girls,—that from childhood upward their souls have been laid bare to her, every secret of their hearts made known to her.

The Mother the Keeper of Her Children's Hearts.

The true Christian mother will be such by the very force of nature, if she is only true to that great law of which mention has just been made. There will be no need of urging the boy or the girl, the young man or woman, to come to mother for advice or direction. A mother who is prying, or unwisely exacting, or deficient in tact, or lacking herself in spirituality or the supernatural character belonging to Christian motherhood, will not obtain this ascendency over her children, or draw them to her with that spontaneous and irresistible attraction exercised by the pure, the wise, the loving and devoted mother over every child of hers.

Nor will this beautiful and unreserved confidence, begotten of perfect love, interfere with the action of God's minister in the sacrament, as confessor and guide. Such mothers are his most valuable auxiliaries; they prepare chosen souls for the action of the divine graces.

How a Solid Religious Character is Formed.

It is such mothers as these whose enlightened piety will enable them to lay in the souls of their children the foundations of a solid religious character. They are careful to give to each practice of domestic or individual piety the importance which belongs to it. Their mind's eye takes in so clearly and vividly the infinite greatness of that Divine Majesty in whose presence themselves and their dear ones are privileged to do service, that every practice of piety is deemed a thing of infinite importance; such mothers judge, and judge rightly, that nothing is little that is done for One so great, so loving, so magnificent in his generosity.

From the mind and heart of the mother, this sublime and true conception of the divine service and of the piety which should be brought to it, passes into the souls and the lives of her children. Hence there will be, comparatively, but little danger of their neglecting in manhood and womanhood the practices of devotion made so sweet in childhood, or of their failing in that reverential awe in approaching the divine presence which was instilled at their mother's knee.

Piety Founded on Principle, How Lasting.

Piety grounded like this, by a true mother, on the very substance of a child's intellectual and moral nature, will not be likely to be shaken or overturned in after-life. It is impossible, where all that is most delightful in the knowledge of God and in one's earliest fellowship with him, and with his bright court of angels and saints on high, have been wound up in the pure joys of childhood, and the most rapturous visions of youth, that the hollow maxims of worldly wisdom, or the sneers of the unbeliever, the voices of one's equals, or the scandal of example within the sanctuary itself, can detach such a soul from its allegiance to God. Where religion has penetrated with the light of its principles the whole of man or woman's intelligence, and made the heart strong and happy by its practice, the inconsistencies of its professors or its ministers cannot have the effect of killing the roots of faith in mind or heart.

So, let mothers who read this be encouraged to make themselves all in all to their dear ones in their practices of piety as in their amusements, in every pursuit, in every enjoyment, in every trial and difficulty, persuading themselves firmly all the while that God is with them doing their work, which is, after all, his own dearest and most glorious work. They are sanctifying their own home, and filling it with God; at the same time he will fill themselves and their children with his light and joy. The day will come when such true mothers, looking back, will remember these beautiful lines of one whose mother was more solicitous about her boy's worldly advancement than about his spiritual welfare:

"Oh, what a pure and sacred thing
    Is beauty curtained from the sight
Of the gross world, illumining
    One only mansion with her light!
Unseen by man's disturbing eye,
    The flower that blooms beneath the sea

Too deep for sunbeams, doth not lie
  Hid in more chaste obscurity.
A soul, too, more than half divine,
  Where, through some shades of earthly feeling,
Religion's softened glories shine,
  Like light through summer foliage stealing,
Shedding a glow of such mild hue,
  So warm, and yet so shadowy too,
As makes the very darkness there
  More beautiful than light elsewhere."[27]

Yes, in the "chaste obscurity" of a home where a true mother moves, the embodiment of all that religion holds to be most lovely to the interior sense, men of the world will not feel repelled as they might by the austerity of the cloister, but attracted and subdued by all the virtues and graces which they behold shining with such "softened glory" in the lives of parents and children.

Be Invariably Cheerful.

We must have failed to convey our true meaning in what has just been said about the inculcation of early piety, if any shadow of gloom is thought to rest, even for a moment, on the home of the true Christian mother, any more than on her own brow or the brows of her little angels. Oh, no! Piety is ever joyous, sunny, and bright. And, as to the mother,—even when she is suffering or burdened with care, or carrying in her heart a heavy load of grief,—she must put the cloud away from her when in presence of her dear ones. There are generous husbands and fathers who never allow their business cares to cross their threshold; they leave them at the doorstep, and go into their home-sanctuary with unclouded face and warm smiles and words of love for all. They will not have the storm which pelts their own hearts so mercilessly in the outside world make its mutterings heard near the warm nest where wife and children are sheltered. So must it be with respect to the mother and her household cares and difficulties; let them never be known to her children.

---

[27] Thomas Moore.

Keep out Gossip and Scandal.

Much more careful ought she to be to close her doors against mere idle gossip; and still more so to exclude the echoes of the scandals which are rumored abroad. Hence the necessity of selecting carefully the circle of those who are to be admitted to the intimacy of the home. Not all who call on the mother are fit persons to converse with the children. Not all who consider themselves to be on a footing of friendship with either parent, are safe friends for children, who have never yet beheld evil, or heard the sound of its voice. The acquaintance with it must always come too soon: it is the inevitable misfortune which a watchful mother will stave off as long as possible.

We once remember a stranger who had been warmly recommended to an admirable family, and who had been welcomed to all the hospitalities of the home: it was soon apparent, however, that he was not what he pretended to be, or his outside friends had represented him. The evening had passed, and all honor had been done to the guest, when some one, in presence of the younger children, made a remark unfavorable to the stranger. This called forth an indignant rebuke from the mistress of the house, who reminded the offender that, as she never intended to invite the stranger again, such censure was needless; and that, moreover, it was unpardonable, as she never allowed any one admitted to the family circle, even for the once, to be spoken of unkindly.

And this naturally brings us to say how scrupulous mothers ought to be to discountenance every thing approaching or leading to

Uncharitableness.

On this point the true mother must be inflexible. We suppose her to be thoroughly enlightened with regard to the transcendent excellence of charity,—that divine virtue practiced after the manner of the Master who gave himself to us, who shields from every eye our own unworthiness, and treats our guilty souls with such infinite reverence in his merciful methods of reconciliation: we suppose that the true Christian woman, with that deep sense, characteristic of her sex, of all that is most divine in humility as well as in charity, ever keeps before her mind the knowledge of God's infinite liberality toward her soul and of her own very inadequate return. This conviction of the infinitude of that love so unsparing of itself and its graces, and of her own indebtedness to the divine benefactor, will prevent her from looking down on others, from judging, or, still less, despising, even the most guilty.

It is one thing for Christian parents to keep away from the innocent souls intrusted to them all persons known to be not edifying or open to serious suspicion, and quite another thing to allow such persons to be spoken of in their home. Such persons should not be admitted to the intimacy of the home-circle; that is a matter of prudence, most frequently of absolute necessity; but no less imperative is it that the faults, the failings, or the conduct of others should never, under any pretext, be made the subject of conversation in the family.

The mother is queen there; her will, in all that pertains to the proprieties and the charities of life, no one, not even her husband, should be permitted to question. Indeed, we suppose, in what we say here, that both parents have long ago resolved to be of one mind on this as on all such matters. Whosoever, therefore, should dare to trespass by word or bearing against the cardinal virtues of the home, should be rebuked by the mother and mistress.

It is a mistake to allow the fear of offending or making an enemy to prevent one from doing one's duty. The person ungenerous enough to take offense at a remonstrance gently, delicately, but firmly administered, would be got rid of very cheaply. The generous-minded,—who are often led to gossip inadvertently by custom or the desire to please, will only conceive a higher respect for that home and a deeper esteem for its mistress.

We know of more than one person who has been radically cured of uncharitableness by the firm but gentle rebuke of a mother at her own table.

As to making enemies,—when a mother has used tact, courtesy, and a gentle firmness in repressing scandalous gossip or uncharitable conversations,—she must trust to the innate sense of right and duty in the persons rebuked, as well as to God's good care of her home and its welfare.

A person in authority having been persuaded by some gossips who had his ear, that a lady visiting in a family very dear to him was unworthy of such intimacy, thought himself bound to warn the mistress of the home. She listened without answering one word, perfectly certain that her informant had been imposed upon by mischief-makers. Six months afterward he came back with a conscience very much troubled, and begged to know how far the information he had given—and which deeply affected the moral character of the person aspersed—had been communicated to others, determined, as he said, to repair the injury done, no matter how widely it might have spread. "Have no fear," the prudent and charitable lady replied; "I have not even mentioned the subject to my husband. Indeed, I could not in conscience do so, knowing that the report you heard was pure calumny."

This is the rule of the saints, never to mention what is or may be detrimental to another, except when it is necessary to do so for the welfare of that other, or to shield the innocent from the imminent danger of contagion. It is related in the life of St. Ignatius Loyola, that, in the discharge of his office of superior-general of the great society he had founded, he received serious charges against one of his subordinates. He immediately laid the subject of complaint before his council. At his nightly examination of conscience it occurred to him that he might have brought about an effective amendment in the other's misconduct by a reproof privately administered and without discussing the matter with anybody;—at any rate, his conscience seemed to tell him that it had been, at the utmost, quite enough to consult one or two persons, without exposing a brother's infirmity to a larger number.

In his grief he scourged himself most severely for what he considered a serious want of discretion, if not of charity, and then lay down. But he could find no rest, and had to rise and awaken his confessor,—though it was past midnight,—before whom he laid his fault with many tears and bitter self-accusation.

We must not be tempted to accuse these great and holy souls of excessive rigor toward themselves, or of unduly exaggerating faults comparatively slight, and committed, as in this last instance, through a little precipitancy at most. When we reflect how much mischief,—fatal and irreparable mischief,—may be done by judging hastily and speaking rashly, we shall be slow to condemn St. Ignatius, and feel disposed to judge ourselves rather, and call ourselves to account for making light of matters in which the neighbor's good name is concerned. It is, some may think, but a trifling imprudence, while passing through a field of ripe corn, to cast away thoughtlessly the end of a lighted cigar. Perhaps he who did so never bestows a further thought on the matter till he hears on the morrow that the poor farmer's crop has been ruthlessly swept away by fire, that his little home shared a like fate, while he and his family barely escaped with their lives.

Alas, we know by the experience of all time that slander, beginning in a thoughtless word, spreads as rapidly as fire in the ripe corn; and that while the field thus ravaged may bear a richer crop next year, and while the burned cottage may rise from its ruins, nothing can adequately repair the ravages of uncharitableness, or build up anew a reputation ruined by an evil, an idle, or a foolish tongue!

So let the mothers for whom we write add the horror of uncharitableness and impropriety of every kind to the joyous and bright spirit with which they train their children during this first stage,—and what a preparation will be made for the thorough education of the noble boys and noble girls, who are soon to develop into the full perfection of manhood and womanhood!

Baptismal Names.

We should be untrue to our own most cherished convictions, as well as to our duty to Christian families, if we did not, before concluding what concerns childhood, state what is the mind of the Church, and the uninterrupted custom of nineteen centuries of Christian civilization, with regard to the names given in baptism to each child newly born. Let no reader judge hastily of what he fancies we are about to say. Rather, let our words be read attentively and our reasons carefully weighed; then, if we mistake not, but few who have done so will differ from us in opinion.

The whole history of revealed religion, both before and after Christ, brings before the believer an immortal society existing simultaneously on earth and in heaven, into which enter with the three adorable Persons of the Trinity and the faithful and glorified angels, the saints already resting in eternity from their trials here below, and the body of believers scattered over the earth and following the divine law handed down to them. This, of course, is not an adequate definition of the Church. It is only an imperfect description sufficient for our purpose and satisfactory to all who have present to their minds the correct idea of the Church as it embraces earth and heaven.

From the earliest dawn of historic times there is apparent in that portion of the race to which God had intrusted the primitive revelation and the promises attached to it, a deep veneration both for the great patriarchs or ancestors who had, from age to age, been faithful to the truth in the midst of infidelity and corruption, and a no less veneration for the glorious spirits who from the beginning held intercourse with men, and were the messengers of the Divine Goodness in their behalf.

Hence a very natural tendency to bestow on newly born children the name of some one of these glorious ancestors or of the mighty spirits who had been sent on some memorable errand of deliverance or mercy. This tendency, though much less remarkable among the Hebrew people before the Christian era, became very speedily a common custom among the followers of Christ; and to the names most popular and venerated in the Old Testament period, were substituted or added those of the men and women most conspicuous in Christian story,—the names of the Blessed Mother, of the apostles and disciples, of the most illustrious of the early martyrs and teachers of the gospel, and, from age to age, of the persons instrumental in propagating Christianity in different countries, as well as of those who had been most venerated in life, and after death, for their holiness and eminent services to the flock of Christ.

The ancient Hebrews incorporated the name of God in their language with most of the names which they bestowed on their babes, both for the purpose of placing them thereby in a special manner under the protection of Jehovah, and for that of stimulating them when grown up to be worthy of the name they bore. Such, in a certain measure, was also their aim in bestowing on their children the names of men or angels.

Nor was the object of the early Christians substantially different, when they showed a predilection for the names of Mary, Martha, Peter, Paul, John,—or in later ages when they called their sons Augustine, Cyprian, Basil, Gregory, Patricius or Patrick, and their daughters Monica, Agnes, Cecilia, or Scholastica. The babe who was incorporated with the Church of earth under the good omen of such a name, was held to have a claim on the protection of the great saint in heaven who first illustrated it by godlike virtues, and an obligation to emulate the sanctity of the patron thus given in baptism. Indeed, among the ancient Irish, the custom was common of adding the word *Gilla*, "servant," to the saint-name, to declare positively this profession of honoring and serving the saint given to one as patron.

While, therefore, the family or clan name, whether glorious or obscure, continued to be borne by all the members as a common appellation, the individual was distinguished by some sweet saint-name from every other among the kindred. Thus in every Christian land the entire population was connected in fellowship and spiritual intercourse with all that was most glorious in the past, all that was greatest and highest in the divine society of heaven: thus the earthly Jerusalem, by the very names born by its members, was the image of the city of God on high.

There is in this venerable and time-honored custom of giving saint-names in baptism to every new child of the Christian family, a something so beautiful, so deserving of all reverence, so deeply rooted in the holiest and far-reaching affections of the race, that it is unaccountable how any family calling itself Christian should overlook it, and sacrilegious in a Catholic family to violate it by bestowing on their babes some name of modern notoriety, and, not seldom, of very doubtful fame.

The Reformers of the sixteenth century set aside the beautiful Christian customs of the preceding ages, rejected the saints, and substituted for them Biblical names. The Independents and Puritans went further, and showed an almost exclusive predilection for Old Testament heroes and heroines, and for many names which were those of any thing but heroines or heroes. From this extreme there has been a reaction among the descendants of the Puritans in America, and now the rage is for the names of modern distinguished men and women, or for every name of man and woman which may tickle the ear or please the fancy of fathers and mothers who delight in "Dime Novels," and worship the names they find therein.

It is the custom of the universal Church, and a positive ecclesiastical law in many countries, that one at least of the surnames given in baptism, should be that of a saint.

We are writing in a country where, unhappily, with some of the objectionable customs of the sturdy old Puritans, other most laudable customs, having their roots far back in the past, are fast dying out. Catholic families who have come hither to cast their lot with the posterity of their bitterest foes of old, are—and it is a pity—forgetting not a few of the traditions of their fathers,—traditions dear to the "Old Land," and blessed of God and man. Their children in this liberty and novelty loving generation would blush to bear the name of Patrick, so nobly borne by the soldier-President of France; they disdain the name of John, or James, or Paul; while young girls are ashamed of being called Bridget, or Winifred, or Margaret, or Monica,—names which shall eternally remain in human history as some of the most glorious ever borne by woman. We say nothing of the ever-blessed name of Mary,—or only mention it to protest against seeing it disfigured by the abominably vulgar rage for "pet names," which has seized on all classes of American women. Let the sweet and hallowed name of her who is the Mother of our Life, the true "Mother of all the Living," remain unchanged and unvailed in our Catholic households. Blessed be the mothers who bear it nobly, and who teach their daughters to honor it with all the virtues and graces of true womanhood!

CHAPTER XI.

A Digression, Which May Serve as a Rest, and a Preparation for What Follows.

Felix qui propriis œvum transegit in arvis,
Ipsa domus puerum quem videt ipsa senem.
Blessed who in his own fields his life hath passed,
Whom the same house both boy and old man sees.
CLAUDIAN.

Good Heaven! what sorrows gloomed that parting day,
That called them from their native walks away;
When the poor exiles, every pleasure past,
Hung round the bowers, and fondly looked their last,
And took a long farewell, and wished in vain
For seats like these beyond the western main;
And shuddering still to face the distant deep,
Returned and wept, and still returned to weep.
GOLDSMITH.

If to any it should seem that the instructions given in the preceding chapter were more fitted to the intelligence and leisure of wealthy homes than to mothers overburdened with toil and pinched with the care of the morrow,—we shall not deny that we had principally in view therein parents left free by affluence, or at least, by competence, to devote themselves to the sacred duties of motherhood. We also supposed that the father, in every such household, gave his most hearty support to the mother's plan of government.

Nevertheless, the general principles we have laid down and illustrated, apply to all homes and all mothers, as it will be easy to convince one's self by an attentive perusal of the chapter. Lest, however, a single mother dwelling amid the necessities of hard daily toil, if not the pressing needs of poverty, should deem herself to have been overlooked in these pages, or reproach us justly with passing her by and not uttering either a word to cheer her at her task or a word to point out the better road, we shall address ourselves to the wives of laboring men in what we are about to say.

Only, anxious as we are to make the general reader understand some of the greatest obstacles which mothers who are not wealthy have to overcome in the performance of their motherly duties, we crave permission to turn aside one moment from our direct path, in order to explain in what consists one great difference between the homes of the majority of our English-speaking Catholics in the Eastern and Middle States and the homes in which they were born and reared "in the Old Country."

Home Culture in Catholic Lands.

Be it said here, once for all, it is an error but too general among a certain educated public, to think that the peasantry and the laboring classes, in what were once called Catholic countries, are devoid of all culture, all refinement, all the courtesies and graces of life,—and that, too, in consequence of their not being able to read! There is indeed a very marked difference between the country people and the townsfolk nowadays, and the difference is not in favor of the town. But,—and we speak of what was or what is in places and among populations where religion has had her full legitimate influence, and where civil intolerance has not tied the tongue as well as the hands of the Church,—we say it most emphatically, there always is in the most modest farmer's cottage, or the poorest laborer's dwelling, refinement, intelligence, courtesy, chastity, truth and honesty, dignity of manners, in one word, all traceable to religious teaching.

Let readers, whoever they may be, allow the writer to pour out his full heart here, to tell what he has seen and what he knows by life-long experience of the homes of the laboring classes, whether in town or country;—the description will enable him, and the reader with him, to grasp the true reality of education during boyhood and girlhood in the lowly homes where God is still feared, and father and mother reverenced. Let us go back to these homes, in which ancestral faith and piety, with their sweet train of domestic graces and customs have never ceased to reign. The memory of childhood, with its golden sunlight lending to all things a glory and enchantment, brings back

"The house where I was born,
The little window where the sun
Came peeping in at morn;"

or with one who was himself born on that dear soil, and who, early and late, had tasted of the bitter as of the sweet of poverty:

"Blest be that spot, where cheerful guests retire
To pause from toil, and trim their evening fire;
Blest that abode, where want and pain repair,
And every stranger finds a ready chair;
Blest be those feasts, with simple plenty crowned,
Where all the ruddy family around
Laugh at the jests or pranks that never fail,
Or sigh with pity at some mournful tale;
Or press the bashful stranger to his food,
And learn the luxury of doing good."

Homes in Ireland.

The secluded cottage, set in its wealth of green fields and flowering hedges, is now distinctly before the eye of our soul, with the calm little lake near at hand, and the hills rising beyond and sloping away to where one gigantic form towered in mid-air, its top crowned with some ruin of far-off ages, and at its foot a cluster of villages nestling, as if the generations which once peopled them had found protection in the now ruined stronghold. There was, just where the lake ended, and a young brook ran wildly out, like a school-boy from school, an ancient mill, which still did service to farmers for many a mile around; while at the opposite end the ivy-covered walls of the ancient abbey or parish church lifted itself above the silver mirror of the lake, and around the ruin slept untold generations of men and women who had "kept the faith," and whose descendants still wished to rest by the side of their parents till the final wakening. There, too,—God knows,—he who pens these lines would fain repose, near the ruined altars of his ancestral faith and by the side of her who gave him birth and was taken from him while he was still a child.

Villages Changed into Pasture Lands.

We know not what change the hand of time has made in the scene thus indelibly stamped on heart and memory. Famine has been busy there also, with fever always following in the train of famine; and many a ship, like that which bore away the writer well-nigh fifty years ago, has sailed from the glorious neighboring bay crowded with the sorrowing but hopeful men and women who followed across the deep in the track of the westering sun! And so the dear homes were made desolate or swept away ruthlessly from the face of the land, as being the too eloquent witnesses to secular misrule and oppression. So be it! We recall their memory not to stir up the bitterness of so many hearts made sore by unmerited wrong, but to celebrate the sanctities and the virtues which bloomed immortal in those lowly homes, and whose roots still cling to the soil as tenaciously as the ivy to apse and chancel-wall in the once beautiful church on yonder lake shore.

There was not a village on the populous plain, or along the shores of its many lakes, or hidden away among its wild mountain tracts, which had not its own traditions of honor, bravery, and honesty, nor a home in these villages which did not possess an inheritance of spotless purity handed down from mother to daughter since the days of St. Bridget and before, which was not surrounded by an atmosphere of ancestral piety and uprightness that was the life-breath of father and son from age to age. The ancient race had been despoiled of almost every right and franchise; of all property in the soil, even of the freedom to cultivate it;[28] they had been left without the comforts of a civilized home; and in their squalid huts the ruthless bands of Elizabeth and Cromwell had not even left what is to this day the pride and consolation of the Icelander in his turf cabin, their ancient native literature. How it fared with the churches, the monasteries, the countless schools, the benevolent institutions of every kind which covered the land, and were the well-springs of culture and highest civilization,—even Protestant historians may tell sorrowingly.

---

[28] See Hall's "Ireland, Scenery, Character, etc.," vol. iii., p. 361 and foll.

Home Atmosphere and Virtues.

But, despite all this ruin, and the religious and civil oppression of three hundred years,—every family in the land had its name for fidelity to God, for spotless chastity, for honor unimpeached,—and to that *name* it clung with a worship as unwavering and a watchfulness as sleepless as the ancient Greek or Roman had for his household altar and the sacred fire.

The authority of father and mother was sacred in the eyes of all, and most sacredly obeyed; their will and their word were rarely, if ever, questioned. The father was king within his home,—though it might be in appearance scarcely one degree above the hut of the savage; but, though stripped of all earthly goods, and barely tolerated on the land which had belonged to himself and his ancestors, the father had lost none of his self-respect, no part of the reverence and love which were wont to be paid to him and his in other days, and in a dwelling befitting a freeman and a soldier. It was the patriarchal ideal of home-authority consecrated and elevated by the Christian faith: all who were born amid this home-atmosphere will remember how absolute was the sway of that paternal rule. But superior even to that, because founded on equal reverence and arising from a love all unmixed with fear, was the authority, the sway of the mother in those humble but holy households. Who ever thought of rebelling against the father's rule, even when it bore most heavily on its unoffending as well as its offending subjects? Who was ever heard to set aside a mother's will and to be blessed of God or happy among men?

Domestic Education in These Homes.

We can never forget the band of children, often composed of those of several relatives, crowding together into one of these hospitable homes to partake together of the instruction imparted for a season by some itinerant master of repute;—and of the implicit obedience all yielded to the dear mistress of the house. The dominie's rod,—sharp as it was known to be,—had less terrors for any of us than a look of displeasure from auntie's gentle but watchful eye. And even when no dominie was there, she could keep us to our tasks, not all unwillingly, push us forward more rapidly, kindle by her sweet smile and soft, low voice a more intense emulation in the breasts of all. It was like a beehive; all labored silently, unceasingly, under the influence of the queen of the hive: she did not seem to see or hear, and had no monitors or spies about the school-room or the house. But we worked hard from morning till night to have one word of praise from her or one motherly kiss. And then at night there was a chapter read by her from the Life of Christ by St. Bonaventure, illustrated, too, by some delightful tales of her own,—some miracle of protection performed during the evil days of the Commonwealth, or Elizabeth's devastations, or during the atrocious reign of the soldiery of Cornwallis in 1798, which had utterly ruined every one of our families.[29] We almost beheld with the eyes of the body the angels who kept watch and ward over the ruined abbey and its church, with the crowded cemetery that hugged its walls; we believed they could be seen upon the lake at Hallowe'en, Christmas, and Eastertide. We knew they watched over us day and night, and through awe of their presence we kept silence after night-prayers and till after morning prayers the next day.

But, oh the happy houseful swayed by that loving heart and that unfailing tenderness, and the bright look of that gentle woman from whom no sound of anger or loud reproof was ever known to come! God rest thee,—who wert a mother to the orphan, and more than mother to thy own! Gratitude cannot inscribe a monument to thee; but let thy work live in these humble pages, if God's good blessing should bestow on them any lasting utility!

These Traditions to Be Cherished in America.

What is the purpose of this narration? This: to show that families who boast,—albeit only the families of the laboring poor,—their descent from this ancient stock of believers, must not allow the most precious and venerable traditions of their former home, the home of their fathers far away, to be lost in the homes they create for their dear ones in another land. On the contrary, amid the civil and religious freedom enjoyed in their adopted country, it behooves them to give to these traditions, home virtues, and home education, which are or ought to be the jewels of their heart, a fairer, a more magnificent setting than they could have had in the homes left behind.

---

[29] See Hall's "Ireland," *ibidem*, pp. 379, 380, 381.

This, then, is what we would impress upon the minds and hearts of our readers, that the new home in America, in Australia, in Africa, in Asia,—wheresoever the dividing wave may have cast the exiles,—should be (for it *can* be) more Christian, more supernatural, more lovely, than the homes on the banks of the Shannon or the Moy, on the shores of Loch Corrib or Loch Neagh.

The question is, whether or not the home of the Catholic farmer throughout the length and breadth of North America, or that of the laborer in city or manufacturing center, or of the merchant and tradesman anywhere among us,—has preserved the traditions of reverence for parental authority, of that simplicity and unsuspecting innocence in boyhood and girlhood, of sensitiveness in guarding the honor of mother and daughter, and the incorruptible honesty of father and sons,—so characteristic of the former family life.

Each Home Had Its Ancestral Honor to Guard.

We all know,—and it is a most blissful recollection,—that the jealous watchfulness with which each family in the old land guarded its unstained reputation,—was, under God's providence, the main preserver of family honor and happiness. Where each family was known to its neighbors throughout a wide and populous circle, and was far more careful of the unstained honor of its members than of life itself,—far more ambitious of having the good opinion and good word of every man, woman, and child for many miles around,—any act entailing dishonor or shame must have been of very unfrequent occurrence. Indeed, the infamy attached to any such stain was such, and the disgrace so intolerable, that the individual had to go into voluntary and perpetual banishment, and very often the entire family had to disappear.

The Basques and Their Ancestral Coats of Arms.

In a former chapter we mentioned a beautiful custom of the Basques relating to their manner of bestowing alms. Let us,—before we go further in this most important matter,—compare in another respect this most ancient Catholic race with the Celts, their brothers in religion, and, not improbably, their associates in flood and field in the far-off period when both migrated westward from Mesopotamia.

In Biscay every family is noble. Nor is this an idle or unfounded boast of a warlike and liberty-loving race. Their right to have armorial bearings is one admitted from time immemorial. Hence every house has its coat of arms; and some houses of peasants, mechanics, or fishermen along the coast have on their shield more quarters than the proudest escutcheons of England or France. We have heard and read much of late of the obstinacy with which, all through the present century, the Basques have fought against every government for their just and ancient privileges; but we have but little conception of the lofty and indomitable love of freedom with which they have so battled from before the dawn of Christianity, or of the incorruptible spirit of faith with which they defend their Catholic altars.

All honor to that heroic race whose struggle for liberty has been one of two thousand years! Hence the pride,—a noble and a legitimate pride,—with which that vigorous, healthful, comely, and Catholic race looks upon every homestead in the land, and upon the shields,—ancient and venerable, and often numerous,—which adorn the outside of their homes.

The Basques Cannot Transplant their Ancestral Homes.

Take the Basque away from his native mountains in Guipuzcoa, he will be, wherever he goes, the same energetic, brave, and believing man. Transplant whole villages from among their ancestral hills or their glorious historic strongholds along the coast, and you will have, whithersoever you lead them, some of the noblest specimens of humanity to be found on the earth. But can you transplant with them the homes consecrated by so many unbroken centuries of domestic virtue, and honored by so many recorded deeds of public worth? Can you transfer the interior and exterior atmosphere of these homes?

What the Irish Emigrant Cannot Find in His New Home.

So is it with that other race of which we are now solicitous. Emigration not only scatters the members of the same village and neighborhood, even when they chance to migrate together; but it separates widely and forever members of the same family and household, and thereby the wholesome and priceless restraints and safeguards of neighborship are lost to the emigrants in their new home.

The evil thence resulting might be only a half evil could neighbors "at home" continue to be neighbors in their new home. There seems to be a strong current of opinion running or tending in this direction at the present moment. But it only points to future possibilities, and we are dealing here with the realities of the present. The tide of emigration has been toward the great cities, where the facilities of daily labor appeared greatest, and higher wages enabled the new-comers to provide many comforts and luxuries hitherto unknown to them. Thus the wretched agricultural life they had formerly led contrasted unfavorably with the ease of their present condition.

And so,—not unnaturally,—the great mass of emigrants from Ireland settled down in the cities, leaving the rich unoccupied lands of the interior, with their certain prospects of health, longevity, independence, and substantial political power to other races, happier both in the experience of better social conditions and in the wiser direction given to their present aims and energies.

A Crowded City Fatal to the Former Home-Life.

But a family transplanted from a quiet country district in Ireland, or from the scarcely less quiet suburb of one of its cities, finds itself utterly lost in a large city in the New World. Their coming only adds one unit more to the vast sum of uncertain labor and certain indigence. Whatever may be their chances of finding employment and forcing their way to independence,—they are, generally, utter strangers; all the ties, affections, and holy influences of the ancient home and neighborhood are gone forever. Their good name, the stainless honor of the family in the past, is a thing of but little account to the hungry, anxious, bustling crowd which daily pours out from the streets among which the new home lies buried, to seek for work and for bread. In that crowd there are hundreds who are glad to have their past concealed, and who care but little what stain may fall upon their next-door neighbors.

There is in the social atmosphere of this neighborhood a tone of morality far lower than that which reigned in the native village; there are many things in what the newcomers see and hear which shock their sense and alarm their conscience. But who does not know that one gets soon accustomed and indifferent to this sort of atmosphere, just as one becomes gradually acclimated in the bitter cold of the north, or the torrid heat of the tropics and the equator?

Our readers will then admit that very many, if not most of the families whom this book may reach, are laboring under sad disadvantages in the work of rearing and educating their boys and girls.

This Is No Reflection on American Institutions.

Let us not be misunderstood. We are not undervaluing in any one respect the many priceless blessings which flow from American liberty and the working of our free institutions. We are not depreciating American manhood and womanhood. Our purpose, well-weighed according to the light of our best judgment, is to aid to our utmost, before we go to our account, in the sacred work of rearing from among the laboring masses armies of true men and women who will build up the glorious America of our dreams.

Those who are apt to take fire at any allusion to the deterioration of races in our country, are, generally, persons born of emigrant parents, and who fancy that any comparison instituted concerning the degree of physical vigor, the level of intellectual culture or moral worth of the first and second generations born on American soil, conveys a personal slight on every one so born.

Preserve Your Home Inheritance of Virtue, and Add to It.

No, no, we are here trying to consider carefully what are the obstacles which are found in the homes of our laborers, of our tradesmen, of our poor, toward the successful education of men and women fitted to be themselves the best of parents in their turn, and to rear children of their own, inheriting, with the qualities and virtues of father and mother, a superadded stock of true manliness and womanliness,—the highest wealth which can be brought to the service of any country.

We are endeavoring to point out to father and mother in every home into which this book may go, how to preserve sacredly every particle of their ancestral inheritance of faith, of morality, of honor, honesty, and that true pride founded on the consciousness of unstained descent, personal integrity, independence, and legitimate ambition. Most anxious are we, moreover,—and in this we believe we are discharging both a priestly and a patriotic duty,—to increase tenfold in every one of these dear homes their precious inheritance of piety, purity, fear of God, self-respect, self-reliance, and incorruptible integrity. Toward this we shall contribute not a little,—if we can convince all minds of the wholesomeness of the teaching here given.

How Poor Mothers Might Be Aided by Their Wealthy Sisters.

The *home of the really poor*, in particular, is now present to our mind, as well as the need which the mother, in such a home, has of the efficient co-operation of her more favored sisters in fulfilling the duties of her condition. We remember, during a brief stay at Roxbury, Massachusetts, in August, 1860, of learning, among other admirable good works carried on under the direction of the Sisters of Notre Dame, of their calling together on Sunday afternoons the poor mothers of families who stood most in need of instruction, direction, and special assistance in the management of their homes. The good Sisters used to visit them on week-days, gently teaching the untaught or overworked creatures how to make every thing clean, tidy, and bright about them; helping them to have the children regular in their attendance at school, neatly dressed, with their clothes mended and all marks of degrading poverty removed; watching over the husband's good conduct and his fidelity to his religious obligations; and, especially, aiding every wife and mother to be herself, to husband and children, a model of sobriety, thrift, and gentleness. It was a most admirable good work. Add to the salutary reform thereby effected in so many homes, the influence exercised by the hundreds of children educated in the incomparable schools of that edifying sisterhood, and one sees at a glance what an amount of good can be achieved by true women when obeying the impulse of the Divine Spirit.

The sodalities named after the Holy Family, established in Quebec and throughout Canada by the early Jesuit missionaries, had a purpose not very dissimilar to this. They were chiefly, if not solely, composed of married women, who lent a tender but helpful hand to their poor, sick, or overburdened sisters, and thus secured the children against the evils of neglect, ignorance, and dangerous associations.

Looking abroad over this great and growing city of New York and its adjacent populous cities, and counting the many thousand needy and neglected homes to which some such helpful influences as this would be most timely, or most necessary,—we ask ourselves what could not associations of married ladies in the largest parishes, or in every parish, acting in co-operation with the sisterhoods who minister to the needs of the poor, not effect under God's blessing?

We must endeavor to make the home of the poor laboring man cleanly, comfortable, bright, attractive, and happy, for his own sake as for that of his grown-up sons and daughters. We must exert ourselves to aid every poor mother to make her home such that her husband and older children will love it and prefer it to any other place on work-days as well as during the repose of the Sunday.

This is a suggestion made with all diffidence in our own judgment, and all due deference to the judgments and sentiments of others. And having thus explained our object in submitting the foregoing remarks to the reader's calm Christian sense, we feel more confident in addressing ourselves to the task of instructing the wives of the mechanic and the laborer in their motherly office toward boyhood and girlhood.

CHAPTER XII.

THE MOTHER'S OFFICE TOWARD BOYHOOD AND GIRLHOOD.

O little feet, that such long years
Must wander on, through doubts and fears;
  Must ache and bleed beneath your load!
I, nearer to the wayside inn,
Where toil shall cease and rest begin,
  Am weary thinking of your road.

O little hands, that, weak or strong,
Have still to serve or rule so long,
  Have still so long to give or ask!
I, who so much with book or pen
Have toiled among my fellow-men,
  Am weary, thinking of your task."

LONGFELLOW.

The Boys and Girls in the Laborer's Home.

Deep as ever must be the sympathy of a priestly heart for both parents and children in the home of the laboring man, and solicitous as every true priest must be of the future of these little ones born to toil and hardship,—it is principally with the much-tried father and mother that his concern lies. Theirs is the hard and often hopeless battle of the present; and worthy of the admiration of men and angels is the struggle they make to keep suffering away from their nestful, or to provide for their dear ones comforts, education, and a position in life from which they had themselves been debarred.

We do not mean in thought and affection to separate such praiseworthy parents in what we have to say; sure are we, that every father will bless our endeavor to make the burden of the laborious mother lighter, her task more pleasant and easy, and her every-day path of duty less rugged and thorny. It is the feet of such as she is that "must ache and bleed beneath" her load: it is the ever-busy hands of such a mother that, "weak or strong," must work at her unceasing task through "such long years!"

Nor, near as the writer may be "to the wayside inn," shall he yield to any sense of weariness after having "toiled so much with voice and pen," but put his whole heart in his present effort to cheer and enlighten so many mothers who have the long road of life all before them.

Courage and Generosity of Laboring Women.

Those only who have gone habitually among the families of our laboring classes, who have their full confidence, and are initiated into all their secrets, can know what treasures of goodness, of generosity, of courage, and patience are concealed by the homely or patched garb of a mother with five or six mouths to feed, and not always a dollar a day to count on for rent, clothing, and other incident expenses in the poorest of homes. While we write these lines, such is the outlook in the households of most laboring men of this great metropolis and the adjacent cities. Such, if we mistake not, is the hard lot of most fathers and mothers in manufacturing centers, and all through our Eastern States.

And this has been the condition of the laboring man among us for years, and such the miserable pittance from out which his wife has had to provide necessaries and comforts for the entire family, with something also for the poor and the church! If persons more favored by fortune and unvisited by such pinching want as is described in this simple statement, ever felt disposed to blame such a mother, or to turn away with loathing from the inevitable squalor in home and dress and countenance of these toilers for our comfort and luxury, let them pause and reflect.

There is more of heroic endurance in the heart of such a parent than in the bosom of the bravest soldier in a beleaguered and famished city. There is in such a life of incessant battling with the wants of the day and the hour, with the fears of what the morrow may bring forth, a fortitude and perseverance far above our sterile admiration. When one has seen much of such homes and such hearts, one begins to understand why the soul of the Master went forth to these toilers, with this sublime exordium of his first recorded discourse:

"Blessed are the poor in spirit: for theirs is the kingdom of heaven!" This was to point their eyes heavenward to the certain prospect of a rest and a reward which the present could not afford. But He would not have them devoid, amid their long and ever-recurring daily struggle, of the sweetest consolation and most coveted recompense of generous souls. "Come to me, all you that labor, and I will refresh you!"

Divine Aid in Dire Need.

In such a family and during a long and severe winter, when labor was scarce, provisions dear, and charity as frozen as the lakes and rivers, a poor father of seven children fell on the ice, while returning home after dark, and broke his leg. His youngest babe was but six weeks old, and the mother was in very feeble health. It was thought, inflammation having set in, that the fractured member would have to be cut off; but the poor sufferer would not consent to the operation till he had made his confession. What a spectacle was that poor home, when the priest, following the oldest child, a boy of eleven, reached the door at midnight during a fierce snow-storm! A loft or garret served as a sleeping-room for the elder children, and the lower part of the wooden shanty contained a little kitchen in front, with a bedroom for father and mother behind it. There were three physicians, one of whom was a surgeon, present and awaiting impatiently the arrival of the priest. The house was a picture of neatness, and the bedroom especially, in which the poor sufferer lay, was like an oratory curtained with spotless white, with a large and very old engraving of Christ carrying his cross, by Raphael, over the bed, and so placed that the patient might look at it. The wife, overcome with grief, struggled hard, when the priest entered, to keep back her tears. After the usual salutations and a few words of comfort to herself and her husband, the latter, seizing the priest's hand, exclaimed, as he looked toward the picture: "Father, I know that He will be with me and with her, too! That beautiful face has been like a book to me for many a year: I could look on it forever! But, sure I know"—and the speaker's voice trembled with emotion—"that the real face is more beautiful than the sun, and that the heart we were all taught to come to is one that will pity the poor man,...and the widow,...(here he broke down)...and the little orphans." Even the stern face of the surgeon quivered with an emotion he could not suppress, while these sentiments were uttered in a firm, low tone.

During the operation, the children were taken to a neighboring house, all but the infant, which remained with its mother, and she could not be persuaded to leave the house, praying in the outside room with one of the neighboring women. Ether was then in common use, but the sick man would not take it: he held, instead, the priest's crucifix in both hands, which the physicians left free, and with his eyes intently fixed on the thorn-crowned head, while the inner sight seemed to behold somewhat of the divine reality,—the sufferer gave himself up to the surgeon. Not a murmur or sigh escaped the silently moving lips, till toward the end, when the pain wrung one groan from him and his head fell back in a swoon on the priest's shoulder.

A few days afterward a crisis came, and the worst was feared. The last sacraments were administered,—the wife seeming to have gained sudden and preternatural strength from the very extremity to which her brave husband was reduced. "She knew"—she assured the priest ere he left the house—"that God would not try her further: something whispered to her heart that her good man would be left to her." He was, as usual, heroic in his calm submission to the Divine Will; only,—such were his words,—he prayed to be left a little longer with his young children. The picture ("The Spasimo" of Raphael) had been taken down from the wall and lay on the white covering of the bed, and the beautiful face of the humiliated Redeemer was the book in which the sick man read night and day.

What the Heavenly Physician Did.

The next morning the priest returned, expecting to hear that all was over. But, to his unspeakable surprise, the wife met him on the threshold with countenance all aglow with rapturous gratitude, and said that her husband was better, "Oh! so much better!" It was wonderful. The patient had slept sweetly,—had even lost consciousness while gazing at his loved picture,—and dreamed that Christ had come to him as he lay sore and weary and faint by the roadside, and had smiled on him, blessed him, and shown him the gap in His own side, and then disappeared.

So, when the burden was heaviest on these stricken ones, He who bade us go to him in our extremity, and who yearns to reward our faith even by miracles when needful, had stretched out his hand and opened his heart to the call of that husband and that wife.

Theirs was a long and a brave battle thenceforward. But every trial seemed light to souls so near to God. The brave man applied himself to learn a trade—he had been hitherto a stevedore—and though there was never surplus of money or of creature-comforts in that home,—there was contentment, and love purified in the furnace, and noble children to gladden the hearts of struggling parents, and that piety which seemed as natural as the very air they breathed.

Treasures to Be Found in the Poorest Homes.

Yes,—there are poor homes, laborious homes, where from earliest dawn till night, and often far into the night, the wife and mother has to work, work, work, without cessation or repose, to do the housework, and, that done, to complete some other task from the outside in order to help the ill-paid husband to keep off or pay off debts, to have decent raiment for the good man and his children, to keep some at least of these at school, to have substantial food for all, and something for the need of the suffering poor who know well her door as well as her heart:—and such mothers *believe* that God's eye is ever on themselves and their dear ones, that his blessed angels are there counting every hour and minute of that loving toil, counting every beat of these generous hearts, every moment so well filled,—and ascending at night to lay the record of such a day before Him who said, "Blessed are the poor!... For theirs is the kingdom of heaven!"

Blood tells, it is said, when noble deeds are to be performed,—that is, perhaps, when the eyes of men watch the performance: but there is inherited piety, which is a something nobler still,—the supernatural piety of Christians. Are we not born, in our second sacramental birth, of the blood of a God-man? Think of this, brave-hearted mothers, and remember it is that blood which is applied to us in every grace we receive, and which strengthens us to do the work before us.

Your boys, your girls must be trained early to be industrious. Not that they must be set to work before their time; God forbid! But it must be your care to give them, from the very beginning, habits of cleanliness, order, industry, self-respect and self-reliance. You must be careful not to allow them to fancy for one moment that there is in your own laborious habits or in their father's occupation or trade, any thing that is not most honorable, praiseworthy, and pleasing to God.

Teach Your Children the Dignity of Labor.

Recall to them frequently that the most glorious names in heaven or on earth were those of men and women whose daily life was one of toil like your own: how Adam and the great patriarchs who succeeded him were tillers of the soil, husbandmen, and shepherds; that such were the great men and women who founded God's people in the Old Law, Abraham and Sara, Isaac and Rebecca, Israel (or Jacob) and his wife Rachel, Joseph who ruled Egypt after having been like his brothers a farmer and a shepherd, as well as Moses, the figure of our Lord, who kept the flocks of his father-in-law. Labor was most honored always down to the days of our Lord, who himself learned the carpenter's trade and worked at it with his foster-father, Joseph,—a prince of the royal blood of David.

Teach them to look upon idleness as a shame and disgrace, upon sloth as most degrading, and as leading to all manner of evil courses. You can always keep them joyous children, while you make them industrious and laborious children; you can make them and keep them bright, pleasant-faced, and cheerful while coaxing them to learn something new every day and to apply themselves heartily to the tasks you set for them at the appointed hours.

Know How to Praise Them.

We have already seen what good a true wife can do by praising generously and judiciously her husband, and encouraging him thereby to rise every day higher and higher in her esteem and in his own.[30] Far greater is the good she

[30] See Chapter VI., pp. 57, 58, 59, and 60; and Chapter X., p. 144.

can do every one of her children by judicious praise. We say "judicious;" for praise bestowed at every moment and for trifles loses its value by becoming common. Praise only when something is done which deserves it, and praise in well-weighed words. Never give praise when it is not well deserved; for then it would be unjust, and you would make your children suspect your truthfulness and your honesty.

Be Gentle, Low-Voiced, and Patient.

Be gentle. That does not mean to be spiritless. It means to be the opposite of violent, irascible, ill-tempered, and moody. Study to be so, for your own soul's sake, and as if you lived in God's presence, always keeping down for his holy love every movement of anger, irritability, ill-temper, or moodiness. And be gentle,—precisely because you have much to do, much to bear, many cares to burden you, many things which continually try your temper.

Be low-voiced. It is wonderful what effect a mother's gentle manner and low voice,—when she teaches, or corrects, or praises,—will have on a band of children. Take a school-room filled with very young boys or girls. Let their teacher be nervous, fidgety, and irritable; you will see all these little ones thrown into a ferment and fever and agitation, which is nothing more than a kind of disorder which they catch from the teacher's manner. Let her be loud-voiced, teaching or speaking in loud, quick, nervous tones, and it is ten to one but you will see within a few minutes all these children becoming restless, talkative, inattentive, and ungovernable.

Now, let some quiet, gentle, calm-mannered, and low-voiced person come in, and all these children will become quieted, stop talking, listen, and be ready to give their whole attention to what is said, or to set to work, and work steadily as long as the calm eye is on them and the gentle, low voice is directing them.

You will spare yourselves and your dear ones much trouble and much unhappiness by laying this lesson to heart. You can do what you like with them,—if you are perfectly mistress of yourself. Besides, what a service you do *them*; and how they will bless their mother in after life for having taught them this gentleness!

Be patient. Not only when you are suffering from aching limbs and head and heart, but when you do not succeed in making your dear ones all that you would wish. There are certain dispositions and characters which seem naturally to defy all control, or teaching, or improvement. They will learn more than you think; and they profit much more than you can see by your lessons, and especially by your example. Even should son or daughter of yours turn out to be every thing but what you trained them to be, the memory of their gentle, patient, loving mother will remain in their souls to their dying day, like a silent voice from the past bidding them return to God and to the paths of their childhood.

Some say that steel beaten into its due form and given a keen edge while cold, is more apt to preserve both form and edge forever. So is it with the temper your patient gentleness will impart to your children's souls. And this firmness, which is only one of the most precious dispositions of true manhood and womanhood, will be both of infinite value to them and of indispensable necessity.

In What Consists True Independence of Character.

To no one more than the child of the hard-working mother is true independence of soul,—that is, true nobility of character,—necessary and useful. Indeed, the all-seeing Author of our nature, who governs all our ways, has made every element of greatness in our souls and conduct necessary because he knew they would be useful; and he made them all the more necessary that he foresaw they would be more useful.

In what does this independence of soul and character consist? In this: that a boy or a girl brought up by a truly God-fearing mother, is so filled with the fear of that Great Majesty, in whose hands we are at every moment, and into whose hands we are sure to fall after death, that they look up to Him in every thing, seek to please him in all they do, and find it impossible to do any thing which is wrong in his sight and contrary to the voice of their own conscience.

Let us understand this well. You rear your boy and your girl, from the very first moment you can make them understand any thing, in the conviction that God's truth, God's word, God's will is to be the sole measure by which they are to weigh and estimate every thing; so that it will be practically impossible for them to do any thing contrary to his truth, his law, or his will. We say every day that such a man is a noble man, a truly independent man, because he is incapable of doing wrong to any one, of violating truth or honor or honesty, of going in any thing whatever against his conscience and his known duty.

Hence it is—and this is the golden lesson which our forefathers learned so well and practiced so nobly, that they made their moral greatness and independence consist

In Depending on God Alone and Their Conscience.

They were poor in this world's goods,—for they had been stripped of every thing,—they were deprived of civil and religious liberty and honor, and were thus, in the eyes of men, degraded to the level of the serf or the slave. But nothing could shake their dependence on God, or their implicit and invincible obedience to the voice of their conscience and their faith.

Now such are the noble men and women that can in our days,—in this generation as in the next,—go forth from the home of every laboring man among us, as they went forth in past generations; men attached to conscience, to honesty, to honor, to truth, to duty, to righteousness, and to God in all things and above all things, everywhere, in all employments and positions, though never so high or never so lowly.

Let us have men and women incapable of telling a lie, of wronging the neighbor in thought or word or deed, of wronging their employer in the meanest trifles or the weightiest matters, of betraying the trust placed in them, whether in the last place in lowliest office or in the highest that can be given in city, State, or Church; men and women who fear God alone, and, after him, fear only what is contrary to truth, honor, and purity!

Dear mothers who read this, you may never be able to give your boys and girls at your death wherewith to buy a suit of clothes or to pay for their meals on the morrow. But if you labored morning, noon, and night till your dying day—because you would allow no dishonesty to taint your lives, and for the sole purpose of making of your children such godlike men and women as this,—you have left them a treasure ten thousand times more precious than all the hoarded millions of our wealthiest.

Make Them Choose Their Companions Well.

In order to do this, you must be careful about two things: the choice of what your boys and girls read, and that of their companions at home or in the street.

Choose well the books which you put in their hands, or which you permit them to bring home with them. Public libraries are like druggists' shops or public dispensaries; they are like them in this, that they contain all manner of poisons as well as healthful medicines; and they differ from them in this, that, whereas conscientious druggists will give what is healthful to all, they will only deal out what is poisonous in small quantities and to responsible and properly authorized persons;—while libraries and librarians have no conscience, and let the innocent child take away and devour what kills purity, innocence, and conscience forever.

Scarcely less baneful are, taken and read promiscuously, the daily and weekly papers. They are not only dangerous and hurtful to the young mind and heart as mere *newspapers*, because they reveal in their hideousness and obscenity what should never be known to youth, and what were better ignored by age itself; but they are still more hurtful as teachers and dogmatizers on religion and morality, either reducing the doctrines and practices of revealed religion to the same level with infidelity, and thus producing practical indifference toward divine truth; or they affect and profess to have an authority which can judge the Church of Christ herself, and enlighten her as to the way she ought to teach and to govern.

Thereby the mind is imperceptibly but inevitably filled with prejudices or preconceived opinions distrustful of the Church or hostile to her, and which act on the intelligence as the foul and poisonous air of coal-mines acts on the lungs: they fill the organs with deadly exhalations which prevent the entrance into them of God's pure vital air.

Just as you are careful of what books or papers your children read, even so be watchful over the companionships they form. It is impossible to take kindly to the lowminded, corrupt-hearted, or ill-bred and ill-mannered, without laying aside one's own good manners, good breeding, purity of feeling, and innocence of mind in habitual intercourse with them. There are worse consequences, as you know, which soon follow this familiarity with the low and the unworthy.

Precisely because the great majority of young people around you are without sound moral education,—untruthful, intemperate, and as careless of honor and honesty as they are of decency,—it is your most pressing interest and duty to keep your treasures away from such contact.

The Two Nests.

Do not seek, while you are struggling against poverty, or even when you have reached a comfortable competency, to expose your home to the eyes of your richer neighbors, or to seek their children as companions for your own. But take well to heart the lesson of the following parable:

"A nest there was in a bonnie May tree,
    In the fairest of fairy bowers;
And methought how happy the bird must be,
    On her nest amid the flowers.
But the children came, and together they vied
    Who should pluck the best branches of May;
And the bird's little nest very quickly they spied,
    And they ruthlessly bore it away!

"A nest there was in a dreary tree,
    In a dark and dismal holly;
And methought how weary the bird must be
    Of her nest so melancholy.
But the children came, and they passed it by
    To rifle a fairer tree;
And the bird in the holly I then confess'd
    The wiser bird to be.

"In the forest of life two different glades
    Are lying before me to tread.
Shall I push my way through the darker shades,
    Or follow the flowers instead?
I will think of the bird and her nestlings' doom,
    And keep to the lonelier way,—
Lest enemies come where the fair flowers bloom,
    And carry my treasures away."[31]

---

[31] Claribel.

As you would not go beneath you for the ill-bred and the vicious, so must you avoid allowing your children to choose their companions and friends above them. This would be to show a want of that proper self-respect, self-reliance, and independence which we have just been praising as in themselves a fortune. It would, by giving your children a desire to enter the atmosphere of a wealthy and luxurious home, tempt them to despise their own home, to be dissatisfied with their condition, with their parentage, their education, their labors,—their whole existence. This temptation is a terrible one,—in a country such as ours especially, where birth and hereditary rank do not place between the poor and laboring classes and the wealthy above them, the separation walls existing in European countries. But only think of what misery for you and what ruin for your children the temptation yielded to would be sure to work!

Besides,—and apart from the despising of the old home and the being ashamed of father and mother,—this intimacy and companionship with the children of wealthy parents would beget other temptations and dangers. Companions, like friends, wish to dress alike and to be able to spend alike. Hence the road open to the approach of that Evil One who prompts to steal in order to gratify vanity, or to enjoy the pleasures accessible to one's friends.

CHAPTER XIII.

How Mothers Should Train Their Boys and Girls (continued.)

Early in years, and yet more infantine
In figure, she had something of sublime
In eyes which sadly shone, as seraphs' shine:
All youth—but with an aspect beyond time;
Radiant and grave, as pitying man's decline;
Mournful, but mournful of another's crime,
She looked as if she sat by Eden's door,
And grieved for those who could return no more.
She was a Catholic, too, sincere, austere
As far as her own gentle heart allowed,
And deemed that fallen worship far more dear
Because 'twas fallen; her sires were proud
Of deeds and days when they had filled the ear
Of nations, and had never bent or bowed
To novel power; and, as she was the last,
She held their old faith and old feelings fast.
She gazed upon a world she scarcely knew,
As seeking not to know it; silent, lone,
As grows a flower, thus silently she grew,
And kept her heart serene within its zone.
There was awe in the homage which she drew;
Her spirit seemed as seated on a throne
Apart from the surrounding world, and strong
In its own strength—most strange in one so young.

Byron.

Such, in many respects, will be the ideal form which will be present to the reader's mind in perusing this and the succeeding chapter.

The best preservative against the dangerous ambition described in our last, is found in the supernatural notions and virtues which a Christian mother is careful to inculcate from the earliest dawn of reason in her children. We insist once more upon it—the royal and rich poverty of Christ, of his Mother, and of his foster-father Joseph, must be made the theme of constant remark and praise in the homes of tradesmen and laboring men. And, next to that, the mother must fill the souls of her little ones with that scorn and loathing of all dishonesty and untruthfulness, which will, with the ever-present aid of grace, render them incapable of telling a lie or wronging any person, no matter how slightly.

Children to Be Taught Simplicity in Dress and Sobriety in Food.

This is another golden rule to be enforced early. Nor need we, while the passion for rich attire, showy ornaments, and jewelry is developed so precociously in our girls, and allowed by mothers to grow unrepressed and unrebuked,—point out how timely and needful this rule is.

A venerable lady, who died in November, 1870, in her seventy-second year, and who came of the best blood of England, wrote thus, in her last years, of her early training: "The dress of these days (about 1806) was very different to that which children have now. My white frocks were of lawn or Irish cloth, without any work or ornament; and when I went out, I used to wear a little green-baize coat. My food was also of the simplest kind, consisting principally of buttermilk and potatoes."[32]

The girlhood trained in these habits of simplicity and wholesome austerity led to a lovely womanhood, to a life of spotless devotion to duty, and to the exercise of these private graces and influences which enable a woman, ever living in the privacy of her home, to win the admiration, the respect, and the veneration of all who approach her. We quote her words and her example to show how women were brought up in the days of our fathers, and how little difference, even in Protestant homes, the deep-seated Christian customs of so many preceding centuries allowed to prevail in the dress, the food, and all the external training of children in all classes.

---

[32] Augustus J. C. Hare, "Memorials of a Quiet Life," vol. i., p. 6.

Mothers in those days, who wished to do their duty conscientiously by their children, did not dream of having for them in the beginning any teachers but themselves. So was it with this lady's mother; although prostrated by paralysis and consumption, she would daily teach her little girl.

"She taught me in all my lessons except French, but her weak health and bad headaches often prevented her hearing me, and many a time I had to stand outside her door waiting till I could be heard, which fretted me a good deal. When the lessons went ill, I was sentenced to sit on the staircase till I was good, and the task perfect. I imagine that though my mother was most gentle, she was firm in her management of me." Some lady-friend having "suggested my doing something because it would be *pleasant*, my mother appealed to me, 'I think my little girl has a better motive for it. What is it, Mia?' and 'Because it is *right*,' was my reply."[33]

How Early the Sense of Duty—of Right and Wrong, Is Found in Children.

The answer given by the child shows how early what philosophers call "the moral sense" is developed in a child, in little girls especially, whose intelligence is so much more precocious than that of boys, and whose sense of right and wrong is much quicker and keener. The sick,—hopelessly sick and infirm mother, here mentioned, while cultivating her child's memory and understanding by teaching her the usual elementary branches, was careful to form her judgment by making her in all things act for a purpose, and to develop her moral sense by giving her in all she did the notion of duty, as her stimulant in doing both pleasant and unpleasant things.

The Moral Sense Is but the Sense of Duty.

Duty is the fulfilling of an obligation toward one's self, or toward another in compliance with His will, who being Creator and Lord has a right to bind our wills to do certain things and to refrain from others.

---

[33] *Ibidem*, p. 4.

Duty is always toward God, even when the immediate object of the action performed is only one's self, or one's neighbor. The very duty of cultivating mind and heart, which regards every intelligent being, is a duty imposed by the Divine Will; so is the obligation to keep one's soul and body free from every defilement. We own it to be a duty to learn, to know clearly and fully what concerns our condition, our profession, or the office we may hold in Church or State, and a corresponding duty to live up to this indispensable knowledge. But Christian philosophy teaches us that in acquiring this knowledge, and in acting up to it, we are only doing what is *due* to Him who has an essential right to every thought and aim and act of ours.

Uprightness is the perfect performance of duty;—and uprightness, in its Christian and supernatural meaning, is the perfect discharge of duty in view of Him who is our Lord and Judge and final Beatitude. The firm look of the soul, in every act of duty or in the gratuitous generosity with which the sons of God go beyond what is of obligation—is upward to God.

Cultivate This Sense of Duty.

in all your children. Make them understand that they are to do certain things most unpleasant, and to abstain from other things most pleasant, *because it is right to do so*; because it is their *duty*, because this is due to their great and good God. Experience has taught that of all characters, in men as well as in women, the most trustworthy, the most honored, the most noble in the estimation of mankind, is the man or woman who always acts according to this sense of duty, and whom no love, no fear, no passion, or temptation can turn aside to do wrong,—that is, what is contrary to duty and conscience.

If mothers will only accustom their children to act, not according to their inclinations, but in obedience to this sense of duty, pointing out what is right to do and what is wrong not to do,—they will buckle round them a suit of armor which will enable them to come victorious out of the terrible battle of temptation. And never was this noble sense of duty more needed than in our day,—when men think little of right or wrong, and a good deal of the surest and quickest road to success;—and when, in the estimation of our public, success once attained makes the wrong right, while failure makes right itself wrong, and the sacrifice to duty foolish sentimentality.

Cultivate the Hearts of Your Children.

This is more particularly needful in the case of your girls. It is by the right or wrong in their affections that women become so powerful for good or evil. Not that their intelligence is naturally inferior to that of men,—on the contrary, in many respects the female intellect is remarkably superior. Intelligence dawns earlier in girls and ripens at a very precocious age. Hence the wisdom of cultivating the judgment and forming the imagination of girls during their fifth, sixth, and seventh years. One will often be astonished in conversing with a little girl of that age, on questioning her closely, to see (when she has been carefully watched by an intelligent and virtuous mother) how completely she will master the great scheme of the creation, the fall, the redemption and reparation, the necessity of a visible and infallible teaching authority, the beauty of the sacramental system of help toward all the purposes of the supernatural life in the individual soul as well as in the body of the Church. All this can be made so clear and so attractive to the childish intellect, without wearying it with theological terms or definitions.

The idea of God is connatural to the mind, as well as that of his providence, of moral good and evil, of rewards and punishments. No child but can be made to ascend from the familiar notion of her father's house, well governed by firm laws, by love tempered with justice, to the great family of nations under one almighty ruler and judge. These and a thousand other notions are so quickly taken in by the youngest girl, that one is reminded forcibly of the famous theories about innate ideas.

It is impossible in a really Christian family that the head should be wrong if the heart is right. The teaching of the Church is so complete, embraces in one firm grasp our origin in the past, our duties in the present, and our prospects for all time and eternity; our doctrines are so positive, so clear, so satisfactory, and so comprehensive that they set the mind at rest, and thereby leave the soul free to direct and control its own affections.

Generally speaking, boys and girls in Catholic families have such a clear sense both of what they have to believe and what they have to do, that when they are led astray it is by their affections.

We have explained in the preceding chapter how mothers are to win and to keep the love of their boys and girls. This is one necessary step toward cultivating their hearts and training their affections. You cannot repair or beautify the interior of a house unless you secure an entrance and be in so far the master in it that no one shall disturb you while you are occupied in your labor. The heart has been endowed by its Maker with so mysterious and so great a power,—that even a babe in arms can shut its heart against its own parent, and that a child of seven can form, rightly or wrongly, likings and dislikings which may last a life-time.

It is for the mother to study from the very beginning the dispositions of her precious charge. We say commonly that some natures are richly endowed, and others but poorly; that some persons are all head and no heart, while others are all heart and no head. That is to say, there are souls in which the intellectual powers seem to predominate and to absorb into themselves the affective powers; while there are others in whom the affections seem to run away with the understanding and the judgment.

There is some truth and a good deal of exaggeration in these estimates which we pride ourselves in forming of the innate faculties of children as well as of grown-up persons. Doubtless, through some physical accident of formation or birth, the brain may be affected and the reasoning powers partially or almost totally paralyzed;—but there is no instance of this total paralysis of the will or the executive and affective powers in the soul where the mind retains its full vigor unimpaired. Some persons are less sensitive, less affectionate, less imaginative, less passionate than others; but in all persons of sane mind there is imagination and sensibility and affections and passions,—though in very different degrees of intensity.

Now where a faculty or special power in the soul is known to exist, it can be developed, strengthened, increased almost indefinitely by exercise and proper culture; just as a faculty neglected either dies out or lives on in a sort of rudimentary condition for want of proper exercise. The hand and arm of one man becomes as terrible an instrument of destruction as the arm of the tiger, by long muscular training. While another man, though more powerfully built by nature, will have a hand as soft as a babe's, and an arm as feeble as a girl's, from the absolute lack of exercise. Women, above all other persons, are familiar with the success which so often attends the cultivation and development of the voice, and how young persons, seemingly deficient in all aptitude for singing, will exhibit, under careful culture and practice, the most splendid vocal powers.

"Heartlessness" the Effect of a Wrong Education.

There is no such thing as natural heartlessness. Cold as certain grown-up women, as well as men, seem to be by nature,—we may be certain that neither nature nor its Author is to blame for this lack of genial warmth and affection. No child is born without the disposition to love and the power of loving warmly: this may be not so apparent at the surface in some children as in others, or exist in the same degree of energy; or, again, this coldness in some may be only such as contrasted with the passionate and impulsive fervor of others. But let mothers rest assured that the heart is there, with its natural and essential powers of returning love for love, and of practicing, not only the virtue of supernatural charity so indispensable to the sanctity and salvation of the adult Christian, but all the other charities of private and public life, with the many virtues which never fail to adorn the soul in which true charity reigns. Indeed were it possible (which is not so) that any human being could be born without natural affection, the Creator Spirit, coming into the soul in baptism, would most surely repair the defect.

But comparatively feeble (and we use this expression most reluctantly) as the power of loving may be supposed to be,—it *is* there in the soul for the mother's tender hand and fostering charity to nurse into fullness of life, into perfect bloom and fruitful maturity. And God's abundant and unfailing help is secured to the mother in this training of her child's heart.

But the real heartlessness which shows itself so offensively in the girl and in the woman is, you may be sure of it, the result of neglect in the parent, or of a training in every way vicious.

For this heartlessness is but undisguised selfishness obtruding itself upon us in all its own repulsive deformity. The mother's eye had failed to detect this weed in her child's soul, or allowed it to grow up during infancy and girlhood, under the delusive hope that the good qualities in her girl's nature would choke out the bad when she grew up to womanhood. But it is the contrary which happens, unless God should interfere and perform a miracle in favor of the neglected or petted child. Selfishness is pretty sure, when continually ministered to and nursed by all around it, to absorb and draw to itself all the vital energies of the soul.

In the tropical forests,—in the West Indies particularly, there is a formidable species of parasite creeper whose power becomes fatal to the mightiest trees in the forest. It first shows itself like a little green plant on a sturdy branch of the forest tree, or a hole in the trunk, whence it sends down thread-like feelers to the ground. There they take root and reascend along the trunk, increasing in number and size, till not one feature of the parent-tree is visible. The whole is now inclosed in a network of serpentine forms so firm, so robust, and so vigorous, that the tiny plant has become a giant, strangling in its embrace the generous trunk which fed and supported it, and hanging high in mid-air, above the topmost branches of its dead benefactor, its brilliant clusters of flowers. Thus does selfishness prosper and flourish!

Examples of Heartlessness.

In a family noted for high culture, refinement, and deep religious faith, the death of a father brought to his home a near relative, a venerable lady of most exemplary life and unselfish devotion to the good of others. Indeed this noble generosity of soul had prevented her from accepting when young, beautiful, and accomplished, the many offers of marriage made to her, prompting her to give her whole existence to the comfort and happiness of her nephews and nieces.

She had been looked up to by the dead man with that union of respect and love which we call veneration, and his wife shared these sentiments. Their respected relative had come to the widow in her bereavement, to offer consolation which no other could, and to spend, as was the religious custom of her country, the night before the burial in praying beside the dead. Her arrival was greeted with heartfelt gratitude by all the mourners, save one, a girl of thirteen or fourteen, who was busy, when the visitor arrived, in dressing a doll for some little girl of the neighborhood. The presence of death in the house, the grief which overwhelmed her mother and sisters, found this girl perfectly callous; the outburst of emotion with which their cherished relative was received did not move her in the least, or only caused her to look up with an air of annoyance from her self-imposed task of sewing. Presently her mother begged her to go and help prepare a room for their aunt. But at this interruption she flew into a rage, and in the hearing of the aged and sensitive lady herself, the selfish vixen burst forth: “What on earth brings this old woman here? I am sure she is not wanted”...and other such amenities. The wound which these cruel words caused was a deep one, and was never healed in that most generous heart. They filled it with forebodings which she hardly ventured to breathe into the ear of any member of the family.

They were, however, not to remain unfulfilled. She was the youngest child, petted, indulged, spoiled. Her natural selfishness blighted and overtopped every other quality in her character. When its fearful manifestations alarmed both parents, the weak mother attempted in vain to check what was now utterly beyond her control. The heartless girl became the more heartless woman, without affection for husband or children, without a particle of love for her mother or her sisters. She has divided, darkened, and ruined the home which her too fond father had labored so hard to render happy and bright for all his dear ones.

Were the bitter fruits of heartlessness to be tasted only by the parents through whose criminal neglect and indulgence grew up the evil plant which bore them,—it would be a most just retribution. But the heartless woman proves a bane and a destroyer to others as well as a heart-sore to her parents and nearest relatives.

Where with this most odious form of selfishness in a woman she also possesses the terrible gift of beauty, she becomes a curse to every man who falls under the fatal spell of her fair face. Love she cannot, for, love being the gift of self, is impossible to the heartless and selfish. The vanity begotten of the selfishness which is conscious of the charm of beauty, only yearns for admiration, and gloats on every fresh addition to the number of admirers. The pains endured by the thrice-foolish men who allow themselves to believe in the warmth of a heartless woman's smiles, or to trust to her promises, are of no account to her. We remember once to have seen a gigantic ivy all in bloom on a part of the ruined walls of Laon. The odor of its flowers is so sweet and the nectar which they distill so intoxicating, that the flowering mass was covered with a cloud of various insects which struggled and fought for a taste of the delicious food, while the earth beneath was covered with the carcasses of countless victims.

The Punishment of Heartlessness.

The selfish and heartless make no friends,—for they cannot inspire any one who knows them with that enlightened esteem and solid respect which are the first requisites for true love in any being. Christian theology, when well analyzed, shows that the greatest torment of the damned is not only the loss of God and of the blissful society of heaven, but the being placed eternally face to face with one's self, with that self which is the creation of one's own will, the work of one's own hands. And, while yet on earth, the most terrible torture of the utterly selfish woman (say the same of man), is, when admiration and enjoyment have passed away, to find herself in presence of *herself*,—of her own false and hollow heart. This is the hell of the heartless, even in this life.

But one or two other examples of this monstrous perversity in the moral formation of certain persons may contain an instructive lesson for more classes than one.

A Heartless Wife and a More Heartless Husband.

Two young people had married early in their native country, with the understanding that the husband would go forthwith to America and there provide for his young wife the home which the misfortune of the times and the circumstances of the country made it impossible to obtain at home.

A few months after his departure, however, his wife was induced by a neighboring family, who were going to New York, to take passage with them,—thinking in her simple heart that, once in the great city, she could find her husband as easily as in her native village.

The poor little woman's disappointment and dismay on her arrival here can be easily conceived. She was penniless, and no inquiries she could make availed to obtain tidings of her husband. After knocking at many doors she was directed by the clergy of the Nativity, in Second Avenue, to a family up town ever ready to interest themselves in cases of distress. So one morning the mistress of the house found in her waiting-room a plainly but neatly dressed young person of striking beauty of countenance, "like one of these lovely Irish girls whom a painter would select for a Madonna." Her story was soon told.

"Her husband had promised to send for her when he had got a little place for both, and she was to wait at home for his letter. But,"... And here the young creature broke down. She told the kind motherly lady who questioned her most affectionately, that she was soon to become herself a mother, and her impatience to join her husband was very intelligible. She had found a protectress, however: a safe temporary home was provided for her, she was given sewing and other such work to do, and every care was taken of her welfare till her babe was born. "It was a most beautiful child," said our informant, "and the happiness of its young mother would have been complete had the efforts made to discover her husband been successful."

A few weeks after the birth of her child, she called on her kind benefactress and told her that she had been advised to go into some good family as a wet nurse, and had put for that purpose an advertisement in the daily papers. "I am sorry you did so without consulting me, Mary," said her kind friend. "It is a thing I would never advise any mother to do. And, besides, we could have found you plenty of good work to do, while attending to your babe."

It was too late; the persons with whom Mary was staying had persuaded her to this course, and the poor inexperienced young thing hoped to gain money to help her struggling husband in his efforts to secure a home of their own. And then again, she was assured that her babe would be well cared for in a family a little out of town, which they designated. And so the fatal step was taken.

Mary was accepted as nurse in the family of a minister in Brooklyn, whose name, as well as the denomination to which he belonged, it is needless to mention. After some three weeks had elapsed, this gentleman called one day on Mary's New York benefactress, to inform her that he should have to part with the nurse.

"Part with her?" replied the other; "why so? are you not satisfied with her?" "Oh, she is a very good woman—neat, quiet, respectful, very careful of our child—and our family physician, after examining her, pronounces her a remarkably healthy person. But there are certain things about her we do not like." "When did you make up your mind to part with her?" "The first week she came to us." "And you did not tell her of it then?" "No, because we have not been able to get a suitable person to take her place." "That seems unkind to her. She could have then returned to her own child in good time. But now she will find that it has been weaned... But, pray, what fault in her could have justified a delay which, to say the least, is cruel?" "Oh! she moans in her sleep, and seems unhappy away from her child, and we do not want to have our babe nursed by any one who seems unhappy." The lady gazed at him in utter astonishment, mixed with no little contempt for the heartlessness of both himself and his wife. At length she said indignantly: "Is it possible, sir, that you could expect any woman with a true mother's nature to be able to give up her own child, and give the nourishment she owed it to that of another mother, without feeling her heart breaking, or without moaning in her sleep?" He persisted in saying that he saw nothing to blame in his wife's or his own conduct. The feelings of poor Mary or the fate of her babe never cost either of them a thought. "At least," said the lady, as he rose to take his leave, "you must promise me to send Mary back to her babe at once. For to keep her longer in your house, or in ignorance of your intention, would be wrong and criminal." A promise was made, but was not kept. Mary was detained a week or ten days longer, and then dismissed with the heartless indifference which characterized the minister and his spouse. At least a full month had then elapsed since Mary had intrusted her beautiful babe to the out-of-town nurse, giving two-thirds of her wages to secure it every possible care and comfort. All this time she had not been permitted to visit it.

Her feeling of joy at the prospect of seeing it overcame every other sentiment in her heart, and without a moment's delay she flew to its side. It was summer-time; she found the woman with whom she had left her treasure dressed in the most slatternly fashion, and a baby, fat and rosy, fast asleep in a cradle. Poor Mary's heart sank within her, and a great faintness came over her as she looked about for her own. She dared not, indeed she could not, inquire... On a wooden washboard she saw a dirty shawl in a bundle, and covered with flies, from which a feeble moan proceeded. And going over she found her babe lying neglected there, so emaciated and so feeble that it had not strength enough to cry for the food it needed.

Of course the unnatural monster with whom she had left it was confounded at the sudden apparition of the young mother. Had she waited a day or two longer it would have been out of pain and soon buried away out of sight, and a story found to cover its slow murder. But poor Mary had no time to waste in explanation or accusations. She must save her child.

Away she flew to her benefactress. She was at first unable to utter a single word, and the former thought the child was dead. But when she heard how the case was, "Go back instantly," she said, "and bring your baby here." While Mary had been in the service of the heartless minister and his unwomanly wife, the home to which Mary was hastening to bring her dying child had been visited by death, and in the gentle mistress's own bedroom a cradle was empty, which she knelt by more than once each day to ask for strength from on high, and to beseech her little angel boy among the choirs above to protect his mother's home.

That cradle was now prepared and decked for the stranger child. So when it arrived the entire household was interested in helping the mistress to save the little starveling. A bath of spirits and water was ready, and when, with infinite tenderness, the noble-hearted lady had bathed it, she arrayed the little sufferer in her dead boy's most beautiful dress, and laid it in his cradle, while her daughters knelt around to look upon the tiny feeble thing, and to pray that it might live. Who can paint the ecstasy of poor Mary as she too knelt by its side, and believed that in the heavenly atmosphere of that room her babe must soon recover.

Presently the great-hearted husband of her benefactress returned from the courts, and on entering his wife's room was greeted with the words: "Oh, do come and see what I have got for you." The other approached the cradle around which he saw his bright-faced children gazing delightedly, and the strange young woman absorbed in watching her sick infant. The tears filled the eyes of the Christian gentleman as he took in the full meaning of what he saw, and kneeling down reverently by the side of the cradle he kissed the sufferer there as he would the feet of the Divine Babe of Bethlehem. "Darling," he said to his wife, as he rose from his knees, "God will bless you for this!"

Meanwhile no time was lost in seeking a new position for Mary as nurse in a good family. Her infant could take no nourishment from her, and she was assured that where it was every care would be lavished on it. Indeed, it was thenceforth looked upon as the child of the house. Within a few days a gentleman called, in answer to the advertisement in the papers,—a Mr. Robinson,—who felt both touched and deeply interested by what he heard of Mary, and by the genuine charity exercised toward her by her benefactress. But he would have Mary not separated from her own infant, and took it in the carriage with her to his home, where the little flame of life, which had flashed up fitfully under the loving care of a true mother, soon went out forever.

Will the reader ask, if from the home where that dying child was taken in and nursed as tenderly and reverently as if it had been the Babe cast out on the roadside at Bethlehem,—true women and true men went forth in good season to gladden the souls of the generous mother, and the no less generous father, of whom we have had a glimpse? We can answer: Ay—true men and true women every one of them—because their hearts had been trained from childhood to the pursuit of every thing that was unselfish, and devoted to the divine honor and the good of others.

A Heartless Mistress's Terrible Fate.

This heartlessness is all the more criminal that it is found in persons making a special profession of piety; and it is simply monstrous in all who have taken on themselves to be the religious guides of others.

Some quarter of a century ago two excellent girls living out at service in good families supported their aged mother,—one of these ideal women so frequent in the dear old Irish homes described elsewhere. When the last illness visited their parent, the eldest girl, Catherine, was living in a family noted for the active benevolence of its young mistress, while the younger, Mary, resided with a near relative and friend of the former. Catherine had no difficulty in persuading her worshiped lady to accompany her to her parent's sick bed; in truth, it would have been impossible to prevent these visits. For, one powerful means employed by divine grace, in bringing this young wife and mother into the Catholic Church, was the supernatural beauty she had remarked on the features and in the bearing of so many poor women of the sufferer's class. She described her as not naturally handsome in countenance, but her snow-white hair inclosed a face stamped with such heavenly sweetness and resignation, and through her meek and modest eyes shone a light so marvelous that it seemed to come from a something divine, and to fill the soul of the beholder with thoughts of God and promptings to godlike deeds. Of course Catherine remained by the side of her sick mother, and every thing which her mistress could do to show her respect for the dying woman or to alleviate her pain, was done without stint or cessation.

Mary had some difficulty in obtaining permission to remain a single night with her dear parent, who, thanks to the generous and intelligent nursing already secured to her, soon rallied so far that both daughters returned to their situations. Catherine, however, was sent back with peremptory orders to remain until the doctor had declared there was no further need of her presence. A second attack, more alarming than the first, soon afterward summoned both girls away, Mary being explicitly told that she could not stay away a single night unless she wished to give up her place. The lady who showed this disregard of the feelings of a daughter and the sacred claims of filial duty, was not considered a bad woman, nor an uncharitable woman. She was pious in her own way, and gave liberally toward works of beneficence. But she had been reared to look upon the poor, even upon her servants, as upon a caste who had no right to have deep affections or refined feelings.

The sick mother rallied a second time, only to be seized with the symptoms of a near dissolution; and as poor Mary presented herself to obtain permission for a third visit, her mistress could not restrain her ill temper. "Well, I declare"—were the cruel words which fell from the proud rich woman's lips on the heart of the poor and lowly dependent—"well, I declare your old mother takes a long time to die!"

The poor weeping girl only reached her mother's home to find that the pure spirit had gone to its eternal rest; and when the funeral was over she accompanied Catherine to their common benefactress,—and declared amid tears and sobs, that she dared not, could not return to her mistress. Then she reluctantly told of the cruel words uttered by the latter. The lady, shocked to hear such a tale told of one of her own kinswomen and oldest friends, tried to console the weeping girl, and prophesied in her just indignation.

"Mary," she said, "go back and stay with your mistress, and pray much for her; for, something tells me, that before a single year is over God will punish her in some dreadful way, and that when she dies not one of her children shall be at hand to comfort her."

A few months after this incident the heartless woman, with her youngest daughter, went to Europe on a pleasure trip; the vessel which bore them perished,—and was supposed to have been wrecked amid the icebergs off the coast of Newfoundland. No tidings or details of the catastrophe ever reached the public. Ah! what would not that mother in her supreme agony have given for the comforting presence of the dear ones at home, or for one short hour of respite from the pitiless jaws of the deep!

Unselfishness the Treasure of the Laboring Poor.

The directions here given will serve to warn mothers in the home of the laboring man, as well as in that of the most wealthy or well-born, against the fatal fruits of their own neglect in cultivating the hearts of their children. Oh! let mothers begin early to destroy in the souls of their dear ones every root and fiber of this dreadful bane of selfishness! We have watched with admiration one mother, blessed in this respect with uncommon skill, accustom an infant to give back to her the toys which it fancied most. It was only the beginning of the golden habit of generosity, ever ready to take from self and give to others. Later the child was taught never to enjoy alone any thing given to it as a plaything or a dessert. Then, out of the first pennies received for pocket-money, it was made to give at least the greatest portion to the poor; while the most touching stories of other children's distress and suffering were told by the parent to awaken within the tender soul of infancy the sense of pity and the virtue of mercy by these pictures of woe often near at hand. And will not God aid and bless these industries of motherly love?

Let us say it at once: the soil of the laborer's heart is one especially rich in the growth of all the divine virtues that claim kinship with generosity. No one knows it better than he whose hand writes these lines, and to whose memory so long and rich a record of the generous and heroic charity of the poor and the laboring classes is now vividly present.

Whence has come the rich and seemingly exhaustless fund out of which have arisen the Catholic churches, colleges, academies, convents, orphan-asylums, hospitals, and homes for the aged and infirm which have sprung up in the English-speaking world within the last half-century? Mainly from the scanty purse of the laboring man, from the very need of the poor man, and from the incredible generosity of servant girls! Within this great city of New York how many thrilling anecdotes could be told by every priest who has had to build a church, to found a school, or some institution of beneficence!

Let mothers see to it that this rich inheritance of generosity be transmitted to their children, to their daughters particularly, so that the coming generation be as royal-hearted as that which went before it.

The blessed root of this undying generosity must be laid in the early love of Him who "also hath loved us, and hath delivered himself for us, an oblation and a sacrifice to God." This has been already insisted on in the preceding chapter, and it only remains that we should once more urge upon the attention of mothers the necessity of making their children do generously whatever they do for God, for their parents, their brothers and sisters, for the poor, the widow and the orphan.

CHAPTER XIV.

The Mother's Office Toward Boyhood and Girlhood. Culture of the Heart—(continued.)

Magnum donum Dei, donum cordis!

A great gift of God is the gift of heart.

St. Thomas Villanova.

We have been like travelers on their way to the Pacific coast, borne swiftly along tracts most rich in treasures beyond all price, at which they could only glance through the narrow windows of their temporary prison, as steam hurried them onward to their goal. Even though we should devote this entire volume to this beautiful and vast theme of the culture of the heart in childhood and youth,—we should be far from exhausting it; and after traveling never so leisurely over the road, we should leave many rich underlying veins of thought and consideration untouched and undiscovered. At least must we direct the attention of every mother who will follow our guidance to a few additional points.

The heart of youth can be most truly likened to these rich deposits of mineral wealth which the hand of the Creator has accumulated for our use beneath the surface of this globe, or to the mighty elements of fire and water out of which the science of man is developing daily such beneficent or destructive forces. There is no limit to the wealth of goodness and generosity which lies hidden within the heart of any one of your boys or girls; and this fund every mother has to study and bring to light, enriching therewith first of all the soul of her child, and then teaching it to bestow its treasures of goodness and generosity on others,—on the members of the family circle first, and then on all who stand in need of generous words and deeds. There is more power for good stored up in the heart of a babe,—power to lift itself upward to God by heroic goodness and godlike works, and to lift others with it to God's level,—than there is of electric force in the ocean. And yet science tells us that a tiny cup full of water contains undeveloped electricity enough to blow up a fortress.

The forces which education—the true education given by a Christian mother—calls forth in the soul of her child may be destined, in the designs and with the aid of God's almighty grace, to save and sanctify as many souls as St. Ignatius Loyola, St. Francis Xavier, St. Vincent de Paul, or St. Teresa. These same forces neglected or perverted by a wrong heart-culture, may destroy as many souls as a Lucifer or a Mazzini.

Let not mothers who read this,—no matter how poor or overburdened with care,—say: My child is born in obscurity, and cannot be designed by Providence for such a great work and such mighty results as are pointed out here. Shall we look at one or two examples near our own times, of men and women who have lived in our generation?

Here is a poor cooper's family in a little town in the midst of a vine-growing country. There are two children: a boy who is working hard to gain promotion in the parish school, with the hope of being then sent to college and becoming in good time a priest,—and a timid, sickly little girl, whom it requires perpetual nursing and all the industry of a mother's love to save from the hand of death. The mother is a God-fearing woman, who makes of the practice of solid piety the first care and pleasure of both her children; and the father—in the midst of the deluge of irreligious doctrines and revolutionary tendencies which have crazed the laboring classes in town and country—holds firmly to the faith of his fathers. From the dawn till late into the night the townsfolk see him toiling away at his trade, varying his occupation with the culture of a small patch of vineyard at some distance in the country. In the terrible times during which their boy has grown to manhood and is approaching the epoch of his ordination, and while their sickly girl is budding into womanhood, both parents have had to fight a hard battle with the dire distress and famine which sweeps over their country like the breath of the Divine wrath, and with the tempest of impiety, blood, and fire which sweeps before it throne and altar, king, queen, nobles, bishops, priests, and every man and woman on whom suspicion of loyalty or religiousness can light.

The brother, concealed in his lowly paternal home, has undertaken to cultivate the mind and heart of his sister, and he teaches her all he knows, the languages of Greece and Rome, together with those of modern Europe. It seemed a folly to the parents, a folly to friends and neighbors, this high schooling of the poor cooper's sickly, shrinking daughter by a brother whose ambition was to cultivate both mind and heart, in man and woman, to the highest degree,—*and for God's service!* And so, while parents at home murmured, and outside acquaintance sneered, the twin souls grew under the silent training of that Spirit, who only asks of man to turn to good purpose "the late and early rain" of the present day, and will Himself give the increase and the ripe fruit in due season.

That brother's soul was not of the temper which could permit a priest to tarry idly or lie hidden beneath the shelter of his father's workshop, while Paris streamed with the blood of priests and bishops, and souls in hourly peril of death sought in vain the saving aid a priestly hand could alone bestow. But to Paris he did not go alone. The timid, sickly maiden bore within her bosom a heroic soul, and she would share her brother's dangers, and, so far as she might, his glorious labors.

When the great social earthquake was over, European society was like a city overturned to its very foundations. Unbelief and the most hideous forms of anti-christian error had invaded hearts and households among every class, and the work of conversion had to be begun over again by the patient apostleship of education,—more laborious a hundredfold and more difficult than the first great mission of the Twelve, when they went forth from the Upper Chamber to overthrow Roman and Grecian idolatry, with all the barbarous paganism of the tribes lying outside the empire of the Cæsars. And new worlds were also opening beyond the seas, where woman's devotion and heroism were called to vie with the most fervent zeal of priestly workmen.

The brother had been but the instrument in God's hand training and preparing that little sister, till the memorable day, November the 21st, 1800, when Providence made her the corner-stone of a society of apostolic women whose ranks now extend from Paris to the ends of the earth.

She was in the very springtide of her maidenhood, when he who is now seated on the chair of St. Peter was first laid a babe on the knees of Countess Caterina Mastaï; and on May the 25th, 1865, when that nobly-born child, after passing through the furnace, had borne for nineteen years the thorny crown of the Pontificate, that great-souled woman passed to the city of God on high, where thirteen hundred and sixty-eight of her associates in the world-wide apostleship were waiting for her, and nearly thrice that number were still on earth carrying on throughout both hemispheres the divine purpose to which she had devoted her life.

We have not forgotten that bent and venerable form as we were privileged to behold it just before the Angel of Death had given the first warning of his approach: the face which seemed to shine with the radiance of the blessed, the words so full of the Spirit of God and which burned into the listener's soul, the atmosphere of holiness which surrounded her, making one feel as if "a virtue went forth" from the very hem of her garments. We could and would fain have knelt for a blessing from that great servant of God,—the little sickly maid brought up in the cooper's poor cottage in Burgundy!

And how many others like herself, born in poverty, but trained to that divine generosity, which is the soul of Catholic spiritual life, were drawn to the saintly foundress by the charm of her humility, her gentleness, her greatness of soul, her consuming love of our Crucified Lord!

Who has done most for His glory and for the true welfare of the race, the lowly-born French girl, who was worthy to be the parent of so wide-spread and so thrifty a spiritual family, or the noble scion of the Mastaï-Ferretti, raised so unwillingly to the papal throne, and governing the Church amid trials far more searching and destructive than the persecution of Decian or Domitian? Their lives have run parallel for three-quarters of a century, and were both animated by that same heroic generosity which knew not how to refuse aught to God or to the neighbor's need.

Education a Creation.

The beautiful languages of the nations once the most Catholic in Christendom,—Spain, Italy, and Portugal,—express the idea and work of education by that equivalent to "create." And a recent traveler in the last-named kingdom, who speaks most highly of the civilization of the "unlettered" peasantry, deserves to be quoted here. "To say of a Portuguese that he is *mal creado*—ill brought up, ill-bred—is still the greatest of reproaches. The exceptions to this universal good-breeding are to be seen among the lower middle-classes, with whom liberal ideas are happily (?) become common, but who appear to think, with liberals elsewhere, that discourtesy is equivalent to an assertion of equality. It has frequently been noticed that, in Portugal, the best manners are to be found in the very highest and the very lowest classes. The middle classes, as a rule, however, sin rather from an excess than from a want of manners; they are, like some vulgar people at home, far too anxious to show that they know how to behave. They are too ceremonious to be perfectly courteous."[34]

We are glad to insert this extract here, both to show our readers what the genuine notion of education is, and what effect it produces on men's manners and speech in their intercourse with each other. We shall revert to this perfect courtesy a little further on. At present our object is to show the effect of education on the soul itself. And here it is that we beg parents to consider seriously how divine a work is theirs.

Education does literally complete in the child the work of the Creator. Only think of it. It is a wonderful thing to see how from the acorn planted in the ground a little pair of leaflets will bud forth, and then a tiny stem, which will grow taller and taller each day, each month, each year, putting forth branches, when in the open, to catch the rain and the dew, and to balance itself against every wind that blows, waxing strong in sunshine and in storm till it becomes the ornament of the field or the hillside, and outliving for centuries the man who planted it and nursed it in its helplessness.

See how the sculptor will take a block of marble from the quarry, and from this rough and shapeless mass with mallet and chisel form a figure so beautiful, so life-like that it seems to speak to you and almost about to move. And see, also, the great painter Leonardo, at work on a naked wall in a refectory of monks. He wishes to represent the Master seated at table for the last time with the Twelve whom he had chosen to be the teachers and parents of a new spiritual world. Figure after figure is sketched and colored along that table, and on each side of the Master, till the whole is completed; and when the great workman unvails his masterpiece to the gaze of the long-expectant brotherhood, one rapturous cry of admiration bursts forth: "It is a creation!" The Divine One is there, his heart preparing to bestow on them, and on the world through them, his divinest gift, and he foresees how, within a few hours, one of those present will deliver him up to his enemies, and how all will forsake

---

[34] John Latouche, "Travels in Portugal," pp. 64, 65.

him in his need. You almost hear him say mournfully: "Amen I say to you, that one of you is about to betray me." While the figures which start up around seem to reply by look or gesture: "Is it I, Lord?"

All these wonders of art and industry are, in their importance, not to be compared to the divine work of education, its effects in the soul, and its consequences on the life of the individual and all dependent on his good or evil deeds.

It is for the mother by her intelligence, patience, gentleness, and unwearied love to call forth in the soul of each of her children the mighty virtues lying there as in a rich soil only awaiting the skillful hand of the husbandman.

We are principally occupied with the culture of the heart. Create generosity in it: we have already seen how a beginning can be made in the babe; now let us study its further progress in the boy and girl.

Generosity in Conquering Self.

We know as well what are the baneful fruits of selfishness and self-indulgence. We have laid down unselfishness as the primary virtue not of motherhood only but of true womanhood. Should any one of the mothers who may be interested in these lessons, find, on examining her conscience, that she is still too much in love with self, then let her learn to overcome herself while teaching her child this indispensable virtue of self-denial. There is not a moment to be lost. Bad habits take root with fearful rapidity even in the richest natures. They grow and ripen and bear their fruit, like southern vines and weeds, almost in a single day and night. Crush them, pluck them out pitilessly from their very first appearance, and do not weary of the labor of rooting them out again and again. For, your child's salvation depends on your sleepless watchfulness and perseverance.

The most successful method, however, consists in accustoming your child to continual acts of the virtues opposed to selfishness.

Teach them not to yield easily to the natural sympathies and preferences which arise among brothers and sisters, and which often prove so fruitful a source of domestic discord, strife, and misery. It is, even in the child, selfishness which inclines it to love all who are of its own disposition, who please it and pet it. Make the child be kind to every one of its brothers and sisters without distinction. But should it so happen that it have a dislike for any one of them in particular, accustom it to show this one some special mark of affection and kindness.

No little strength is imparted to the childish character by thus early accustoming it to be generous in overcoming its likings and dislikes where these are unfounded, or of a nature to breed mischief when allowed to grow. Besides, the exercise of this same generosity of will is of scarcely less importance toward the child's outside playmates and acquaintance. Many a fatal friendship has sprung up at the age of ten or twelve. This very morning's papers record the sudden death from heart disease of a poor hard-working and virtuous mother, whose son,—perhaps an only son,—had contracted, in spite of repeated warnings and chastisement, an intimacy with a boy of his own age. The latter exercised a sort of fascination over all those of his years in the crowded quarter where they lived, organized a band of juvenile libertines, thieves, and burglars; and gave the police a world of trouble.

A burglary was committed and traced to the two lads; and the tempter and his victim were seized by a detective just as they were about to enter the latter's home. The poor anxious mother had been watching all the livelong night near her window for her absent boy—he is only a boy—judging that he was in some trouble or danger. She had fallen into a slumber toward morning when the noise at the door startled her; and, on opening her window, she saw them handcuffing her child. There was a faint scream which awakened the husband, and then a low moan, while she pressed her hands on her heart. "Oh! the pain I have here!" And she was dead.

Had she been neglectful of her duty toward that child? Alas, but few, very few among mothers of that class, living in such awful neighborhoods, are careful to do what we are here endeavoring to inculcate,—to check the very first beginnings of intimacy and companionship with all who are not thoroughly good.

Teach Them Generosity in the Exercise of the Home Charities.

Home is, or always should be, the school where the child should learn this practical generosity. There are aged persons in the home; and what household is complete or completely blessed without venerable age? There is nothing so beautiful among men as age: its very wrinkles and infirmities are eloquent of the battle of life well fought and the glorious victory won. The fruit tree in spring, when it is covered with the tender green of its leaves and the lovely tints of its blossoms, is a charming object to the sense; but this bloom only lasts a few days, the blossoms drop with the first blast or the first rain,—and then all nature's labor through the remaining spring, summer, and autumn is to increase and ripen the fruit. When they hang in all their mellow richness from the branches at the end of the fine season, do not complain that the flowers are no longer there, that the few leaves left are discolored or shriveled, and ready to fall to the ground. Leaves and flowers, dew and rain and sunshine, the rich moisture of the earth and the blessed warmth of the air,—all worked together to bring forth fruit on that tree. Is the fruit there? Are the branches bending beneath their load?—Then is there not in garden, field, or forest a more precious or beautiful object than that tree with its golden load of fruit!

Even so with a long life all filled with brave struggles against poverty and loss and treachery and discouragement,—with victories over one's own weaknesses, and virtues ripened in the soul to the full maturity of Christian holiness,—what is more glorious, more lovely, more worthy of affection and reverence, than these long lives with their merits and pregnant lessons,—just as the sun of this world is setting for them and the first brightness of the Eternal Day is on their close?

We could kiss the maimed hands and feet of the soldier who has given his limbs and exposed his life for the defense of our liberty and our honor! Even though the battle in which he received his wounds lasted but a single hour, his glorious scars deserve perpetual remembrance and gratitude. But when the hands of a dear mother, after serving us so long, after having given us so lavishly and lovingly of the fruits of her late and early toil, and having been lifted, morning and night, for our dear need to Him from whom all good descendeth,—when these hands that have nursed our helpless infancy, supported and directed us through childhood,—are now infirm with excess of labor and trembling with the chill of age,—shall we ever touch them without kissing them with infinite reverence? For the hands of a mother are the visible image near to us on earth of that Almighty hand,—all wisdom and tenderness, which never ceases to toil for us throughout the unwearying years.

Or, when the wearied feet of a father linger, benumbed and leaden, near the hearthstone, shall we not call to mind with swelling hearts the long and rugged road over which they have traveled, burdened with the load of our manifold wants,—aching and bleeding many times,—and yet unable to pause for rest, for the love of us urged them onward through sun and storm, through ice and snow,—till nature sank exhausted? O blessed feet,—how well might every true-hearted child not only venerate the sores which time and long travel have left behind, but kiss your prints along the rugged paths through which you fared unfalteringly for our dear sakes!

And other aged are often in the home,—venerable relatives who cast their lot with the family, or on whose own hearthstone there is nothing left but the cold ashes of a former warm and generous hospitality;—or the stranger given a place by the hearth in Christ's name, and to be reverenced as his own person!

O home-charities of the Christian family, what deep and heavenly love you lay open to the soul, and what visions of the dwelling of the Common Father above the skies,—where love eternal decks out its most royal mansions for those who are poorest and lowliest here below!

With all the voices of our soul we beseech you, O mothers, to inculcate reverence for the aged,—whom God has given you to love and venerate in His own stead. Beautiful, most beautiful is this tender and worshipful regard which our holy faith bids us pay to gray hairs. It was a living part of the religion of our fathers, it was the honor of every Catholic fireside: oh! let us cherish it here as the sure pledge of God's blessing on our homes, and the fulfillment of the promise of "long life in the land" to all who honor father and mother and old age to the end! Teach your boys and girls also to

Reverence and Worship the Sick and Infirm an Your Home.

To the lessons contained in the seventh chapter of this book, it may suffice to add here, that of all the blessings God may send to the home of such as love him truly, none is more precious than the presence of the sick.

Children and young people (at least where these have not been already perverted by self-indulgence) are naturally inclined toward the needy and suffering. The pale and emaciated features of the sick plead eloquently with young and generous hearts, and their moans find a ready echo in souls from which sin has not banished the spirit of charity. It is for mothers to foster and train aright in the bosoms of their boys and girls this touching sympathy toward every kind of infirmity and disease. There is One in the soul of your child who will not fail to help you powerfully. Only recall, when you are teaching your dear ones, how the Master loved the sick, and how he would have it that if they only touched the hem of his garment with a lively faith they should instantly be healed.

Was it not his own mission of healing mercy to our souls that he described so divinely in the parable of the Good Samaritan? Is not the office of that love which bore us in its heart from all eternity, and which ever stoops to the need and misery of each, as if each were alone in existence, painted by the divine hand in that alien in blood and religion who forgot the whole world to care for the wounded man found by the roadside,—while priest and Levite, the fellow-countrymen and fellow-worshipers of the poor forlorn one, went to the other side of the road, lest it should be thought they saw his blood or heard his groans?

Make every child of yours know and feel that he or she is the poor lost one, cast all wounded and dying by the roadside, and so near the eternal death,—and that the friend in need was He who came from the throne of heaven to heal, to restore, to lift up to the height whence he had himself descended. Make them understand,—that, on leaving earth again, he wishes and bids every one of us to do for the sick in body, in heart, or in soul, what he did for us.

The Mohammedans look upon idiots and the insane as upon persons specially privileged and loved of God, and treat them in consequence with the most religious reverence. Our Christian faith teaches us, as it taught our fathers from the beginning, to consider Christ himself as being concealed beneath the rags of the beggar, the emaciated or disfigured form of the sick, or the touching helplessness of the idiot or the insane.

In the Rhone valley a hideous form of swelling in the neck brought on by the mineral qualities of the waters they drink, and called "Cretinism," is accompanied, after a certain time, by imbecility; and the Catholic piety of the population leads them to look upon this awful scourge as a blessing from on high, as a mark of predestination. Even the images of our crucified Lord are made with this deformity,—as if they applied to the letter the prophecy of

Isaias: "There is no beauty in him, nor comeliness: and we have seen him, and there was no sightliness... Surely he hath borne our infirmities, and carried our sorrows: and we have thought him as it were a leper, and as one struck by God and afflicted" (ch. liii.). Hence, too, the unspeakably touching custom during the Ages of Faith to place in leprosy hospitals paintings representing our Lord as covered with that most loathsome form of disease.

We have seen religious communities where the room of a member afflicted with chronic disease was a kind of sanctuary to which all sought, as a special privilege, the permission of paying a daily visit,—and with what exquisite refinement of politeness and charity! We have known homes where the presence of some such incurable disease or life-long infirmity was hailed by parents, children, and servants as a priceless favor of the divine goodness: and how every act and industry that the fondest love could devise was practiced for years and years to render the lot of the stricken one bearable, to make the sick-room bright and cheerful, to fill it with the most pleasant sights and sweetest sounds! The most delicious fruits were sought for the sick one, and the most beautiful and fragrant flowers,—and we have known the master of that home to permit no one but himself to bathe the feet of the sick man,—and on bended knees, as if Christ himself were there. We have seen high-born ladies permitting no hand but their own ever to make the sufferer's bed, or decorate the room with gay colors, or wash and dress the disgusting sores. Think you the children of such parents will fail to inherit this sublime spirit of faith and piety? Or that peace and contentment, deeper than the ocean and sweeter than all joys that can be tasted outside of that vast bosom of God which is to be our home, will not flood such hearts and such households forever?

So, Christian mothers, you will train your dear ones to treat the sick and the infirm with a respect and a tenderness equal at least to their heartfelt reverence for the aged.

Let Children and Young People Generously Overlook Infirmities of Temper in the Aged and Sick.

This will be the crown of your home-charities. For, if there are aged and sick persons of so sweet a disposition and such conversational charm, that the pleasure felt in one's intercourse with them more than repays any service rendered, any effort at generosity made in attending to their wants or their gratification,—there are others whose manners disgust or whose temper sorely tries all who approach them.

This, however, is an extreme case. But, be that as it may, it is the mother's duty, where there are such persons in the family, to prepare the children to expect that old persons should have certain peculiarities which are to be borne with. The reverence with which she will have taught them to regard age in all persons, will prevent her dear pupils from turning into ridicule whatever might strike them as ludicrous. Nay, the true politeness which comes from the culture of the heart, and is the offspring of piety, will teach them to submit gracefully and lovingly to the whims and oddities of old people,—as well as to the irritability of the sick.

This generous self-restraint and devotion to the need and comfort of others is an admirable discipline for the young, as well as a rich source of merit before the Divine Majesty, whom the true children of God profess to serve, and believe they serve, in ministering to the infirm and the aged.

Generosity in Forgetting One's Pain, to Please Others.

This last and most important form of the home-charities can be practiced by children every day of their lives. A mother well accustomed, in her unvarying attention to the happiness of all around her, to forget the pain that is torturing head and limbs, the carking care which is gnawing at her heart, and the grief which is seldom absent from the life of the purest and the best,—will easily succeed in making her daughters remember that they too must forget their little aches and griefs to make all pleasant for their brothers and sisters, or to show perfect hospitality to visitors. Nor will they have any difficulty in making their sons, every day and hour of their lives, give up out-door pleasures or pursuits in order to contribute their share to home enjoyments or to its generous hospitalities.

One instance of such self-denial in a child of twelve summers may conclude not unaptly this fundamental doctrine on generosity. She, as well as her older sisters, had been taught by the example of both her parents to devote herself, in spite of headaches or other such slight ailments, to make the evenings in the family circle delightful or to give up her whole time to the entertainment of guests. In the absence of the mother this became the all-important duty of her daughters; and they, to gratify their worshiped mother, vied with each other in leaving no one of the home-charities unattended to while she was away.

It so happened that during one of these enforced absences the fatal disease which carried off our little maiden so suddenly, seized her at the very time when two girls of her own age and dear friends of the family, were visiting her. The child was in an agony of pain all day, trying the while to wear her sweet smile, to play and sing with her friends;—and lest she should seem inhospitable, she carefully concealed her torture from her sisters,—going for a few moments to the kitchen, where no one could observe her, and giving way to her tears. She made the cook promise that no one should know she was suffering.

And thus the day past,—and the long evening came. But then, the pain in her limbs became so dreadful, that every now and then she would cast herself on the sofa to find a moment's relief. She took her share in all the amusements of the drawing-room; it was only remarked that her eyes shone with a preternatural brightness and that her color went and came very rapidly. She had, however, no sooner bidden her two little friends good-night, than she became insensible.

They laid the unconscious child on the sofa, applied in vain restoratives, and then bore her to her room. But she was to rise no more from her bed. During an entire week she raved in the grasp of the malignant and mysterious disease which had seized upon her, unable to recognize even her father, but calling piteously and continually for her absent mother. She, with her eldest daughter, was hundreds of miles away by the sick-bed of her own parent. The latter, when the telegraph summoned her visitors away, would not even hear of her grand-daughter's remaining with her, and chose to suffer alone in her widowed home, bidding her children imperatively not to delay one moment.

They did not arrive a moment too soon. It was midnight when they entered the sick-chamber; the terrible spasms of the preceding days had now given place to a deep lethargy, the evident forerunner of death. The poor mother, who expected every minute to be the last, sat tearful but resigned to the coming of the dread angel, praying with her whole soul that her child might recover consciousness, were it only to know that her mother was by her side. Suddenly, at the first break of dawn, the little sufferer opened her eyes, a preternatural light overspread her features, and stretching forth her arms, "Oh, mama!" she said, "I am so glad you have come home again!" Then raising herself, she clasped her weeping parent round the neck and drew her down on the pillow. "Dear mama," she continued, "I have been very ill since you went away." Her parent tried to soothe her; but as the patient perceived her youngest sister standing near, "Oh! L—," she said, "you can now have my blue ribbon" (a favorite ornament). And with one look of inexpressible tenderness at her mother, and drawing what seemed a deep sigh of relief, she closed her eyes, and gave her soul to the embrace of the divine messenger.

She had been preparing, with angelic fervor, for her first communion, and would have made it ere the end of the month. On the Sunday before her illness she had, as usual, gone to early mass in her parish church. She begged her brother and youngest sister, when the service was ended, to go home without her, while she remained to pray a little longer. To their remonstrances she replied that she wanted to ask for the grace of a happy death. "You know, dear," she pleaded, "that one may die suddenly." The malignant pustule which soon manifested itself gave no sign of its presence when the words were uttered.

Scarcely four hours had elapsed after that most innocent soul had been borne away, when the body was so blackened that it had to be inclosed in a casket. Yet from the very moment of her passing away so sweet and strange an odor filled the room that the whole household as well as strangers marveled at it,—so unlike was the fragrance to any perfume of earth. And when, later, the family changed their residence, two of the deceased child's sisters visited her room to ascertain whether the odor still clung to it. It was there still like an atmosphere of purity and virginal holiness!

Well might the gentle mother, for whom this bereavement was only the beginning of a long series of visits from the Holy Angel, Death, console herself with the remembrance of the angelic goodness and generosity of which her own life was an eloquent lesson.

> "She came, as comes the summer wind,
>   A gust of beauty to my heart;
> Then swept away, but left behind
>   Emotions which shall not depart.
> Unheralded she came and went,

Like music in the silent night—
Which, when the burdened air is spent,
Bequeaths to memory its delight.
Or like the sudden April bow
That spans the violet-waking rain,
She bade those blessed flowers to grow
Which may not fall or fade again;
For sweeter than all things most sweet
And fairer than all things most fair,
She came, and passed with footsteps fleet,
A shining wonder in the air![35]

What a recompense for all a mother's generous nurture! But more lasting among men than all the glory of heroic deeds is the memory of holiness in youth, the "sweet odor of Christ" embalming not only the household amid which the sweet flower of generosity and self-sacrifice bloomed,—but every home into which the influence of such examples penetrates.

Generosity in Practicing the Out-Door Charities.

As every mother,—whether her home be that of the laboring man, or that of the rich man or the noble,—has a deep interest in the poor round about, and a divine obligation to fulfill toward them in proportion to her means, so is it her duty to train her children to aid her in ministering to them. We remember a baker's wife, with eight children, girls nearly all of them, and whose husband was not troubled with much money in bank,—who never failed during the most inclement winter's weather to go out with one of her children to bring bread to a number of poor families in pressing need of relief. Winter and summer, long before the break of day, she and her companion, with their full basket, would sally forth, making their visits rapidly, and then stopping at the nearest church to hear mass, before they broke their fast. To be mother's companion in this early excursion was a privilege eagerly contended for by all her children, and often granted as a reward for success at school or steady amendment at home. And the baker himself, when his oldest

[35] Buchanan Read.

boy could superintend the business during the early morning, would joyously take the basket and trudge along beside his wife, through rain and sleet and snow! He "wanted," he said, "to have a kind word and a blessing from the sick as well as his wife;" and when almost paralyzed by rheumatism, he still persisted in taking his turn,—he would reply to the pleading of his sons and daughters: "Rest! and sleep a little longer!—no, no! I shall have a long sleep in the grave; and heaven will be a good place to rest in." He was called to it all too early, the royal-souled man... But he left behind him children who made it their happiness and glory to imitate him, and to be thereby worthy of their mother,—the guide of both father and children in every good work and every home-virtue.

A Patriarchal Family.

Let us conclude our instruction on this matter by mentioning a family whose name is still held in benediction throughout the North of France—the family of M. Dubois of Valenciennes. This man, one of the angels of God to the poor and the persecuted during the great French Revolution, had been twice married; but, as we were assured by one of them, the children of the second wife grew to manhood and womanhood before they knew that she who was their mother was not the mother of their elder brothers and sisters. Twenty children had sprung from these two marriages; and, at the epoch of the father's death, nearly one hundred of his descendants knelt around his bed to receive his blessing.

Though he was then the possessor of a large fortune,—far more than he possessed had been distributed to the poor or bestowed in good works, during his lifetime, by himself and his sons and daughters under his direction. Indeed he was known and revered far and wide as the father of the poor.

After his funeral, and the reading of the will, his sons and grandsons would not separate till they had agreed to take on themselves, each some one of the favorite good works and charities of their parent. The eldest son allowed all his juniors to make their choice; "and," said our informant, "they seemed to have all of them quite enough in what was allowed to them; while to the eldest fell the 'discipline' or scourge, and the hair shirt used by the saintly dead to keep his own body in subjection. But to every one of that noble race had descended unimpaired the faith and generosity of their heroic ancestors."

Such are the results of Catholic piety where the Spirit of God is allowed to reign both in homes and in hearts; such the generously-tempered souls, in the palace as well as in the cottage, which true Christian mothers form when they do their work well. But what shall we think of such women as are painted in the following passages:

"When we observe women for whom silk is too rough, whom a rose-leaf wounds, who swoon at the least sound, who cannot pronounce their words whole, who, forgetting their own affairs, attend to those of others, whose lives pass in visiting their pretended friends, who are found at all parties, who are pleased in worldly societies, in splendid entertainments, and cannot live retired in their houses, who must know all the stories of the town, whose curiosity impels them to go everywhere, who can invent false reports, and can rekindle old hatreds,—when we consider what these persons ought to be, and what they are,...it is difficult not to feel an indignation which is itself admonitory and instructive; for then we shall call to mind that the Catholic religion, which denounced such manners as infamous, furnishes the best security against their recurrence."[36]

A Terrible Lesson for the Self-Indulgent.

Finally, should our readers be tempted to think that the piety and generosity of M. Dubois and his family are not suited to our climate or our epoch, we should commend to their attention this one example:

"A Duke of Venice had for a wife a lady of Constantinople, who lived with such delicacy that she actually disdained to use common water for her ablutions; but her servants were employed to collect the dew from heaven, with which her baths were formed. In eating she would use only golden forks; and her chambers were all perfumed with every kind of precious odor. How hateful to God was such pride appeared afterward from the horrible maladies with which He visited her, so that no one could approach her without a sensation of horror."[37]

---

[36] Luis de Leon, quoted in *Compitum*, b. i., c. iv., p. 107.

[37] *Ibidem*.

Make Not the Bread of Hospitality Bitter.

And so, with one other word of exhortation, we close this chapter. Among the many outside of one's home to whom charity in its most blessed form will prove a most welcome visitor, there will be found persons too proud to make their wants known, and too sensitive about accepting any aid, even when at their utmost need. And such persons are as numerous among the poorer classes as among the rich and the well-born.

Find out these shrinking ones. Approach them with more respect than you would show to king or queen, or pope or president. Your heart will teach you how to make the much-needed relief acceptable. For the heart has infinite delicacy. And when you have discovered these hidden sufferers from want,—not only must you be careful not to pry into their lives or to show a curiosity which would be resented because it wounds cruelly,—but you must conceal names and facts from everybody as sacredly as you would guard the secrets of your own soul.

There are families unwearied in their efforts to find out such cases of distress and meritorious charity as we here point out, and who, when the sufferers belong to their own class, are most ingenious in making their own homes acceptable and delightful to these homeless ones. Oh! it is the luxury of doing good rewarded by an interior sweetness beyond the power of expression.

But let us remember, when such sufferers are admitted to our hospitality, that no act or effort should be neglected to make the bread we break to them sweet and the wine of our generosity not bitter, by cold looks or any thing that might savor of weariness or neglect.

Familiar to all during the last six centuries has been the cruel inhospitality of the Lord of Verona to the exiled Dante, Italy's greatest poet, as well as the immortal lines in which the latter has preserved the memory of his entertainer's baseness.

"Yea, you shall learn how salt his food who fares
Upon another's bread,—how steep his path
Who treadeth up and down another's stairs."[38]

---

[38] *Paradiso*, xvii.

A modern poet has commented the tale in verse not unworthy of the Great Florentine.

"Arriving only to depart,
  From court to court, from land to land,
  Like flame within the naked hand
His body bore his burning heart
  That still on Florence sought to bring
  God's fire for a burnt offering.

"And Can La Scala marked askance
  These things, accepting them for shame
  And scorn, till Dante's guestship came
To be a peevish sufferance:
  His host sought ways to make his days
  Hateful; and such have many ways.

"Therefore the bread he had to eat
  Seemed brackish, less like corn than tares;
  And the rush-strown accustomed stairs
Each day were steeper to his feet;
  And when the night-vigil was done,
  His brows would ache to feel the sun.

"He went and turned not. From his shoes
  It may be that he shook the dust,
  As every righteous dealer must
Once and again ere life can close:
  And unaccomplished destiny
  Struck cold his forhead, it may be.

"Eat and wash hands, Can Grande;—scarce
  We know their deeds now: hands which fed
  Our Dante with that bitter bread;
And thou, the watch-dog of those stairs
  Which of all paths his feet knew well,
  Were steeper found than Heaven or Hell."[39]

[39] Dante Gabriel Rossetti, "Dante at Verona."

The retribution which the noble heart of man or woman would fear most for rendering so bitter the bread given to the exile, or the stranger, or even the relative, received into their homes, would not be the contempt of others, or even the contempt of their own thoughts, so much as the wrath of that good God who is the certain avenger of violated hospitality and of charity turned into cruel unkindness.

CHAPTER XV

Special Training for Girls and for Boys.

She was a phantom of delight
When first she gleamed upon my sight.
I saw her, upon nearer view,
A spirit, yet a woman too!
Her household motions light and free,
And steps of virgin liberty:
A countenance in which did meet
Sweet records, promises as sweet;
The reason firm, the temperate will,
Endurance, foresight, strength, and skill;—
A perfect woman, nobly planned
To warm, to comfort and command—
And yet a spirit still and bright,
With something of an angel light!—Wordsworth.

Along with great qualities and admirable talents, I find in him these virtues without which all excellence is deformity—namely, modesty, meekness, tranquillity, religion, sanctity, and integrity.

Leonardo Aretino.

Thus far the instruction given applied almost equally to children of both sexes. What is said in this chapter addresses itself first to girls and then to boys, purposing to aid the mother in perfecting the education of her daughters and sons, according to the requirements of their future avocations.

I.
What Is Special in the Home Education of Girls.

There are not a few persons, of great experience in directing souls, who have been so dispirited at seeing the result of the public education given to boys, that they would have parents and all persons interested in teaching bestow their chief care on the training of girls. Whatever may be the little or the much of truth in the theories, arguments, and facts set forth by these persons and their opponents, it is none the less indisputable that the ill training given to girls, whether at home or in our public schools, has made them the abettors and counselors of the dishonesty, the corruption, the love of extravagance and dissipation which are producing among men of every class in the community the frightful crop of crime which is the most alarming symptom of the latter half of this nineteenth century. The forgeries, the wide thirst for ruinous speculation, the gambling on the stock-exchange, the betrayal of sacred trust in offices high and low, the open and shameless organizations of public men in almost every department of general or local government aiming at bribing in order to rob the public, and robbing in order to supply the inconceivable extravagance of their wives and daughters;—all this is due either to the early lack of strong moral home-culture, to the neglect of woman's holy influence over boyhood, or to the baneful influence of women ill trained or taught to look upon pleasure and enjoyment as the prime end of life.

Assuredly if mothers are only such as we have been describing them,—if their children and their young people are brought up in the convictions, the principles, and the conscientious practice of the virtues we have been detailing,—our young girls will be any thing but vain, extravagant, heartlessly fond of admiration and enjoyment,—while their brothers must be every thing rather than the wretched crowd of untrustworthy spendthrifts, forgers, thieves, gamblers, and drunkards whose doings are daily chronicled in the press.

But apart from these degrading and discouraging manifestations of the result of our wide-spread educational systems, there remains to the Church of God, and to the priest who does her work faithfully, the mighty influence of Christian motherhood training an army of true women to withstand and cry down untrustfulness, dishonesty, and corruption, and an auxiliary army of true men, to be in their lives the embodiment of truth, honor, and incorruptible integrity.

We do not know whether this little book may ever reach the firesides of Episcopalians, Presbyterians, or Methodists, but we fervently hope, with His blessing who knows how to use the lowliest instrumentalities for the highest purposes, that it may be of some utility in the homes of our Catholic millions, and thereby leaven their hearts and minds with that loftiness of aim and purity in performance without which neither public liberty nor national greatness is possible.

So then, O mothers, we are now in the very heart of our subject; and no words we can use are at all able to express the intense desire we have to fix your whole attention on what we are about to say.

The Girlhood and Boyhood of To-Day the Twin-Roots of the Society of The Future.

The spirit and practice of simplicity in dress, in food, and in furniture,—the practical and continual self-denial, which we have laid down as the very soul of womanly virtue (as they are in very deed the soul of Christian life), must be made the groundwork of the education you give your girls. It will be for them, as it must have been for yourselves, health of body as well as health of soul; it will be, for the men and women of whom God destines them to be the mothers, the principle of strength of limb and energy of will, of clearness of intellect and purity of life; and these are the men and women for which America and the whole of Christendom are yearning and praying, and without whom, within a century, our civilization will be worse than heathenism.

Simplicity and Self-Denial.

There never yet existed a perfect man,—one possessed of that moral excellence in which there is no flaw,—who was not distinguished by simplicity of character and a life of self-denial. Much more is this true of woman. And why? Because the true woman, the perfect woman, values before and above every thing that virtue, that strength of mind which seeks to make the soul like unto God, by the possession of perfect knowledge and perfect holiness, and by considering external advantages,—beauty, wealth, dress, ornament, and the homage of others,—as only an accessory to greatness of the soul, and as utterly valueless when that greatness is not there. These things do not make the woman or the man, no more than the magnificent robes of a feeble, decrepit old king,—when a pageant or state-reception is over,—can help to conceal the palsied limbs, the shrunken frame, the weakened mind, or to pacify the conscience mindful of a long life of debauchery and tyranny.

You have often seen women,—poor women, too,—so beautiful that no splendor of dress could have added to the charm of their beauty: simplicity alone befits those things which God has made most beautiful and most perfect. Ornament is there superfluous, or the Creator would have added it; and ornament is only called in to aid in concealing the poverty of nature or of art.

You have also seen women,—nay, you know such in every neighborhood,—to whom, naturally uncomely, or even ugly, goodness, innocence, holiness lend a charm so heavenly that they are more than beautiful. The light of the beautiful soul seems, in such persons, to pierce the rude bodily covering, and overspread the features, transforming them, making them shine with a splendor which is not of earth.

Oh! aim, then, at possessing first of all this unearthly glory which, though "all within," sheds a luster on the bodily frame that ravishes the beholder. We remember in one of the dear old Catholic homes of Maryland to have seen an aged slave-woman, who had a merited reputation of exalted piety, so transformed while expressing her anxiety about the spiritual welfare of her husband and son living in Louisiana, that her face shone like that of an angel. Indeed it was impossible to see this gentle creature without being impressed with a feeling akin to veneration,—so visibly did the light of holiness irradiate the dark and wrinkled countenance! So was it with the venerable Mother Barat, the foundress of the Ladies of the Sacred Heart; and so with many and many a soul to whom we have given the Bread of Life at the communion table: rays from behind the vail seemed to illumine their countenances with a glory that sent a thrill to the soul of the beholder.

Simplicity in Dress.

Beauty, the highest beauty, does not consist so much in outline and form as in expression; and what ineffable beauty does not the expression of purity and holiness give to the homeliest countenance and the frailest figure! Certain old earthen-ware vases were covered with designs so exquisite, and in colors so cunningly disguised to an ordinary observer, that, in his estimation, they possessed neither beauty nor value. But when, at night, a light was placed within them, the whole artifice of the maker was plain, and they were pronounced most beautiful and of inestimable price by the beholder.

Be ambitious to place that light—the light of that supernatural love you know of—within your daughter's soul; and fear not but when lighted up with it face and figure will charm all who look upon them. The first labor of yours will only be the beginning of the formation of

> "A perfect woman, nobly planned
> To warn, to comfort, and command—
> And yet a spirit still and bright,
> With something of an angel light!"

If you continue to add to this sweet simplicity and purity of soul that other sister and guardian virtue, self-denial, as you have been taught in the preceding chapters, rest assured that, at fifteen and sixteen, your child will add to that angelic expression of countenance

> "The reason firm, the temperate will,
> Endurance, foresight, strength, and skill,"

every thing, in one word, which can make her "a phantom of delight" to the beholder.

What man—no matter how high-born—if his heart has not been corrupted by vicious indulgence, would not prefer such "a vision of purity," though wearing the simplest attire, to a gaudy worldling dressed out in robes and jewels worth a fortune, and from whose eyes flashes only the fire of earthly passions?

It is not the child rich in the priceless treasure of the virtues you thus inculcate who is likely to be unsought for or unloved, or who, when she has been found by the man of God's own choice, will fail to make his home a paradise, and his whole life one long blissful bridal day.

If you are a wealthy mother, you will understand that by insisting on this early love and practice of simplicity, we do not condemn the richness of attire suitable to one's condition, or the occasional wearing of suitable ornaments.

The habit of simplicity in girlhood and maidenhood will be certain to lead to appropriateness and good taste in every thing, and throughout life. It is not the well-born or the well-educated, the simple-minded and pure-hearted maidens of our true Catholic homes, who are to be seen before marriage bedizened like the queens of a country theater with flashy gold ornaments added to the horror of the loudest colors; it is not the married women who have come from such homes, after having been trained by true Christian mothers, who will be seen going through the markets with trains fit only for a drawing-room, and their fingers all aflame with diamonds and emeralds,—or astonishing the motley crowd packed into a street-car with their diamond ear-rings, their diamond brooches, and their diamond necklaces,—all which flaming ornaments in such places advertise the wearers as "shoddy," as plainly as if they bore the word placarded on breast and shoulders.

Suitability in Dress Is Not Extravagance.

This beautiful simplicity in dress and ornament still remains as a relic of ancient Catholic customs even in the countries that have cast off their allegiance to the Roman See. All through maidenhood girls of the highest rank dress with extreme simplicity,—which its very suitableness and good taste compel one to consider as elegant;—unmarried young ladies, though never so nobly born, do not wear jewels, even on solemn occasions. And it is no small surprise to Europeans to see the fair representatives of Young America displaying such a wealth of ornament on their travels,—as if they were jewelers' daughters sent in advance of their fathers to advertise their pearls and precious stones!

It should be known, however, that old American families are just as chary of displaying their family jewels on any but extraordinary occasions as the ancient aristocracy of England, France, Italy, or Spain.

This same habit of simplicity and sense of appropriateness have another remarkable effect in old Catholic lands. In Spain and Portugal women of every rank, young and old, married and unmarried, never attend church save dressed in black and deeply vailed. The highest and wealthiest have a little mat brought with them to the church, on which they sit or kneel during the service. There are no pews, and no carpets, to preserve the worshipers from contact with the cold marble or tiles of the floor. The gentlemen always stand, no matter how long the service or tedious the sermons.

The same custom prevailed all over Christendom before the Reformation: one not unlike it rules in many parts of Italy and France, in spite of the sad changes brought about by revolutionary impiety. At any rate, the practice points to the beautiful discipline of the Church in times when she was powerful enough to enforce her own regulations; and the austere simplicity and sentiment of equality which underlie the custom, embody her doctrine and feeling.

They are in marked contrast with the luxuriousness with which so many of our fashionable churches are fitted up, and with the extravagance of the women who frequent them at late service,—the wealthy dressing as if the house of God were the temple of Vanity, and the poor either excluded by their very poverty or shamed into staying away lest their poor attire should provoke the sneers of the rich. With Protestant denominations, among whom this scandal is so general, where the church edifice belongs to the society of worshipers, and where a wealthy few own and furnish it and hire the preacher,—we have nothing to do. We only pray that the day may be far distant indeed when the Divine Sacrifice of the New Law, at which all Catholics are bound to be present, shall fail to have around its altars the crowd of the poor and the lowly so dear to the heart of the Great Victim!

But the very mention of this Victim and this blessed daily sacrifice, with all the sublime and comforting realities which cluster around it,—should be enough to recall to the mind of every believing man and woman how monstrous it seems to make of the solemn celebration of the death of Him who died hanging naked, humiliated, and soul-stricken on the bitter tree, an occasion of displaying vanity in dress and levity in deportment.

Oh! how true to the divine reality of the sacrifice is the beautiful Spanish custom, which bade women come to mass attired as if they were there to mourn with the Mother of Sorrows, and men to stand upright in their strength, as if they emulated the beloved disciple, who stood with Mary beneath the cross during the three long hours of His terrible agony! And shall we Catholics in this nineteenth century allow the glorious piety of our fathers to die out in our souls, and our churches to be other than the temples of the Lamb, where we should meet half in joy and half in sorrow beneath the shadow of the cross and its Victim, to taste in our heart of hearts the bitter-sweet of the great commemoration?

Always Dress Simply and Modestly for Mass.

Do so yourselves, mothers,—and for the deep reasons we have just given; and never fail to make your daughters do so from their earliest years till they pass out of your control. If you are rich—and we suppose you are—your sense of piety and of propriety as well will dictate to you what is suitable. As to the poor, let them, if they choose, put on their best for the Lord's day: their best will scarcely be on a par with your simple and becoming attire,—and thus there will be less of apparent inequality before that altar, which is the table of the common Father in his earthly temple, representing the banquet of the eternal life. And, O mothers, love yourselves and teach your children to love to have the poor around you and near you, at least in the house of their Father and yours; and let no tyranny of fashion or prevalence of unchristian custom ever induce you to overlook these central teachings of Catholic faith!

What Your Daughters Are to Read.

Akin to the fatal passion for dress is the still more fatal and no less general passion for light reading. We have already warned you against the danger of reading every book and newspaper they may chance upon.[40] What then shall they read? It would scarcely be possible, even if it were wise, to give a list of books and publications adapted to family reading and specially suited to the minds of children and young people. Vitally important as early religious instruction is, and great as is the help derived from reading books treating on religion and the men and matters connected with its history before and after Christ,—it is hard, and it might seem invidious, to point out those which we deem the very best for the purpose now in view.

English-speaking Catholics labor under no slight disadvantage in that the standard works of English literature are for the most part either not Catholic or bitterly anti-Catholic. Our language had been formed, just as the genius of

---

[40] Chapter XII., pp. 174-175.

the nation had been trained, by the Catholic education of the eight centuries preceding Elizabeth. Just as the diction of Chaucer and Robert Grossetête had ripened into the style of Spenser, Shakespeare, and Sir Thomas More, the archenemy broke up the unity of Christendom and separated England from the Holy See. The classic tongue which Catholic England had been perfecting and polishing then became the mighty weapon of triumphant heresy and the vehicle of a spirit hostile to the Church of Saint Bede and Alfred the Great. It is only within the lifetime of the generation not yet passed away, that the Catholic worship was free under the British crown, or that the English tongue was taught to utter Catholic truth or convey to men's minds the history, the doctrines, and the ascetic theology of the Great Mother.

Still we have in the works issued within three-quarters of a century on both sides of the Atlantic a great wealth of Catholic literature. We lack, indeed, many, very many—not to say most—of the beautifully illustrated and otherwise attractive books destined especially for childhood and youth, and in which Protestant literature is so rich. Still we have enough, and more than enough, to place in the homes of the wealthy, as well as in the least favored homes. For, during childhood and early youth, educated and zealous mothers, truly Christian teachers, and well-conducted Sunday-schools, will know how to provide ample food—wholesome and nourishing—for the young and studious mind.

It is most important that girls should be even better grounded than boys of their age in the clear and full knowledge of Christian doctrine, the Bible history, the history of the Church, the lives of the most glorious saints in every age, and in that beautiful portion of Christian history which relates the rise and progress of Church architecture, with the dependent arts of painting and sculpture. Such eloquent works as those of Montalembert,—the "Life of St. Elizabeth of Hungary" and "The Monks of the West,"—will open up for the generous mind of youth prospects so enchanting and a world of heroism so beautiful and elevating, that no boy or girl who has begun them can help reading to the end and returning to the lecture again and again, like the thirsty traveler to the delicious spring;—and those who like such works will be impatient to read more,—the works of Rio on Christian art and poetry, those of Ozanam, of Dom Guéranger, and many of Dr. Newman's most beautiful volumes.

Girls to Be Taught in Good Time the Weakness of Heresy and Unbelief.

Your object in training, instructing, educating your girls is to rear women thoroughly enlightened in all that can make them love the faith of their baptism and enable them to explain and defend it; to rear mothers able to be the first and most successful teachers of their children in all that pertains to faith and the true life,—the life of the soul. When girls have reached their thirteenth year, they must be given the history of the heresies and schisms which still live and set themselves up against the authority of Christ's infallible Church.

They must be enlightened with regard to the present universal war waged against the independence of the Papacy, or rather against its temporal sovereignty, without which no Pope can exercise freely and independently the spiritual functions of universal pastor. "What, indeed, is it," says Bellarmin, "which is brought into question when there is question of the pontifical supremacy? It is, in one word, the very existence of Christianity. For then the question really is, whether the Church should continue to exist, or fall to pieces and disappear."[41] All the Protestant sects unite with infidelity and revolutionism in urging on public opinion and the States of what was once Christendom against the Holy See. But they do not see how their own existence, and that of the Christian religion itself, are involved in the extinction of this independence. "The churches at enmity with the universal Church," says Count de Maistre, "subsist notwithstanding only by means of the latter, although they may little imagine it; like those parasite plants, those sterile excrescences which live only on the substance of the tree that supports them, and is impoverished by them."[42]

It would not be prudent to allow one's children to go forth into the busy world and have their ears assailed by the many objections which the sects bring against the Church, without having prepared them beforehand with a proper answer to all and each. This, of course, applies mainly to educated women, who have had the leisure and opportunity of well studying these doctrinal differences. But we have met beneath the roof of the laboring man and the

---

[41] *Præfatio in librum de Summo Pontifice.*

[42] *Considérations sur la France*, p. 33.

artisan with mothers thoroughly read up in these matters, and well skilled, too, in the use of their theological weapons.

Young girls are also to be warned in time against the arguments used by infidelity and materialism under the name of "Modern Science." They are to be told that, apart from the very imperfect deductions of some hostile geologists, there is not an argument used by Darwin, or Tyndall, or Huxley, that has not been rehashed from the works of the ancient Greek philosophy; not a form of error which has not again and again been denounced, refuted, and anathematized by the Church.

At the close of the last century, and during the Reign of Terror in France, Count de Maistre wrote: "The present generation is witnessing one of the greatest spectacles ever offered to the eyes of men,—the mortal combat between Philosophism and Christianity. The lists are opened, the two adversaries are engaged, and the whole world is looking on."[43] Girls, as well as young men, are thus more firmly grounded in their faith and prepared to defend it against all comers. They see in the present designs of Darwinians, radicals, and revolutionists only the continuance of the old warfare against God and his truth, and in their pretended "new" theories and discoveries the old, old tales of the father of lies re-echoed from age to age throughout all time.

What Girls Are Not to Read.

Together with this solid and religious instruction, impart to every one of your girls a deep horror of the licentious and romantic literature of the day. Their inborn good sense will enable them to feel that it is just as dangerous and as fatal to allow the mind to feed upon the thousand and one "Dime Novels," "Illustrated Weeklies," and "Fireside" or "Seaside Libraries" as it would be on entering forest or fields in summer or autumn to eat of the bright-colored berries of unknown kinds, or of the beautiful and tempting forms of mushroom that cover the earth all around.

Let their rule be to read only what they know to be good, and never to touch what they know to be bad, or what they suspect is so. One of the first principles of morality is, that all rational beings accountable to God for their

---

[43] *Ibidem*, p. 79, published in 1796.

actions should be able to assign a lawful motive for every act of theirs. It is no justification for me, either in presence of my own reason, or before the divine judgment, that I have the power of doing such or such a thing, *if I choose*;—I must further justify my doing it by the reason that it is good, useful, and lawful to me to do what I am impelled to. If I have any fears as to the act being wrong or hurtful, I am bound to suspend my action till I am better informed.

This applies to the works which in every shape and at the lowest prices are continually poured on the book market to entice the appetite of our boys and girls. Mothers cannot be too careful in protecting their dear ones against this impure deluge, and in cautioning them, when they are grown up, against the dreadful effect of these literary poisons.

Inspire Them with a Horror of Indecent Prints.

Just as a conscientious, God-fearing girl would not read one page or one line of a book she knew to be bad, even so must she be taught to turn her eyes away unhesitatingly and instinctively, from an indecent engraving, or painting, or sculpture,—no matter where she happens upon it. Make her understand that this is a matter of high principle,—a matter between her soul and the All-Seeing;—so that even when alone she stumbles on such objects, she would turn her eyes and her whole mind away from the object,—as she would withdraw her hand or arm from the contact of red-hot iron.

Exceeding Care in the Choice of Engravings, Paintings, and Statuary.

We Catholics are not to forget that Christian art,—that all art, indeed,—during the ages of faith, was exquisitely chaste, modest, angelic, and tending to inspire heavenly thoughts and feelings,—while the introduction of the nude, the fanatical worship of the old heathen forms of art, and the abuse poured on Christian painters and sculptors,—dated from the second dawn of Pagan philosophy and literature (the Renaissance of the fifteenth century). Italy and France are expiating at present their having turned aside from the sweet and lovely paths followed by their Christian forefathers. We, in the New World, and at the beginning of a new era in the world's history, must be careful not to imitate what is most blameworthy; we must in the culture of art and literature, as in all else, be guided by the supernatural light within us.

Nor need we fear in replacing on its pedestal the pure and lofty ideal of the beautiful worshiped by so many Christian generations, to be accused of being reactionists or retrogrades. It is no shame to any man, when he has, knowingly or not, gone astray from the only royal road of righteousness and truth, to confess his error and retrace his steps. It is no shame, when one has openly and consciously sinned and led others astray as well,—to retract one's error and repair it so as to make the reparation as public as the offense. The shame is in the conscious and voluntary wrong-doing; the very height of shame is to persevere in wrong-doing, when one sees the full ruin it brings on one's self and on others. There can be no shame in going back to the right.

One may admire the genius of Michael Angelo and Raphael without ceasing to admire still more the heavenly purity of Fra Angelico and Fra Bartolomeo and Bernardo Luini, or the chaste and exquisite grace of Donatello and Luca della Robbia, and one greater than all perhaps, Leonardo da Vinci. We are only anxious that in every ornament of the home, and in every object of art placed before the chaste eyes of girlhood and youth, there should be a beauty lifting the soul above earth and reminding it of that heavenly abode where all things are made beautiful in the light of the Uncreated Truth. Children, with the sure instinct of truth and beauty which is so marvelously quickened by the indwelling Spirit, are not deceived by the cheat you put on them when your statue of an angel is only that of a coarse, overgrown boy, with excrescences called wings, or when your pretended weeping Magdalen is but a very unspiritual and very ill-dressed female. Their unsophisticated sense will make them turn away from the most "classic" crucifixions of the Renaissance, to kneel before the simple and sublime beauty of that painting of the Spaniard Velasquez, in which the scourged and bleeding Redeemer lifts himself from the ground on which he has fallen exhausted, to look back at a boy who kneels behind him and sends up a cry of grief and adoration. The face of the Divine Sufferer is more eloquent than any commentary ever written on the Passion, and from his head a single ray of light shoots forth to pierce the heart of the little worshiper.

Is not such the effect, O mothers, that you would have your dear ones experience from contemplating every book and engraving and picture and statue that you place before their eyes to help you in your labor of lifting their minds to his, and of bringing down one ray of light, one spark of the sacred fire from his heart into theirs?

It is not the purpose of the writer to discuss the comparative merits of national schools of art, or, indeed, to enter into any thing like a formal judgment on artistic productions. He is only considering here the effect which works of art produce on the educated and pure-minded. Without depreciating the productions of any one school, or the artists of any one nation, he may be allowed to say that no painter of any school or nation seems to have caught the true spirit of Christian devotion in a higher degree than the comparatively little known Velasquez,—the most glorious representative of Spanish art.

Girls to Be Taught the Value of Time.

Not less important to the future welfare of your children than any thing you can teach them is the priceless value you should accustom them to set upon time. Mothers,—wealthy mothers, in particular,—cannot weigh too seriously and conscientiously how strictly the just Judge will call them to account for the use of the hours and days and years which are wasted in idleness, even though not misspent in vice and dissipation. There are some persons who live as though they never had been taught when young that the Great Giver of life and time and hourly opportunities would surely exact of them one day a minute account of the use made of every sun that rose upon them, and of every hour that marks his course.

Mothers such as we suppose our readers to be, cannot plead ignorance of their early knowledge of the sacred obligation of employing every moment of time to good purpose,—and, surely, they will not allow son or daughter of theirs to be ignorant in so vital a matter.

It is in childhood, and in youth especially, that every day is of priceless value, when, in simplest truth, every precious hour well employed is a seed sown in the furrow and covered over with the fostering earth, and blessed of God from on high to bring forth certain increase in due season. But every day and hour idled away or misspent in doing any thing and every thing but what one ought to do, is an opportunity thrown away for self-improvement, for progress in all true goodness, or, what is infinitely worse, given to the service of the archenemy of souls and of their Almighty Creator.

We beseech women of culture to read and ponder well those lines of a man of the world, and to read them to husband and children,—to their young daughters above all. The timely regrets which their perusal is calculated to awaken may prevent eternal and unavailing regret

"The lost days of my life until to-day,
    What were they, could I see them on the street,
    Lie as they fell? Would they be ears of wheat
Sown once for food but trodden into clay?
Or golden coins squandered and still to pay?
    Or drops of blood dabbling the guilty feet?
    Or such spilt water as in dreams must cheat
The throats of men in Hell who thirst alway?
I do not see them here; but after death
    God knows I know the faces I shall see,
Each one a murdered self, with low last breath.
    'I am thyself,—what hast thou done to me?'
'And I—and I—thyself' (lo! each one saith),
    'And thou thyself to all eternity!'"[44]

Innocent girls, with their quick woman's wit and the unerring instinct of pure hearts, will easily seize the poet's pregnant meaning. Our lost days are dead leaves strewing the street along which we daily travel, lying as they fell and never to bloom or live again. They are "ears of wheat" given to us to sow for food of life eternal, and which we have not cast into the furrow, but thrown on the highway to be "trodden into clay." They are "golden coins" confided to our husbandry, with which the Giver intended we should purchase eternity, and we have squandered them against His will! But they are "still to pay."... And presently, when youth has quickly passed, and old age is before us,—like the dry bed of a river out of which almost the last drop has been drained,—we would fain go back to drink of these sweet waters of our life;—but they are like "spilt water" thrown on the burning soil, and cheating the ever-thirsting throats of "men in hell."

---

[44] Dante Gabriel Rossetti.

We must not deceive ourselves: every moment of time is ourself living during that brief space, every hour and day,—is our own soul filling that hour and that day with its deeds of good or ill.

You have heard of the "transit" or passage of a star across the sun's disk: astronomers watch it with their telescopes, and count by minutes and seconds the apparition of a little black speck on the bright round luminary while it moves rapidly across it to the opposite side to be apparently lost in the unmeasured heavens beyond. The span of our life,—as compared with eternity, is like that bright broad face of the sun projected on the immensity of space behind it; and the stages of our passage through life are as brief and as rapid as the transit of yonder planet across the sun. At every minute and second it is "myself" who am moving before the eye of the all-seeing and all-remembering God. I enter life like one emerging from the boundless void behind me, and appear moving, moving across the narrow circle of my life during the few fleeting years given me to exist,—and then I pass out of the sight of mortal man into that other limitless eternity beyond.

But brief as is my passage across the narrow sphere allotted to me,—I can merit, while it lasts, to shine forever "from eternity to eternity," or to disappear forever from that heaven where my glory might have been commensurate in duration with that of the sun's Creator. Yes,—to God's eye,—every moment of my existence here below is "myself passing over the circle of this life of trial,"—it is myself living for God, or forgetting him, or working against him, while the resistless motion of the heavens hurry me from my birth to my death, from time to eternity, from the use or abuse of the golden moments and days and hours to the terrible, unavoidable, and most righteous judgment of the eternal God.

When "my time" is past, and that judgment is at hand, I shall look back upon the misspent years,—each year shall be *myself*, looking my conscience full in the face,

> "'I am thyself—what hast thou done with me?'
> 'And I—and I!'"

And what I have made myself, by actual deadly guilt unrepented of, God will adjudge me to remain unchanged and unchangeable throughout all eternity!

We have known men, born, alas, amid wealth, and nursed in the lap of unlimited indulgence, who, having grown up in vice, without any other god but their animal appetite, and without any apparent sense of responsibility for youth and manhood wasted in eating, drinking, and dreaming,—would say to their own young children as these reproved them for their sloth: "What sin am I committing? I am doing no one harm!" Had they passed out of life, as these words were uttered, into the hands of Him who giveth *to every one according to his way, and according to the fruit of his devices,*[45] they would have known what is the terrible and irreparable guilt of a wasted life.

Minutes Are the Golden Sands of Time.

Elsewhere, in your office of mistress of the home, we have pointed out the necessity of order toward a proper and fruitful economy of time; this love of order you must make a second nature in every one of your dear ones. And, besides, you must begin early to impress them with the priceless importance of having neither idle hours nor idle moments. Of course, we count not these hours as idle or ill spent which follow the day's toil, and are devoted *by all* in the home of the laboring man, as well as in the mansion of the wealthy or the halls of the prince, to pure and blessed family recreation and enjoyment. If mothers and fathers, children, visitors and guests, would only make it a rule to join heartily in these "fireside entertainments,"—they would find these sweet evening hours to be the source of the purest domestic happiness, the preservative of family innocence,—blessed of God and praised by all friends and acquaintance.

What we urge upon the attention of mothers is the value they should teach their children to attach to what the French call "lost moments," *moments perdus,*—the little leisure moments or intervals that occur during the daily hours of labor, study, or occupation. *They*, too, ought to be applied to some special and profitable use.

Such moments in the day are like the grains of gold carried down from the mountain in the river streams and mixed up with sand along their shores. Each grain in itself is of little account; but the miner knows its value, and his

---

[45] Jeremias xvii. 10.

husbandry teaches him how to separate the grains of the precious metal from the dull valueless matter in which it is buried,—till at the end of his day's toil, he has amassed the beginning of a treasure; and with the persevering industry which adds together the gains of many successive days, he soon acquires a fortune. Do not the wise men of the world repeat to you daily that time is gold? Assuredly it is,—even for the ends of the lower earthly life; but for the higher purposes of life, and, in particular, for the highest of all, is not every second of time a grain of the golden sands? And are not these sands the "golden coins" with which we may purchase not only all intellectual and moral excellence, but His friendship to whom alone belongs eternity?

What Can Be Made out of Odd Moments.

This industrious husbandry of time joined to persistence and perseverance in carrying out any good purpose, is, in itself, more than a fortune for every son and daughter of yours whom you will teach and help to acquire it.

We remember once traveling with a noble French lady and her husband, bearing one of the great historic names of his country,—and from the moment the train left the station till it arrived in Paris, she and her daughter never ceased their knitting,—thus preparing sundry articles for an orphanage they befriended. Every "lost" or "odd moment" of theirs was thus devoted to the poor. It is also well known how many useful arts, languages, and sciences have been and are daily acquired by turning to good account these otherwise "lost moments." Indeed it is on record that some of the most splendid monuments of which letters and the sciences can boast were begun and accomplished during these odd moments, which else would have been truly lost moments.

One sort of industry can be acquired by girls during these intervals between work and meals, or between one set occupation and another,—and that is needle-work, including, of course, embroidery. Needle-work in our day is becoming rather a comparatively rare accomplishment; machine-work tends to supersede the deft cunning which belonged to the fingers of our grandmothers. If sewing-machines only lightened the burden of our poor seamstresses and milliners! But we know that the hearts of our millionaire merchants become pitiless in proportion to the number of machines they employ, and as unfeeling toward the wants and hardship of the poor slaves who work them as the very steel and iron which replace the human hand.

But precisely because mechanical operations tend in every department of industry, and in many departments of art, to take the place of handicraft, we ought to cherish in all good families intelligent skill in all kinds of handiwork. There are many, very many ladies, the most distinguished by birth, position, and accomplishments, who can do every thing, and have taught their daughters to do every thing, from painting, embroidery, and sewing of all descriptions, to the minutest details of cookery. Are they less dear to their households on that account? or are they less worshiped by husband and children? or less respected by servants and dependents? Our readers can answer for us.

Value to Be Attached to Practices of Devotion.

If there is a most skillful and thrifty husbandry in thus employing time, and in acquiring the skill and habits which make one's existence most useful to others and most delightful to the home-circle,—there is a spiritual husbandry and science which are to be practiced early and late by mother and daughters. Of the number of what are called "practices of devotion," or of their nature, this is not the place to treat; it is the province of the enlightened spiritual guide to direct the individual soul in their use.

We, therefore, confine ourselves to saying that it would not be wise in mothers to cumber their daughters with too many of these practices. But in these, as in morning and evening prayers, the recitation of the "Angelus," the preparation for the sacraments, the devout attention during the divine offices,—it is impossible to insist on too much earnestness, reverence, and fervor.

Even the "devotions" which are not performed generally in non-Catholic countries, like the "Angelus," have a sublime sense to the Protestant mind when properly explained. For what can be more magnificent, in Catholic lands, than the custom when the Angelus bell sounds at dawn, and noon, and sunset, to see every man, woman, and child stand still, every head uncovered, and every knee bent, to worship the incarnate God, the author of the Christian faith, the Second Parent of the human race, and to renew toward the Second

Eve, the Mother of the new life, Gabriel's salutation, "Hail, full of grace! the Lord is with thee!" It is as if the united voice of Christendom, and in it the voice of the entire race, went up thrice each day to thank the incomprehensible Goodness who sent his only begotten Son to be the teacher, guide, and consoler of the entire human family.

When the wise men in the gospel had come from the far East to Bethlehem, and had been directed by the star to the wayside cave in which the Mother and the Babe had found a refuge, they—first-fruits of heathendom—as if in the name of us all, "falling down adored Him" on his Mother's knees. Is it not what we do still? And in this great city of New York, how many of our professional men, of our hard-worked business men, who interrupt every occupation when noon is nigh, to lift heart and silent voice to the throne of that same incarnate God, and unite their prayer with that of the Church the whole world over!

It was the universal custom in Catholic countries, at the sound of the Angelus or Ave Maria bell,—that all labor and all conversation should cease in street, in field, on highway, in court and camp;—all uncovered to join in the salutation. The great heart of the busy world stood still thrice a day, and forgot its pursuits and its cares, to salute Christ's Mother and adore himself! Was it not a sublime custom? And are those lands in aught the better to-day that so many do not worship Christ, or pay daily reverence to the true Mother of all the Living?

We were touched to the heart last February, while enjoying the hospitality of the Bishop of Buffalo, to hear the bells from the cathedral tower ring over the half-silent city at night, and over the adjacent lake, calling on the faithful to pray for the souls of the departed. Is not all this most beautiful?

And most beautiful, instructive, and improving are all these sweet immemorial practices of popular devotion,—the sign of the cross, the use of holy water, of blessed candles,—the devotion of the rosary, that of the way of the cross, and the love which the Church is laboring to enkindle and spread on every land toward that Heart which was pierced for us in death, and in which our names are written.

Let mothers be zealous not only in obtaining themselves full instruction on all these points, but in communicating it to their sons and daughters. Sons thus taught will not be apt,—though going forth from never so poor a home,—to forget the early piety which lies so deep in mind and heart, or to turn away from the faith of their mothers; and such daughters will be its true apostles everywhere.

The Mother's Guidance with Respect to Matrimony.

There are two things which the true mother will not fail to do in order to save her child from a wrong choice, and from the irreparable misery it would bring.

The first is to accustom her to attach no importance whatever to a handsome face or fine personal appearance as compared with the higher qualities of goodness, purity of life, honor, truthfulness, temperance, and fortitude,—all of which go to make up the one attribute of manliness in its true sense: add to this,—that which in God's present providence, constitutes the perfection and glorious crown of manhood,—enlightened and practical faith,—and you will have placed before your daughter's mind the ideal husband to whom alone a true Christian maiden could give the worship of her love.

Nor need you,—nor, indeed, ought you,—to paint true manliness to the young girl with the avowed purpose of describing the only desirable husband, or even a husband at all. Form her judgment by making her prize the qualities that enter into such a character, and giving her a contempt of their opposites. That will be sufficient to prompt to a good choice when the proper time has come, and to keep her back from a wrong choice. Of course, when the thought of matrimony has come, it will be a no less sacred duty for you to pray yourself and to make your child pray, and seek in the sacraments new light and strength never refused to all who ask for such in this momentous crisis of life.

The second is, without warning your child, to keep away from your home all young men who would not be desirable matches, and to invite or admit only those who are, in your judgment and that of your husband, most likely to be worthy companions for the innocent girl you have reared. Remember that you have to consult your child's happiness infinitely more than your own; and in selecting the man whom you would have for son in your family, select him unselfishly,—for his own real worth and his pure devotion to your daughter, as well as because of her disposition, her heartfelt love for him, and the likelihood of their being truly devoted to each other through life.

If God has blessed you with a good husband,—if your mutual affection and your being all in all to each other, have been, under God, the source of all your wedded bliss, and the secret, too, of your prosperity,—then see to it well whether or not the young people whose union you desire are sure to be companions for each other. If not, let no inducement make you encourage a friendship or an acquaintance between them.

On this point,—every mother who has both a true womanly heart and the fear of God before her eyes, will avoid with the utmost care the guilt and folly of so many women, who, in choosing for their daughters, consult nothing but their own selfish liking or dislike, their worldly interest, the temporal advantages which may accrue to themselves and the other members of their families,—leaving entirely out of the question the inclinations of the poor girl herself or her prospects of happiness or unhappiness.

Such conduct is highly criminal, and is sure to bring swift retribution with it.

Vocations to Religious Life.

As to those of your daughters who feel called to the higher, the Virginal Life,—do not presume to put obstacles in the way. There are many certain indications pointing out to a pious and unselfish mother's eye that her child is called to the divine service. There are rules laid down by God's Church, and sanctioned by the practice of so many centuries,—all directing both the child herself in the examination of her own heart and its motives, and enlightening the priest and the theologian in his appreciation of all the reasons for and against such a vocation. If both your child and yourself are guided by the sole desire of doing God's will, and if you fervently pray him to make that will known, there is little danger of your going astray.

If the mother, in a matter so weighty as this, really seeks to find out what God wills, and is resolved to fulfill it, and not to prefer her own to it,—then she will not manifest anger toward her child, abuse her as if she were attempting to do what is wrong and unlawful, or treat the priest who directs her as if he were stealing away her heart's treasure unjustifiably and unwarrantably.

You have brought up your daughters to love all that was best and holiest, to consider God's will as the supreme law of angels and men, and God's service as the most honorable and blissful occupation of man or angel. Bless God when you have quietly and surely found out that your child wants to give herself to Him all the days of her life: take your child yourself to the altar, as Anna of old took her first-born, Samuel,—her only one,—and offer her to Him who will be her portion forever, and reward your generosity with untold blessings.

II.
Special Care Needed in Educating Boys.

While bestowing such constant care on her girls, the Christian mother must be mindful of the special difficulties which attend the education of boys, of the terrible struggles which await men in the battle of life, and of the imperious necessity of so arming their soul in advance as to put all the chances of victory on their side. Your boy is doomed to battle with the general corruption, the low thoughts, the low aims, the low tastes, and the lower manners of the generation among whom his lot is cast; he will have to battle with inveterate and powerful prejudices against his faith, with a current of scientific opinion gathering daily fresh depth and width, and tending to sap the very foundations of revealed religion; against the influence of a literature and a press bitterly hostile to all that he has been taught to look up to with reverence and worship; against a "human respect" more seductive and degrading than the witchery of the fabled enchantress of old, who only held out to thirsting lips a cup full of all delights, and then changed all who tasted it into beasts and kept them beasts forever:—and, what is worse than all, he will have to battle with his own heart and its inclinations amid a world solely occupied in ministering to sensuality and passion. God alone, with His fear and His love firmly seated in the heart, while it is as yet free from sin and evil habits,—will be all-powerful to give courage and strength and perseverance and final triumph even to the best and bravest against such a combination of adversaries.

See how many of the boys you behold yearly kneeling in our churches for first communion or confirmation fail to hold their virtue or even their faith firmly till manhood. If your eye could follow each generation as it grows up, the few who remain steadfast in the piety or faith of their youth are like the rare ears of corn on the harvest-field when the sickles of the reapers have disappeared and the sheaves have been housed.

It is of all duties the most important as well as the most difficult to ground your boys in true piety and in that true Christian manliness of which piety is the beautiful crown. Think of the heroic temper which the great Christian soldier mentioned in the following passage must have received from his mother's teaching, and consider well how you are to imitate her in your training of every boy of yours.

"When the venerable Marshal de Mouchy was led to execution for having protected priests and other devoted victims,—as they were hurrying him from the Luxembourg, a voice was heard from the crowd saying, 'Courage, Mouchy! Courage, Mouchy!' The hero turned to them who were by his side, and said: 'When I was sixteen years of age, I mounted the breach for my king; now that I am eighty-four, I shall not want courage to mount the scaffold for my God!'"[46]

Is not your purpose to form such true men as this—men so filled with *the sense of duty* that at sixteen they would be ready to brave death at the call of country, and in extreme old age brave the rage of an impious crowd and the horrors of a public execution to maintain the faith of their boyhood? Yes,—here is the model man: one who has been taught and is accustomed from infancy to fear God alone, to serve him in the performance of every civil and every religious duty, ready at any moment, from boyhood to the feeblest old age, to discharge conscientious duty fearless of every consequence. Whoso is true to God all through life cannot fail to be true to country and every trust imposed on him.

We have said above (pages 223, 224), that the life of every Christian man must be an intellectual and moral warfare against error and infidelity. There are countries, too,—Russia, Germany, Italy, Switzerland, and France,—where persecution is abroad and likely not to end with the present century,—and where, consequently, Catholic men must go forth from their mothers' homes filled with the spirit of the ancient martyrs and the more recent crusaders. Will

---

[46] Mazas, *Vies des grands Capitaines Français du Moyen Age*, tome iii., p. 220 —as quoted by Digby in his "Broad Stone of Honor."

you, mothers, who read this, prepare your sons for the strife, and fill them with the glorious spirit which shone in the Seven Macchabee Martyrs,[47] or that which St. Symphorosa poured into her seven boys?[48]

The Spirit of Christian Chivalry.

"To be always ready was the maxim of chivalry, which would accord well with its religious duties. This was also the principle of the saints, whose death, precious in the sight of God, is often observed to be premature and sudden. Some have accomplished their course at twenty, others at sixteen, others at a still earlier age. One is preaching on the love of God, falls into an ecstasy and sinks to the ground; on being raised up, he is found to be dead: such an instance lately happened in the cathedral of Rennes. Another dies in the act of blessing the people, with the monstrance in his hands; another while beginning to say Mass, with the words *Introïbo ad altare Dei.* He thought he was about to mount to the material altar, but it was to that which is in heaven. The Duke de Montmorenci, in 1827, died in the act of kissing the Cross on Good Friday, in the church of St. Thomas d' Aquin in Paris. To be attentive and prompt to answer the call of duty was another quality essential to chivalry; and what advantage might not be expected from such a disposition in regard to religion? *Amanti sat est indicare* ('A sign is enough for one who loveth truly'). Behold the character of chivalry: it knows not the word 'to-morrow,' as St. Augustin says of a Christian."[49]

And do not fancy that this glorious spirit is dead. Thank God it still fires the breasts of millions. "Take a recent instance. At the first assault by the French, when Rome was in the hands of the new Pagans, the aide-de-camp of the general Levaillant fell mortally wounded. After confessing to the Abbé du Cosquer, the general came to see him. 'Do you suffer much, commander?' he demanded. *'Beaucoup, mon général,'* he replied with simplicity, *'mais pas encore assez pour Dieu'* ('Much, general; but not enough yet for God'). The general fell on his knees and wept."[50]

---

[47] See "Heroic Women of the Bible and the Church," ch. xix.

[48] "Lives of the Saints," July 18.

[49] Digby, "Broad Stone of Honor," vol. i., pp. 106, 107.

[50] Idem, *Compitum*, b. iv., c. ii., pp. 106, 107.

The Ideal of True Manhood.

There was, at the most hopeless period of the history of Christendom, and when the deluge of Barbarism seemed to have utterly swept away with the Roman empire the first growth of Christian civilization, a man who went forth from Ireland at the head of a band of missionaries, and undertook to begin anew the labor of reviving throughout all Western Europe the love of religion, piety, letters, and gentleness. France, Germany, Switzerland, and Italy have never ceased to treasure the remembrance of his glorious services. It was an age of violence, lawlessness, lust, and blood; and Columbanus set himself with his companions to raise high, high, and ever higher still, the level of divine love and supernatural excellence in their own hearts and lives,—that they might thereby be enabled to raise the level of all goodness and excellence in the dark, warring, sensual mass of humanity around them. And thus these model men, the apostles of their age, passed through Gaul and Northern Germany and Italy like a vision of supernatural beings exalted between heaven and earth, compelling men to look up and admire and envy such unearthly goodness,—drawing after them—as the vision passed to and fro—the hearts of the multitude and crowds of imitators, and thereby renewing slowly but surely the face of the earth.

Swarms of devoted disciples were left behind by the great Irish patriarch, in numerous monasteries and monastic schools,—which became in the surrounding districts centers of a new spiritual and intellectual renovation, till the earth began to rest once more from the convulsions and wars of centuries,—and God's work through his Church began to prosper anew in peace and beauty and holiness of life.

It was an age of ruthless warfare and lawless violence, we have said; and these men had schooled themselves under their heroic leader to the use of weapons and methods which might beat down the lance of the robber and break the bloody sword of brutal power.

Would you know what was the IDEAL Columbanus set before himself, before those who gave themselves with him to a life of apostolic abnegation and labor, and to all who studied in their schools or sought to walk in the paths of Christian manhood under their direction? Here it is in brief. The Christian youth and man of that age—so much like our own in the deluge which sweeps over Christendom—should be:

"Fearless in the cause of Truth, but shrinking timidly from worldly contentions;—before the Divine Goodness like a beggar seeking alms, in presence of the wicked like a soldier unconquered;—docile as a babe toward his elders and superiors, running in the race of virtue with the ardor of a giant along with one's juniors;—loving to be all in all to his equals, but straining every nerve to rise up to the level of the Perfect; meanwhile never envying the excellence of those above him, nor showing jealousy of the swifter in the race, nor speaking ill of those who had kept him back; but responding promptly and generously to the voice of those who called on him to advance."[51]

Here, then, O mothers, we place in your hand a mirror in which you can view at a glance all the chief characters of that true manhood on which you have to form your boys. Let each one of you call your son to look into this mirror with you,—so that he may become enamored of the divine likeness pictured therein. And let us take every one of these lineaments separately, and study it well,—just as some painters do before copying a great master-piece, dividing the whole surface into small squares, so that they may be sure to reproduce exactly every feature and line.

Fearless in the Cause of Truth.

On this leading feature of Christian manhood, we need not dwell at much length: what has been already said about the spirit of faith, and a life of faith, supposes that your boy has not only been thoroughly instructed in all that pertains to his religion, but that you have labored to inspire him with an enthusiastic love of it, and a chivalrous zeal in its defense.

This chivalrous zeal is, however, the very point on which we would have you dwell for a few moments. The forms of ancient knighthood, as blessed by the Church in the ages of faith, have passed away; but the spirit of chivalry has not and never will so long as the faith of Christ is a living reality on earth. Hear, then, what is meant by that spirit, what virtues it supposes in the man who

---

[51] *Audax in causa veritatis, timidus in contentionibus, supplex bonis, insuperabilis malis, senioribus obediens, junioribus concurrens, coæqualibus coæquans, perfectis concertans melioribus non invideus, præcurrentibus non dolens, remorantibus non detrahens, provocantibus consentiens.*—Bibliotheca Patrum, xii., Instruct. xiv.

lives up to it, and what are its high practical obligations. We take the lesson from authentic history.

We are in 1257, at Cologne, and assisting at a solemn ceremony, the knighting by a papal legate of a young prince, elected king of the Romans, and soon to be crowned as emperor of Germany. Mass has been celebrated, and William, Count of Holland, who has only reached the preparatory degree of squire, is presented to the legate in these words: "We place before you this squire, humbly beseeching that in your fatherly kindness you would accept his desires that he may become worthy of associating among knights."

To which the cardinal-legate replies, addressing himself to the young prince: "What is a knight according to the meaning of the word? Whoso desireth to obtain knighthood must be high-minded, open-hearted, generous, superior, and firm;—high-minded in adversity, open-hearted in his connections, generous in honor, superior in courtesy, and firm in manly honesty. But before you make your vow, take this yoke of the order which you desire into mature consideration."

"These are the rules of chivalry: 1st. Before all, with pious remembrance, every day to hear the mass of God's passion. 2d. To risk body and life boldly for the Catholic faith. 3d. To protect holy Church, with her servants, from every one who will attack her. 4th. To search out widows and helpless orphans in their necessity. 5th. To avoid engaging in unjust wars. 6th. To refuse unreasonable (excessive) rewards. 7th. To fight for the vindication of innocence. 8th. To pursue warlike exercises only for the sake of perfecting warlike skill. 9th. To obey the Roman emperor, or his deputy, with reverence in all temporal matters. 10th. To hold inviolable the public good. 11th. In no way to alienate the feudal tenures of the empire. 12th. And without reproach before God or man, to live in the world.

"When you shall have faithfully attended to these laws of chivalry, know that you shall obtain temporal honor on earth, and, this life ended, eternal happiness in heaven."

When the solemn oath on the Gospels had been taken, the rank of knighthood was conferred on the kneeling suppliant in these words:

"For the honor of God Almighty I make you a knight, and do you take the obligation. But remember how He was smitten in the presence of the high-priest Annas, how he was mocked by Pilate the governor, how he was beaten with scourges, crowned with thorns, and, arrayed in royal robe, was derided before King Herod, and how he, naked before all the people, was hanged upon the cross. I counsel you to think upon his reproach, and I exhort you to take upon you his cross."

The Chivalrous Spirit Most Needed in Our Day.

Most instructive and consoling are these monumental teachings of the past. They show how our ancestors considered our dear Lord as the model of all manly generosity, devotion, and self-sacrifice. Looking over these rules,—and substituting for the words "Roman emperor or his deputy," those of "lawful supreme authorities," and for "feudal tenures of the empire," the expression "national territory,"—we have a complete code of religious patriotism adapted to the sore needs of our own epoch, and most acceptable to every young man in love with the interests of religion, country, justice, and humanity.

We cannot trust ourselves to dwell at length on so rich and tempting a topic. Many occasions will offer themselves before the end of this book for recalling now one rule and now another.

But no one can give a more eloquent and satisfactory illustration of this first point of his own legislation than Columbanus himself,—the fearless, the heroic, the invincible amid persecutions which compelled him to go from province to province, and kingdom to kingdom. When driven from Burgundy by Queen Brunehild, and forced apparently to renounce forever the apostleship in the countries which he had so immensely benefited, he writes to one of his disciples whom he had appointed to govern his monasteries during this enforced exile:

"I had intended at first to write you a sad and tearful letter; but, knowing the weight of labor and anxiety that oppresses you, I have changed my style and sought to dry up your tears rather than bid them flow. I have allowed nothing but sweetness to appear in my words, and have locked up my grief in the bottom of my heart."

"But lo! my own tears break forth!... They must be driven back, however; for a good soldier may not weep when just about to combat. After all, our misfortune is not a new one. Is not our fate what we so often preached to others to be continually prepared for? Was there not once a philosopher, excelling all others in wisdom, who was cast into prison for having maintained, in opposition to the popular belief, that there is but one God?"

"Besides, the gospel is full of such encouragements as we need. And, truly, one might think that they were chiefly written to exhort the true disciples of Christ crucified to follow their Master bearing each his own cross. Our dangers are many; the war which threatens us is raging fiercely, and our enemy is in every way formidable. But there is glory to be gained by the struggle...

"Take away the enemy, and there is no struggle; and where there is no struggle there is no crown... Where one has to struggle, there one finds courage, watchfulness, earnestness, patience, fidelity, wisdom, firmness, and prudence. In the absence of this warfare there is but unhappiness and disaster."

"So, then, no struggle, no crown! And I add: no liberty, no worth or dignity!"[52]

The old man had been sent down the river Loire under escort to Nantes, in order to be thence sent on a ship to Ireland. While there, and waiting for the craft that was to bear him to his native country, he poured out his soul in exhortations and directions to his disciples in Gaul. His unbending firmness and fearlessness,—which recall so vividly the Prophet Elias,—were united to a tenderness of heart, which remind one of a mother's love for the dear ones she is leaving behind.

"While I am writing these words"—the glorious old champion of Christian truth and morality says, in conclusion—"some one comes in to say that they are getting my vessel ready, the vessel that is to bear me toward my own country. The end of the parchment also forces me to make an end of writing. Love ignores logical order, and that is what makes this letter so confused. I wished to say every thing in brief, but in vain... Pray for me, dear hearts, that I may live for God alone!"

---

[52] Translated from Montalembert's *Moines d' Occident*, vol. ii., pp. 507, 508. We add the last lines of the Latin text in favor of our young classical scholars. *Si tollis hostem, tollis et pugnam. Si tollis pugnam, tollis et coronam... Si tollis libertatem, tollis dignitatem... Nunc mihi scribenti nuntius supervenit, narrans mihi navem parari. Amor non tenet ordinem; inde missa confusa est. Totum dicere volui in brevi. Totum non potui... Orate pro me, viscera mea, ut Deo vivam.*

God, for whom alone he lived and labored, interposed miraculously, and the vessel was driven back by the waves and stranded on the beach,—while the apostle and his companions were sent to another of the Frankish kingdoms to continue their work of regeneration.

But from that classic beach at the mouth of the Loire does not that voice of power come to us across the deep, across the wide gulf of twelve centuries,—to repeat to every Christian mother, and to every son she rears, the thrilling words: "Be the soldier of Truth... Our dangers are many; our enemy is formidable; and the war in which we must share is raging fiercely. But the field of battle is the field of glory. No struggle, no crown! No liberty, no honor or dignity!"

Summary of the Remaining Traits of True Manhood from St. Columbanus.

This fearless advocacy of truth and justice and enlightened liberty,—is to be inseparable from an aversion for loud wrangling, for mere worldly contentions, and the miserable squabbles for political place and power, which seem to fill up the existence of so many men in our midst. The fearlessness and chivalric spirit which dispose a noble-minded young man to assert the truth which he holds most dear when he sees it attacked, and when its advocacy is both timely and needful,—are not incompatible with gentleness; on the contrary, to render that advocacy efficacious, one should be as gentle and firm as fearlessly outspoken.

Godfrey of Bouillon, the hero of the first crusade, the conqueror and first Christian king of Jerusalem, is thus described by Radulphus, his contemporary: "He was rich in virtues,—in those that become the man of the world as well as those that adorn the man of God,—bountiful to the poor, merciful to the erring; distinguished by humility, humanity, soberness, justice, chastity. You would have thought him rather the light of monks than the commander of warriors." The Archbishop, William of Tyre, says of him, that he was "a religious man, clement, pious, and fearing God; of spotless life, departing from all evil; grave, firm to his promises,...assiduous in prayer and works of piety; remarkable for liberality, gracious and affable, kind and merciful; in all his ways commendable and pleasing to God." This was the gentle, humble prince, who refused to wear a royal crown in Jerusalem, where Christ our king had been crowned with thorns.

And this beautiful union of intrepidity in presence of the enemies of God and of his truth, and of gentleness and meekness, it is which renders all these great heroic characters so lovely.

This is what you must impress on the young souls you are forming—to be as brave as a lion when truth or justice demands it, and as meek and gentle as a babe in the bosom of one's family and the common intercourse of life.

The other virtues and qualities commended by Columbanus to his disciples are no less necessary to every young man of our age and country;—the dependence on God which makes one look up to him with humble and prayerful gratitude in prosperity, and the invincible fortitude which no adversity or persecution can cast down (*supplex bonis, insuperabilis malis*);—the prompt disposition to yield respect and deference to one's seniors, obedience to one's superiors, will be joined to the willingness to vie with those younger than one's self in all manner of good deeds; the spirit of true humility will never shrink from feeling one's self on an equality with all who are earnest in serving the good cause, no matter what may be one's wealth or one's rank. The youth in whose heart burns the love of true excellence will ever seek out men who are the most perfect models, and bend his whole strength to rise to their level. Nor will he be envious of the superior talents or acquirements of others, or jealous of such as have attained eminence, or even speak ill of those who have been the cause or the occasion of his own backwardness in virtue, learning, or position; but, anxious as he is to serve God and his country well, he will excite himself by the examples of those above and before him to make a good use of his own talents and opportunities,—showing himself in all things ready to profit zealously and gratefully by the advice and assistance of those who take an interest in his advancement (*provocantibus consentiens*).

This is only one way of interpreting the pregnant synopsis of the great monastic teacher. A mother who will weigh each word well cannot fail to find much more. We have only "opened the rich vein" for her and her pupils; their own labor will discover its full wealth of instruction.

In the rules laid down for knighthood will be remarked the fourth and seventh,—the former binding the true Christian man "to search out widows and helpless orphans in their necessity,"—the latter obliging him to be the protector and avenger of innocence, of female innocence and virtue particularly. And this leads us to a most important consideration.

Let Your Sons Be Their Sisters' Devoted Servants.

We cannot impress too earnestly this lesson upon you,—whether you be the poor toiler in the cottage, or the wealthy mistress of a palace. Be such in your life, in your whole deportment, that your sons may believe that there does not exist on earth a mother or a woman like you. Let them be made to understand, as early as possible, that men are to treat all women with a sovereign respect. We once saw in one of the public conveyances of Paris a young nobleman, a foremost member of the Society of St. Vincent de Paul, get out of his place to help a poor infirm old market woman into the omnibus. She was cumbered with a large parcel, which he took from her, raising his hat to her as if she were a duchess, and then gracefully and gently helping her to a seat. As we passed the market in which she worked, he got out before her, holding her parcel with one hand and giving her the other to assist her to alight; and then, taking off his hat, he kissed her hand to the no small astonishment of more than one of the passengers. She was only one of the many that he was in the habit of visiting weekly to distribute alms and spiritual comfort in the name of the Society. We did not venture to question this noble Christian youth about this demonstration of reverence to one beneath him. But a friend who knew him well said that he had been taught to reverence his own mother in every person of her sex, in the aged particularly, and to that he added the veneration which Christian piety inspires for all who are the recipients of our charity.

In such Christian families as his the familiarity which exists between brother and sisters is always accompanied with that feeling of profound respect for the weaker sex, of that invariable deference and courtesy which will keep a well-bred brother always on the watch to help or serve his sister in every thing,—even though no stranger or any other member of the family happen to be present. He is taught to be devoted to his sisters wherever they are, at home or abroad. And one who has that true reverential feeling toward his mother and sisters, cannot help extending it to every member of their sex as long as he lives. Is there nothing here that appeals to your motherly sense of self-respect?

The Necessity and Value of Home-Bred Courtesy.

Home is, after all, the great school of virtue, of faith and piety, as well as of that gentleness and devotion to the comfort of others, which constitute the soul of courtesy. It was because the lower classes of old Catholic countries were so full of deep faith and sincere piety, that they displayed before the woful changes wrought by revolutionism such mutual respect, such gentleness, such inborn courtesy. "God bless your work!" was the salutation which every stranger or wayfarer passing along the road addressed to the laborer at his work. And "God bless you kindly!" was the gentle response, as the plowman looked away from his furrow, or the mason looked down from the wall he was rearing, or "God speed you safely!" was the answering prayer. No matter how poor the cottage, or how comfortable,—no one crossed the ever-open door without the greeting, "God save all here!" and without hearing in return, "God save you kindly!" and "You are heartily welcome!" These forms of greeting are but straws on the surface of popular life and manners; but surely they indicated the direction in which the current ran, and were significant of a warm deep feeling of faith and neighborly charity.

Are we in aught the better for dropping these and so many other salutations and locutions from our vocabulary? Is our life in aught the happier, the more elevated or refined, because these currents are frozen or stand still? or because "freer, easier, more independent and careless manners" usurp the place of the sweet customs of Catholic ages? In the harvest-fields of Spain and Portugal, the laborers will salute each other with words of praise and adoration in honor of the Holy Name, or in honor of the Immaculate Mother. And in conterminous fields one man or woman will take up the first verse of a well-known hymn, or of one of the glorious national ballads, and all the others will sing the next, and so on to the end, mixing religion with the popular songs which preserve the memory of the heroic achievements of their ancestors. Who does not see that such customs presuppose the highest civilization in the masses, and the very essence of that courtesy which can be and is high-bred in the peasant and the cottier, because bred by faith and piety and the love of all that is ennobling in the memories of the past?

Home-bred courtesy is necessary from husband to wife and from wife to husband, from brother to sisters, and from sisters to brothers, else in what does the home of a Christian differ from that of a pagan, or even from the hut of a savage? And to be true courtesy it must not be a mask put on for an occasion and then laid aside, but a habit springing from the interior life, from the thoughts of the mind and the affections of the heart,—just as the veins of the maple-wood, and the rich tints of the mahogany, and the lovely colors of the rose are the work of the vital sap in tree and flower, not the artifice of human industry.

But we specially insist on the necessity of home-bred courtesy for boys, and from their earliest boyhood, if you would have it become a second nature. We plead this necessity to every mother of the laboring and the middle classes. For,—be it said without offense to any,—the courtesy which distinguished the ancestors of these classes in the old European homesteads has been sadly forgotten in the new. People who rise in the world,—and here it is free to all classes to rise,—are anxious to show that they *are* rising or *have* risen,—and hence that offensiveness of self-assertion or the no less offensive display of excessive politeness which are meant to tell the beholder that "we are somebody!"

Young people are quite earnest in claiming to be "ladies" and "gentlemen;" but the important thing is to be *gentle*, to possess that habitual *gentleness*, the sister of piety, which is sure to produce courtesy, and without which there never has been and never will be a true lady or gentleman. Go into Andalusia: the Spanish farmer there will start from his home amid the mountains to carry his crop of wine twenty, forty, sixty miles or more to the nearest town, or further still to the best market. He will hear early mass before he starts, and fill his pockets with dried figs and peppers of which he will make his noonday meal on stopping at a well-known fountain or well on the road. The water is his only beverage,—and there is not a well or a spring within hundreds of miles whose qualities he is not familiar with. His mules are laden with the rich wines which fetch so high a price in London and New York. But he never dreams of tasting them on his way. Speak to him on the road and you will be charmed with his dignity of manner and highbred courtesy. Converse with him in the posada or inn where he spends the night, and you will have a still more favorable opportunity of estimating his real civility and intelligence. You will say that such a race is a race of gentlemen.

It behooves the poor man and the laboring man among us to see to it that these qualities once believed to be inborn in his own blood shall not disappear in his children and grandchildren. And surely it behooves the well-born and the wealthy that true courtesy shall not disappear from their homes with true piety.

We commend this reflection to mothers and fathers alike: can true piety be where a passionate temper rules the house, and where a blow and a curse are the usual accompanyments of reproof or punishment? We beseech parents to think well of this. Let them never suffer themselves to be rude toward their children; and let them never tolerate in these anything approaching to rudeness toward each other.

Mothers Must Not Allow Their Daughters to Be the Servants of Their Brothers.

There are sad examples of the fatal mistake made by certain unwise and weak mothers in giving their boys, as these grow up, so large a place in the house that their daughters either seem in the way or are obliged to devote themselves to the pleasure and caprice of their brothers.

Two families are now present to our memory in which were contrasted the principles of a truly Christian education, as set forth above, and the fostering in the sons of this spirit of selfishness.

The latter was a home distinguished for its wealth; and when the sons, grown up and coming home from college, brought their young friends and acquaintance with them, they were allowed to be the absolute masters of the house, and to make their slaves of all persons in it,—parents, sisters, and servants. These boys, thus made the gods of the household, whom all therein had to worship and obey, became utterly reckless of the comfort or happiness of everybody about them. Brought up in selfishness, they gave themselves up in manhood to self-indulgence and dissipation, broke the hearts of their foolish parents, beggared their sisters, married beneath them, and went every one of them to ruin.

Not so their next-door neighbors. They had seen better days before they came to their present abode. But the mother was the embodiment of all the gentle virtues that ever made home delightful. The sons, when the day's toil was ended, forgot, or seemed to forget, their own fatigue in making their mother and sisters happy. Every device that rare culture adorning heartfelt piety could think of was brought nightly into play to make the ladies believe that they were the princesses of a fairy palace. And this courtesy and gentleness of manners followed all of them through life. The eldest brother, in particular, distinguished for his masculine strength and chivalrous patriotism, was blessed with a wife, nurtured like himself by a wise, firm, and gentle mother. Their children, from the first dawn of reason, were sweetly habituated to that unselfishness and gentle courtesy which the unobservant stranger might mistake for weakness, but which, to the eyes of those who knew them well, were like the graceful and lovely creepers trained to adorn, but not to conceal, the fair proportions, rich material, and exquisite workmanship of some massive classic edifice.

It is thus that you have to work, O mothers. Where what seems but is not courtesy or genuine politeness appears in a man or a woman, the least shock or commotion will show how superficial and hollow is the quality you might be tempted to admire. False courtesy is like a light veneering of beautiful wood, laid over the coarse grain of common material, or like the thin layer of plastering placed on the front of a building and painted to resemble marble or granite;—but a slight knock will break this veneering and lay the natural coarse grain bare to the eye, and the first rain or the first thaw after a frost will show that what you mistook at a distance for a marble palace was but a wretched sham.

It is the solid material of nature, enriched by a long and thorough nurture, that can receive a high polish and keep it for ever. Be it your care, mothers, to form in the heart of hearts of every son and daughter of yours the solid, substantial piety and gentleness of which we have been speaking. This is the structure that you have to raise. Its solidity and its beauty, fear it not, will resist the pelting of rain and hail, survive the action of the summer's heat and the winter's frost.

Make Home the Only Center of Amusement for Your Sons.

The training of daughters is, comparatively, an easy and a delightful task for mothers,—for their daughters are ever at home; but it is far otherwise with boys. An irresistible impulse leads these to seek companionship and amusement outside of the home. Hence arise most of the serious dangers and temptations for boys.

One of a good and wise mother's most useful industries is to make home *necessary* to her sons. Let her provide for them there everything which can amuse and delight as well as instruct; and let her also encourage her boys to bring their young friends and companions home. She will thereby be able to see who and what these are, so as to select such as may be profitable companions and safe friends for after-life.

We need not insist on the prudence which a mother must use in keeping away from her home and companionship with her children the rude and the vicious. She has to avoid giving offense; she alone can find means to unite firmness, decision, and gentleness in guarding her dear ones from evil.

At any rate, when your boys have grown up, it must be a part of your duty to entertain hospitably such friends as they may invite to your home. Should you see in these qualities which render them unsafe companions for your children, your tact and motherly love will surely find a way to warn these against such associations. Only, let it be apparent in your whole conduct that you are solely guided by your sense of duty and the purest love for every child of yours.

Make it also your duty to accompany your grown-up sons and daughters to every sort of public amusement which you may sanction. If this precaution is a most necessary one in the case of your boys, it is indispensable in that of your girls. Oh! if parents among the laboring classes only knew the irreparable ruin caused every year by their permitting their young sons and daughters to frequent these abominations called low theaters and free dances, without a father or a mother's eye to overlook them! We say the same of "excursions," gotten up for no matter what purpose: no mother should allow her daughter to go to such places without accompanying her, and no father, who fears God, and has at heart the perseverance of his son in piety and purity, should permit him to mix with such gatherings without being there himself to protect him. Indeed,—and the most enlightened and experienced will support us in the assertion,—the less the children and young people of the laboring classes know of such assemblages and amusements the better will it be for the health of body and soul.

A Concluding Advice.

We hear, on both sides of the Atlantic, of women of fortune founding institutions of charity or rearing splendid churches at their sole expense. It does seem a noble undertaking on which to bestow one's fortune and one's labor,—this rearing of a perfect temple to the worship of the most high God. But the formation in piety, in knowledge, in the practice of all goodness of a single child is, in the sight of God, a something far more glorious, far more meritorious. Time lays low the most solid, beautiful, and costly structures planned by human genius, reared and decorated by the rarest skill; but the soul of your boy is to outlive time itself, is destined to be happy with its Creator in eternity, when the sun himself will be quenched in the firmament, and the starry heavens folded up and cast aside like a worn-out garment.

Will you labor to enrich that dear soul with virtues whose energies shall fail not when even fire shall cease to burn and light to be needful to the eye? Will you adorn it with these charities of earth and heaven which will form its ornament and its crown near the throne of God long after the last star will have ceased to shine in the immensities around us?

Oh! what temple can be compared to your child for whom Christ died, whom he purchased from hell with his own blood, and whom he wills you to help in making a godlike man!

For this you need no fortune, no riches,—nothing but the love and devotion, the industry and perseverance of a true woman's, true mother's heart.

When the poor, persecuted, but fearless prophet, Elias, had to fly his own country and take refuge among the enemies of his God and his race, he was bidden to go to a poor widow-woman at Sarephta on the sea-coast. "When he was come to the gate of the city, he saw the widow-woman gathering sticks,...and said to her: Give me a little water in a vessel, that I may drink. And when she was going to fetch it, he called after her, saying: Bring me also, I beseech thee, a morsel of bread in thy hand. And she answered: As the Lord thy God liveth, I have no bread, but only a handful of meal in a pot, and a little oil in a cruse; behold, I am gathering two sticks, that I may go in and dress it for me and my son, that we may eat it, and die."[53]

---

[53] 3 Kings, chap. xvii.

Surely here was poverty on the part of the mighty prophet who could shut up the heavens for seven years, and the very extremity of destitution on the part of this generous-hearted widow. She gave to the man of God all she had in the world,—all that stood between death by hunger, and her boy and herself!

God repaid her well, however: hunger was provided against by the prophet's miraculous power, and a still greater miracle rewarded both mother and son, for the latter was brought back by Elias from death to life.

How, think you, after this wonderful providence over herself and her only one, ought this mother to have reared her boy? In the full knowledge, the unbounded love, and the faithful service of the God of Israel. Indeed the Jewish traditions say that she gave up the lad to Elias to be his servant and inseparable companion ever after. She is mentioned by our Lord in the gospel; her memory and that of her boy shall live among men as long as the world itself; and in eternity they shall shine like twin stars among the hosts of the blessed.

So this poor but great-souled woman made her son like herself—ever ready to give everything, even life itself, for God and the poor! Do not say that you are too poor to rear godlike sons.

Are you a wealthy or a noble mother? Then remember the widowed mother of the great St. John Chrysostom. She lost her husband, a general officer in high command in the imperial armies, when she was in her twentieth year. Though solicited, and pressed to marry again,—being very beautiful and wealthy,—the noble lady resolved to give her life to God and the education of her infant son. Thenceforward her whole time and industry were devoted to that divine labor of forming a man worthy of being a true follower of Christ. Other masters aided her, when early boyhood was over, to cultivate his mind. But the culture of that great heart was her work. And how beautiful was that heart, how godlike the life of St. John Chrysostom, the admiration of fourteen hundred years can attest.

But you may think that the examples of these remote ages do not apply aptly to our own; that the heroines of Scripture or the heroic women of the early Church are too far above the mediocrity, the commonplace virtue of modern times. This we do not admit. Soldiers in a vast camp covering many miles of plain and forest can see but little of what is passing around them, and hear only the voices of their immediate neighbors. Those who come after us will be like people looking down from a lofty vantage-ground on camp and battle-field, taking in at a glance whole armies and their positions, and marking the actions of the most heroic. A hundred years hence the names of the saintly in life will be brought out distinctly in the annals of God's Church by the action of the Spirit of Truth, who abideth with her evermore. And who can say how many heroic souls may thus shine forth resplendently from what seems to our near-sightedness a mass of undistinguishable mediocrity?

A Poor Mother and Her Two Noble Orphans.

Take the facts in this short narrative as illustrating one instance of true motherly love, rewarded by heroism in very young children.

A lady of high social position, but far higher in God's favor, rich in charity and in all the merits of manifold good works, but not overburdened with worldly wealth, was summoned away from the head of her table and the delightful conversation of her large family by a pressing case of want. "A little boy, weeping bitterly for his dead mother, was"—so the servant said—"asking for the good lady in the reception-room." She went to him without a moment's delay, heard the pitiable tale which the child's stifled sobs made more eloquent than any words, and without going back to the dinner-table, she hastily got ready to accompany the little mourner. On the way to the house of death the lady was struck by his beautiful features, his air of gentility and good-breeding, as well as by the scrupulous neatness of his poor threadbare clothing.

She was ushered into an upper room, where some neighboring women had already washed and laid out the corpse,—a young woman about thirty, seemingly, on whose thin emaciated features dwelt, together with the awful beauty and serenity which the Angel of Death bestows, a purity and delicacy of outline that bespoke good blood, and that sweet radiance which the joy of a happy soul leaves behind on its companion clay, as the sure pledge of a blissful resurrection. There was a little girl between five and six, most fair and angelic to look upon, dressed scantily, but with the same neatness that was apparent in her brother's clothing,—while the room and its furniture all wore the same air of exquisite neatness and tidiness. It was evident that the surplus articles had been parted with, one after the other, to support life and pay the doctor's bill.

The lady was deeply touched by all she saw, and drawn at once to the two fatherless and motherless orphans. She embraced them tenderly, provided for all their immediate wants, furnished everything necessary for a decent funeral, and then took counsel with her husband as to how the two children should be disposed of.

They were of Anglo-Irish parentage. Their father, unfortunate in business at home, had come to New York with the hope of improving his fortunes. But overwork, a severe cold, and a climate of extremes had brought on rapid consumption, and he died, leaving his children penniless and his wife heart-broken. She bore up bravely, however, doing with her needle whatever she could to keep a temporary home above her orphans, and devoting daily a specified time to their education. Her noble boy, William, beginning his eleventh year, was to her both a great comfort and a great help. He did all her errands and most of her marketing,—for, alas, the double hardship of her lot told speedily on a very delicate constitution, and it became soon but too evident that she was about to follow her husband.

Too proud and independent to seek or to accept aid from the humble families of her poor neighborhood, she parted with everything but the most indispensable articles; and then the end came.

No sooner was the funeral over, than steps were taken to have William complete his schooling, and his little sister sent to an institution where she would be cared for and brought up by one of our admirable Sisterhoods. When, however, Willie was informed of his kind protectress's intention, he was overwhelmed with grief, and besought the lady in the most piteous terms not to separate him from his sister. "She is all I have in the world," he said: "I can work for her. If I only had a few dollars, with a basket, some books and pamphlets, or other things, I might go about selling. I could earn money enough to support us both after a few weeks... Only try me, dear madam," the manly little fellow pleaded; "and if you will only be kind to us, and see my little sister every day, I know God will bless me. My dear mama promised me He would; and oh! I know she is praying for us both in heaven..." How could he be refused? Besides, both the lady and her husband saw here a character so noble, a spirit so manly and self-reliant, and so pious withal, that they at once resolved to foster these admirable dispositions. The house-rent was paid three months in advance, a supply of fuel and provisions was laid in; and the furniture was made more comfortable for the little ones, warm clothing and linen was purchased for both, and Willie got his basket well stocked with all the articles which he was likely to dispose of. His delight was as unbounded as his gratitude.

His benefactress, on her way to early mass one morning, called in to see her interesting charge. The children were up, the room was swept and clean as a new pin; the little tea-kettle was singing on a bright fire, and the little table for two was covered with a snow-white cloth, with bread and butter waiting for young appetites. As the lady entered and took all this in at a glance, Willie was standing over his little sister, chatting merrily with her while he combed her long golden locks. It was a pretty picture, and went to the heart of the true woman who stood looking at the pair.

Another morning a lady of the family called about the same hour, and found the brave-hearted boy washing his sister's white apron! For he could not bear to have her wear anything soiled. Indeed, the boy's spirit of self-respect and independence had led him to resolve to wash his own and her linen till such time as they could afford to pay for the washing.

The story of these little orphans was soon known among their benefactress's large circle of acquaintance, and many were ready to befriend and assist them. Still she thought it better to spare the praiseworthy pride of the boy, and help him quietly to make his own way to fortune. He was sent to a night-school, and himself and his sister were taken on Sundays to the home of their generous friend, where every one vied to teach them, and make them happy. The mistress of the home allowed some of her lady friends the privilege of replenishing Willie's basket from time to time. And so the boy prospered. His delight was inconceivable to be able thus to support his little sister, while she, emulating his generosity of spirit, kept steadily to her room, locking the door against all intruders, learning to keep the fire burning brightly for Willie's return, watering the flowers on the windows, and applying with her whole heart to improve herself in reading. And was there not an angel there, albeit invisible to the bodily eye, who knew how to whisper bright thoughts and sweet hopes to the childish soul,—the germs of future noble aspirations and generous deeds?

In this way several months elapsed, when a letter came from England informing the orphans that they had been left a very handsome fortune. They parted weeping from her who had been to them a second mother: who knows but ere she dies she may yet have glorious tidings of Willie and his sister?

Let Your Sons Be God-Fearing and Self-Reliant.

We pause here. There is no home that our voice can reach in which this simple lesson may not be thoroughly appreciated by even the most poverty-stricken, and taken to heart by her sons, if the mother will only understand aright her own best interests even in this world. No man is braver than the God-fearing man, no man has more self-respect and true self-reliance. Were we to succeed in making the sons of our laboring poor to be at once God-fearing and self-reliant, we should not begrudge devoting to the illustration of these noble qualities every hour of life God may spare us,—so deeply are we convinced that the fear of God is the strong foundation of all true manliness, and that one of the most precious attributes of Christian manhood is that humble self-reliance springing from the certainty of His ever-present grace and the continual generous sense of duty.

We resume our teaching in this chapter, by repeating that if mothers will only be faithful to co-operate with the Holy Spirit in this great work of making of their sons true children of God, together with the natural "great qualities and admirable talents" bestowed on them by the Creator, the culture we have been detailing will be sure to result in producing noble Christian men and model citizens. Every one who will know a son of yours brought up in this fashion will say of him in life and death: "I find in him these virtues without which all (natural) excellence is deformity,—namely, modesty, meekness, tranquillity, religion, sanctity, and integrity." What a panegyric such praise would be both for mother and for son!

No less perfect and admirable would be the women sent forth from every home in our midst. Let young girls take the following words, as they would a nosegay of rarest and sweet-scented flowers, and enjoy again and again their delicious perfume:

"All virtue lies in woman, and the health of the world. God has created nothing so good as a woman. No one can find a limit to the praise of women.

He who can tell where the sunshine ends may also proclaim the end of their praise. Women are pure and good and fair, they impart worthiness and make men worthy. Nothing is so like the angels as their beautiful form, and even the mind of an angel dwells in woman."[54]

Truth in Action Inseparable from the Profession of Truth.

To your sons and daughters alike,—to such noble young men and women as the Church expects you to prepare for society, we commend these golden words of one of the greatest men of all time, and the loveliest saint of modern times:[55]

"For all the estates of Savoy and France, and for the whole empire, I would not carry a false paper in my bosom. I belong to the blood of the ancient Gauls. What is on my tongue is precisely what comes from my heart. The prudence of the world and the artifices of the flesh belong to the children of the world; but the children of God have no double meaning and no dissimulation."

Or, again: "The spirit of chivalry (common to all true Christian men and women) is to the highest degree delicate and susceptible: once convince it that an action is base and criminal, and it shrinks from it with a depth of moral feeling such as leads the poet in the Indian legend to represent sin as something so incapable of concealment that every transgression is not only known to conscience and to all divine spirits, but felt with a sympathetic shudder by those elements themselves which we call inanimate, by the sun, moon, fire, air, the heavens, the earth, the flood, and the deep, as a crying outrage against nature and a disarrangement of the universe."[56]

---

[54] Ulrich von Lichtenstein's *Frauendienst*.

[55] St. Francis of Sales.

[56] Digby.

CHAPTER XVI.

DUTIES OF THE MISTRESS OF THE HOME TOWARD HER PARENTS AND HER SERVANTS.

The sons of Wisdom are the church of the just; and their generation, obedience and love... He that honoreth his mother is as one that layeth up a treasure. He that honoreth his father shall have joy in (his own) children... He that feareth the Lord honoreth his parents, and will serve them as his masters that brought him into the world.

Ecclesiasticus iii.

In the house of a just man living by faith, and still journeying far from the Celestial City, even he who commands is the servant of those whom he seems to command; for he does not rule through a passion for domineering, but through the desire of fulfilling his duty; not through the pride of authority, but through the mercy of providing for others.

ST. AUGUSTINE.

If thou have a faithful servant, let him be to thee as thy own soul: treat him as a brother.

Ecclesiasticus xxxiii. 31.

I.

It will not, we trust, be deemed superfluous if we close these chapters treating of the dignity and the duties of the mistress of the home as wife and mother, by reminding her that she stands herself in the relation of child to those who are her own or her husband's parents. Marriage among us, and by virtue of the laws which govern us, dissolves the tie of obedience which children till then owed to their parents. But the obligation of reverence and love remains through life.

The patriarchal system, which prevailed in the first ages of the world, made the parental authority much more absolute and persistent: the married groups, though living outside of the patriarch's home, continued none the less to pay him, as long as he lived, not only love and reverence, but entire obedience. That his wife had her full share of his authority there is every reason to believe, though it was restricted to the sphere of purely domestic duties. There remains, however, among one of the most ancient races on earth, the Chinese, laws and customs dating from time immemorial, which throw no little light on the probable nature and extent of maternal authority and influence in the remotest historical times.

The ancient laws of China give a father the fullest power over his children,—all power, indeed, save that of life and death,—and this power lasts as long as life, and follows the children in every position or rank they may occupy. The son of a peasant may become a mandarin, the governor of a province, a prime minister, a commander-in-chief; but the son, though never so far in rank and social position above his parents, is still bound to the same rigorous obedience, the same duties of reverence and filial piety.

A commander-in-chief will come down from horseback in presence of his whole army to do homage to his father or mother, a magistrate will descend from his seat of authority as soon as he perceives his parent in the audience. In the imperial court the person most honored and revered by sovereign and courtiers alike, is the emperor's mother. And this holds good in every family, high or low, in the kingdom; the parents are the absolute sovereigns of their own little home-empire.[57]

This universal reverence for parental authority is the very basis of social and domestic life, as well as of the political constitution of this vast empire, comprising one-third of the entire human race. And second only to this deep-seated filial piety is the respect for old age.

"Honor as you would your own father, whoever is twice as old as yourself, and respect, as if he were your elder brother, the man who is ten years older than you." Such is the prescription of the *Li-ki*, the great Chinese Ritual. Hence natives of that country will bestow the title of *lao-yeh*, "venerable father," on every man whom they wish to treat with respect.

---

[57] See most instructive details, in F. Le Play's *Ouvriers des Deux Mondes*, vol. iv., p. 116. Paris, 1862.

Again, when a man has rendered illustrious services to his country, or deserved in any way to be raised to the rank of noble, the rank is conferred on his parents, not on himself. "The reason is," says the *Li-ki*, "that we easily persuade ourselves that the parents of a virtuous man must have been themselves models of virtue."

"The more I consider," says the Emperor Kang-hi, "the principles which induced the ancient emperors to govern the world by the sentiments of filial piety, the more am I convinced that they wished thereby to go back to the original form of government, and to insist on what is essential to it. Filial piety is the principle and the term of all virtue."[58]

This reverence for father and mother is also the foundation of the Chinese religion. It is the center of public and private worship. "The hall of ancestors," says the *Li-ki*, "is the first structure erected when a palace is built, the vases destined to the commemoration of the dead are the first to be purchased: no matter how poor one may be, one must not sell these vases, nor cut down the cemetery trees." At Pekin, in the ancient "red city," still stands the Taï-miao, a spacious temple covered with red brick, and dedicated to the ancestors of the reigning family. And in the remotest provinces of the empire an apartment may be found in the peasant's hut, appropriated to a like purpose.

We have gone out of the beaten path of illustration to show how ancient, wide-spread, and deep-seated is this beautiful sentiment of filial piety, the religion of the sweetest and holiest gratitude.

No mother who is true to nature but will, as age advances, and as her dear parents draw near the grave, exert herself to show them all love, honor, and reverence. In the last chapter we have shown her how necessary it is to impress these sentiments on the heart of her children. Let her believe it;—it is her own interest we were then pleading. And it is her own happiness we wish to promote by what we say here. The young and active and energetic mother of to-day will be the aged, feeble, helpless invalid of to-morrow,—to whom the loving looks and loving words, the heartfelt reverence and veneration of her dear ones, will be the sweetest of all rewards.

One can have a father and a mother but once: while they are yet with us we prize not as we ought the treasure their presence is to us, and we often allow

[58] Quoted by Le Play, *ibidem*, p. 122.

the preoccupations and pangs of the day to make us overlook the duty of giving ourselves heartily to making them comfortable and happy. We hope to be in a better mood on the morrow. But that morrow never comes with the hoped-for opportunities, and brings with the grief of their loss the keen regret of having neglected those who never neglected us.

In the Chinese family, most minutely described in the work mentioned above, "the most striking characteristic, as indeed in all Chinese families, is the respect shown to parental authority. The elder brother maintains this duty most rigorously by his own example. At table he never tastes food till his mother has done so; and he respectfully offers her, first of all, every fresh fruit or vegetable on the board. From his children he receives in turn these same marks of respectful deference, the omission of which would be considered a crime. While a father may beat his son, no matter how old the latter may be, the son, from the age of sixteen upward, never calls his parents by any other name than *dajun*, 'my lords.'"

We do not insist on the practical conclusions to be drawn from all this. Will parents exact from their children some such show of respect as this? Will they so demean themselves toward their dear ones, from the earliest infancy of the latter, that this respect may be well merited and heartily accorded? Will they, especially, practice toward their own parents this fundamental and sovereign duty of love and reverence? Surely, if there be a country on the face of the globe, in which this sentiment of reverence is fast dying out from heart and home and social life, it is the country in which we live,—so proud of its Christian name and its advanced civilization, but in the appreciation and practice of the beautiful home-virtues infinitely below the heathens of China.

Never Put Yourselves in Your Children's Power.

We formulate our advice this way, in order that all our readers may examine their consciences on this point.

"Give not," says the Divine Book, "to son or wife, brother or friend, power over thee while thou livest; and give not thy estate to another, lest thou repent and thou entreat for the same. As long as thou livest and hast breath in thee, let no man change (dispossess) thee. For it is better that thy children should ask of thee, than that thou look toward the hands of thy children."[59]

There are but too many eloquent examples around us of the unwisdom of parents who heed not the voice of the inspired teacher; of parents who left native land and gave a whole life of earnest and uninterrupted labor to making a fortune and creating a comfortable home for their children,—slaving and almost starving themselves to give them education and a position, and whose great heart could not withhold their hands from giving their dear ones every thing with the new homes in which they saw them wedded and well to do. And how many such fathers and mothers have been and are still left to pine in neglect and poverty by the very children they loved all too unwisely!

"A wise son maketh a father joyful: but the foolish man despiseth his mother. Honor thy father in work and word, and all patience. That a blessing may come upon thee from him, and his blessing may remain in the latter end. The father's blessing establisheth the houses of the children: but the mother's curse rooteth up the foundation. Of what an evil fame is he that forsaketh his father! And he is accursed of God that angereth his mother!"[60]

The real practical difficulty in the way regards not so much, perhaps, a woman's reverence toward her own parents, as what is due to those of her husband. Nor does the discharge of this duty offer so much hardship when parents retain their own home, and are independent of their married children. Heart-burnings mainly arise when they have to look to these for support,—and often become unbearable when they have to reside beneath the same roof.

Then it is that the mistress of the household needs to look up to God for her motives and her rules of action. We put aside the case of women who are so unnatural and so unchristian as to forget what is due to their own aged parents, to their husbands, and the venerable persons to whom these owe their birth, and, it may be, the very roof which covers the ungrateful wife. A husband's father and mother become, by marriage, the wife's father and mother; policy, mere worldly wisdom and practical good sense, in the absence of the divine law, ought to teach her that her peace and her interest would be best secured by loving her parents-in-law.

[59] Ecclesiasticus xxxiii. 20, 21, 22.

[60] *Ibidem*, iii.

We suppose the mother who reads this is most anxious to have God's blessing, the love and respect of her husband and children; all this she can only have by showing a true and heartfelt affection for the persons who stand, within her home, as the representatives of God's fatherly power and love. No blessing can rest upon a home where the wife and mother makes life a burden and the bread of life most bitter to the parents she is privileged to have near her.

To encourage all good mothers,—women true to the noblest instincts of nature and the most solemn teaching of the divine law, let us rather warm our hearts in the light of heroic examples,—such as very many in all classes may behold around them daily.

Two young people, of excellent family both of them, had married, with the full approbation of the wife's parents, who were wealthy and much respected, but sorely against the will of those of the husband, of his mother especially.

There was perfect equality on both sides. But the young man, during a tour on the continent of Europe, had embraced the Catholic faith, and this circumstance, on his return home, had led to his intimacy with the family into which he married. Bitter religious prejudice lay at the bottom of the opposition made by both his parents, while his mother persisted in saying to every one that he had been inveigled into a change of religion by his beautiful bride. The truth was, that the young people had scarcely been acquainted when the change took place, and there certainly was then no attachment on either side.

The young man was disinherited; but this cruel treatment did not shake either his faith or his affection. He was further driven to hasten his nuptials by a cruel and scandalous report concerning the lady, started, too, by his own mother. Never was scandal so unfounded and so malignant.

But it only injured the originators. The innocent child herself was kept in total ignorance of the rumor, and the other relatives of the gentleman's family vied with each other in showing their detestation of the slander.

The bridegroom was too high-minded to beg favors from his bigoted father, and too independent to accept from his father-in-law the handsome settlement which the latter wished to make in his favor. He had a good and lucrative profession; he was himself accomplished, self-reliant, and trustful in God's protection; he loved his young wife with that deep love of pure hearts which is deepened tenfold by the grace of the sacrament. And, not rashly confident of his own ability, he fixed his residence in a large city far away from his native place. Success came to him with the divine blessing, which they both sought so earnestly, and year after year he rose higher and higher in his profession and in the esteem of all who knew him. His wife looked up to him with a sort of worship, founded on the intimate knowledge of his worth,—of the talents and learning which were sanctified by a piety so enlightened and so simple. No home could be happier than theirs—no bliss, the little wife and mother thought, could equal hers. She was afraid of its very excess,—and begged our dear Lord daily to send her a cross which should temper the unalloyed sweetness of her lot. It came in His good time.

She had been several years married, when an accident made her acquainted with the scandal about herself set afloat by her mother-in-law. Its real malignity, however, only dawned on her by degrees, and thus the terrible force of the blow was broken. Nevertheless it nearly crushed her; and it required all her husband's tenderness and all her own piety and strength of soul to sustain her. She had a very serious illness; for the rumor in its worst aspect only reached her a very short time after the birth of her second child. While she was thus in serious danger, her husband wrote to his father informing him of the critical state to which the innocent young wife was brought by an infamous slander originating with his own mother.

The father, who had not lost all feeling for his son, and who, besides, was proud of his rising fame, was heart-stricken on receiving the letter. He had heard of the report against his daughter-in-law, but never fancied that the vile slander had his own wife for author. He for one did not and could not believe it. His fault lay in his bigotry, his exaggerated notions about a father's authority over his son's conscience, and in the obstinacy with which he adhered to a determination once taken. From every direction he had heard his daughter-in-law praised for every quality of mind and heart and person, for all the sweet virtues that can make a perfect woman, wife, and mother; and more than once he felt disposed to relent toward his son. The letter filled him with equal grief and indignation.

But his wife only met his reproof and his questions with haughty scorn and a fiercer denunciation of her son, as a most ungrateful child, and of his sick wife as a crafty, scheming hypocrite. Leaving his partner to the evil passions that possessed her, he hastened to his son's home, atoned with manly frankness for his own harsh conduct, embraced his daughter and her babes with all a father's tenderness, assured the patient sufferer that no one among all his kinsfolk or acquaintance ever gave credit to the absurd report, and by his generous reparation recalled the sick one to health and happiness once more. His wife, he said, would not delay to see the wrong she had done and to atone for it, and thus the happiness of his children seemed complete.

But the inevitable atonement was to be made sooner than he anticipated, and in a way that he could not foresee. During his absence his house—the ancient home of his family—was burned to the ground. No one could tell how the fire began; and as it was in the country, with a high wind blowing at the time, no effort of servants or neighbors availed to save the building, with its precious furniture and library. The mistress of the house was, it was said, herself severely injured in the confusion.

These tidings reached her husband when halfway on his homeward journey, and seemed to his conscience like a judgment on his wife's unnatural cruelty and his own harshness and obstinacy. No sooner, however, had his son and daughter-in-law heard of the calamity, than the latter, with the impulse of true charity, besought her husband to fly at once to his parents, and to bring his mother back with him, that she might receive from their hands all the tender care her misfortune and injuries needed.

With what eagerness the young husband hastened to comply with his wife's God-inspired entreaty, the Christian reader will easily conceive. He found his mother only slightly bruised, though sorely afflicted in spirit. The hand of God, in striking her in its justice, had also touched her heart in its mercy. She had done many acts of true charity in her life, and these now pleaded for her with that Wisdom which disposeth all our ways for its own ends.

No mother ever received from the most tenderly loved child so warm a welcome as she received from her daughter-in-law. It was truly a merciful dispensation. Soon after the burning of his mansion, the sturdy old gentleman learned that the bulk of his fortune, invested in what had till then been a most prosperous venture, had been utterly swept away by the failure of the concern. This news brought on a fit of apoplexy. He lingered, half-paralyzed, in his son's house, where the most devoted care of his angelic daughter-in-law, and all the comforting assurances of his son, availed not to raise the crushed spirit. He died under the effects of a second stroke of the fell disease, but not till he had again and again prophesied to the angel who watched by him night and day, that she would surely be blessed in her children. "You are more than a perfect woman, my love," he would say; "you are an angel, and the very atmosphere of your house is heavenly." So he passed away, finding in death what he had not else known, the perfect road which leads to God, and that perfect peace which worlds cannot purchase.

His widow survived him for several years. She was given time to expiate her sin. A cruel cancer in the neck tried her patience to the utmost and proved the generosity of the daughter she had so deeply wronged, and whom she had learned to love with a love she had never known till then. Month after month did that devoted one and her husband lavish on their parent every mark of the most untiring affection. The side of the house in which her apartment was, had to be given up to her, so nauseating was the odor which the frightful sore emitted. Yet her room was kept like a paradise. One of the young wife's sisters, worthy of her in every way, volunteered to assist her in taking care of the sufferer. She, too, felt like her husband, that this was true charity, and wished to die in the faith of her forefathers. She needed all the sublime consolations which it imparts. For the priest who ministered to her frequently in the last stage of the terrible disease, often declared afterward that, accustomed as he was to every form of human suffering, he never had beheld anything comparable to the appalling loathsomeness of that death-bed.

And yet there the heroic son would remain with his parent, hour after hour, reading her some sweet passage from the "Imitation of Christ," a few verses from the history of the Passion, or reciting with the agonized patient some favorite form of prayer. There, too, the angelic forms of his wife and sister-in-law moved about silently, whispering from their pure, brave hearts such words of love and comfort as true women's hearts alone can find.

"Read me these beautiful words once more," she could barely say in an almost imperceptible whisper to her daughter-in-law, as midnight on Good Friday was at hand. Her son was absent on most urgent business, and no one was in the sick-room but the devoted little wife. And she read from the "Imitation" the 21st chapter of the third book, beginning: "Above all things and in all things, do thou, my soul, rest always in the Lord, for he is the eternal rest of the saints." When the other had read down to the words, "In fine, above all angels and archangels, and all the host of heaven," the dying woman pressed the hand held in hers. Then, as the other looked up, she motioned to her to continue, and just as the last words, "above all that is not Thee, my God!" she repeated thrice audibly, while a light seemed to overspread her features, "Thee,—Thee,—my God,—my God!" and expired.

II.
Duties Toward Servants.

It would be a strange inconsistency if a truly Christian mistress, fearing God herself, and making his love and service the chief purpose of her life, should fail to be toward her servants much more of the mother than the mistress.

Among God's people, before the coming of Christ, though the servants in the family were either slaves belonging to the master, or free men and women who had bound themselves to temporary service, the heads of the household were obliged not only to treat these dependents with humanity, but to secure to them all the precious benefits of the faith and hope in the Redeemer. Thus the true religion formed a bond of brotherhood between the inferiors and the superiors. Under Christianity slavery was gradually done away with by the very force of the doctrine and sentiment of brotherhood working on heart and mind among all classes.

The beautiful sentiment of Ecclesiasticus, "If thou have a faithful servant, let him be to thee as thy own soul: treat him as a brother,"—sounds almost like some gospel precept. But this last verse in the chapter is preceded by several injunctions or practical rules concerning stubborn or vicious servants, that a slave-master might easily pervert to his own purposes.

St. Paul and the Fugitive Slave.

Compare with this the divine charity which shines forth in St. Paul's Epistle to Philemon. This man, a citizen of Colossæ in Phrygia, and a convert to Christianity, had a slave called Onesimus, who fled from his master to Rome, after having wronged him in some serious manner. In the great city the fugitive came within the influence of St. Paul, then imprisoned, but left a certain freedom to preach the gospel and help in spreading it among all those who had recourse to him. Onesimus became not only a convert, but a most zealous and efficient assistant to the great apostle. For, in these days, the fortunes of war reduced the vanquished to bondage, and thus men of the noblest birth and the highest culture were brought down to the condition of slaves. Onesimus, apparently, was anxious or willing to repair the wrong he had committed toward his master; at any rate, he consented to fulfill the prescriptions of the civil law, which compelled the return of fugitive slaves to their masters.

But in the case of Onesimus, the conversion to Christianity of both master and slave entirely changed the sentiments with which each regarded the other,—although it did not do away formally with the power of the former over the latter. So the aged Paul, from his prison, sends back Onesimus to Colossæ, intrusting to him a letter or epistle for the young church springing up in that city, and another to Philemon in commendation of the bearer himself.

"Paul, a prisoner of Christ Jesus,...to Philemon our beloved and fellow-laborer... Though I have much confidence in Christ Jesus to command thee that which is to the purpose: for charity's sake I rather beseech, whereas thou art such an one, as Paul an old man, and now a prisoner also of Jesus Christ: I beseech thee for my son, whom I have begotten in my bonds, Onesimus... Do thou receive him as my own bowels (my own heart)... Not now as a servant, but instead of a servant, a most dear brother, especially to me... If therefore thou count me a partner, receive him as myself."

The Doctrine of Universal Brotherhood in Christ.

This was a language never heard before. The sentiments it expresses, the great doctrines of universal brotherhood and a common calling to the inheritance, with Christ, of an eternal glory, leavened thenceforward the hearts and minds of men, and changed the face of the world. In our day there are found men who would set aside this divine brotherhood and all its humanizing influences, and bring back the reign of the darkest Pagan materialism. Christian homes and hearts sanctified by all the charities which a living faith in Christ begets, must be the firm bulwark against this impure and rising tide.

Imperious Necessity of Winning the Hearts of One's Servants.

It behooves every Christian mistress and mother, as she loves her own children, and labors to make them live up to the sublime duties of their religion, even so to love her servants dependent on her motherly charity, and looking to her, under God, for instruction, edification, care, and comfort in health and sickness.

Later, in a separate chapter, we shall see what are the special duties to be fulfilled by servants themselves, and the special excellence to which they can attain. Be it sufficient in this place to hold the mirror of her own duty up to the true woman, so that she can see in it the model of a perfect mistress, as we have already shown her the image of a perfect wife and mother.

How Servants Should Be Bound to Their Masters.

"I have collected certain instructions," says an old author,—"and composed almost an art of friendship between rich and powerful men and persons poor and of low condition, to whom has been applied the odious name of servitude. What domain is more fertile than domestic charity? Is it not better that our house should be in the charge of true friends of good will, rather than in that of men who evince, I do not say love, but not even the shadow of love? Such servants have only one object—to steal and get rich as soon as possible; but if you lift them up into the sphere of friendship, of free and kindly regard, what immense utility shall we not derive from their assistance? For then they love their masters tenderly, spare no pains, and expose themselves to all dangers for them. This friendship, if we do not trample humanity under our feet by our pride,...will certainly spring up of itself and increase; for nothing is more natural than to love those who dwell under the same roof with us; and, certes, nothing can happen more advantageous to a man than to live in the same household with another man, when of suitable manners."[61]

---

[61] Della Casa, "Treatise on Duties."

The Golden Rule.

"I knew a lady, who now lives in heaven," says Luis de Leon; "the persons who served her never left her without being prized the more for having lived with her. It happened once that she was obliged to dismiss one of her servants without having done him all the good that she desired, and I often heard her say, that she was disconsolate at the thought of a person, once intrusted to her by God, departing from her house without having been benefited by the stay."[62]

Unquestionably these are the ideas by which every head of a household ought to be governed in her relations with her servants. They are "intrusted by God" to her that she may do them all the good she can, and make them in every way as good as she can. They are a charge committed to her, not to be kept in the ignorance and moral deficiencies with which they came to her service, but to be improved in every way not merely for the sole motive of self-interest, as Della Casa suggests, but because they are a trust for which we must be accountable to God.

Aim High in Performing Your Duty.

We know by our sad experience that we seldom succeed when we aim high in hitting the mark we aim at. We fail in our best and calmest resolutions to do exactly as well as we purposed; indeed, it is to the most generous a constant source of regret and self-reproach that their performances fall short of the promises made to their own soul.

In the performance of one's duty toward one's servants, then, how can one best secure a high degree of merit and a great amount of good done to them? The first extract we gave exhorts masters and mistresses to make "friends" of their servants and dependants,—because "then they love their masters tenderly, spare no pains, and expose themselves to all dangers for them." This attachment being based on a motive of self-interest, may not be either very lasting or very exalted. There are servants deeply attached to vicious masters, because the attachment is founded on community of enjoyments, pursuits,

[62] Quoted by Digby.

and vices. We shall secure a more exalted, permanent, and purer friendship, and a more loyal and generous service, by following the practice of the noble Spanish lady mentioned by Luis de Leon,—by considering every servant who enters our household as a needy brother sent us by the Shepherd of souls,—that we may receive the stranger as we would Christ himself, that we may guard that soul, and respect it, as we would the Body taken down from the cross and given over to our care, or the pierced Heart taken from out the yawning side. This is the model,—the only practical rule to set before ourselves,—to keep the deposit of that precious soul sent to us, as we would keep the sacred treasure of Christ's heart.

Consider Each Servant's Soul as a Sacred Deposit.

What would you think good enough as a repository for such a treasure? What gold could be refined enough to inclose it? What gems so rare or valuable as to be fit to adorn it?

What precautions would be taken to prevent profanation or defilement? But let us apply this ideal rule, supplied by the charity of Paul in chains for Christ, to the real need of your servants.

The Spanish lady considered that every servant sent to her by Providence had to be dealt with as a child of her own;—loved and reverenced as a thing which had been saved from the eternal death by the utmost love and agony of the Sacred Heart, purchased by all the blood it contained. The soul of each was in her eyes therefore of equal value to the infinite price it cost, and to be cherished accordingly. Wherefore was that soul thus confided to her? that she might merely keep it from evil, from sin? That surely;—but not that alone. She was, moreover, instructed by her faith to do all the good in her power to that soul, and to make that soul as good as she could.

Hence "she was disconsolate at the thought of a person once intrusted to her by God departing from her house without having been benefited by the stay therein."

There is no Catholic woman but will immediately take in the full meaning of this lesson. It is a magnificent one; and let us not part with it too speedily. Look you, when a bee on a summer morning lights on a garden filled with sweet flowers and untouched by a single sister-bee, she thinks not of returning to the hive until she has taken her fill of honey. Nay, she will go back again and again to that privileged spot, till not one flower is left that has not been rifled of its treasure.

Lofty Views of Duty in Catholic Spain.

Let us be wise after this fashion, and thus draw from these pregnant truths of our holy faith all the honey they contain. No nation ever surpassed the Spanish in the lofty sentiments which they conceived of Christian duty. The noble poet, who is the Shakespeare of that nation, with more than Shakespeare's elevation and purity, and none of his sad blemishes, makes a servant say to his ungrateful master: "Consider that I have always served you well, and that negligence is not a crime with a Catholic Christian."

And why was negligence a crime unknown to Spanish servants, if not because neglect of the welfare of servants,—either spiritual or temporal,—was a thing unheard of among Spanish masters and mistresses. Elsewhere[63] we have seen with what respect and reverence the Spaniards treat the poor, the beggar, and the sick. We must be prepared, therefore, to find them extending to their household servants and dependants the same feeling of honor and true friendship.

How Servants Were Treated in All Catholic Countries.

Nor was this religious sentiment of brotherhood and equality in Christ confined to the Spanish peninsula; it reigned throughout all Christian nations. In every princely and noble family lived a chaplain, whose special care and duty it was to devote himself to the spiritual welfare of the servants and dependants, to instruct them thoroughly in the Christian doctrine, and to afford them every facility and encouragement for the reception of the sacraments, and the advancement in holiness of life. Nor did this dispense the lord and lady from seeing to it in person that the chaplain did his duty, and that their household was one in which God, before and above all things, was served and honored. The Sundays and feasts of obligation were duly sanctified

[63] Chapter VII., pp. 81, 82, 83.

by all; and in more than one country the law of the Church and that of the State enjoined, that, on the eve of these days, servants and others should be allowed to retire early in order to be up in time for Mass the next morning. How many Catholic masters and mistresses sin grievously in this respect in our day and country!

Masters and Mistresses Anxious for the Progress of Their Servants in Holiness.

More than that, in these ages of faith of which modern ignorance and fanaticism speak so sneeringly, all Christian masters and mistresses were anxious that their entire households should have the very same advantages for instruction which they had themselves. St. Paulinus, Archbishop of Aquileia, thus instructs his immediate sovereign, Henry, Duke of Friuli: "Entreat all who are in your house to do whatever they do humbly before God; for whatever a man doeth with pride can never please God. In all their actions let them be humble; for no one can come to the kingdom of God unless by humility. All labors, prayers, alms, fasts, and vigils, if performed with pride, are accounted as nothing before God... Prescribe to all your domestics, and those subject to you, to abstain from pride, and to live temperately, justly, piously, and holily before God; for Christ shed his blood not alone for us clergy, but for the whole human race. There is no acceptation of persons with God; for the celestial palace opens its doors to the laity who keep the divine commandments, as well as the clergy and those who bear the monk's habit; for we are all one in Christ... Love your Head with your whole heart, and the members of that Head. How can the hand hate the hand, or the foot the foot? All the members ought to grow up lovingly together into the perfect man.[64]

This sentiment of Christian equality made masters and mistresses in the highest households call all their servants "children," and the custom still survives in lands where faith and piety have long since waned. More than that,—it was held wise and proper to make both sons and daughters mix with the servants in the performance of the menial household duties. The heroic

[64] Quoted by Digby.

Bayard relates that he had to do so in his father's house; and Marina de Escobar says that her mother, although having a numerous retinue of servants, "used, as a prudent woman, always to make her daughters apply to domestic exercises, along with the maids."

The Charity of the Mistress Begets Love in the Servants.

Where the old Catholic spirit, the true spirit of Christian charity, reigns in a household—thanks to a pious and zealous mistress—servants cannot fail to become attached to their masters, to consider themselves as members of the family, having the same interests, affections, hopes, and fears, as they have the same faith, returning love for love in view of him who is the Elder Brother of us all. Our ancestors were not fond of changing servants, precisely because the servants were not fond of changing masters. The charity which bound together the entire household was utterly opposed to the selfishness of our times. Our grandmothers had a saying which we would heartily commend to the meditation of their daughters and granddaughters: "The herb one knows, one ought to tie well to one's finger."

An author of the early part of the last century cites, for the instruction of after-ages, an example of this mutual attachment of servants and masters. "What a charm," says he, "when masters and servants grow old together! What a joy to old age, when it is served by ancient domestics, accustomed to its mode of life! There are families thus favored. I have known no house happier in this respect than that of the great Séguier, Chancellor of France. All his servants had grown old with him; so that if one did not always see the same faces, one saw always the same persons. As their constitutions were not so strong as his own, most of them broke down on the way; and he saw them perish before himself, leaving but little behind them, though after forty years service in the house of a chancellor. All this must be regarded as a part of the felicity of this great man, adding to the sweetness of his old age."[65]

---

[65] Le Baron de Prelle, *Considérations sur les avantages de la Vieillesse dans la Vie Chrétienne*, p. 314. Quoted by Digby.

The Tie of Charity Loosened in Modern Society.

Certain it is, that the spectacle offered in any of our cities, when, in answer to an advertisement for a servant, hundreds of ill-clad, half-starved, and most uncomely-looking creatures besiege the door of the advertiser, and crowd the street and the sidewalk,—was a thing unseen and unheard of a century ago, even in European countries, far less in this New World of ours. It is a sight which might have been witnessed near the great marble palace of one of our prince merchants twenty-four hours before this was written; and it is a sad commentary on the Christian charity which is supposed to govern the relations of masters and servants in this land of fraternity and equality.

How is this gulf, which selfishness and uncharitableness have opened between the wealthy and the poor,—between the class which counts masters and mistresses, and the poor who have to serve and to work, to be housed and fed and clothed,—this gulf which unbelief and radicalism are deepening and widening with all their splendid theories about humanity and fraternity and equality,—how is this gulf to be filled up or bridged over? By the hearts of true Christian women!

How Kind and Charitable Mistresses Can Prevent Socialism.

Your influence, your action within your homes and outside,—on your servants, on the poor and sick, on your own daughters,—on all minds and hearts that come within reach of your voice, within the magnetic circle of your goodly deeds,—all this will help to heal the wounded hearts into which the hatred of the rich, of the Church, of religion, of God himself, is every day sinking deeper.

Say not what can one woman do,—but say what could not all true women do, if each within her home were to kindle in her own heart the fire which Christ came down on earth to kindle? Fire like that cannot be kept hidden within the vessel that contains it. God intended it to burst forth and warm and inflame all hearts that come near it. The days are coming,—nay, they are at hand, when the very men in whose souls that dreadful hatred we have just mentioned will be the only religion. Ministers of the Christian faith will have no influence over these mortally sick souls. Their voice will not be listened to, their authority will be derided, and their interference repelled like an insult or a crime. But you, women, you, mothers—will still be God's instruments for staying this dreadful plague, and restoring to Christ and to charity all their influence. This is the mission in which the Church will employ you.

An Illustration of True Women's Influence.

Say not, then, what can women do? Travelers over our southern seas tell us of the manner in which a tiny little insect, called the coral insect, prevents the last traces of submerged continents from disappearing forever beneath the waves. These worlds, sunk beneath the ocean surface long, long ages ago, left visible here and there only a few of the crests of their highest mountains, and by degrees even these were worn down by wind and rain and the ceaseless lashing of the waves. Just when the last summits had passed out of sight, God sent these armies of tiny creatures to labor together and build in the shallow waters which covered the sunken crests these beautiful structures called corals, with their marvelous forms and colors; generation after generation of these little toilers of the deep succeeded in doing what all the might and ingenuity of the race of man could never compass,—they erected structures so solid that the rage of the mightiest storm could neither destroy nor shake them. Higher and higher they rose, till the tide left them bare, and other agencies then came to aid in making an island. Elsewhere existing islands are preserved from the destroying action of the ocean by these same little workers, which build their barriers or walls of coral all round to break the force of the waves, and save the islands with their inhabitants and lovely growth of vegetation.

If God accords such marvelous results to the united action of insects invisible almost to the naked eye, what blessings will he not bestow on mothers laboring within their homes to make husbands, children, servants,—ay, and the neighbors all around,—true children of the living God?

Do all the good you can to the souls God gives you to work upon: if you are a faithful laborer, He will surely give you more,—and this number will go on increasing in proportion to your goodness and the charity burning within.

Practical Rules.

In this spirit you have only to see what are the simple rules taught by experience and which are to guide you in your conduct toward your servants. As in the case of your children, so here impress every one in your service with the conviction that his or her single soul is as dear to you, as if none other claimed your interest and your care. This personal interest in the welfare, the comfort, the progress of every individual in the household, works like a mighty spell. Nor, by kindly inquiring into the concerns of each, will their respect for you be diminished, if you are careful to be kind without being familiar. Servants like their masters to keep a proper distance. We have known the rudest, the most impertinent, and ungovernable, to be tamed and made respectful and well-mannered by this prudent mixture of kind motherly interest and reserve. It is necessary always to address one's servants with a simplicity which is far removed from a proud, imperious tone, but implies a certain degree of regard for them; and still more necessary that they should never be permitted to address their master or mistress, or any member of the family, otherwise than respectfully.

Persons really well bred will never permit themselves either rudeness, haughtiness, or familiarity toward their dependants; and it very rarely happens that these show themselves disposed to be otherwise than respectful toward such masters.

We repeat it, then, take a real interest in each one of your servants.

Encourage Them to Seek Your Advice in Difficulties.

Remember how little of present joy or happiness such persons have outside of what your home affords them. They have had, very many of them, a hard lot in the past; their stay with you may decide of their whole future; they are all gifted with some share of affection, some of them, at least, with warm and deep affections; among these hearts there may be one that is sorely bruised, and which your motherly hand can soothe and heal. Your own womanly tact will not be slow in discovering such as need especial kindness, nay, very great delicacy of treatment. Let them be encouraged to come to you; and let them feel that their secret, whatever it be, is safe with you.

It not unfrequently happens that a certain moodiness or irritability which you perceive in servants, otherwise excellent, arises from concealed grief. There may be a fearful struggle going on against despair beneath that vail of sadness or that cloud of ill-temper. A single kind word from you,—a word from your heart,—will make these clouds dissolve in tears of sweet relief, and the whole soul will be laid bare before you.

Do Not Judge Them Hastily.

Even where there is neglect of duty, be not hasty in condemning or punishing. You will,—if still young,—find out before you die, that the harshest and most pitiless of mistresses, the quickest to think ill of the delinquent, to judge severely, and punish without mercy,—is the woman who is most remiss in the fulfillment of her own sacred duties, and who stands most in need of the mercy of God and man.

When complaints are made, do not lend a willing ear, so as to encourage informers, nor hasten to act upon the information. Let all under you know that you never condemn before inquiring carefully, and that your inquiry is always conducted without noise or partiality.

Surround Your Servants with Objects Which Can Elevate Them.

The feeling of inferiority and dependence, and the nature of the services they render, are, in themselves, sufficient to humble persons who may be naturally proud, high-minded, or sensitive. Do not debase or degrade your servants still further by allotting them rooms to work and sleep in where all is discomfort and meanness. Our forefathers were wont, when the beggar asked for a night's lodging, to give him, in the name of Christ, a place at the common board, a seat near the warm hearth, and a clean and comfortable bed,—all for His dear sake who for us "came unto his own, and his own received him not."

We have just seen that the servant in the Christian household is to be treated as a something holy and precious;—do not, then, while you give warmth and comfort to the passing beggar, and while you lavish luxury and all honor on a guest,—leave the servant who labors for your interest and who is one of your family, to what is as inhospitable as the cavern of Bethlehem,—

as cold and as comfortless and as unclean almost. For there are mistresses who care not how wretchedly furnished may be the miserable garret or cellar in which their servants pass the night, after a hard day's toil.

See you not that the very necessity of accepting such a resting-place is felt as a degradation? And every thing which degrades is remembered as an unpardonable wrong. Let every thing in their sleeping and working rooms tend to elevate them; let there be both cleanliness and comfort; and let the walls be ornamented with such pictures and other simple decorations as may lift mind and heart above the sights and sounds of the street.

Insist on it that their food shall be wholesome and abundant, and that every thing about the meal shall bespeak a motherly care for their health.

Do Not Overburden Them with Work.

Just as persons who have no conscience are harsh and merciless in dealing with the weaknesses and faults of others, even so do persons who have never known what it is to work hard, or work at all, show themselves pitiless or most unreasonable in the amount of labor they expect and exact from their servants. There are, unhappily, but too many masters and mistresses in all large communities, who have more than one trait of resemblance to Sampson and Sarah Brass. Such abominable meanness and hard-heartedness are not, however, consistent with any one Christian virtue in man or woman. Still there is in many households a carelessness and callousness as to the hardships, the diet, and comfort of servants, that result in like suffering to these, and create the same bitter hatred in the sufferers, and call down from a just God the same inevitable retribution.

Where servants are loved and cared for, they work lovingly and conscientiously for their masters, and repay with ample interest the generosity shown by these in providing for the health and comfort of their dependants.

In Sickness Care for Them Tenderly.

Do not send them out of the house when they are ill, unless the disease be a contagious one, and you have near at hand an hospital in which they are sure to be well cared for.

When the sickness has been contracted in serving you faithfully, this care on your part is simply an act of justice. In every case it is a duty imposed by charity; and where the soul of the sufferer needs more tender nursing than even the body, it is far more urgent that you should not give over to others the duty God wishes you to fulfill in person.

During many years of ministration to the sick we have had occasion to witness the unsparing devotion of many mistresses to their sick servants. One instance, that of a generous Protestant lady, did not fall under our own observation, but was related to us by an eye-witness. She was the most distinguished personage in her native city, and her example may serve as an exhortation to many tepid and remiss Catholics.

One of her servants fell ill of a most malignant fever; the nature of the disease and the imminent danger to her large family were clearly pointed out by the physician. The lady, however, had no thought of sending the poor patient away; but made an hospital of one-half of her large mansion, isolating it as far as she could from the rest of the household, and shut herself up with the sufferer, an Irish Catholic girl. She would permit no one but the physician and the priest to enter, all that was needful to herself and her patient being left outside the apartment adjoining the sick-room. Night and day the courageous woman watched over her charge; but it was all in vain. The terrible fever claimed its victim.

The generous mistress bestowed on the dead the same loving care she had lavished on the living. She dressed the corpse in her own raiment, gave orders to have every thing done as if the deceased were one of her daughters, had the body in its beautiful rosewood casket laid out in her best parlor, and invited all the friends and co-religionists of the dead girl to pay their respects to her remains. The funeral was a touching demonstration, attesting by the numbers of those present and by their quality that all appreciated this noble example of Christian charity.

Her daughters and granddaughters inherited together with this self-sacrificing spirit their parent's claim to a still higher grace.

We have quoted in the first part of this chapter the beautiful charity of two sisters to the woman who had wronged them so fearfully; and elsewhere[66] we

---

[66] Page 136.

glanced rapidly at the death-bed of a young martyr of charity. We have seen, in families blessed with parents who deemed the tender care of sick servants an ordinary but most sacred duty, what mother and children can do to make a sick-room delightful. There was no thought of expense, or fatigue, or fastidiousness. The best physicians in the city were in attendance, the most costly articles from the druggist, the grocer, or the market,—the most generous wines when needed, and what was more than all that, a love and untiring care, inspired by true religion, was lavished on the patient even though he or she had only been a few days in the family.

Could it be a matter of surprise that servants living in such a house never could speak of their master or mistress but with tears of gratitude and expressions of heartfelt veneration?

Know How to Praise Your Servants.

This is only the application to your dependants of the rule given with respect to your husband and your children. It is a serious defect in a mistress not to know when and where and how to praise her servants. Praise, however, is a sweet reward, and most coveted, too, by those who labor conscientiously,—a reward often more prized by affectionate and generous natures than the miserable compensation called wages; and it is a most powerful stimulant to the sluggish, the careless, and even the perverse. What transformations have we not seen in school-room and kitchen, and workshop and field, effected in natures hitherto rebellious to all stimulants, by the gentle words of praise bestowed by a wise master or a kind mistress!

We once more remind you that the judicious and generous bestowal of praise is a most beneficial and meritorious almsgiving. It is more than gold or silver to the receiver, and it never impoverishes the giver. Do not stint those who thirst for it. It will be more welcome to many a famished heart than a draught from the cool spring to foot-sore and fainting wayfarer. It will inspire good resolutions and give strength to execute them. It will be like the first steps of that divine ladder which the Patriarch saw reaching from earth to heaven; your kind words will raise the weak soul up one step, or two or three,—thereby showing it that the ascent to higher goodness and virtue is not only possible but sweet. God's angels then will do the rest; and the God of Angels from on high will look down and bless you for the help you have given to the faint-hearted.

And so we have been teaching you to be the teacher, the dispenser, as well as the pattern of goodness. May those who know you, long years hence, say of you as they recall all your gracious words and deeds!

> "For thou art still the poor man's stay,
> The poor man's heart, the poor man's hand;
> And all the oppress'd who have no strength,
> Have thine at their command."

If we love the poor, and give them our heart and our life, shall we not have, in our turn, their strength at our command in the hour of our direst need? Let one last example, quoted by the illustrious Count Molé in a memorable discourse before the French Academy, serve as an encouragement to all good mistresses, and a model to all true-hearted servants.

Catherine Naville, a peasant girl, entered the family of Madame de Létan, in 1808, at the age of eighteen. "Finding that the family was sinking into distress, the young girl devoted herself to assist it; became the nurse of her sick mistress, who died in her arms; the nurse of the widower, who then fell into a state of debility, and who, unable to pay her any wages, received even his nourishment from the fruit of her former savings; after his death, the guardian of their orphan girl till her marriage.

"Then, on distress visiting the former home, she returned to her devoted services, giving up all claim to her arrear of wages, refusing to accept service in a house where she was basely offered 20,000 francs ($4,000) if she would leave her unfortunate master and mistress; then, on their falling sick, she watched them through a long malady, and closed their eyes when they expired. After this she transferred her devotion to their helpless orphan daughter, whose education she is at this moment (1842) carrying on, at the age of fifty-two years, which have been thus spent in assisting an unfortunate family, with whom she had first become acquainted by accidentally entering their service."

"We can judge"—says Digby—"from such narratives how well the old poet painted from living manners, when in the *Miracle de Notre Dame de Saint Jehan le Paulu*, he represents the hostess saying of her maid-servant: 'If

I and my husband should die on our pilgrimage, this sweet creature has, I know, such courage, that she will not keep all our money to herself, but will give alms for us also.'"[67]

May the number of such maids and such mistresses increase amongst us through the light of your examples!

[67] *Compitum*, b., iii., c. vii.

CHAPTER XVII.

OBSTACLES TO THE RIGHT GOVERNMENT OF THE HOME.

Where Faith has stamped its character on the maiden's heart,...man is reminded of the graces of her whom he delights to serve, woman's divine air and her countenance, her words and her sweet smile, can so separate him from all evil influences, that no obstacles on the road to truth will be able to detain his feet from pressing forward to embrace it;—and then hand in hand he is led to his second Home, where Love and Truth made one with Love, will remain with him thenceforth forever.

—KENELM DIGBY.

Whence I more carefully my answer frame,
 That he who weeps on yonder bank may feel
 A punishment assorted to his shame.

Through the bounty of celestial graces

So gifted in his early life was he,
 Each virtuous germ implanted in him, would
 Have flourished in a marvelous degree:
But soil untilled and sown with noxious seed,
 The more with native vigor 'tis endued
 The more malignant yields the noxious weed.
Long time my look sustained him:—to his sight
 The luster of my youthful eyes displaying,
 I led him with me in the path of right.
Scarce had I reached life's second state, when he
 Betook himself to others—rashly straying
 From better guidance and forgetting me.

His steps he turned into an erring way,
 Pursuing false appearances of good,

Which promise fair, but ever lead astray.
Nor inspirations asked for him availed,
By which in dreams I fain would him recall;
Such slight regard he paid them:—wholly failed
The means I often used (so low he fell)
To insure his safety and redeem his fall,
Save leading him throughout the rounds of Hell.

WRIGHT'S DANTE, Purgatory, canto xxx.

The Ideal Home.

When wife and husband are what God wills them to be, one mind and one heart, having but one purpose in life—to be devoted to each other, walking hand in hand in the divine presence, seeking to know the divine will clearly in all things, and yearning to accomplish it perfectly—then their home cannot fail to be an ideal or perfect home, and their united work in life a perfect work; because it is as much God's work as their own.

In such a home,—when all the ordinances left by Christ to his Church have sanctified it as well as the hearts of its master and mistress,—the wife is most truly the embodiment of all natural and supernatural excellence designed to keep her companion faithful to God and the Truth.[68] We again recall the attention of all mothers to the exceeding care and reverence with which they should prepare their sons and daughters for the reception of the (to them) all-important sacrament of matrimony. In the world-wide warfare made at present on the Church and her most sacred institutions, not the least mischief is done by making of marriage a mere civil contract and lay ceremony. As we believe firmly in the perpetual union of Christ with his spouse the Church, so let us be faithful and fervent in profiting by these divine ordinances designed to hallow our homes, our hearts, our lives.

The conception of the great Florentine poet, where his political and personal passions do not cloud his judgment, embitter his heart and poison his pen,—is that of Religion (or Revealed Truth), under the form of perfect

[68] Truth is defined by De Bonald as "the knowledge of beings and their relations." This is truth in our *mind*; but truth in our *life*, or truth in action, would be the fulfillment of all the duties imposed on us toward all beings—God, ourselves, and the neighbor.

womanly grace and supernatural virtue, saving man from himself in youth, and guiding him step by step to the highest excellence and felicity. The Catholic religion,—in his mind,—is the true Beatrice (Latin, *Beatrix*, "bestower of bliss"), the guide, the enlightener, the loving, devoted friend and companion, who never quits the side of the faithful man till she has led him to that "second home" on high, where God, who is both Love and Truth, takes the pilgrim to his own bosom,—the only home worthy of the children of God.

In treating[69] of the qualities and virtues of a true wife, we did little more than point briefly to the fact of so many husbands being saved from ruin, temporal and eternal, by her agency who is the angel of the home. Presently we shall see how hard it is to achieve the redemption from inveterate vice of a soul so dear. But there stands the mighty lesson in all its divine meaning,—that just as Mary the mother of the New Life gave the Saviour and salvation to the world, just as the Church, the spouse of Christ, evermore performs the divine office of motherhood here below toward the nations,—even so true woman in every home is the saviour and sanctifier of man.

Hence the mighty import of the duties assumed by the teaching orders of women in the modern world. Their schools are not merely a nursery from which their own numbers are recruited, but they are the nursery of the true Christian mothers who are to rear the priests as well as the citizens of the future.

Where husband and wife are united by the deepest of all natural affections—deepened still more, purified and intensified by the great gift of the special sacramental grace—they set before themselves, like Christ and his Church, one mighty work to do, to make their home a paradise and their children saints. And when we say "saints" we mean true men and true women,—faithful, perfect, admirable in every possible relation of life.

Let every one of you, wives and mothers, who read these lines, pause here and say, whether or not she has seen such homes among the poorest day-laborers, among tradesmen and merchants, among the wealthy and the nobly born? Where there is living faith in the twin souls knit together by the sacrament, and that most blessed union of minds and hearts and wills,—even

---

[69] Chapter VI., pp. 62-69.

poverty is sweet and hard toil is welcome, and husband and wife find in each other every day that dawns on them new qualities which delight and new virtues to increase their mutual love: each is to the other a continual exhortation to trust in God, to piety and uprightness, to the patience and energy which bear with unavoidable ills and aim at the possession of true good. There is happiness with a dry loaf, a warm fire, and the love which enables each to be all in all to the other; and there is wealth above all price in the contentment based on this mutual tenderness and on the all-sufficiency of the devoted husband to the wife, and of the devoted wife to her husband.

The home of the poorest man where such love is, and such goodness is known to all around, is most truly like a bright light in a dark place.

But where this union of hearts exists in the home of the wealthy and the great, the life-labor of husband and wife can be productive of incalculable good. Such people, with their ample means, their position, and their influence are, in truth, God's stewards in high places, with an arduous mission before them; but who can describe the reward kept in store for their fidelity?

Aim at Making the Ideal Home an Hereditary Home.

This is the last suggestion which we make to those who have succeeded in rising to affluence. In the days of our forefathers it was the ambition of every high-souled man, whether born in poverty or in a palace, to create a home for himself and his children after him, or to preserve and adorn the home of his parents.

To every father and mother whom our voice can reach, we say: Make your home so happy, so honored, so hospitable, and so substantial that your children shall vie with each other as to who can possess it, keep it, and transmit it more honored still and more substantial to their dearest. Love to have your married children settle near you; encourage and help them to build homes like your own. Give them to understand, by your advice and example, that the fortune which they may make in their turn is not to be spent by the possessor in mere personal enjoyment, but laid up for his children and the poor and God's Church, in their need.

> "This small inheritance my father left me
> Contenteth me, and is worth a monarchy.
> I seek not to wax great by others' waning,
> Or gather wealth, I care not with what envy;
> Sufficeth that I have maintains my state,
> And sends the poor well pleased from my gate."[70]

This spirit is not that which animates in our day nations and individuals. The universal tendency is to make the most of the present, and to let those who come after us take care of themselves. Families in the olden time, even those of farmers and tradesmen, were most ambitious to leave a home and a name after them,—the home and the name they had received from their fathers. Men of all classes resembled the banian or sacred tree of India, which sends down from its lower branches air-roots into the earth. These in their turn grow up to be strong props, supporting the horizontal branches and remaining connected with the parent trunk. Thus does the latter multiply itself till it covers many an acre of land, and affords shelter to thousands.

But fathers among us care little about founding a house; nor do their sons preserve any lasting affection for the home in which they were born. Families nowadays resemble the solitary trees left behind by the settler when ax and fire have swept away the forest from around his abode. They pine alone, graceful and stately it may be, amid the waste, but they leave no descendants behind them.

"There is nothing more expensive and injurious," says a wise author, "than changing one's residence. Things are lost and broken. It has an influence even on the mind; ideas are discomposed and troubled, and some time must elapse before they resume their wonted order. I wish that all who are mine should lodge under the same roof, warm themselves at the same hearth, and sit at the same table. The united family obtains more consideration than if it was dispersed. If divided and less numerous, it will never arrive at the same esteem, authority, and importance."[71]

Let fathers and mothers forgive these earnest wishes we form for seeing their homes ideal homes, most blessed homes; for seeing them also

---

[70] Shakespeare, "Henry VI.," part ii., act iv., scene x.

[71] Angelo Pandolfini, *Governo della Famiglia*.

substantial and permanent homes,—not like tents set up for the night and struck with the next dawn, but homes that will continue to be loved and revered by many a generation of noble Christian men and women,—to whom every stone shall "represent the ancient honor and venerated virtue of the family," and the dwelling itself shall be "the heart of loyalty and the sanctuary of honor."

Such it can and will be with the cordial co-operation of a husband possessed of manly spirit, devotion to his wife, and a conscientious desire of fulfilling the divine will. Fathers, whoever you are, let it be your purpose to make your home such that every son of yours in passing it would uncover his head and almost bend his knee, as if it were the temple of the living God, and honored with the presence of his vailed majesty.[72]

Obstacles to the Wife's Good Government.

If the home is what it ought to be, what God intends it should be, its mistress and sovereign is so not only by the nature of things, but by the supremacy of her own goodness, and the free and loving homage of her husband. He is to be, throughout his whole life, the first servant of her he has made queen over his household and his heart.

What happens, when, instead of this loving service done to his wife, instead of being her willing and docile instrument in furthering the happiness of all subject to them, instead of co-operating with her in the divine work of educating and elevating both children and servants,—he becomes her chief obstacle, the ever-present and insuperable difficulty which no one can remove from her path?

We do not wish to cast a shadow on the spirit of the reader by dwelling for one moment on the extreme cases—alas, all too frequent among us—of habitual intemperance, or unfaithfulness in husbands, bound by the obligations inherent to their state to be models of virtue and the guardians of the sacred honor of their homes.

---

[72] "Groenveld on his way to execution, when passing by his father's house bent his knees looking toward it, and then courageously met his death."— DIGBY.

The wife whose heart is not broken, whose life is not shortened, and whose spirit is not utterly prostrated on discovering her companion to be the slave of intemperance, his affections to be given to another, or his soul to be a loathsome moral ulcer,—must be sustained by the hand of God. We have shown one example of such a sad lot in a preceding chapter;[73] but how many young wives possess the angelic piety and heroic fortitude of Portugal's most lovely flower of sanctity?

There are some, however;—there are, we doubt, many more than we suspect. God knows how to feed the springs of nobleness and spiritual life in the souls most dear to him, in those especially who seek "to make of their cross their crown." In the very homes where the drunkard's beastly life would seem to kill every germ of happiness in the hearts of wife and children, and to blight every promise and prospect of future prosperity,—faith and love will continue to live within the soul of a gentle woman, and hope to survive all the crushing disappointments of the past.

In the frightful cold of the highest latitudes ever yet reached by man, even beneath the ice and the snow which the sun of last year and many preceding suns had failed to melt,—our heroic travelers have discovered, on digging deep to the soil, the beautiful heath called *Andromeda* still living and awaiting a future spring. The hardy little thing has its own internal heat, and thaws the first soft snow which covers it, forming thus a kind of dome or roof of ice above itself; and there it lives on secure, with the buds of its pretty flowers in their sheaths ready to expand when the long winter is over, and the first rays of sunshine fall upon its bed.

And are not immortal souls more a care to the Father of all than the heath-flower of the extreme north, or the queenliest blossom that blows among the wild luxuriance of the Brazilian forest? So, brave hearts, in your desolated homes, over which have settled the darkness and the cold of more than the longest arctic winter, be sure that God the life-giver is with you, and that His warmth,—who is the Sun of all comfort,—will visit you in good season.

[73] Chapter VIII., pp. 107 and following.

Obstacles in the Wealthy Home.

Apart from the extreme case of habitual intemperance and such destroying vices as we have just mentioned, the wealthy wife may have to contend with other difficulties. Her husband,—though neither dissipated nor intemperate, may be entirely out of sympathy with her best and most cherished designs for the education of her children and the government of her household, as well as for all her most legitimate works of outdoor charity and zeal. Thus, especially in the great labor of educating her children, there will be a want of sympathy in what a true woman holds to be most dear and sacred. It is a sad trial.

But if most women are discouraged by this lack of sympathy, or of efficient co-operation on the part of their husbands, there are others,—and they are not so very rare,—who have derived fresh courage and energy from their husbands' apathy, doubling their efforts to secure to their dear ones the highest culture of mind and heart, and employing a God-inspired industry and perseverance to interest the father in the intellectual and spiritual advancement of his children.

A woman of genuine piety will, like St. Monica, know what virtue there is in fervent prayer and tears poured out before the divine majesty in favor of the callous soul. As in the case of Augustine, so in the case of the worst husbands, we should say to the mourner, "It is impossible that the son of such tearful prayers should perish!" But there are other remedies which God wonderfully blesses. Not only must you make your children pray with you and tell them that they are praying for their parent;—you should also stimulate them in their studies and their progress in all goodness by the thought of thereby making their father happy.

Get up in his honor little family festivals,—with recitations, music, and other like amusements; interest the entire household in these entertainments, with such of his friends as he would wish to see pleased. It is rare that the most indifferent and unsympathetic remains uninterested or unmoved by such exhibitions as these. We merely suggest. We have seen the experiment succeed so marvelously that we deem it worth while to counsel a renewal of it.

There is worse than want of sympathy, however: there is interference with the mother's plans and methods in rearing her children, or in caring for the instruction and comfort of her servants. This is a great hardship. But what is to be done?

Not to lose heart; to do as much of one's duty as circumstances permit; to go on from day to day giving to the young plants under one's care as much attention and culture as is possible; and to trust in the divine assistance for a change, sooner or later.

Besides, does not the homely truth of the old favorite ballad, "Love will find out the way," apply to such cases as this most unreasonable opposition from one's husband? Will not the love which survives in a true woman's heart for the man she once loved best of all the world, prompt some one way to bring him to her way of thinking? And even should that wifely love be dead, dead,—will not the mother's love "find out the way" of overcoming the obstacle? Again we remind mothers so circumstanced that He whose work they are trying to do binds himself to aid them, and will surely lend his assistance to their strenuous and persevering efforts. Monica converted her pagan husband, as well as his mother: it was a hard struggle with a weak soul utterly steeped in heathen vices and self-indulgence;—and she ended by winning her son to God,—a still harder conquest, for in the case of Augustine there was the pride of intellect to overcome as well as the terrible power of human respect and a life of more refined indulgence as yet in its prime.

How can you tell what your children may be in God's designs?

In this case,—of Augustine's father, Patricius,—we have touched upon the terrible obstacle offered to the mother's teaching and moral training by the evil examples of a father. We cannot do better than recommend to mothers circumstanced as Monica was the lesson of her life and examples. Let us listen to one page of Augustine's "Confessions,"[74] as if we paused for a few minutes on a toilsome and steep path, to look down on a lovely vale and breathe deliciously the mingled fragrance borne upward to us by the summer air.

"Being modestly and soberly trained, and rather made subject by Thee to her parents, than by her parents to Thee, when she had arrived at a marriageable age she was given a husband whom she served as her lord. And she busied herself to gain him to Thee, preaching Thee unto him by her behavior; by which Thou madest her fair, and reverently amiable, and admirable unto her husband... For she waited for Thy mercy upon him that by believing in Thee he might become chaste. And besides this, as he was

---

[74] "Confessions," b. ix., c. ix., Pilkington's translation.

earnest in friendship, so was he violent in anger; but she had learned that an angry husband should not be resisted, neither in deed nor even in word. But so soon as he was grown calm, she would give him a reason for her conduct, should he have been excited without cause.

"In short, while many matrons whose husbands were more gentle, carried the marks of blows on their dishonored faces, and would in private conversation blame the lives of their husbands, she would blame *their* tongues... And when they, knowing what a furious husband she had to endure, marveled that it had never been reported, nor appeared by any indication, that Patricius had beaten his wife, or that there had been any domestic strife between them, even for a day, and asked her in confidence the reason of this, she taught them her rule, which I have mentioned above. They who observed it experienced the wisdom of it, and rejoiced; those who observed it not were kept in subjection, and suffered... Such a one was she, Thou, her most intimate instructor, teaching her in the school of her heart... She was also the servant of Thy servants. Whosoever of them knew her, did in her much magnify, honor, and love Thee; for that through the testimony of the fruits of a holy conversation (life), they perceived Thee to be present in her heart. For she had 'been the wife of one man,' had requited her parents, had guided her house piously, had brought up children, bringing them forth anew as often as she saw them swerving from Thee. Lastly, to all of us, O Lord,...who, before she slept in Thee, lived associated together, having received the grace of Thy baptism, did she devote care such as she might, if she had been the mother of us all, served us as if she had been child of all."

Wives and mothers who bear the double cross laid on Monica must imitate her faithfully, remembering, each of them, that she too has in the Spirit ever dwelling in a faithful soul "a most intimate Instructor, teaching her in the school of her heart."

Go not abroad to neighbors, or even dearest friend, to tell the story of your grievances, against your husband,—but follow the promptings of that divine Teacher within, bidding you suffer, be patient, pray, labor and wait,—doing meanwhile quietly among the poor all the good you can, that they also may lift up their hands in prayer for you.

Obstacles in the Poor Home.

Whatever hardship a wealthy mother may find in doing a true woman's work within her home,—she has not the fear of poverty or starvation to contend with. That is the fearful lot of the poor woman cursed with an intemperate or idle husband, or burdened with an inefficient or infirm one.

Where intemperance consumes in the home all the fruits of a husband's labor, or where idleness sits at the scanty board and eats up the bread which the wife's hard toil has to earn for her dear ones and herself,—how heavy the heart must grow with the care of the morrow! How weak the hands must feel in doing the work which cannot keep fire enough on the hearth or bread enough on the board! And where is the leisure for teaching the children all too poorly fed and too barely clad to be sent to school? And if the overtaxed mother should find heart and leisure to instruct the little ones that multiply and grow up around her cheerless hearthstone, even should her own examples be most angelic,—can they be efficacious to counteract the words, the deeds,—the profane and blasphemous language, the violent and brutal conduct of a father who is either always intoxicated or always suffering from the irritability and half-frenzy consequent upon habitual intoxication?

Oh! if there were religious orders of men and women whose exclusive vocation it would be to go to the succor of such mothers as these—and they are so numerous! they would yearly save millions, who are willing to be saved, but who must be lost without some such interference of Heaven-sent charity!

Of all the most deserving—so often the most heroic—members of their flocks, none more than these mothers appeal to the priestly zeal of our devoted pastors. Our voice can scarcely reach these brave souls fainting on the road beneath their intolerable burden, or it can only come to them through the generous hearts this page may move with pity for Christ's dearest ones. May he speak to every one of you, and impel you to aid where to aid is the divinest mercy!

If you prefer another voice,—of one most gifted and most blessed,—but blessed with a heart all devoted to the poor, and her life crowned with a death earned in their service,—then read at your leisure the following lines,—and think, while you read, of how many mothers near your own home, perhaps, their every word holds true.

"Hush! I cannot bear to see thee
    Stretch thy tiny hands in vain;
Dear, I have no bread to give thee,
    Nothing, child, to ease thy pain!
When God sent thee first to bless me,
    Proud, and thankful too, was I:
Now, my darling, I, thy mother,
    Almost long to see thee die.
        Sleep, my darling, thou art weary;
        God is good, but life is dreary.

"I have watched thy beauty fading,
    And thy strength sink day by day;
Soon, I know, will Want and Fever
    Take thy little life away.
Famine makes thy father reckless,
    Hope has left both him and me;
We could suffer all, my baby,
    Had we but a crust for thee.
        Sleep, my darling, thou art weary;
        God is good, but life is dreary.

"Better thou shouldst perish early,
    Starve so soon, my darling one,
Than in helpless sin and sorrow
    Vainly live, as I have done.
Better that thy angel spirit
    With my joy, my peace, were flown,
Than thy heart grew cold and careless,
    Reckless, hopeless, like my own.
        Sleep, my darling, thou art weary;
        God is good, but life is dreary.

"I am wasted, dear, with hunger,
    And my brain is all opprest,
I have scarcely strength to press thee,
    Wan and feeble, to my breast.
Patience, baby, God will help us,
    Death will come to thee and me,

He will take us to his heaven,
    Where no want or pain can be.
        Sleep, my darling, thou art weary;
        God is good, but life is dreary."

Such the plaint that, late and early,
    Did we listen, we might hear
Close beside us,—but the thunder
    Of a city dulls our ear.
Every heart, as God's bright angel,
    Can bid one such sorrow cease;
God has glory when his children
    Bring such poor ones joy and peace!
        Listen, nearer while she sings,
        Sounds the fluttering of wings.[75]

[75] Adelaide Anne Procter.

CHAPTER XVIII.

THE MISTRESS OF THE HOME AND HER SOCIAL DUTIES.

Art sets before us the images of some who by the path of love have conducted men to God; for such is the mission of those whom we have already met upon the road of the domestic home and life. —DIGBY.

Oh! beautiful! and rare as beautiful!
  But theirs was love in which the mind delights
To lose itself, when the old world grows dull
  And we are sick of its hack sounds and sights.

See—those are never objects of praise who indulge in delights, who are devoted to worldly dissipations, whose pleasure is in vanity after the manner of the Pagans. But our law is that of the Beatitudes.

ST. EPHREM.

The words "society" and "social duties," as they are to be understood here, have received from the real follies and criminal vanities of worldly-minded women an odious meaning, which must be at once corrected ere we can enter on an explanation of the noble part which a Christian woman has to play in the social circle to which she is born and to which she is bound by so many duties and charities.

The word "society," as understood by the world of fashion and vanity, means simply assemblages of the wealthy, the worldly, and the dissipated, into which women go to be admired and sought after; where the great purpose of life is to display one's self to the best advantage, to outshine one's neighbors, and to decry them by a thousand arts. Women who have never gone into such society but to shine in this way, and who rear their daughters with the same notions of social life, and introduce them to "Vanity Fair" for the same purpose of dazzling and outstripping all competitors in the race of extravagance, will teach their children, as they have taught themselves,—that their sole duty in life is so to dress and to charm in these gatherings that they shall become resistless:—these are the persons who have given an odious and almost criminal sense to the terms "society" and "social duties."

And not without great reason. For such women there is no true home with its sacred duties and godlike virtues, with its serious labor of self-culture and spiritual advancement, followed by the sweet repose and delightful amusements of the family circle. There is no home-life for these votaries of vanity. Home for them only means the retirement in which they rest between one round of dissipation and another, and in which, when they have slept a part of their weariness away, they wearily prepare for the next social meeting. The husbands of such women are only looked up to as the prime ministers of their pleasures, as a happy convenience for providing the moneys necessary to their unlimited extravagance.

The care and regulation of a household, the education of children, when they elect to be burdened with any, the improvement or comfort of their servants, or the needs of the poor who knock at their gate,—are to these weary ones an intolerable nuisance. Vanity,—Self, rather, under another name,—is the only deity these heartless ones worship,—and pleasure is the sole end of their miserable existence. But let them view the deformity of their own lives and the certain ruin of body and soul toward which they are hurrying, by the contrast presented by the life of a true Christian woman of the world, by her notions about society and social duty, and her conscientious discharge of the obligations imposed by her position.

The "Woman of the World" and the "Worldly Woman."

Truth is like the broad light of day in which the eye sees the reality of things. In that light let us behold what is the difference between a woman of the world, in the fair and obvious sense of the words,—that is, a true Christian woman living in the world, discharging faithfully every known duty, and a "worldly woman," who lives for self, for human opinion, and mere enjoyment. We have already seen the dark side of the picture, let us now see the bright.

Most women have to live in the world. It is the sphere of their labors, often heroic, beneficial to everybody around them, and glorious to God and his Church. St. Monica lived all her life in the world, and discharged most admirably all the duties of daughter, wife, mother, mistress of a household, a member of the sorely-tried Church in her day, and of the more than half-pagan society around her. So was it with many others of her contemporaries in the East and West: St. Macrina, the grandmother of St. Basil the Great, and St. Emmelia, his mother, were women of the world, living together in the same house, and together laboring to rear the sons of the latter, three of whom have been revered as saints by all succeeding Christian ages. Near them, in their native province, lived another family of saints, that of St. Nonna, the mother of St. Gregory Nazianzen, who also converted and made a saint of her husband. Nor were such women and their families by any means so rare as one might be led to think. In Africa, we have at the same time the glorious defender of Catholic doctrine, St. Athanasius, whose mother declared that "it was her intention to devote her life to making of this her only child a true servant of the Church." She alone educated him, trained him in learning and goodness, till she made of him the wonder of his age. Under this most wise and loving guide the boy became an apostle even before he had ceased to be a boy. For even then he was wont to assemble the pagan children of his own age, in his home or in the street, instructing them in the Christian faith, and when he had given them the desire of being baptized, baptizing them with his own hand.

And this man, become the bishop of his native city, Alexandria, having experienced the powerful influence of a true Christian woman in his own early formation, employed the Christian women of his church as the most zealous apostles of the truth and the most eloquent denouncers of Arianism.

We have already mentioned Anthusa, the illustrious mother of St. John Chrysostom, who lived and died a woman of the world, without ceasing to be a model of virtue. History has also preserved the names of many of the saintly women who helped John, when raised to the perilous episcopal chair of Constantinople, to combat the vices of the court, to stem the torrent of extravagance, luxury, and corruption which swept over the new capital and the surrounding provinces. At the head of these virtuous and most noble ladies stands St. Olympias, and among them may be mentioned St. Pentalia, St. Sylvia, Percuta, Sabiniana, Bassiana, Chalcidia, Asyncritia, and St. Nicareda, of the highest nobility of Nicomedia, the mother of the sick and the poor, who lived and died in her own house, shedding around her on every side the hallowing influences of her spotless life and her most generous charities.

In the West, Italy offered a like spectacle of womanly holiness and zeal. Rome beheld the great St. Jerome literally enlisting the patrician ladies into the service of the poor and the infirm, or into the ranks of the monastic life. One has only to remember such names as St. Paula and her daughter St. Eustochium, and forthwith a galaxy of glorious Christian women arise before the mind's eye, who made of the Rome of the fourth century the worthy parent of the Christian Rome of the nineteenth, before it became the prey of Piedmontese infidelity and unblushing corruption.

Further to the west and the north we meet with St. Ambrose, the spiritual parent of Augustine. Ambrose,—the great magistrate, become a great archbishop and teacher, owed also his education and holy training to his mother. His father, who was governor of all Gaul and a great part of Germany, died while Ambrose was in his infancy. The mother, left with three children, succeeded in making saints of every one of them, Marcellina, her only daughter, being afterward of immense utility to her great brother in spreading the reign of Christian piety and the practical knowledge of the higher life in Milan and its vicinity.

In the next generation the family of St. Gregory the Great, as well as that of St. Paulinus of Nola, may be quoted as illustrious instances of the heroic Christian spirit sanctifying all the spheres of active life in the world, as distinguished from the life of the cloister.

Need of True Christian Women in the World.

Indeed it is the homes created by such women as Macrina, Emmelia, Nonna, Paula, and Monica which become the fruitful nurseries of the men and women who make the priesthood venerable and monastic life flourishing and fervent, while blessing at the same time the world itself with the sweet active virtues characteristic of Christianity. Mothers who fulfill beneath the eye of God, and with a full sense of their responsibility, the duties of motherhood, will rear the very men God needs from whom to choose both the apostolic priest and the model Christian gentleman and statesman;—they will also form to their own image and likeness the maidens whom the Divine Spirit will as surely direct to follow the Lamb in the paths of his apostleship, or to remain behind to create and sanctify homes of their own.

But the mothers who rear such sons and daughters,—and such of these daughters as God wills to remain in the secular life to perpetuate the precious virtues learned from their parent,—have other duties beside the education of children, the happiness of a husband, the economy of a household. The wife of the laborer or the mechanic has duties toward the neighbor, duties toward the Church, duties toward the various institutions of education and beneficence in which every family and every individual in the community are interested.

But this is much more true of the wife of the wealthy man, of the magistrate, the legislator,—of the large proprietor, the nobleman, and the prince. Beside their most important and most onerous household obligations, these women have others which they cannot dispense with, and which, properly and conscientiously fulfilled, are most conducive to the interests of religion as well as to the benefit of the community at large.

Importance of a Christian Woman's Social Duties.

Treating as we are of the duties of women in the world,—of women of all classes,—it surely will not be denied that the wives and daughters of sovereigns, of chief magistrates under any form of government, and those of public functionaries of all degrees, are bound to receive and entertain, to appear in public on certain occasions, to accept invitations to certain social gatherings. This is, this has ever been, and is likely ever to be, considered a real and most important duty inherent to the position filled by all such persons.

In our own age,—not to seek examples too far off,—we all have known or read of women, at once most exalted in rank and most exalted in virtue, who felt themselves bound to honor their position by showing a courtly grace in every circle in which duty compelled them to be the central figures, by dispensing a right royal or princely hospitality on every occasion,—indeed on every day of their lives;—who knew on these very days, early or late, to visit our Lord in the persons of the needy and sick. In the queen, the princess, the noble lady of whatever rank, in the gentlewoman, the merchant or the mechanic's wife, the Spirit of God will be sure to manifest his presence by the light on the features or in the eye, by the words dropped in conversation in the reception-room, at table, or even in the strictest privacy.

Every one knows,—even France which upset the throne of the husband has not forgotten the angelic virtues and noble charities of the wife and her daughters,—how the late Queen of the French, Marie Amélie, was the light of Louis Philippe's court, and "the providence" (as they were wont to call her) of the poor far and near. There never was one word of scandal uttered about the royal circle. She was a devoted and worshiped wife; and the sons she has left behind show by their lives how well she discharged her motherly duties. But her daughters reflected in an especial manner the virtues of their admirable parent. One, above all the others, walked closely in her mother's footsteps, Louise, Queen of the Belgians, whose memory to this day is venerated in every Christian home in the land. Such women were worthy of the blood of St. Louis.

Not less admirable were the princesses of the royal houses of Savoy, Bavaria, and Austria. More than one of them are at this moment candidates for the honors of canonization. What though the king who disgraces in the Quirinal, his line, his faith, and his station, should be the son of a saintly mother? Solomon was the son of David, and Roboam was worse than Solomon. The virtues which adorned so many princes of the ancient house of Savoy reappear in the prince who resigned the crown of Spain, and is now content, like another of his near ancestors,[76] to become, after his young wife's death, the humble member of a religious order.

No one who has approached the ladies who grace the thrones of Austria, Bavaria, Belgium, and Portugal, or who are the companions in exile and in private station of the royal families of France and Naples, but are as cordial as they are unanimous in praising in them the courtly graces which lend a luster to their exalted rank, and the unaffected piety which adorns their private life. Wherever they are, the poor far and wide soon learn to bless them.

Catholic Ladies Everywhere True Christians As Well As Women of The World.

Our American travelers who have spent a single season in London must have been struck by the multiplicity of good works to which English, Irish, and Scotch Catholic ladies of high rank residing there, devote themselves.

[76] Charles Emmanuel II. died a Jesuit lay-brother.

Indeed one has only to glance over the notices in the London *Tablet* or *Weekly Register*, to see how active they are in promoting public charities of every kind. And yet only a few of these appear on the surface; the greater number, the most costly to the noble patronesses or founders, are carried on quietly, far away from the public eye. One of these noble women, Cecilia, Marchioness of Lothian, died in Rome during the month of June. It is only since her sudden and lamented death that most men have heard of her unlimited generosity and indefatigable zeal in providing for the manifold needs of the London poor. But Scotland had also most touching stories to tell of that charity which could not help giving, but loved to give in secret, like the life-giving warmth of the sun which works through the long hours of the spring and summer and autumn, long after the great luminary has withdrawn his light. Another, no less noble and no less devoted, was with Lady Lothian when God gave her rest in the City of the Holy Apostles; of her numberless charities England as well as her native Ireland could tell many a thrilling tale. But she is still among the living; and so is another of world-wide fame as a writer, as good as she is noble,—a passionate lover of poverty, devoting to the poor not only the proceeds of her literary labors, but every thing she can spare from her necessary household expenses. And these are only three among thousands on both sides of the Channel who do not think they can dispense themselves from complying with the duties of their social position, while being most exemplary in the accomplishment of every obligation of family life.

American Ladies Models in Public and in Private.

Although American society is not divided into distinct and acknowledged classes, there has been, from the beginning, in every one of the colonies out of which the republic has grown, a well-defined and recognized "good society," which is almost if not quite as exclusive in its intercourse as any of the aristocracies of Europe. Families which rise from the laboring and industrial classes are not always easily admitted into the home circles of the old families.

At any rate, the cities which had originally a large Catholic population, such as Baltimore, St. Louis, and New Orleans, have also had at every epoch a large, distinguished, and influential Catholic society. Other cities throughout the Union do, indeed, surpass these in the numbers of their Catholic inhabitants; but these do not possess the charm of comparative "antiquity," are not looked up to by "the Americans of the Americans," and have to establish their social credit by culture, public services, and a sustained reputation.

Nevertheless there is in every large city throughout the country a steadily increasing population, whose educated classes could form among themselves very creditable social gatherings, but who, very properly, prefer to mingle on all social occasions with families belonging to other religious denominations.

The first occasion, for instance, in which the best elements of the Catholic population of New York City were brought together conspicuously, was during the great charity fair for the Eleventh Street Hospital, gotten up in the Crystal Palace in 1856. The numbers and respectability of the Catholic population were only then revealed to the persons most interested in ascertaining them. But, save when some great purpose of religion or charity happens to call Catholics together, they wisely abstain from forming among themselves exclusive social circles, and mingle with neighbors and acquaintaince of their own class like other citizens.

How Charity and Religion Are Promoted by Social Gatherings.

One thing is certain,—that where mothers have been careful to educate their sons and daughters in the elevating and refining atmosphere of "the Gentle Life," which is born of enlightened piety, they cannot fail in a republican country to be welcome guests in every circle. Where a man of good standing and education shows himself to be truly "the scholar and the gentleman," there is no circle into which he may not be admitted; and where his sisters have all the solid and graceful accomplishments of the true Gentle Life we have been sketching under so many forms, there is no circle which they cannot ornament, shining wherever they appear with a light which will hurt the eyes of none, while it serves to diffuse the influence of genuine goodness and gentleness.

Every true Christian mother who has had herself experience of the power of such goodness and gentleness in an accomplished woman, will deem it her duty to prepare her sons and daughters for their appearance in society. If her home-life, her home-education and amusements have been in conformity with the rules laid down here and there in the preceding chapters, their "coming out," as it is phrased, will be no sudden and abrupt transition from obscurity into dazzling light, or from simple, homely manners to the strange stateliness and ceremonial of a superior world.

As these remarks are addressed, principally at least, to educated women of position whose sons and daughters are supposed to display in their daily home-circles the accomplishments of music and song, there will be for them but little of novelty and no strangeness in their displaying their best powers for the delight of the first great company assembled in their own honor, or for the amusement of any circle, even the most brilliant and cultivated, in which they may subsequently appear.

The piety they have drunk in with their mother's milk, will be a sure preventive against the foolish vanity which troubles some light brains. Where singing, playing, and all the conversational arts are an every-day exercise in good families and in presence of guests who are good judges of proficiency, there is as little ground for vanity in the display as there is of novelty. What is done habitually is soon done unconsciously,—and with the naturalness arising from habit come that ease and grace which are the great charm of those whose home has ever been for them the school of "the Gentle Life."

Of course, while an experienced and thoughtful mother is thus training her sons and daughters within her own home-sanctuary, she is fully aware of the importance of the social duties for which such training so admirably prepares them; but she is also most careful that they shall not know that their education is directed toward any such purpose. If this long home preparation be carried on beneath the eye of God, with a final view to his honor, by making his religion lovely in the person of its professors, and by thus drawing to the truth souls for whom Christ died,—will this not be the highest charity? And will not religion win the only triumph aimed at both by the pious mother and her worthy children? And,—in very truth,—how many souls, among the best, the purest, the most gifted have been gained in the past, and are still daily won to God by the unconscious charm of an accomplished but innocent young man or woman.

So long, therefore, as society exists, the charities of neighborly intercourse must be a duty incumbent on all, and, above all, on the professors of the true religion; for true religion there cannot be without true charity,—active, practical, and aiming at the highest good of others. Neighborly intercourse means for each mistress of a home that she will exert herself to make it a center of attraction for all who can benefit her children and herself, or who can be benefited by them, and that her visitors shall go away delighted to return again and again. It also means that she and her children will, in their turn, grace the family circles of these same friends and neighbors.

The influence of the Christian mother's home-circles, and the very charm which she and such as she exert in the social gatherings where they appear, are the only possible and the most powerful corrective to the corrupting influence of that world so well denominated "Vanity Fair."

Eloquent Facts.

We shall suppose,—both to instruct and to encourage the reader,—a young woman, a wife and a mother, reared exactly in such a Christian home as we have been painting,—to find herself led by the hand of Providence where public wants and abuses of every kind demand the labors of superhuman zeal. We shall not suppose it to be a new settlement in our Western wilds, or an infant colony in Australia or South-eastern Africa, where all has to be created, and where every living soul is but too glad to obey the voice and follow the lead of a young and noble-hearted woman. Instances there are on record of the good achieved by such women in such places in past times and within this present year of grace. But we shall take a concourse of circumstances far more formidable to the bravest heart,—a scene where, to all appearance, woman's influence will be as feeble against the adverse influences around her as the current of the Mississippi, the Orinoco, or the Amazon to freshen the bitter waters of the South Atlantic Ocean.

Here is a country long settled, with an upper class belonging to the proudest, most sensitive, and unchangeable of the ancient European races, with an inferior population of the pure aboriginal natives, and a mongrel mixture of half-breeds. The climate is a most enervating one, rendered unsafe by fatal endemic diseases and by the most terrible visitations of the plague. Commerce has no marts or outlets, industry offers no stimulus to labor, invention, or progress; morality is low, and religion is both hampered by state legislation and rendered powerless by the ignorance, the inertness, or the vices of its own ministers. The institution of matrimony, as the Church intends it and as it operates on home-life and public society, where religion is free,—has long ceased to be respected in this God-forsaken land. Unions, among several of the wealthiest, the most influential, are mere engagements formed on convenience or inclination, to be broken when the parties weary of each other, or a new passion arises; and the inferior classes are not slow to imitate the examples of their betters. And so, unblessed of God, and with but little thought of craving his blessing, the current of social life moves sluggishly on in its impure channels. Add to all this, that sanguinary political revolutions are as frequent there as changes in the moon.

One of the noblest sons of this unhappy country is sent for his education to a great distance, and, while breathing its free religious air, is drawn within the influence of a Catholic home where all is purity, peace, piety, and refinement. The eldest daughter is remarkable, not for striking beauty of person, but for that indefinable charm of superior goodness which is felt like a most potent spell by all who approach her, for extreme grace of manner, rare intellectual culture, and that divine gift of song which, possessed by angelic virtue, becomes in the possessor a charm that can tame the wildest and soften the most obdurate.

The stranger wins this gifted maiden; she prefers him to many men more wealthy and more attractive, because he is good like herself and holds out to her,—already in her own native city the apostle of the poorest of the poor, of the outcast and the slave,—the prospect of their laboring together to improve the social condition of the country in which he was born. And, her young heart filled with such God-given hopes, she tears herself away from her idolized parents, her brothers, sisters, home, and the many hearts her charities had bound to her,—to labor in the far-off field where there is no apostle to aid, to direct, or to encourage her.

In her new home the magnetism of her presence draws to her every member of her new family, and their numerous dependants; the children and the poor have soon found her out, and thenceforward continue to besiege her. The impression made by her charming manners is more than confirmed by the first song she sings. Have we not read in youth of the famous Thessalian who sang so divinely that the very wild beasts trooped after him from mountain and forest? But it was not merely the untutored and sadly neglected Indians and half-breeds who would crowd to the, till then, forsaken church when she woke the organ and poured forth her magnificent voice in prayer and praise; but, from far and near the best families, one and all, would come to hear the little enchantress. For enchantress she was by the magic of her humility, her gentleness, and the ardent love she felt for these neglectful and erring souls. They came to see, to hear, to be delighted, and went away subdued, edified, thinking of better things, and longing to return to their lovely kinswoman once more.

The children were attracted,—and a Sunday-school was soon organized by the young missionary, some of the most zealous of the neighboring ladies and gentlemen lending their cordial assistance. A choral union was also formed, which comprised the most distinguished and cultivated in the local society, and its members were induced to make the Church offices more solemn and attractive by their voluntary services. The public celebration of mass was, at the time, forbidden to all priests who did not sign the schismatical terms dictated by the head of the government; and in consequence many churches were closed altogether. But our little apostle, trusting to her quality of an American citizen, either evaded the prohibition or openly defied it, and thus succeeded in restoring to divine worship more than its wonted splendor and a pious feeling unknown there since the days of the ancient missionaries. Even the priest, who had suffered himself to float listlessly down the current of evil custom, was recalled to a sense of his sacred obligations by the eloquence of such examples in one so young and so devoted to God's interests.

And so the hallowed springs of piety were reopened in church and homes and hearts. The ladies far and wide were enlisted in pious associations designed to foster individual piety and the virtues of home-life, to promote the religious and secular education of the poor and the instruction of the Indians, to care for the sick and the needy,—as well as to keep alive the sweet neighborly charities which had begun to revive and to produce such incalculable good on every side.

Without noise or outward effort on the part of her who was the soul of this great revival, all who were living together in violation of the divine law hastened to repair the mischief done. Weak souls, in high and responsible position, who had sacrificed conscience in the hour of persecution, were led to recant their error. And so the little stranger, while suffering severely from the dreadful climate and fulfilling with a calm, joyous spirit all the duties of her large household, found time and means to urge on and accomplish good works innumerable.

Meanwhile a fearful civil war had broken out, blood was being daily shed, and there was no one to care for the wounded and the sick. Though sick herself, and having her infant daughter to care for, the brave little woman lost not a moment in organizing a band of nurses; and, though naturally so timid as not to be able to bear the sight of blood, she nerved herself to follow the surgeons from sufferer to sufferer, as they did their dreadful work, helping to bind up a shattered limb or to dress the festering wounds of some poor wretch who had been too long overlooked in the torrid weather.

It were needless to recall the superhuman fatigues of these terrible days. God alone could have sustained her, for it was for him that she worked and to him she looked up for the needful strength to endure what else she could not have borne for a single hour. That she was praised and blessed and worshiped by the townspeople, as well as by the sick and wounded themselves, was to be expected.

When death called her away from the labors she had so lovingly assumed, there was a proposal made to erect, at the public expense, a monument over that early grave. But that would have been utterly in opposition to the spirit which had guided the little heroine, as well as to her own well-known wishes. Her memory lives in every home in the land, and the good she did has not perished with her, while one of her most cherished hopes has been realized since her death,—that of seeing her adopted people governed by a truly apostolic bishop.

Social Virtues of American Women.

The lessons of the young and fruitful life, so prematurely closed, are lessons repeated throughout our country in the north and south from the Middle States to every portion of our territory bounded by the two great oceans. Women to whom Providence has given a superior social position, women unmarried as well as married, feel the responsibilities of their rank, and devote themselves heartily to the good works within their reach; and they have met with a most generous co-operation from their less favored but no less devoted sisters. It is a matter of notoriety that the foundation and support of our numerous and splendid establishments of charity and education, without mentioning the churches themselves, are chiefly due to the self-sacrificing zeal of women of position in each community, heartily sustained by the wives and daughters of the tradesman and the mechanic, by the exhaustless charity of our unmarried laboring women,—shop-girls, factory-girls, and house-servants. God alone knows and he alone can adequately reward the toil, the hardship, the humiliations, the sacrifices of time, money, health, and self-love which the women of every Catholic congregation within the land have had and still have to face, year after year, in their joint industries and endeavors for the support of church, schools, convents, asylums, hospitals, and other local charities.

Work of the Woman of the World Outside of Her Home.

With all these the woman of the world has to become acquainted; an interest in them is as much her own interest as the education of her children or the well-being of her household. Who does not know that in France the magnificent Society of the Propagation of the Faith, with the millions raised annually, penny by penny, from poor and rich alike, with the fruitful missions founded and sustained in both hemispheres,—on every point of the English-speaking world as well as among the heathen,—is mainly the work of French women? And so is the "Association of the Holy Infancy," founded by the chivalrous De Forbin-Janson, Bishop of Nancy, and which yearly rescues from death so many heathen infants in China, and provides for their education? These are only two of the great works carried on in France by women of the world. Their sisters in Canada do not belie this well-earned reputation. One has only to live a single week in Quebec or Montreal to feel that the heart of woman there is ever open to all the noblest impulses of charity, her head quick to conceive generous plans, her tongue ever ready to plead them, and her hand well practiced in working for every form of distress.

Woman's Work in Italy and Germany.

We are not to believe that the women of these two great countries have been idle lookers-on while their respective governments were either destroying with a sort of impious rage all the fair and glorious institutions of eighteen centuries of Christian life, or ruthlessly cutting down at the very roots the noble tree of clerical and apostolic zeal. Long before the names of Bismark or Victor Emmanuel had come to be ranked with those of a Pombal and a Henry VIII., Germany and Austria had their own admirable associations rivaling in efficiency the noblest organizations of French religious zeal, while Italy was covered all over with guilds of women—the highest in rank and foremost in virtue—who only kept up by their charitable labors the traditions of so many centuries of ancestral piety. The breath of revolution—albeit as keen as the blasts which descend from the glaciers of Monte Rosa on the vine-clad hills of Upper Lombardy, and as destructive in their course as a tropical tornado—has neither killed nor chilled the soul of charity in the women of Italy. As the storm grows louder and fiercer, and the Radical crisis becomes more and more imminent, the women who, from the Alps to the southernmost cape of Sicily, boast the blood of hosts of canonized saints, display more courage and energy in pleading the cause of Religion defamed and despoiled, and in providing for the needs of the countless poor, whose increasing numbers and sufferings are the one unquestioned result of Radicalism. Even the fell persecutor Diocletian was wont to refer the distressed Christians of his empire to the charity of the Roman Pontiff, whom he knew to be looked up to as the common parent, and whose benefactions he wisely encouraged. But our modern Levelers will not allow the Church or the priest either the right or the means to relieve the poor or to comfort the distressed. And so to Catholic women alone is left the divine mission and ministry of seeking out Lazarus at the gate of Cæsarism or Radicalism,—where even the dogs are not allowed to lick the sufferer's sores. To them it is given and permitted to raise him up, and house him, and feed him, and to prepare his soul for that eternal repose where all wrongs are righted and all the ills of time most amply compensated.

Bismark may succeed in imprisoning or banishing the last faithful bishop and priest in the German Empire,—but he can neither banish nor imprison the zeal and heroic devotedness of German womanhood. Victor Emmanuel, or the Mazzinian Radicals who misgovern Italy in his name, may suppress the last monastery and convent, and sequestrate the last remnant of the once magnificent patrimony of the poor; but the spirit of St. Catherine of Sienna and St. Frances of Rome cannot be suppressed; the generous piety which the Deacon St. Lawrence inherited from his Christian mother will defy all the edicts of the Italian parliament and outlive not only Victor Emmanuel and his dynasty, but the last representative of Young Italy and the Revolution.

Let our readers only peruse the accounts which reach us of the noble doings of Italian, Swiss, and German women, and they must be convinced that we have not exaggerated the importance of woman's social duties and social mission at the present time and in every Christian land.

Part of the Working-Man's Wife.

But have we not,—it may be suggested,—left the woman of the laboring classes a very unimportant part to play in social life, and in the discharge of what we have termed "social duties"?

By no means. The advice so frequently given, and the rules addressed to women of these classes in the preceding chapters will teach them how to make of their own homes so many schools of "the Gentle Life," of their sons and daughters apt and accomplished scholars in the true courtesies and graces of society,—how to make their evenings at home most delightful, entertaining, elevating, and refining to their own as well as to the guests attracted to their fireside by this twofold charm of refinement and bright cheerfulness. The pleasures,—pure, heartfelt, ever fresh and welcome,—which the good wife of the laboring man is as careful to provide each evening for her dear ones, as she is to prepare them a wholesome and plentiful meal,—will encourage others of her neighbors and acquaintance to follow her example. And thus there will be other firesides, regulated in all things on her own pattern, which will be a safe and welcome place of enjoyment for herself and her children. To such alone ought she and they to go.

Are such homes as these very rare among our people? No, thanks to God's fatherly care over them; and all due praise be to the wisdom and piety of so many true women well known to their religious guides, and better known still to all of their own class who love true goodness!

How the Good Are Drawn Together.

For, there is an occult freemasonry among the good, among those who truly live as becomes children of God, just as there is among worldlings. They find each other out in a neighborhood, they are drawn to each other in a crowd, their lives seem to be governed by the laws of a "supernatural selection," which unconsciously and irresistibly throws them together. Have the good angels anything to do with this? Most certainly.

Cast a handful of gold dust into a vessel full of coarse sand, and shake it,—if presently you seek for the shining speckles of the precious metal, you find them not,—they have sunk to the bottom, and there they cluster together. Nay, place the vessel on some place where it may be heated slowly, without melting the golden particles, and after a time the mysterious laws of affinity will draw them together, separating them from the earthy mass, and impelling them downward, away from the surface. Again, watch a flower garden in springtide, when your plants are in full blossom; you will not find the bee and the wasp sucking the same flower. The bee seeks the honey to bear it home to the hive, fasting and toiling herself the while; she is thinking of others while she is abroad and seeking the loveliest and most fragrant daughters of the spring; and she hastens homeward laden with her treasures, only to hoard them up for her sisters during the long winter months. On the contrary, the wasp seeks the honey to enjoy it. Unselfish, unworldly, and motherly women are like the bees; they go abroad to make honey for their dear ones, not for the purpose of gratifying their appetite, like the wasp, or of displaying their beautiful wings, like the butterfly; and God gives them the instinct of knowing each other and trooping together, while they work with one accord and untiringly, as long as the day lasts, to treasure up sweet stores of enjoyment for others. Wasps, like selfish and pleasure-seeking people, also know each other; but they do not work well together,—they quarrel and sting each other to death, or victimize some innocent, harmless bee, because it incautiously seeks the same flowering shrub with themselves.

Even so will true-hearted women, guided by the divine instinct within them, seek each other's society to encourage each other in living godly lives, to learn how they can improve their methods of educating their dear ones and of brightening their homes, as well as to plan means for relieving the poor, for providing for the needs of a church in debt, or of saving from want, temptation, and ruin the youthful and destitute of their own sex.

Oh! blessed shall be the day when, in this great city of New York, we shall see such women as these forming associations for the purpose of protecting innocent and inexperienced girls arriving on our shores, from the many snares set for them by fiends of their own sex, and by men who can never have known a mother! There has always existed in Catholic Italy associations of this sort, which provided asylums for the homeless and unprotected, where they could learn trades and work for their own benefit till they found a suitable match; then the association added to the little store laid up by the bride, and thus secured her a handsome marriage portion. Moreover, it has been the immemorial custom for sovereigns, for popes, for noble ladies of every degree to bestow yearly, on certain feast-days, a dower on a number of poor but portionless girls. This was often done by noble ladies on the day of their own bridals, or on some such joyous occasion, or in thanksgiving for some great favor from on high.

We dare not make a suggestion. These lines may inspire some generous womanly heart with a noble emulation of the charities of other lands.

In our own there are surely souls ready to respond to every breath of the divine inspiration. For we have in our midst women of the world who seem to have no other occupation but that of benefiting others,—women who give up every pleasure to open homes for the young and houseless of their own sex. What though their labors do not always prosper as they wish? or though men do not praise or befriend their efforts? Is He for whom they work blind or forgetful or ungrateful?

Generous women, whoever you be, forget not that you labor for the eternal God, and that your reward is not to be enjoyed on this side of eternity. To all of you, being what you are, we would fain commend these lines on "Hoarded Joys," should you be tempted to repine at the slowness with which either success or repose cometh for you:

"I said: 'Nay, pluck not,—let the first fruit be:
  Even as thou sayest, it is sweet and red;
  But let it ripen still. The tree's bent head
Sees in the stream its own fecundity
And bides the day of fullness. Shall not we

At the sun's hour that day possess the shade,
And claim our fruit before its ripeness fade,
And eat it from the branch, and praise the tree?'"

But to the worldly women, who, born of Christian mothers and reared to the knowledge and practice of better things, allow the spring and summer of life to pass away without a single flower or fruit of ripened goodness for themselves or others,—what shall we say? They have resolved, and resolved, and resolved, and not one resolution has ever ripened into performance. Their virtues are like the fruits buried long centuries ago in the royal sepulchres of Egypt: they fall to dust on being brought to the sunlight.

CHAPTER XIX.

MAIDENHOOD.

Unto God's will she brought devout respect,
Profound simplicity of intellect,
    And supreme patience. From her mother's knee
    Faithful and hopeful; wise in charity;
Strong in grave peace; in pity circumspect.
So held she through her girlhood; as it were
    An angel-watered lily, that near God
    Grows and is quiet.

DANTE GABRIEL ROSSETTI.

Mind'st thou not (when the twilight gone
Left darkness in the house of John),
Between the naked window-bars
That spacious vigil of the stars?
For thou, a watcher even as they,
Would'st rise from where throughout the day
Thou wroughtest raiment for His poor;
And, finding the fixed terms endure
Of day and night which never brought
Sounds of His coming chariot,
Would'st lift through cloud-waste unexplored
Those eyes which said, "How long, O Lord?"

THE SAME.

Girlhood of the Virgin-Mother the Model of Maidenhood.

The virtues and qualities which the poet attributes to Mary in her girlhood, are those which every Christian mother will endeavor to develop in her daughters: the deep-seated piety that makes conformity to the divine will the first and last study of every hour and day and year, till the vail is removed and the dutiful soul beholds face to face Him who through all eternity will study to fulfill her will;—the "profound simplicity of intellect" which is but the illumined eye of faith beholding God first and last and middlemost in all this wondrous world and in the complicated course of human history;—the "supreme patience" which springs from the certain hope that such faith begets, and makes the trials of time seem as nought compared with the eternal possession already begun in faith;—these twin virtues of Faith and Hope, like the wings of the soul, lifting the maiden to the divine bosom even "from her mother's knee;"—that "wisdom in charity" which consists in filling the heart brimful with the chaste love of the Supreme Good, in order to pour all the unselfish devotion it inspires on the home first, and then on all outside the home, according to the enlightened laws of charity;—the invincible fortitude that nerves the soul to struggle unceasingly against the warring desires of earthly concupiscence, while bearing with unruffled serenity the ills which befall, no matter whence they come;—and that "circumspect pity" which makes the soul careful, while succoring the distress of others, and showing divinest pity to their most loathsome ills, not to be herself defiled,—just as when mercy leads one to plunge into a roaring flood to save a poor drowning wretch, one takes care not to be swept away by the swift waters.

With all this strength of soul the Christian maiden must be near the maternal bosom and beneath the sweet light of a mother's love, like a lily within the close of some august sanctuary watered daily by angelic hands and growing up in gentleness and the perfection of all loveliness.

Mary's Public Life the Model of Womanhood's Trials.

This gentle nurture within the home will give a girl's soul that adamantine firmness as well as purity which will bear without injury the terrible trials of after-life. Maidenhood had scarcely begun for the Most Blessed One, when the divine purpose was unfolded to her, and her share in the Work of Ages[77] was foreshown, the bitter road from the Manger to the Cross; and then the long stay on earth after him in the house of John, with her full participation

[77] Habacuc iii. 2.

in all the manifold woes of the infant Church. She who was the Mother of the Bridegroom,—who had pillowed his infant head on her bosom through the long journeying, back and forth, of his exile, and who, at the foot of the Cross, received on that same agonized bosom the dear thorn-crowned head taken down from the wood, was predestined to watch over the birth and growth of His Bride and our Mother.

As she suffered in Him when scourged at the pillar and nailed to the bitter tree, so she suffered in his members during the first persecutions,—was scourged in Paul and John, and beheaded in James, and stoned in Stephen, being meanwhile the model of all in faith that never faltered, in hope that never was dimmed, and in that all-bearing love which waiteth for His coming throughout the interminable years.

How true a mirror of maidenhood and womanhood! How clearly can one view in the life of that Mother of Sorrows the lot which all true women must accept! And how consoling for all these classes of toilers, sufferers, and waiters whose trials, labors, duties, and virtues we are now going to set forth.

I.
The Daughters of the Wealthy Home.

We have no further concern here with maidens who remain beneath the roof of their parents till they have chosen a home of their own in matrimony or in religious life. What has been said must suffice for them, inasmuch as we suppose their mothers to have faithfully discharged toward them all the offices of motherhood. Our present concern is with the daughters of wealthy families, on whom poverty has fallen while still unmarried.

Girls Reared in Affluence and Forced to Labor.

1. We approach this large and most interesting class with a feeling of infinite reverence. We know that their numbers have much increased of late years even in our midst, and in spite of all the securities which surround the wealthy in a country untroubled by socialism, in spite, also, of the facilities afforded in a young and prosperous community for recruiting impaired fortunes. And our reverence is founded on the magnanimity with which so

many young girls, brought up in luxury and with the most splendid prospects, accept the reverse that befalls them, and set to work to lighten the hard lot of father and mother,—and, not unfrequently, to provide for the wants of their whole family.

Resolution and Fortitude Characteristic of American Women.

It is one beautiful feature of American womanhood, this resolute facing the inevitable, this heroic determination daily manifested of undertaking any kind of honorable toil, in order to be self-supporting and to be a help to the dear ones at home. Men are born to be the providers in the home: they are formed by nature and still further fitted by education for every species of toil. Theirs is the battle of life on sea and land. The home with its quiet, its obscurity, its sanctities, is for woman: she is made to grow up in the shade. Man's strength of soul and body, his physical and moral qualities, liken him to the mountain-oak which waxes strong in the sunshine, the wind, and the blast. The sturdy trunk, the rough bark, the gnarled and wide branches,—like mighty arms stretched out to contend with the storm,—all bespeak struggle, strength, and victory over the elements. But woman is like the lowly vine, which needs support for itself and the delicious clusters that it bears, and needs, too, whether in valley or on hillside, to be sheltered against the fierce cold winds that may happen to sweep over its native soil.

Heroic Women in Adversity Like Choice Vines on a Barren Soil.

It will serve our purpose to pursue this comparison a little farther. The vines which bear the most renowned fruit and produce the wine most eagerly sought for, are not those that grow on the rich and sheltered lowlands; just as the women most admirable for heroic endurance and perseverance are those who have to grow up in toil and trial and self-reliance. Let us listen to this description by a recent traveler of the port-wine district in Portugal:

"As I ascended the ridge of mountains which separates the valley of Villa Real from the port-wine district, I became entangled in a network of paths... On either side of the river Douro lies a district about twenty-seven miles in length and six or seven in breadth, of steep hills, with narrow, ravine-like valleys; the soil a naked, yellow-brown, slaty schist... Looked at from where I now stood, and seen in the thin atmosphere of early morning, with every detail sharp and clear as in a photograph, with hill beyond hill extending confusedly below, the appearance was that of a wilderness of utterly bare and arid peak and valley... All over the sides of each acclivity stone terraces have been built, in lines running parallel with the horizon; and in the poor schistous soil thus kept from being washed away by the rains of winter, the vines which make port wine are grown... If Portugal were to lapse into an uninhabited wilderness to-morrow, this monument of man's accumulated handiwork would probably outlast every single work of Roman, Goth, Saracen, and Portuguese...

"The flavor of the wine here produced depends upon the nature of the soil, certainly not upon its richness; for the surface of the vineyards looks like the rubbish thrown up from a stone quarry; and it depends also upon the great heat of the summer in a district shut off by lofty hills from the north and the northeast. The cold of winter among these high-lying lands, is, however, for Portugal, very considerable; snow falls and lies, even in the valleys, and frost often lasts for the whole twenty-four hours. This comparative cold arrests the winter-growth of the vine, and gives it the rest which the plants of temperate climates require, and is probably one cause of the superiority of produce of these vines over those grown in other parts of Portugal... The upland vine is less productive, but makes a finer wine than that grown in the plain."[78]

Instances of this Superior Virtue Developed in Adversity.

If ever the history of this phase of American womanhood is written, it will show that during the momentous years which elapsed from 1861 to 1878, the severe trials which fell on so many homes during the Civil War and afterward, only served to call forth in our women,—in those especially born in affluence,—qualities worthy of the highest admiration. The political whirlwind which swept over the country ruined the upper classes in the seceding States, upset many solid fortunes in every portion of the others, while the fearful loss of life among both belligerents left thousands upon thousands

---

[78] John Latouche, "Travels in Portugal," pp. 121-123.

of homes dependent upon the sole industry of women, accustomed till then to ease and luxury.

While men, suddenly stripped of wealth and thereby fallen from their position, or compelled without due preparation to face the manifold hardships of a career they have never tried, are not rarely tempted to give way to discouragement and intemperance,—these noble women, with the self-denying fortitude which is an attribute of their sex, offered themselves to any sort of remunerative labor.

The Federal Government gave employment to a few,—very few in comparison with the number of applicants, and fewer still in comparison with the claims of so many widows, wives, and mothers, who had given their dearest to the country in her need. In France, after the desolation and distress brought to so many firesides by four years of slaughter,—the Government would have thrown open to these most deserving women every position they could possibly fill in the treasury, post-office, and other departments; this was a laudable practice introduced into the French administration long before 1870. The local State legislatures among us should have urged upon telegraph and railroad companies the patriotic necessity of handing over to women the many posts which they could have filled most advantageously to the public service.

It would have been—it would be now—an administrative reform full of wise economy and large-minded forethought. But Congress, at that epoch, in spite of all the noisy professions of patriotism made by the dominant party, cared as little for the economical interests of the nation as it does at the present hour, and held the most sacred debts of justice and gratitude toward the families of the patriotic dead or disabled to be very cheap in comparison with the claims of the ravenous political following that beset the doors of every Federal minister, senator, and representative.

It is time still to do justice to so many families reduced to want and destitution by the very devotedness of their male members. And we raise our voice here for the twofold purpose of claiming that some justice be done, even at the eleventh hour, and of urging on the attention of statesmen and other public men the wisdom of giving up to women, trained for the purpose, so many positions of labor and trust, in which men have shown so little of laborious husbandry, and so much of untrustworthiness.

Admirable Conduct of Impoverished American Women.

Much is known to the general public of the hardships so patiently and silently borne by these two armies of American women impoverished by the war; but that much is but very little indeed of the distressing reality.

Even now we could point out the descendants of men who filled with honor the very highest offices in our State and Federal governments, reduced in old age to seek a precarious means of subsistence by the exercise of some liberal or industrial art. And how many others pine in obscurity and neglect, after having sought in vain for honorable and lucrative employment!

We have said there were "two armies" of such women: for if this distress is so widespread and so deep in the States which remained faithful to the Union, how incomparably more so has it been among the once wealthy classes of the South and Southwest! Southern women, whose every male relative fell in defense of what they considered the honor and independence of their homes, had nothing to expect from an administration bitterly hostile to them:—and even had it been possible to secure them any portion of the places at the disposal of the Treasury or the General Post-Office, they would neither have asked for them nor accepted them.

Hence the distress and destitution among the very best classes of Southern women were, and are still in very many places, a something inconceivable. It will touch their sisters at the North to know, that, amid the long and hopeless darkness which settled on these once bright and ever-hospitible homes, their mistresses allowed no complaint or murmur to escape them,—no despondency to cast them down; but with a firm trust in God and a calm resolve to bear what could not be remedied, they set themselves to make thrift out of their very poverty, and to share generously with the many poorer than themselves all around the scanty store of comfort they could still dispense. How many stories have reached us, from every point of the vast territory over which the contending armies swept successively, of a but now reduced to bare walls, with the adjoining plantations ravaged or occupied by some insolent intruder! Woman was there standing a queen amid the ruins of her once happy kingdom, but still a queen, with loyal hearts to worship her, and with a right royal soul to share with these the unfailing treasures and resources of a love that is only strengthened by adversity!

How Women Are Often Treated by Federal Officials.

Before we offer a few words of practical advice to the persons who are fortunate enough to obtain positions under government, one little trait will afford the reader a glimpse of the most unmanly spirit of intrigue and treachery which, we fear, is not altogether a thing of the past in Washington or in any of the great centers where the Federal patronage is extensively felt.

A widow lady, belonging to one of our oldest and most honored families, had been utterly ruined by the civil war. She had five or six children absolutely dependent on her exertions, and, though highly accomplished, her talents could avail her nothing in a community where all her acquaintance had been, like herself, reduced from affluence to total indigence. She was as devout a Christian as she was a devoted mother, and, after sacrificing every thing she could dispose of to keep a roof above her children and to provide them with needful clothing and food, she had recourse in her extremity to Him who is at once the protector of the widow and her orphans, and the inspirer of men's hearts. She told Him in her prayer that he must befriend her in her utter need;—and, trusting in him, she applied for a clerkship in one of the departments of the capital, and obtained it, to the great surprise of her friends. The place thus given her was one of great trust. She filled it, as she would have discharged any duty, with the most conscientious fidelity, and was looked up to by all the other officials with unfeigned and involuntary respect. The emoluments of her place enabled her to complete the education of her children, applying herself, with the sagacity of a true-hearted mother, to form every one of them to be self-reliant and self-supporting in the future. Besides, as her salary was barely sufficient to cover the most necessary expenses for her household, she was advised to do what the misery of the times forced so many of her class to do,—to accept a few select boarders. One of the persons thus admitted into a family circle far above his own in social standing, was an under-secretary in the department. He was charmed at first with all he saw in mother and children, of goodness, piety, innocence, and the thousand charms diffused by that gentle life which is the natural atmosphere of truly Catholic homes.

Like many other of the superior and inferior officers of government, this young man had his own "following" of needy and greedy dependants. They had cast their eyes on the very office filled by the devoted lady with whom he boarded; and as she was connected with the "Lost Cause" through her family, it needed only some trumped-up charge to have her dismissed. Thrown as this young man was, into the intimacy of that home, he could not but hear both the children and the friends who visited them expressing their sympathy with the South, or their dissatisfaction with the acts of the Federal administration. A man of gentle birth, and with the high honor of a gentleman, would have died rather than disclose to the outside world any of the secrets of the family in which he lived. But the soul of the undersecretary was not so highly tempered as this; he revealed not only what he had heard, but much more than he had heard. As he possessed the unlimited confidence of his chief, the poor lady's fate was soon decided.

Suddenly, without warning being given or any reason for the act, she was dismissed; and no pleading availed to obtain an interview with the high and mighty secretary. This was utter ruin to the widow and her orphans. They were literally on the verge of starvation, suffering from hunger, when, three or four months afterward, chance brought to Washington a gentleman much esteemed for his public worth, but unconnected with any branch of government. His wife was with him,—high-minded, independent, like her husband, and the fervent, fearless advocate of right against wrong.

Both had rendered great services to government during the war, and their authority was such as could not be set aside. The wife was no sooner informed of the wrong done to the widow and her orphans, than she flew to the secretary, insisted on an instant interview, and set before him in the clearest light the wrong, which had been done under his name, and which had not, in fact, a shadow of justification. The order for dismissal was immediately canceled, and the under-secretary was directed to reinstate the widow in her former office. He, however, trusting to the speedy return to New York of the enemy who had discovered and denounced his treachery, deferred from week to week the execution of his chief's instructions, keeping the latter meanwhile in complete ignorance of his disobedience, and watching incessantly the approach to the secretary's door, lest a second visit should disclose his delinquency.

Meanwhile the poor widow was almost driven to despair. Day after day she had to stint herself and her children, doling out to them what was barely sufficient to keep them alive. While in this condition she heard that her benefactress was still in Washington, nerved herself to go to her hotel, and gasped out her tale of woe.

There was not a moment to be lost. Her friend, leaving the sufferer in her own room, after ordering her refreshment and giving her means to provide her children with temporary relief, went forthwith to the secretary. She found his aid watchful at the door and determined that she should not go in. But she walked calmly by him into his chief's presence and related what had occurred. This time disobedience was out of the question. The widow was reinstated that very day, and held the office till her latest hour.

But she was careful thereafter to avoid any sort of intimacy or social intercourse with the government officials.

And this is the first advice we give to you, ladies, no matter what may be the position you occupy in any department of the administration.

Hold No Communication with Other Officials.

There is a twofold reason for this, of which one must be apparent from the facts just related. The other is that one does not always wish to form an acquaintance with the motley crowd whom political intrigue and influence obtrude into responsible offices under government. To be civil and obliging to all, is proper and politic; to be familiar and open to all, is most imprudent, if not most improper in persons of your sex. We suppose you to be true Christians and true women; then respect yourselves infinitely, and others will ever show you infinite respect. With that, be most scrupulously exact in the performance of every part of your duty, and thus you will avoid all cause of blame or suspicion. There is another reason for the extreme and religious reserve of which you must make a cardinal rule; and that is the evil report which of late years has gone abroad from more than one department of government about the relations between high officials and their female subordinates. Necessity,—a sad and sore one,—compels you to seek and accept positions which may have been dishonored. The atmosphere of reserve, modesty, self-respect, and womanly dignity, which you will bring there with you, will honor the office as well as yourself.

Expect to Lose Temporarily Your Own Position in Society.

For the reason last mentioned, and for others, you will be tabooed by many of your former acquaintance,—by the vain, the light, the worldly-minded especially, by some very estimable persons, who are carried away by the current of general custom because they have no weight of character or independence of their own; but not by the good and truly noble who know you, appreciate your motives of self-sacrifice, and honor you so much more for the obloquy you undergo perforce; most certainly not by your religious guides...

The comfort of a fatherly word from these will be one of your needs during this period of labor and humiliation: fear not, God will know to place on priestly lips the very words that will light up the gloom in your soul and make you feel sure that your trials are only rendering you more dear to the heart in whose depths of tender compassionateness is all our sufficiency.

Amid your clerical duties do not neglect either your own cherished devotional exercises and pious reading, nor the other studies favorable to a higher culture. Do not "let yourself down" to the level of the common herd, because you have to consort with them for the time being. Your exercises of piety will always help to lift you up higher and higher; and the studies which contribute to refine and elevate will be a delight to you amid the depressing and intolerable monotony of office-life.

Above all things,—if your health and time in any way permit,

Hear Mass Daily.

We have seen[79] that, among the rules which every Christian knight had to observe faithfully, the very first was, "with pious remembrance, every day to hear the mass of God's passion." If this was a sworn observance of every gentle knight, how much more so was it and ought it ever to be of every true and gentle lady? In the dear old city of Quebec, where the writer was brought up from early boyhood to manhood, one of his most vivid recollections is the sound of the cathedral bell calling the working people,—the market folk

[79] Chapter XV., Part II., p. 241-242.

particularly, who are very early risers,—to mass at four o'clock every morning of the year. And he who took on himself the duty of being thus ever ready at the altar of the Lamb each morning was the most venerable and most learned man among the entire clergy of Canada.

Later, when many years a priest himself, the author remembers being touched to the depths of his soul by the simple and heroic piety of a poor servant girl, who, from year's end to year's end, never could retire before midnight, and "who had made a pact with her Guardian Angel to wake her up daily in time for the first mass" at the Church of St. Francis Xavier. Everywhere in Catholic countries it is the custom to ring the Angelus bell so early that workmen of every description may have time to assist at the Adorable Sacrifice before attending to their daily labor in house or field. Thus, if you chance to be passing up the Rhone valley in June or July, you will see at the first sound of the Angelus bell all who are not already in the village church hastening thither, taking with them their implements of labor, which they leave outside in the porch before entering the sacred precincts. Shall we, in this New World, where we are so free and so encouraged to plant and cultivate the loveliest flowers of Catholic piety, shall we not delight in sanctifying our daily toil after the manner of our forefathers? And will your own consciences, oh Christian women and maidens! not upbraid you with the neglect of such mighty graces as are thus daily within your reach?

"Ah, wasteful woman!...
How given for naught her priceless gift,
How spoiled the bread and spilled the wine,
Which, spent with due, respective thrift,
Had made brutes men, and men divine!"

Believe it: the moral hardship endured in such occupation as we here treat of needs supernatural strength, and how one half-hour spent early before the mercy-seat, in sweet communion with Him who is the bread of life, and whose blood applied to us in the sacrament intoxicates like wine and lifts us above ourselves, will send us forth filled with an energy and a joy all divine to brave every thing and undergo every thing for his dear sake! Be the supernatural woman in your present trial; be a true child of God,—and he will be with you!

Lady Companions and Governesses.

2. Although we did not expressly mention this most interesting and deserving class of ladies, when instructing the mistress of the home in her duties toward her children and dependants, we meant that all that is said in various places[80] should apply in a special manner to those whom she associates with herself as a companion, friend, and adviser, or as an assistant in educating her children.

The lot of most governesses is a hard one; but, nevertheless, it is far preferable to that of the very uncomfortable person known as a lady companion. A governess has work to do, hard work very often, and oftener still most miserably requited. But her very hard work is her salvation from discouragement and despair. A lady companion, generally, has no defined position in the family, no definite duties to perform, no set work at certain hours to which she can give her whole heart and mind,—forgetful of all else, for the present hour, but of the pleasure of doing work and good work on souls or for souls in his honor who is the passionate lover of souls.

A lady companion for the most part is a kind of slave to the caprices of an aged, infirm, and whimsical person,—tied down to every caprice of her selfish old tyrant, unable to apply herself to any improving or congenial occupation, and continually humiliated by the neglect of the family or the petty insults of the domestics, unable to resent either the odious pride and uncharitableness of the former or the studied insolence of the latter.

Happy the sensitive soul, born to better fortunes, often born in a sphere far superior to that of her present employers,—who chances to fall on a truly noble-minded and large-hearted Christian woman! For there are many Christian women whose little minds and selfish narrow hearts, in spite of their long profession and practice of a certain kind of piety, would justify the very common belief,—that they were as surely born with an intellect as narrow as a linnet's, or a heart as small as a mouse's, as some people are born stone-blind or deprived of arms and legs. No education (but such women cannot have been educated!) seems to have enlarged their very small notions of things, and

[80] Chapter VII., pp. 75, 93; Chapter XIII., pp. 184; Chapter XIV.211-212; Chapter XVI., Part II.

no practice of devotion has made a place in their hearts for any thing but their little self.

Advice to Lady Companions.

But no matter what may be the rank of the family in which a lady companion is admitted,—from royalty down to the latest fortune,—she who resolves to accept such a position must expect to find it one of the most irksome servitude. For one elevated and religious womanly soul who will treat a companion with the respect due to gentle birth and breeding and the delicate considerateness due to misfortune, there will be found ten unwomanly natures who will think it is due to their own place and importance to make a dependant feel her inferiority at every moment of the day and night. Where there is great intellectual culture united to solid piety, there is little to fear of the constant humiliations inflicted by those who are conscious of no superiority but that of rank or riches. True piety is always humble, charitable, considerate, kind, and courteous. Happy the young lady who becomes the companion of such a one! She will find motherly care in one who is her elder, and a true sisterly friendship in one of her own years.

But this is a rare case; and when it happens, the fortunate companion has only one rule to follow,—to devote herself, heart and mind, to the comfort and interests of one fitted to appreciate every gift of mind and heart.

God, in his admirable ways, has a most important mission for lady companions,—and that mission is most remarkable in our own days. Numberless families in countries where unbelief or skepticism is general, have been enlightened and converted by the agency of a pious, high-principled, and cultivated lady forced by circumstances to accept the position of companion to the mistress of the house. This occurs not unfrequently among ourselves. But it is of still more frequent occurrence in England and on the European continent. While in France we heard instances quoted of most remarkable conversions effected among the Russian nobility by persons thus selected for their goodness and accomplishments to serve as lady companions in great families. One, however, which happened in France itself, and which resulted in making most fervent Christians of an entire family given over to unbelief, may serve to show both what a thoroughly good lady companion can do by example and teaching, and what is expected that a true woman, well-bred, refined, and alive to the claims of hospitality should do in all cases.

Though some readers may fancy the good fortune of the young lady here mentioned to be an ideal, or, at least, an exceptional case,—it is certainly to our own knowledge not so rare. Let it, however, serve as a mirror for ladies blessed by fortune and in a position to befriend a class of persons most deserving of all their tenderest and most delicate sympathy. We shall see afterward the "reverse of the medal."

True Kindness Rewarded by Heroic Devotion.

While the so-called "Tractarian Movement" was at its height about 1840, an aged English gentleman with his only daughter, a lovely girl of nineteen, had sought during the winter months the mild climate of Southern France, with the vain hope of staying the approach of death. He was of a good family, of cultivated mind and refined taste, deeply interested in the controversy then agitating the English universities, and looking forward with an earnest longing to the day when the churches of Western Europe would be again one in faith and communion. Some years before, while seeking health among the valleys of Tuscany and Umbria, he had been fortunate in forming an intimate acquaintance with a noble and ancient family in which deep faith and practical piety went hand in hand. The Englishman's intellectual objections against the Church of Rome were met with masterly skill by the amiable and accomplished head of the house,—and his inveterate prejudices concerning Roman superstitions and idolatry found an eloquent refutation in the lives of his friend's wife, children, and dependants. Frequent and delightful excursions among the beautiful villages and historical sites which abound in that paradisaical region, enabled the invalid to convince himself that the Italian country-folk were solidly virtuous, that their piety was any thing but blind superstition, or their attachment to religion and its teachers one founded on fear and self-interest. He could not help contrasting the comfort, the refinement, the bright and quick intelligence, and the courteous manners of the mass of the rural population, with the stolidity, ignorance, and coarseness of the same class in his own country.

Still his convictions only led him to see that there were only fewer objections than he had fancied toward the reunion of the apostolic Church of England with the equally apostolic Rome. His stay in France afterward did not tend to bring him nearer to the truth. It was only a few months before his end that the conversion of his daughter became the occasion of his own. She had been a warm admirer of the writings of Keble and Newman. The sweet songs of the "Christian Year" had been favorites with her from childhood; but the celebration of the great feasts of the year in the beautiful churches of Italy, far more than the festivals of France, convinced the girl that the great Reality conceived by Keble was to be found, not in the empty Anglican liturgy, but in the time-honored worship of the Church of Rome. She had also read with deep interest Newman's beautiful sketches of the early Fathers, and of their love of monastic life. She found in France as well as in Italy religious communities of men and women whose life was in perfect conformity with the pictures contained in the writings of St. Ambrose, St. Jerome, St. John Chrysostom, and St. Basil. Father and daughter compared their impressions and their difficulties: she besought and obtained permission to be received into the Catholic Church, and her rapt happiness on the day of her first communion so powerfully moved the parent, that ten days afterward the same happiness was his own. Thenceforward till his peaceful end came, the bliss of both was only clouded by the grief of the approaching separation, and the thought on the dying father's mind that he left his child totally unprovided for.

The estates which he owned were entailed, and, as he had no sons, they descended to his nephew, a Low Churchman, to whose mind both the deceased and his child were the worst kind of apostates. She was informed, a few days after her father's burial, that her family had entirely cast her off, and that she could have no further claim on them for support or sympathy.

The generous girl did not lose heart on that account: she had a firm trust in Him for whose sake she was prepared to make any sacrifice, and was determined to support herself by her own exertions, without ever appealing to her relatives at home, or accepting aid from strangers. She was a proficient in music and painting, spoke five languages, and had been trained during her constant companionship with her father to be eminently practical.

A noble French lady who had made their acquaintance at Florence some years before, happened to live in the neighborhood of the town in which they had been staying. She felt a warm sympathy for the lovely orphan, whose many accomplishments and beautiful character she admired. She was exceedingly kind during the last illness of the parent, made her husband superintend all the arrangements for the funeral, and then insisted on taking her young friend home with her for a few weeks' repose and distraction from her bereavement.

A low fever, brought on by long bodily fatigue and severe mental trials, compelled a stay of several months with the family, at the end of which the lady proposed that she should make the castle her home for the next year, hoping that, in the interval, the relatives of the interesting English girl would relax from a rigor which she could not understand. Her young guest, in her perplexity, seeing no avenue open to her through the difficulties of her lonely lot, yielded a reluctant consent. There were five children in the house, two sons and three daughters, the oldest of whom was a girl of fifteen; they were under the care of an elderly lady, who acted as governess; and these with the grandmother, a titled and stately old dame of the last century, with a large retinue of servants, composed the household.

Not till after a week's stay in the castle did our heroine, whom we shall call Miss Edwards, discover that the old dowager was a rank Voltairian; that her son, the count, was an avowed materialist, while the countess only clung to the religion of her fathers by her attachment to the legitimist cause. The children were brought up in open and avowed unbelief, although the governess still seemed to keep up in private a few simple practices of devotion.

The dowager-countess, who had followed her family into exile during the Reign of Terror, spoke English fairly, and was in all things a great admirer of England, save, as she was wont to say, "the absurd and superstitious reverence of the English for a church establishment which was only Popery without the Mass, and with the reigning prime-minister for Pope." She took a great liking for the beautiful orphan, insisted on her having her apartment next to her own rooms, and put forth all the graces of a cultivated mind and the charm of most fascinating manners, in consoling her during her first grief, in soothing her suffering during her illness, and in amusing her loneliness during convalescence. The old lady was kind-hearted; her skepticism was the result of her early training and associations;—and it was very seriously shaken by the unaffected piety and deep, unquestioning faith of the little convert.

The latter had to relate to her venerable friend the whole story of her own and her father's conversion. This was told in presence of the count and countess, who, for the first time in their lives, felt an irresistible attraction toward the recital of interior struggles of two superior souls seeking for a perfect religious faith, and, when found, giving up the whole world to secure and enjoy its possession. Unconsciously the little convalescent was drawn into giving her own explanations of Catholic doctrine and practice; the perfect harmony history establishes between the Church of the nineteenth and that of the fourth and fifth centuries; the beautiful significance of the sacramental system, and the power of the solemn Church ceremonial in lifting the soul up to God. Then came a most interesting discussion of Catholic theories of art. Indeed the first acquaintance of the count and countess with their eloquent little teacher—for such she now was—had been made while the latter was sketching some of the most beautiful frescoes of the Baptistery in Florence. Now as she progressed toward perfect health, these sketches were exhibited, and the children were invited with their governess to be present at the charming stories about medieval Christian art and artists which the young girl poured forth as one inspired.

And she was. During her fever she had almost vowed—at any rate she had made herself a promise—that she would devote herself to the hospitable family into which, in her extremity of distress, she had been received and treated with such respect and tenderness; she would not quit that interesting household till she had enriched it with the only treasure she possessed in the world,—a living faith.

The countess, who had conceived a true motherly affection for the gifted girl, protested that she would never part with her, and the dowager declared that Miss Edwards had become necessary to her. So, to quiet the latter's scruples and laudable self-love, it was arranged that she would stay in the family as companion to the old countess, who, on her side, wanted to adopt the girl as her daughter.

About ten weeks after her father's death, Miss Edwards received the visit of a young cousin traveling with his mother, and who was all but betrothed to his fair relative. They had spent the winter in Palermo, and had learned in Rome of the death of Mr. Edwards, without, however, hearing then of his having died a Catholic. The son was deeply attached to his cousin; he was the heir to a title and a splendid fortune, and would have laid both at her feet if she consented to renounce what his mother called "the papal delusion." But, though the mother pleaded earnestly with her niece, she found her proof against all the arguments she could draw from theology, love, and ambition; and mother and son left the castle without any offer of marriage being made.

It was a keen pang for the young and fortuneless orphan: she loved her kinsman, though she said not so; and when he had gone, she was found in an agony of tears by the countess, who, touched to the heart, employed all the tenderness and delicacy of a true womanly affection in soothing her friend's bitter distress.

Let us abridge this narrative. The dowager, before a twelvemonth had elapsed, died reconciled to the faith of her childhood, blessing her whom she called her daughter and angel-guardian as the minister of God's mercy in her own behalf. From her son, with her dying breath, she exacted the promise that he should follow his mother's latest example, rear his children as true practical Catholics, and have especial care of the Christian education of his servants and numerous dependants.

The promise was faithfully kept. The conversation, the angelic life of Miss Edwards, the influence which her piety and goodness exercised on his children and the entire household, had made a deep impression on him. Since his first communion, he had never approached the sacraments. But the deep peace which had settled on his mother after her reconciliation with God had recalled the sweet happiness of his own innocent years. Then he gave his cordial support to Miss Edwards while she set about, at his request, instructing and preparing the three oldest children for confession and communion.

Nor was this all; the servants were also drawn to the beautiful young stranger. She took it on herself to instruct them likewise, and said with them the rosary and night prayers every day, explaining so interestingly this beautiful devotion that, at length, the whole household joined in night prayers, the count himself reciting them.

All this while the countess remained proof to every argument and example. Tenderly as she loved and greatly as she admired Miss Edwards,—the worldly education she had received, and her intimacy with one of the foremost female infidel writers of France, seemed to render her impervious to the light of truth and the influence of others' holy life. Nevertheless she consented to aid her young friend in restoring the beautiful little family chapel in the castle. It had been neglected for more than sixty years, and served as a lumber-room. But as she was herself a great lover of art, she gratefully accepted her friend's offer to decorate and paint it with her own hand. Miss Edwards had secretly vowed to do so in order to obtain the grace of the countess's conversion.

So the good count had the chapel cleared of every profane article, had the windows repaired, new furniture purchased, and a temporary altar made, the rector of the parish being invited to celebrate mass. It was quite a family festival for the household and the numerous tenantry.

Thenceforward Miss Edwards and the countess labored together to prepare designs for the frescoes, the illumination of the wood and iron work, and the restoration of the mutilated stained glass in the windows. The two oldest children by this time were able to work at some of the details. For our little apostle had been forced by her noble patrons to open a little school of art in the castle, and she found or created enthusiastic pupils.

And so the years sped by. Inside and outside of the castle the zeal and charity of the two ladies were felt in many a home, and their names mentioned together in many a heartfelt blessing and fervent prayer. It was precisely what our little heroine wanted, that her friend should seem to have herself the initiative in every good work, so as to remove all cause of jealousy,—and that she should have before the people the merit of every charitable deed. Thus all were in reality praying for the noble lady's conversion.

Miss Edwards would persist in calling herself the countess's companion, though the latter loved her and treated her as the dearest of sisters. They spent two seasons together in Paris, where the countess's friends were surprised at seeing her assiduous, together with her husband, at divine service on Sundays and holy-days, devoted to every prominent work of charity, while she continued to be attentive to all the duties required of her by her position in society. Some of her friends affirmed that Miss Edwards must be a female Jesuit, sent by the crafty order to the family of the count to convert his mother and himself, and to make sure after his death of a good share of his property. All this absurd gossip did not serve the cause of unbelief in the estimation of the countess. Still the false shame called human respect held her back from avowing to her husband or to her dear young friend that she yearned to have their faith. For she did not, and, as she thought, *could not believe.* Nor could she be induced to pray.

Such was her state of mind when the revolution of February, 1848, drove Louis Philippe into exile, and inaugurated once more a republican form of government in France. The count was elected a member of the National Assembly, and this circumstance led the countess and Miss Edwards to accompany him to Paris at the very moment the cholera was raging most virulently. The countess, alarmed, was just preparing to return to her family, when she was seized by the plague. Her friend at once, as by a sudden inspiration, offered her own life to God in exchange of that of the countess, on the condition that He would bestow on that dear soul the gift of faith. The sacrifice was accepted, the countess was spared to live and die a most fervent Christian; Miss Edwards was carried off by the pestilence, rejoicing that God had heard her prayer, and beseeching him to remember in his mercy her friends in England, and one above all others, whose love still lived in her faithful heart.

Unladylike and Unwomanly Conduct.

It should never be forgotten by families whom God has blessed with wealth, all the more especially when that wealth has been accumulated from the labors of the poor,—that persons forced to accept the position of lady companions, are, without exception, deserving of the kindest sympathy, and accustomed to be treated with respect. They are not born to such a position, nor prepared or trained for it from girlhood, but compelled to seek for it by misfortunes for which they are in nowise accountable. They are ladies not unfrequently born amid wealth equal or superior to that of the family of which accident makes them inmates,—ladies of refined feelings, sensitive nature, and very superior education.

To such is always paid by the true woman and the true lady the respect due to one's own sex and to the requirements of the former position, as well as the reverence due to unmerited ill-fortune, and the delicate attentions and cordial hospitality which make a shrinking, sensitive stranger forget the old home in the affectionate warmth of the new.

Our kind and generous-hearted readers will easily understand the lesson conveyed in the contrasted conduct of the two women mentioned in the following narrative, every detail of which is taken from real life in our own community. They will appreciate, we are confident, our endeavor to make of every mother who may take kindly to our teaching one able to fill her sons with that spirit of Christian chivalry we have already eulogized. One of its fundamental laws was reverence for woman and life-long devotion to her service.

A family of gentle blood and very superior culture had been involved by the imprudence of one of its members in disasters that swept every thing away but a bare competency. They settled, thereupon, in a remote part of one of the middle Atlantic States, and betook themselves to farming on a large scale, while some of the elder sons pursued the studies already begun in the liberal professions. The daughters inherited from their mother remarkable mental powers, which the most careful home education had developed to the utmost. But with this devoted mother's death other calamities befell her husband and children, and one of the oldest daughters, ambitious to be of help to her younger sisters, and much against the wishes of the whole family, sought the place of governess.

It so happened that the person who first answered the advertisement belonged to the class not then very numerous and called by the French *grands industriels*. His wife was the daughter of one of his business connections. There was wealth; there could, there ought to have been, if not the high breeding and refinement which come naturally with gentle blood and training, at least the gentleness, the delicacy of tact, and the courtesy which are the inseparable accompaniments of a true womanly nature. What there was, and was not, in the wealthy man's home, we shall see presently.

The oldest brother of the young lady, after vainly endeavoring to dissuade his self-willed sister from a course which deeply mortified him, felt himself bound to see that in the family she was going to there should be every thing to secure her comfort and self-respect. The mansion was far away from the city, and, though only a summer residence, it was magnificently furnished and surrounded by beautiful grounds. Both the master and mistress received the young gentleman, already most favorably known in his profession, with the most profuse assurances of interest in his sister, and reiterated promises that she would be treated in every respect as their own sister and a member of their family.

He, however, felt exceedingly uncomfortable amid the loud luxury of this splendid abode, and not at all reassured by the spontaneous promises of its masters. A last effort, on his return to town, was tried to dissuade the inexperienced and simple girl from her purpose; but she persisted.

To her surprise,—almost to her dismay,—she was received with the coldest courtesy; a French maid, destined to be to her a perpetual annoyance, conducted her to her room, notifying her that in half an hour she would be called to dinner. The half-hour of expectation gave the new-comer ample time for contrasting her own hospitable and refined home to the cold and gilded vulgarity which stared at her from every side. When, presently, she went down to dinner, she only found the children in the dining-room; and, though surprised at not finding any other member of the family there, she so far mastered every painful emotion as to greet all her young pupils most affectionately, keeping up a most pleasant conversation with them till the meal was ended.

The mistress of the house, who, in her total ignorance of what good-breeding and courtesy demanded, had deemed it beneath her to welcome a governess on her arrival in the house, now majestically sailed into the drawing-room, over-dressed, for her afternoon ride, and, without further preliminary, informed the young lady (whom we must designate as Miss Porter) of what she was expected to do. Beside her hard and impracticable task of teaching a half-dozen naturally good-hearted, but self-indulged and neglected children, Miss Porter was expected to teach their mother French. She was always to dine with the children, and, as they were in the country, she was to take tea with the master and mistress. But this great privilege was to be withdrawn on the return of the family to the city.

There was, happily, no time for reflection. The girl of seventeen was making her first experiment of self-reliance; and she nerved herself to the work before her. The training which her pious mother had given her enabled her to conceal a proud high temper beneath unruffled gentleness, the habitual result of conscientious self-restraint. She threw herself at once into her work of winning the children, and at once made a conquest of every one of them. This affection at least, she thought, would be one sweet compensation for the trials which she instinctively foresaw; and she would have pleasant and engrossing occupation in cultivating the young minds and hearts intrusted to her, after the same manner her worshiped mother had developed her own qualities.

She was not a handsome girl; but intelligence, innocence, and goodness lit up her refined features with a radiance far superior to mere beauty of outline or complexion. Her simple black dress, too (for she was in deep mourning), lent her the additional charm of interest in the eyes of her sympathetic young pupils; and thus the afternoon was soon passed, to their extreme delight, in a variety of anecdote and illustration, which instructed and charmed them.

At tea, the unwary and unsuspecting girl was drawn out by her host, Mr. Z—, on a number of most interesting historical and literary topics; and she, who had always been accustomed to hear such matters discussed in her own family, very naturally answered him to the best of her power, displaying not only remarkable and extensive culture, but great originality of thought and uncommon conversational power. He was delighted,—but not so his wife. Had the simple-hearted girl but caught the eyes of Mrs. Z—, and noticed the strange light that filled them, she might have been warned in time.

The conversation was kept up after supper; and the sincere enjoyment felt by Miss Porter during this first evening in her new home would have gone far toward removing the feeling caused by her chilling reception, if the mistress of the house had not suddenly and without any apology broken up the little circle by retiring very early.

Once in her own room, the sense of loneliness overwhelmed the poor orphan girl like the sudden rush of a mighty wave, and she gave way to the tears she had so long struggled to keep back. But her sweet exercises of devotion afforded a timely and most blessed relief. A chapter of "The Imitation of Christ," taken at the first opening of that golden book, gave her delicious words of light and comfort, as if they had been just written there for her by the hand of the Master himself; and then came the night prayers poured out as if she knelt visibly before the entire court of Heaven, and she almost felt that the Blessed Mother was interceding for her, and as if a sensation of nearness to her own saint-like parent stole on her soul like a soothing and blissful presence.

Happily, too, she knew not as she lay down to her much-needed repose,—that her mistress had already become her enemy, and that the French maid had sworn to be her foe from the moment she had crossed the threshold. Mistress and maid from that very first evening had exchanged opinions about the governess, and each found that she could make use of the other to render that young life miserable while within their reach.

Ah! if that selfish, under-bred, jealous mother had only known what a treasure she and her children possessed in the young stranger,—a child almost, who had at length lain down to slumber so peacefully beneath the watchful eyes of her heavenly protectors, how much she might have profited by the talents which afterward proved to so many a blessing beyond all price!

But with the very next morning began a series of petty annoyances on the part of the maid, and of vexations and humiliations on the part of her vulgar mistress, which went very near breaking that sensitive young heart and ruining the child's health forever.

The breakfast and dinner with the children,—though she felt the humiliation deeply,—would have been acceptable to the governess, because it afforded her opportunities of teaching her pupils good manners, and of reciprocating the delight her company never ceased to cause them. But the French maid, with a mock humility, found means of informing her in presence of the children, and of one or two servants, that her mistress never allowed governesses to dine with her. When the hour arrived for giving Mrs. Z—her lesson in French, the coarse nature of the purse-proud thing showed itself in some pettish remarks about Miss Porter's not pronouncing French as well as the maid; and to decide the question the latter was called in to give her judgment on Miss Porter's proficiency. Yet the brave little orphan resolved that she would keep both her temper and her place, were it only to improve the children who grew hourly more fond of her. And so she began her term of service, of servitude rather, resolved to work and

. . . "Wait from weary day to weary day."

Shall we detail the trials to which the unprotected child's patience, temper, and self-denying generosity were put by two women tacitly leagued to humiliate and wound her at every turn? And how, under all this unkindness and malignity, the young heart began to faint and sicken, and the brave, self-reliant spirit to grow weary of the intolerable burden it had to bear? For there was no one to whom she could, even if she would, open her full heart.

Then, although the children had their drives regularly each forenoon and afternoon, their governess was never permitted or even asked to accompany them, while the French maid became their almost constant companion in these recreations. Whatever outdoor exercise the poor drooping girl wished to take, she took alone in the grounds. Mr. Z—, it was but too apparent, had been lectured by his wife for presuming to draw out Miss Porter in conversation; and, for peace sake, he was as dull as he could be both at the tea table and in the drawing-room. But what was most galling to one who was a gentlewoman by birth, and accustomed to the very best society, whenever strangers visited the house she was not only excluded from the dinner-table but from the tea-table and the drawing-room.

At length the sad tone of some of Miss Porter's letters to her family awakened the suspicions of her brother; and one afternoon he and one of her sisters suddenly made their appearance in the house. It so happened that at this very moment some of Mr. Porter's most valued friends were visiting Mr. Z—, and the governess, for whom the visitors had a warm affection, had been, with an ingenious cruelty, debarred from every opportunity of speaking to them.

Nevertheless Mr. Porter was received with the utmost courtesy and apparent warmth, and proffered all the hospitalities of the mansion. But there was evident embarrassment in the politeness of Mr. and Mrs. Z—. The cause was soon made known by the young governess herself, who threw herself into her sister's arms with the joy and relief of one who escapes from the rack. And yet it was with extreme reluctance the poor girl told her tale. The brother could scarcely contain his indignation, and would have his little sufferer return with him that very evening. But her three months had not yet expired, and she was determined to fulfill her engagement. So, at her most pressing entreaty he consented to allow her to remain; and it was agreed that no hint should be given to Mr. Z—or his wife, of the revelation Miss Porter had been forced to make. The people were, he justly thought, so much beneath himself and his sister, that they must scorn to show either anger or resentment.

So Mrs. Z—was not gratified by witnessing either the exhibition of Miss Porter's feeling as she wept on her sister's neck, or when she leaned her head on her strong brother's shoulder, and promised him, through her tears, that she would do all the good she could to the children during the remaining weeks of her stay, and seek in prayer and communion with God the comfort which never would be refused to her.

She was thenceforward, if possible, more patient and more devoted; she certainly was brighter and stronger. She felt that the strong current of welcome sympathy flowed daily to her from the hearts of her dear ones at home; and from on high a still more powerful current of interior life lifted the young heart upward and bore it joyously forward amid the increasing persecutions she had to endure.

At length the three months came to an end. Before the end, however, another family at Washington, fitted in every way to prize Miss Porter as a companion and an instructress, had eagerly solicited the privilege of possessing her. They had become acquainted with her brothers and sisters, and were drawn to them by the twofold sympathy of the same religion and the same gentle blood and refined tastes.

Mr. Z—, when it was too late, remonstrated with his wife on the loss of the invaluable governess, to whose worth he had never been blind, and reproached her, very uselessly, with her most unkind treatment of a woman who, he declared, was infinitely her superior in every way. This did not mollify the heart of his partner or dispose her to regard the departure of her victim with any feeling akin to regret. The leave-taking cost the children sincere pain; they had been vastly improved by their beloved teacher, and never forgot her beautiful instructions and still more beautiful character. Her influence, however, was like the passing foot-prints on the sands of a stormy beach, soon blotted out by the next waves and the rubbage they left behind in receding. Their parents have long since been dead, nor shall the mention of their names on these pages lift them up from the utter nullity in which they and their fortune lie buried. Their children have built after them neither a name nor a fortune.

In Washington Miss Porter became in very deed the joy and delight of her new friends. She was loved as a sister by the noble woman who prized to their full value all her extraordinary gifts. The children fairly worshiped their teacher, and made under her uncommon progress both in learning and in the science of self-control and self-denial. But their generous mother, impervious as her unselfish nature was to any thing that savored of jealousy or littleness, seemed to make it her delight to bring forward her young friend on every possible occasion, using every industry to call forth her powers. Thus Miss Porter unconsciously found herself one of the most brilliant stars of Washington society, shedding around her a light and a warmth that created no envy, made her hosts of friends, and left her the same simple-hearted, pure-minded girl she had been at her mother's knee. Of her after career we say nothing. God knows it, and she would not have the world praise it.

Practical Rules for Governesses.

The two preceding narratives must dispense us with much counseling. We have in them touched upon some of the principal difficulties and hardships that this numerous, hard-worked, little understood, and ill-paid class of persons have to meet with. We trust in God's blessing on this book that wealthy mothers who read it,—especially if they be such as would listen respectfully to a priest's instruction or adjuration,—will be touched by His grace to deal kindly, gently, generously,—in all Christian charity and courtesy,—with those to whom they commit the whole or part of their own sacred function of teaching and educating.

Parents, of whatever rank, should remember that young women who fit themselves by long and careful training for the sacred functions of educators in families, are persons whom it is almost sacrilege to treat with any sort of disrespect; what then must the guilt be when such persons are degraded systematically, not only in the eyes of servants and other dependants, but especially in the eyes of the children whom they are expected to instruct and educate.

Surely mothers,—Christian mothers, alive to the surpassing importance of a thorough moral education, and conscious, too, of the sacredness of the duties they devolve on all persons to whom they intrust the training of their children,—ought to be also aware of the absolute necessity of securing to such persons the utmost respect and consideration within their own households. The reasons for this are peremptory. In the first place, these persons represent the mother herself (represent indeed both parents), in her most sacred office of teacher. Now reverence for the mother's person, and for this her office, demands that all who fill her place shall be reverenced in like manner. The second reason, akin to the first, is, that to teach, one must have authority; for, as we have said in another chapter, "without authority there can be no discipline, and without discipline there can be no education." A third reason is, that the dearest interests of both parents and children are involved in the result of this education; the interest of the parents, whose happiness must depend largely on the moral and intellectual advancement of their offspring,—and, above all, the interest of the children, whose future, temporal and eternal, is mostly secured or sacrificed by the training they receive.

It would seem inconceivable, therefore, that even worldly-minded parents should be so blind to what they owe themselves and their children, as not to choose their governesses with exceeding care, and to treat those of their choice with equal affection and respect. But that a Christian mother, fearing God and her own accountability to him, should not deem it a most conscientious duty to have her governess reverenced as she would have her own self, and aid in securing her the regard and affection not only of her pupils, but of servants, friends, and acquaintance—is simply monstrous.

We appeal, then, to the worshiped and zealous mothers whose whole heart is in their home-work,—in making of their sons and daughters children of God,—to welcome to their families the governess they have scrupulously selected as they would an own sister, and to make her feel that she is regarded as such.

This is one of the home charities,—and it is also good policy. We now address ourselves to the governesses themselves.

What a Good Governess Must Observe.

She also must have her heart in her work; loving it for its own sake, and for the sake of Him who is to be both her chief helper and her magnificent rewarder, and for the sake of the children, whose welfare and future ability must depend so largely on her labors.

Bear this well in mind; your success,—even supposing you could succeed without His ever-present help,—would be a barren and a joyless one without having your heart set on seeking and pleasing God before and above all things. This is the sursum corda of the divine sacrifice, the lifting of our hearts and aims to Him from whom are light and knowledge and docility of soul, and progress in all the ways of true wisdom and true happiness. Cultivate and cherish this loftiness of heart.

Be conscious of your own fitness for every branch you have to teach,—and do not rest satisfied with a half knowledge of any science which may be necessary or useful to you. Remember that, so long as you live,—devoting yourself as you do to teaching,—*you must study to improve yourself.* This conscientious desire for perfecting yourself in every thing worth the knowing, and the knowing well,—will be to you a most precious resource should you happen to be with a family where you are left to yourself. In religious orders, one of whose chief labors is that of teaching, professors after their class-hours are left to the solitude of their own rooms. He who writes these lines has himself thus taught for a good part of his life; and he knows by experience how sweet is that solitude in which one may refresh one's heart in brief and sweet communion with God, or in completing one's knowledge on some topic of actual interest or probable future necessity.

Be most conscientious in preparing the matters you have to teach, as well as in taking the very best means to communicate your knowledge to each one of your young hearers. If your heart is in your work, you can scarcely fail in this. Study carefully the characters, dispositions, and ability of each pupil. Love them, make them love you. Omit no art or exertion which can make them consider the school-room as a delightful place, and school-hours as a time of real enjoyment. There will be true enjoyment for them, if each hour and each lesson makes them feel that they have learned something. The ripe fruit from the tree of knowledge, which you will gather for them and present to them daily, you can make the daintiest and most appetizing of fruits, if you only use your woman's skill and cunning in preparing it.

With those who are slow be patient. Do not confound slowness with dullness. In looking back over our own college years, and those spent in teaching, we can now see many, very many boys who were considered dull because they had not the retentive memory or quick apprehension of others among their school-mates. But many of the men of quick wit and powerful memory have come to nothing, like trees blossoming before their time, and dropping their unformed fruit before autumn had arrived; while we now see the slow men, some even of the reputed dunces, foremost in the senate, at the bar, on the bench, or gracing the priest-hood.

Form the judgment and intelligence of your pupils well, without, however, neglecting their memory. Make them understand every thing, give them a reason for every thing; illustrate what is difficult or obscure by comparisons or analogies. All this will give the young minds you are forming a thirst for study, and will attach them to you. For just as women of your age can make the very birds, beasts, and fishes troop together to be fed by them, or even take their food fearlessly from the well-known hand, even so will the minds which you feed daily with sweet and dainty food yearn to be with you for fresh nourishment.

Be gentle, calm, self-possessed, well-bred, and reserved. There is always in a true womanly heart a good deal of motherly affection and tenderness,—which children will feel as they would the sparks from a charged electric receiver. Let them feel that in your heart there is that genuine pulse of motherly kindness, while you restrain it, and keep on it the check of reserve and dignity. Outside of school-hours, let this lady-like and dignified reserve never quit you.

Then, again, never omit an opportunity of increasing your pupils' love for their mother. This is one of your duties, and its faithful discharge will not fail to make her your fast friend. Show her yourself the utmost respect; and avoid seeking to be familiar or confidential, no matter how much you may be disposed to be so.

You will need great patience with all children; with some you will need extreme patience. You must endeavor to school yourself to *supernatural* patience,—practiced for His love who consummated our redemption and bought our souls from Hell by going to the pillar and the cross like a lamb to the slaughter. Few are the souls,—no matter how stubborn, how vicious, how perverse,—which are not overcome and won by meekness and forbearance.

Bear and forbear, then,—if you are sensitive, and know yourself prone to exaggerate or to create, in your trouble, phantoms which disappear with the return of serenity of soul. Precisely because you are thus sensitive and fanciful, never act or speak under irritation or emotion. How often have we to regret what is spoken or done impulsively! How often do over-sensitive and imaginative persons make themselves utterly miserable over a word or a look, to which their own fancy lent a meaning and a coloring without any existence in reality!

Be strong enough, brave enough to bear with a great deal, both because all have to bear with much, and because the very patience practiced at the present moment may purchase for us the grace which shall secure all our future happiness. It often happens that in a family, the mistress whose looks or words offend others, all unconsciously to herself,—is sadly burdened with many cares and griefs, and most deserving of your heartfelt compassion. If the sore heart, which she heroically conceals while filling all the duties of her station, were laid bare to you, you would kneel down to worship its goodness, instead of taking offense at the look of pain never meant for you, or the unconscious word wrung from her as from one on the rack.

And *forbear*,—from judging, from speaking, from acting hastily even on your good impulses. Be *mistress in the house of your own soul*, especially while you are under the roof of another; and this discipline will enable you, when God's good time has come for you, to be truly *mistress of your own house*, governing it patiently, gently, lovingly, and wisely; loved of your husband, your children, your servants. All this will come of that sweet womanly forbearance learned and practiced by you while dependent on others.

Imitate to the utmost of your power the examples of the lovely girl mentioned in the section on lady companions. Should the family in which you find yourself be one lost to all sense of religion, see what your example may do to enlighten them. Perhaps God has sent you to them to be the means of their salvation. Perhaps their conversion may be the sole work on which your own eternal salvation depends. It may even be that there can be for you no place in the Company of the Blessed, save on the condition of having these souls now given to your zeal as a living crown around you there. Is it not worth while to try what you can do with them? And,—then, again,—is not the Divine Workman with you, in whose hand you are only an instrument? Ah! we do not consider often enough, all of us—priests and laymen, men and women, young and old—how much good He would do with us, poor weak instruments though we be, if we would only leave ourselves passively, humbly in the Almighty hand! Nor do we take time to reflect that even a living instrument, a living heart,—which will not obey that wise and loving hand, exposes itself to be cast into the fire...

Persons who have been well brought up, and have had from infancy all the opportunities and graces necessary to form both mind and heart, are but too apt to misjudge families which have never enjoyed these advantages,—families that have risen to opulence through a brave struggle with obstacles of every kind, and in which the parents are either unconscious of their own deficiencies, or deplore them most bitterly. When brought suddenly into contact with such persons, we are shocked and repelled by their rusticity, their rudeness, their apparent lack, not of culture only, but of all religious principle. We judge rashly.

One most dear to the writer, and who is now with God, happened to be situated in some such circumstances as these. A privileged and beautiful soul himself, and blessed from his birth with all the divinest influences of a Christian home and training, he found himself all at once living with people foreign to him in religion, in culture, in manners, even in the way they spoke his language and judged of all things human and divine. There was discontent, aversion, and a repulsion so great that he was on the point of withdrawing from a place to which, as events proved, he had been providentially led for the benefit of this very people.

On the eve of the day fixed for his departure, he dreamed that he was traveling in a mountainous region and had to scale a lofty chain which opposed itself like a wall to his further progress. As he climbed with his guide the fair slope facing the south and east, their path lay through a succession of lordly oaks and chestnuts, to the fir and heath-covered region near the top where every variety of wild flower grew and scented the air. But the steep northern acclivity offered a barren and almost naked wall of rock, on which a ray of the sun never rested, and deep dark ravines running down to the gloomy valley beneath. As our young traveler gazed amazed and impatient at this scene of weird desolation, murmuring against the barrenness and horrors of the place, and contrasting it with the smiling and fruitful slopes they had just passed, he was reproved by his mysterious guide. "See you not," said he, "that the cause of all this wealth of tree and shrub and flower that you have been admiring and praising, is the sunlight which floods it the whole year round,—while not one ray of the beneficent light ever warms these steep walls of barren rock, or cheers the deep gloom of yonder fearful ravines?"

The sleeper awoke to understand that man's soul also needs the sunlight of divine grace to warm its barren and rugged nature, its dark and dangerous sides, into life and fertility and moral loveliness. So he remained true to his post, and the spot where that vision was sent him now blooms with the fairest flowers and fruits of supernatural goodness.

Let us also be warned by our own very fretfulness, impatience, and uncharitableness that it is not the Spirit of God who inspires our distaste or aversion; and let us gain his blessing by applying ourselves, with his aid, to bring light into the dark places, and to make what is barren and naked bloom like the garden of God.

Where this inferiority of culture is apparent in the mistress of the home,—it must be your study never to allow her to feel that you perceive her deficiency or that you are conscious of your own superiority. On the contrary you must endeavor to be more respectful and deferential than if she were your superior in intelligence and accomplishments, as she is in wealth or social position.

Should it so happen, however, that you cannot remain in the family,—no matter from what cause,—there are two things which it behooves you to observe in leaving: the one, that you continue to the very last moment to show yourself the true lady, not permitting yourself either complaint or quarrel, though never so bitterly provoked,—that not a word escapes your lips that can lower you in your own esteem; the other is, to make every sacrifice of feeling, temper, and even interest, rather than not part in perfect friendship with the family.

But, supposing the worst,—that you cannot leave, and that your life is almost made intolerable,—we cannot impress on you too strongly the necessity of strengthening your soul by prayer, by the sacraments, and by an unfailing trust in God. There is a precious lesson in this well-known song:

> "One by one the sands are flowing, one by one the moments fall;
> Some are coming, some are going, do not strive to grasp them all.
> One by one thy duties wait thee, let thy whole strength go to each;
> Let no future dreams elate thee,—learn thou first what these can teach.
> One by one (bright gifts from Heaven), joys are sent thee here below;
> Take them readily when given, ready, too, to let them go.
> One by one thy griefs shall meet thee; do not fear an armed band;
> One will fade as others greet thee, shadows passing through the land.
> Do not look at life's long sorrow; see how small each moment's pain;
> God will help thee for to-morrow,—so each day begin again.
> Every hour that fleets so slowly has its task to do or bear;
> Luminous the crown, and holy, when each gem is set with care.

Do not linger with regretting, or for passing hours despond;
Nor the daily toil forgetting, look too eagerly beyond.
Hours are golden links, God's token, reaching heaven; but one by one
Take them, lest the chain be broken, ere the pilgrimage be done."[81]

Were it given to every one of you,—as to an only and beloved sister in the chivalrous days of old,—to arm your brother as God's own knight, and to send him forth to do and dare and bear the utmost for the cause of the oppressed and the captive, would you hold him back because it might become his fate to be taken prisoner by the infidels or by some rude son of violence and blood and detained in bondage for years? The annals of these glorious ages say that many a brave youth so detained made of his bonds the means of enlightening his infidel captors, or of converting from their evil ways unchristian Christians.

You, women,—you, young women, particularly,—are to revive the chivalrous spirit of old, by arming yourselves with an invincible faith and patience—and seizing every opportunity and employing every occupation of yours to illuminate the dark places, and to plant the cross of Christ and the love of the Crucified in every home and heart to which you have access. So,—be brave-hearted, work, and wait!

"A little longer yet—a little longer,
Shall violets bloom for thee and sweet birds sing;
And the lime branches where soft winds are blowing
Shall murmur the sweet promise of the Spring!

"A little longer yet—a little longer,
Life shall be thine; life with its power to will;
Life with its strength to bear, to love, to conquer,
Bringing its thousand joys thy heart to fill.

"A little longer yet—a little longer,
The voices thou hast loved shall charm thine ear;
And thy true heart, that now beats quick to hear them,
A little longer yet shall hold them dear."[82]

---

[81] Adelaide Anne Procter.

[82] *Ibidem.*

School-Teachers.

The rules given above to governesses, as well for their spiritual advancement, as for their intellectual improvement, their thoroughness in every branch they undertake to teach, their devotion to their pupils, and their general deportment, apply to this most numerous and most respectable class of women,—young women, for the most part, in our country.

To parents who destine their daughters for this most important and most honorable profession, as well as to young girls who feel impelled toward it, there is one suggestion we feel bound to make. Let no influence or temptation ever induce the former to send their daughters to mixed colleges or normal schools, or the young girls themselves to consent to go there. It is one of those extreme cases where parents who fear God, instead of using their authority to throw their innocent children in the way of certain danger, are bound on the contrary to use it in dissuading and preventing them from a course fraught with peril.

Special Training for School-Teachers: in England.

We are addressing our advice to Catholic parents, of course; to those of other denominations we have no right to speak. In England the pupil-teachers who are preparing to graduate as school-mistresses receive a special training from the Sisters of Notre Dame de Namur, or from the Sisterhood of the Holy Child Jesus, both of which were especially selected by the Government, in conjunction, with the bishops, as the persons best fitted to train young girls for this vocation.

In Canada.

In Canada, Government has intrusted the female department of the Laval Normal School to the Ursulines of Quebec, and in Montreal to another sisterhood equally eminent for their method of imparting instruction. The professors of the normal schools repeat their lessons in the convent, a grating separating them from their pupils, and one or two members of the community always presiding during this course of instruction. They, as well as the junior members of their own order who wish to profit by the special lessons thus given, see every thing without being themselves seen by the gentlemen professors.

Let no one say that such a manner of proceeding is prudish or monkish or medieval: all we know is, that it has covered the country with most admirable school-teachers, while affording the latter the inestimable benefit of living beneath a roof which protects their innocence, and of being associated with the sisterhood in their magnificent schools, which thus serve them as a practical training-school.

High Standard of Excellence.

This continual seeking after the highest excellence, both in the sciences to be acquired and in the methods of communicating knowledge to others, has a most elevating effect on the Sisters themselves as well as on the pupil-teachers. It compels the former,—even were they inclined to be satisfied with a low standard of excellence,—to aim at having in their own professors and in their methods the very highest ideal, and of never being satisfied with mediocrity or a wretched system of make-shifts.

It is the wish and the aim of the hierarchy in the United States to have for all Catholic schools teachers trained to this twofold superiority of knowledge and method, as well as moral purity. This is a result which all good Catholics and good citizens are bound to promote by every means within their power. For on our success in forming school-teachers equal at least, if not superior, to all others in attainments and practical ability,—and decidedly superior in living faith and practical piety,—depends not only the welfare of the Republic, but the honor and prosperity of religion itself.

So, in religious communities, where such young girls are formed, no pains or sacrifice should be spared to make them perfect and unexceptionable in every way; every such pupil sent out from our academies ought to be enabled to take her stand at once before the public as an accomplished teacher and a trustworthy teacher. In our parish schools the formation of these young girls ought to be for the pastor, and for all who assist him in the divine labors of education, a matter of unremitting zeal. While directors of conscience, when they have discovered what is the bent of these young girls, ought to bestow on their guidance and instruction in solid and enlightened piety more than ordinary care.

The whole future of the Church and the country lies in this very point.

Importance of Proper Remuneration.

To our magistrates, legislators, and public men who have not only the making and administration of our laws, but the distribution of the public money and the remuneration of every public trust and service,—we would earnestly represent: that of all the professions devoted to the service of the commonwealth not one is more worthy of respect and liberal support than that whose sole occupation is to educate the sons and daughters of the laboring classes,—and not one, at this writing, is more exposed to be sacrificed to the illiberal and ignorant cupidity of our municipal politicians.

Defenseless young women, who have spent all their years since early girlhood in fitting themselves for this most important function of public teaching, are not only overworked, but they are underpaid, and are threatened with a further reduction of the wretched pittance received from the people's money.

They are the daughters of the people,—intrusted with the performance of the labor of all others most affecting the homes and happiness of the people. We appeal to the people to see to it that their hard-earned money go rather to the support, independence, and necessary comfort of this devoted class of teachers, than to swell the already too rich gains of so many functionaries without any thing like a serious function to perform.

Advice to the Teachers Themselves.

To the teachers themselves we cannot too earnestly recommend a sincere love of their profession, a firm determination to rise daily to a higher degree of excellence both in their knowledge and method of teaching, a love of their holy work for the sake of the work itself, and a fervent piety which will not only enable them to see God present in the school-room and aiding their own earnest labors, but God's angels too, invisibly present and seconding every effort to enlighten the young minds and hearts intrusted to them.

Devotion to the Guardian Angels.

Never begin your class without a prayer to the Guardian Angels; make your little ones join you in it. Give them an early knowledge and love of these glorious spirits; teach them what their ministry is toward us,—who are God's adopted children. This will easily seize upon intelligence, imagination, and affections. This sweet and most beautiful devotion to the holy angels appeals easily to the heart of childhood; and, besides, it places the mind of youth in the central truth of the entire supernatural order of which Christ is King, and these great spirits are the administrators in our behalf.

Patience with Perverse Pupils and Parents.

Do not be cast down or discouraged in your divine work of doing the best you can with every child committed to you, either by the rudeness or perverseness of the children themselves, or by the ignorance or stupidity of the parents. Well do we know how much the work of education depends on the sympathy, the support, the cordial co-operation of the parents. Well also know we how dispiriting it is to find any thing but sympathy or support from those to whom one would naturally look for both; how the head aches and the heart burns, when a superior is cold or indifferent where he ought to be fervent in his praise and most zealous in his assistance, or when a stolid father or peevish mother interferes to prevent all reformation or progress in a child, or to ruin discipline by taking away from the teacher all authority.

In Deepest Discouragement Seek Christ.

These hardships,—of general and daily occurrence,—make the load a poor teacher has to bear intolerable: and what can we say to each one of you, who faint beneath your burden, without a voice to cheer you or a hand to raise you up? This: Look to Him who is ever by your side, especially in your hour of trial. "The whole life of Christ was a cross and a martyrdom: and dost thou seek for thyself rest and joy? Thou errest, thou errest, if thou seekest aught else than to suffer tribulation; for this whole mortal life is full of miseries and everywhere marked with crosses... Set thyself, then, like a good and faithful servant of Christ, to bear manfully the cross of thy Lord, for the love of Him who was crucified for thee."[83]

And here is the voice of human wisdom and common sense helping to cheer you on your way:

> "I think we are too ready with complaint
> In this fair world of God's. Had we no hope
> Indeed beyond the zenith and the slope
> Of yon gray blank of sky, we might be faint
> To muse upon eternity's constraint
> Round our aspirant souls. But since the scope
> Must widen early, is it well to droop
> For a few days consumed in loss and taint?
> O pusillanimous heart, be comforted,—
> And, like a cheerful traveler, take the road,
> Singing beside the hedge. What if the bread
> Be better in thine inn, and thou unshod
> To meet the flints?—At least it may be said,
> 'Because the way is SHORT, I thank thee, God!'"[84]

[83] "Imitation of Christ," b. ii., ch. xii.

[84] Mrs. Browning.

CHAPTER XX.

THE TOILERS OF THE SHOP AND THE LOOM.

'Tis also well to tell thy heart
That good lies in the bitterest part,
And thou wilt profit by her smart.
But bitter hours come to all:
When even truths like these will pall,
Sick hearts for humbler comforts call.
Then I would have thee strive to see
That good and evil come to thee,
As one of a great family.
Then strive more gladly to fulfill
Thy little part. This darkness still
Is light to every living will.
ONE only knows. Yet if the fret
Of thy weak heart, in weak regret
Needs a more tender comfort yet:
Then thou mayst take thy loneliest fears,
The bitterest drops of all thy tears,
The dreariest hours of all thy years;
And through thy anguish there outspread,
May ask that God's great love would shed
Blessings on one beloved head.
And thus thy soul shall learn to draw
Sweetness from out that loving law
That sees no failure and no flaw
Where all is good. And life is good,
Were the one lesson understood
Of its most sacred brotherhood.

ADELAIDE ANNE PROCTER.

The Divine Comforts of Poverty and Toil.

Verily, without this magnificent brotherhood between angels and men, and between man and God himself incarnate in the son of Mary and become the elder brother of us all,—there would be but little light to cheer the dark places of perpetual and hopeless toil, but little comfort to warm poverty shivering over the expiring embers on her hearthstone, with scarcely a morsel of bread for to-day and naught but bitter forebodings for the morrow. What would the world be,—even the labor world of our free America,—without the faith in Him who said, "Blessed are the poor!... For theirs is the kingdom of heaven!" Oh! fools, fools that we are ever for one moment to forget or overlook the sublime, the all-embracing REALITY, that we are the heirs of eternal bliss, toiling, suffering, humiliated for a little space of life, to rest, to enjoy, to be glorified everlastingly.

We are drawing near Christmas-tide, with its entrancing memories,—its cavern by the roadside, the crib, the Babe, the two worshiping figures of Mary and Joseph, the exultant music that streams down from heaven, and the poor shepherds hastening to the new-born King. The Church cannot contain the joy which floods her maternal heart at the sight of our Elder Brother thus beginning his life of toil and poverty and suffering, and at the heavenly glory which floods that wretched cave, floods the hills around with their poor weary watchers, floods the crowd of poor worshipers round that manger throne, the royal maid and her carpenter husband, and these shepherds with their garments all wet with the heavy dews of midnight; and so, even after the joyous season has passed, she sings, as her look is upward to the "multitude of the heavenly host," and to the open gates of the everlasting city:

Dies venit, dies tua,
In qua reflorent omnia
Lœtemur et nos in viam
Tua reducti dextera.

"The day returns, this day of thine,
And all's again in bloom arrayed:
Led safely by thy hand divine,
May we the gladsome chorus aid!"[85]

[85] Breviary Hymn.

Hail, then, ye daughters of toil and poverty, infinitely dear to the heart of Jesus Christ, dear to the heart of his poverty-loving mother, and most dear to that of royal Joseph,—Joseph the carpenter, whose existence was devoted to unwearied toil for the support of these two, and whose blissful privilege it was to die in their embrace, cheered by their voice, and made infallibly sure of the eternal joys by the presence and the word of the Redeemer of Israel! May he inspire us with words of light and strength that may find their way to your minds to show you in what a right royal road you are traveling, if yours be the path of hard and unceasing toil,—and reach your hearts to make you love this divine company of toilers in which our Jesus is ever chief, and in which his most beloved companions are the mother who bore him and the faithful man who watched over his infancy and boyhood! We approach the ranks of this great army of women laborers with reverence and awe, seeing at their head these three august personages, the most so of all whose feet have ever touched and hallowed this earth of ours. And beneath the eyes of these three we desire to write every sentence, every word in these remaining pages, that so, the good done thereby and the consolation brought to sorely tried hearts, may be the pleasant crown of our toil in this book.

Toilers in the Shop.

In those Christian ages when religion was free to lighten gradually and then to break forever the yoke of the bonds-man, to lighten also the burden of the laboring man, to give to labor its dignity and to secure to the laborer by her edicts and influence a just remuneration, there was offered to the world no spectacle so sad, so disgraceful to the manhood of Christendom as these millions of women who in the most civilized (!) countries are, at this moment, subjected to labors more intolerable, and accompanied by prospects of livelihood much less certain, than the worst criminals ever condemned to the galleys!

How the Medieval Church Freed the Serf.

It may be well to see, just as our boasted nineteenth century,—the great century of *humanity*,—draws toward its close, how the Church in the year

1060 raised the poor serf, tied down to labor on the soil, to the dignity of a freeman, and in whose name she did it. We are in a monastery where a solemn assemblage of lords ecclesiastical and temporal is held to bear witness to a solemn act of emancipation. Here is the instrument:

"In the name of God, the Almighty Father, and in the name of his only Son, who was incarnate to deliver men from the slavery of sin, and to adopt them as his sons, we, that He may deign to remit us the sins that we have committed, restore to liberty our men who have been subject to the yoke of servitude: for the Lord God has said: Remit and it shall be remitted to you: and in speaking to his Apostles, He said, You are all brethren. Therefore if we are brethren, we ought not to keep any of our brethren in a servitude which they do not owe to us, as Truth himself declares, Let no man call you master,—blaming less the arrogance of human pride, than the injustice of domination: that is why we emancipate from all servitude our serfs, both men and women."[86]

How Servitude Is Restored in Our Midst.

How happens it that in this great city of New York there is an army of women,—young for the most part, some of them scarcely emerged from early girlhood,—whose numbers are daily increasing, and who are as helplessly, almost as hopelessly, the slaves of our wealthy shopkeepers, as if they were born bondwomen on their hearths,—and bound to give their taskmasters unlimited labor without the legal right to be housed, clothed, cared for in illness, or secured by their owners against sheer starvation?

Taking those among the weary toilers who are supposed to stand at the head of their class, the head dress-makers and saleswomen,—though compelled to wear costlier attire than their sister seamstresses, they are not much better off in the way of remuneration. A head dress-maker has to serve an apprenticeship of several years of the hardest labor and closest application before she can hope for steady employment. During this long and laborious preparation she has to support herself and to dress well; and, when she does succeed in finding a position, her scanty wages go almost entirely toward

[86] *Archives de Congues dans les Mémoires sur le Rouergue.*

providing herself with the stylish and costly raiment which her employer insists on her wearing, in order, as he says, to please the fashionable customers who daily pass through her hands for measurement, etc.... Then, again, she is responsible for the work of her aids and of all the seamstresses who work under her direction. Stuffs lost or spoiled, dresses wrongly made, etc., are placed to her account. We say nothing of the jealousies and countless annoyances inseparable from such a position.

Hard Lot of Dress-Makers.

Together with this cruel responsibility there is toil without cessation, both for the head dress-maker and for all under her. How ill requited are these interminable days, and, not unfrequently, sleepless nights, we need not say. The strongest constitutions soon give way, and the ruin thus wrought is irreparable. No medical skill avails to build up again a frame overworked long before its maturity, or, what is more, to raise up the spirit hopelessly broken by a long struggle against fatigue and poverty, intolerable tyranny and utter despair, at an age when a young girl needs the open air and the sunlight, and all that is most pleasant and cheering in God's bright world.

There are other hardships, other dangers—of a still more serious nature, and to which we would fain not be forced even to allude. Let us, therefore, give this class one word of advice and exhortation.

Advice to Dress-Makers and Saleswomen.

Respect yourselves sovereignly; and, precisely because you are poor, dependent, and constrained to do hard work for very little money, never permit any one placed above you in your labor, so much as to breathe a word capable of bringing a blush to your cheek. That you are dependent on your labor is not a shame, nor a disgrace, nor a sin; your poverty is honorable, your anxious desire to make your labor yield aid and support to the dear ones at home as well as to yourself, is most honorable to you;—but your virtue is God's treasure as well as your own most precious fortune: guard it with the spirit, the pride, the indomitable courage that become one who knows herself to be "a child of God."

You need not be told whence these dangers threaten you in your sacred honor: they come from the very necessity, sometimes, of being dressed above your means,—more frequently still from that natural vanity which makes one desire to appear as well as persons of one's own age and class, and whose rich dress seems to make them beings of a different order. "Handsome is who handsome does!" Remember it well.

Then, be punctual to hours, be faithful and conscientious in your labor; be strictly and most scrupulously careful never to keep or lose or waste the most trifling portion of what is committed to you. And to this high-principled honesty add a truthfulness that would scorn to equivocate or prevaricate in any circumstance, even when your horror of falsehood may cost you your place.

There is a class of women toilers worse off even than the seamstresses or milliners; they are the saleswomen, who have to dress very expensively, to be on their feet twelve or thirteen hours daily, without being permitted to sit down once! and yet they are exposed at any moment to be discharged without warning or reason. There is not a morning on which, at their arrival at the shop door, they are not liable to be told that their services are not needed!

Modern Legislation Heedless of This Servitude.

We hasten over these details with an indignation which we can but ill conceal; and yet we only touch very, very lightly on a few points, and not the worst points either, of a system which is daily growing in its oppressiveness, its pitiless cruelty toward the young of the weaker sex; and no manly voice is raised to protect them!

Besides, our indignation is all the more righteous, that our boasted civilization and improved statesmanship aim daily at ignoring more and more the protecting agencies employed in former times by the august Mother of nations and individuals, to shield women of every age,—the girl and the maiden, particularly,—against the tyrannies of labor, the sufferings of extreme want, and the many temptations to which youth and poverty expose the sex. Alas! the day is past when that Mother could raise her voice and compel the manufacturer and the shopkeeper, under pain of ruin temporal and eternal, to be just, to be kind, to be chaste, and fatherly; and compel, if need were, the sovereign, the legislator, and the magistrate to interpose their authority between pitiless greed and helpless indigence!

An Instance Illustrating a System.

One instance may here show both the magnitude of the evil we complain of, and the simple heroism to be met with in the class which are its victims. "Happening"—says our lady informant—"to have some dresses ordered for myself and my family, I went into one of the largest of our city establishments. After purchasing the silks needed, I was taken up stairs to the head dress-maker,—a pale, sweet-featured, and simply dressed person of about twenty-three years of age. She was exceedingly respectful and ladylike, and made quite an impression on me by the air of fatigue which was apparent in her very voice as well as in her eyes, and by the lines of extreme sadness and sweetness about her mouth. It was, however, only on my second visit, and while fitting on some of the new dresses that, finding herself alone with me, the poor girl ventured to open her heart. 'Forgive me, madam,' she said, 'if I make so bold as to address you on something personal to me. I knew, the moment I saw you, that you were a Catholic, and felt drawn to you... Indeed I need counsel and sympathy, for I am almost in despair. Since ever I came to this place, I have labored most devotedly to make myself useful, to please both my employer and his customers; and I have reason to think that in every respect but one they have good cause to be satisfied with my work. This sole cause of dissatisfaction—though they have not expressed it in words—comes from my not dressing as stylishly as they wish. With true ladies or gentlewomen like you, there is no difficulty: they do not object to my plain but neat black dress, and as I treat them with all proper respect and am successful in suiting their tastes, they always go away well pleased and are sure to return to me. But there are other fashionably-dressed ladies, who are not of your class, and do not know much about good manners or the refinement and gentleness that a true lady shows in dealing with her inferiors. These on coming up here and seeing me so simply dressed cannot conceal their contempt and dissatisfaction. This is noticed by my assistants, who, as you see, are much better dressed than I am, and who are, besides, jealous of my position here,—though, God knows, neither look nor word of mine has ever wounded them. I am satisfied that they have reported all this to my employer, for this very morning I saw an advertisement in one of the daily papers calling for a head dress-maker who can afford to dress stylishly..."

"'I have an aged father and mother absolutely depending on me at this moment,—for my brothers have been for more than six months idle, and have vainly sought to find work of any kind. Thus, living as we do, not only economically but poorly, and refusing ourselves every thing that is not strictly necessary, you can imagine how impossible it is for me to dress stylishly. I know that there are others around me who do so, and can no more afford it than I can. But God forbid I should accept rich robes and jewelry at the price they pay for theirs! So, you see, how heavy my heart is, and what a relief it is to unburden it to one like you. For, to my employer I could never make known the distress and poverty of my father's home.'"

How it has fared with this interesting and conscientious girl our informant could not tell us. The case, on the whole, is a very mild one. But it affords a glimpse of the aching heads and weary hearts that are to be found in these great palaces of fashion to which our wealthy women daily resort, without ever knowing or caring to know aught of the tragedies that fill the lives of these heavy-eyed and heavy-souled girls who stand behind the counters or wait on them in the milliner's rooms.

Women in Manufactures.

We have mentioned the words milliner and seamstress; they form an army by themselves. Of the still greater army of women employed in fabricating the rich and gorgeous materials that fill our merchants' warehouses, as well as the hundreds of other articles that are known to trade as the special industry of women,—we could now wish to speak befittingly. It is a hard task. But let us draw a picture of these mighty hosts of women toilers from a work just now passing through the press, and compiled from the most authentic and the best official sources.

The Glorious Side of Modern Industry.

"What is called *la grande industrie* has given birth in the present age to so many wonders, and so many marvelous creations, that we are too apt to forget what has been the cost of all this progress. When we go into one of these exposition buildings where all the masterpieces of strength, patience, skill, and taste lie before us in splendid array, we cannot help yielding to a warm sentiment of admiration and gratitude toward that resistless power which is laboring unceasingly to transform the face of the earth. Here are light, soft, silky tissues whose mingled colors remind one of the brightest flowers,—cloudy-looking gauzes whose warp and woof are invisible to the eye, sparkling gems which the miner dug up from the earth under the shape of a dull pebble, and whose artistic setting combines all the elegant fancies of every age and clime. Over there are still greater wonders;...telescopes, which shall soon leave the firmament without a single unexplained mystery, and render daily the impress of the divine hand more manifest; microscopes, which in exploring the infinitely small almost equal in analytical power the creative power itself. Further on you see these prodigious furnaces that produce weekly as much as two thousand tons of iron, these stupendous pieces of machinery with which you might think you could move the world, these mechanical forces which, if combined, would equal the force of gravitation of this terrestial globe; and then, again, the wonders of steam navigation, of railroad traveling, and photography; in fine, that electric cord which will soon inclose the earth in a symbolic circle, place us in instantaneous communication with our antipodes, and thus enable science to begin to realize the great unity of the human race foreshown by the gospel."

"In presence of such an exhibition one almost feels one's self becoming a pagan, deifying over again human might and genius...

"Such is the song of triumph and thanksgiving which industry breathes into her sons, and which all of us, on certain occasions, find ourselves singing. But we should soon change our language if we could only see the wonderworker at her task in her own laboratory. We should wonderfully moderate our enthusiasm if we only knew how much the masterpieces displayed to our view have cost, and are still costing, of suffering, tears, and blood,—of lives of men and women and children! The inventor has not been the only victim sacrificed to his love of science and humanity; not rarely entire generations have sacrificed their health in bringing about a single industrial progress."

The Murderous Side of Modern Industry.

"What is still worse, the most frequent victim of industry is not man, fitted by his nature for the struggles and dangers of active life and outdoor labor;—it is woman, it is the child which the implacable necessities of trade opposition and of the laws of cheap production sacrifice, against all the laws of nature, to the unceasing toil of the factory...

"Medical science has drawn-up a list of the diseases which women infallibly contract while pursuing this sort of life. We must summon courage enough to read this long and mournful catalogue.

"First of all comes the woman worker properly so called, who belongs to all ages and countries,—the seamstress. Bent over her work during whole days, and sometimes whole nights, she loses her erect form and becomes round-shouldered; she frequently becomes a bloodless, consumptive thing, and almost certainly loses her sight. If she works on a sewing-machine, its continuous pulsations are sure to produce the most serious organic disorders.

"Girls who work at the loom are equally to be pitied: they are often quite young children, and with their little undeveloped bodies, and feeble strength, are forced to spend eleven, twelve, and thirteen hours standing upright near a loom, the continuous clatter of which never fails in the long run to disturb the nervous system.

"The woman, the young girl, whose skilful hands have woven the richly-colored stuffs which delight our eyes, is subject to various ulcers and other serious disorders of the circulation of the blood, arising from this compulsory habit of standing all day; nay, she may be troubled with the painful disease known as the noise of the shuttle evermore re-echoing in her chest."[87]

Diseases of Cotton and Silk Spinners.

We are all but too well acquainted with the chest diseases and hemorrhages caused by the fine cotton dust or film floating in the atmosphere of large factories: they destroy yearly numberless victims. Lace-works and fine embroideries send numbers to an early grave; and so does the manufacture of

---

[87] René Lavollée, *La Question du Travail des Femmes*, in *Le Correspondant* of October 25, 1877.

silk in all its stages. The putrid emanations of the cocoons, and the steaming processes to which the threads are subjected, produce consumption, vomiting of blood, and putrid fever; while the carding, etc., is accompanied by sore eyes, cerebral fevers, and inflammation of the lungs.

Moral Diseases.

We fear to dwell on this point. Moralists and economists have drawn up a far more formidable list of the disorders begotten in the soul by the atmosphere of the factory and the workshop, than the distempers with which the body is afflicted. Nor must we Americans flatter ourselves that we have preserved our manufacturing system and our industrial establishments from the terrible swarm of evils which have settled on them in Great Britain or on the neighboring continent, and have been as fatal to home-life, to the growth of all the fair flowers and fruits of domestic virtue, innocence, and happiness, as the locust plague periodically proves to the fairest and most fertile regions of Africa.

Godless Industry a Social Plague-Spot.

Serious students of history, scientific men, and travelers will appreciate our purpose in thus warning, by these illustrations, the public conscience in our own midst. One[88] whose unrivaled pen has written so many most beautiful and instructive volumes, thus describes the beginning and progress of that fearful plague:

Illustrated by the African Locust Plague.

"His finger was directed to a spot, where, amid the thick foliage, the gleam of a pool or of a marsh was visible. The various waters round about issuing from the gravel, or drained from the nightly damps, had run into a hollow, filled with decaying vegetation of former years, and were languidly filtered out into a brook, more healthy than the vast reservoir itself. Its bands were

---

[88] John Henry Newman.

bordered with a deep broad layer of mud, a transition substance between the rich vegetable matter it once had been, and the multitudinous world of insect life which it was becoming. A cloud or mist at this time was hanging over it, high in air. A harsh and shrill sound, a whizzing or a chirping, proceeded from that cloud to the ear of the attentive listener. What these indications portended was plain... Agellius and his guest looked at each other in dismay. 'It is the locusts,' they whispered to each other, as they went back into the cottage."

"Instances are recorded in history of clouds of the devastating insect crossing the Black Sea to Poland, and the Mediterranean to Lombardy. It is as numerous in its species as it is wide in its range of territory. Brood follows brood, with a sort of family likeness... Even one flight comprises myriads, upon myriads, passing imagination, to which the drops of rain or the sands of the sea are the only fit comparison. So dense are they, when upon the wing, that it is no exaggeration to say that they hide the sun. And so ubiquitous are they when they have alighted on the earth, that they simply cover or clothe its surface... Not only the crops and fruits, but the foliage of the forest itself, nay, the small twigs and the bark of the trees are the victims of their curious and energetic rapacity... They take pains to spoil what they leave. Like the Harpies, they smear every thing that they touch with a miserable slime, which has the effect of a virus in corroding, or, as some say, in scorching and burning it. And then, as if all this were little, when they can do nothing else, they die;—as if out of sheer malevolence to man, for the poisonous elements of their nature are then let loose and dispersed abroad, and create a pestilence; and they manage to destroy many more by their death, than in their life."[89]

Dangers in a New and Free Country:—the Armies of Women Toilers.

To estimate the risk in a new country, with immense undeveloped agricultural resources, the danger to population and to morality, threatened by the probable increase of the manufacturing industries, we have only to glance at the number of women and children employed. In 1860 there were

89 "Callista," ch. xiv. and xv.

already 73,605 women employed in cotton factories alone; in 1870 the entire manufacturing establishments of the Union employed 323,768 women, and 113,088 children. Taking the intermediate year 1865, we find that the single State of New York had 32,000 women in its factories, while Pennsylvania counted 60,000 women, and Massachusetts had 83,000,—women in this last State being as three to one in the woolen and cotton factories. We are now near the end of another decade, with a fearful increase in these numbers, in the proportion especially of women and children,—for manufacturers, not to be driven off the market, will turn out cheap goods, and in order to do so, they must employ the cheap labor of women and children.

Numbers of Factory Women in The United States.

Surely we are within safe bounds when we say, that, at the beginning of 1878, there are no less than 500,000 women and children employed daily in factory work throughout this great republic, without counting that other smaller host of toilers in our city stores and shops from year's end to year's end.

The Prodigious Hosts of Women Toilers in Europe.

Think of these numbers,—and then look beyond the Atlantic to the fearful hosts of the same degraded and sickly toilers to be found in European countries. In Switzerland, where the population is primarily one of farmers and shepherds, manufacturing industry does not offer the physical or moral dangers that it does even in our own Northern States. Nevertheless, in 1870, Switzerland counted in her various factories 62,396 women and 9,540 children.

In Germany, on December the 1st, 1875, there were 257,000 women employed in the various industrial establishments throughout the empire, of whom a large proportion were children. Belgium has upward of 400,000 women toilers; linen fabrics alone occupying 113,000 women. England and Wales, in 1871, had 1,522,000 women workers in their industrial establishments; and of that immense army 428,000 were under twenty years of age. We had rather not speak of Scotland.

Such are a few of the statistics that enable one to estimate what is the lot of the vast majority of women in the new democratic era, and under the benign influence of the socialistic civilization whose approach is daily predicted.

Social Outlook from These Numbers.

The debasement, the enslavement, the physical, intellectual, and moral ruin of woman;—the destruction in the child of the fairest and loveliest promises of womanhood; —the destruction of the poor man's home by the very toil to which industry subjects his wife,—the physical impossibility of rearing children, when the mother cannot be a true mother to her offspring, nor the father the protector of his wife, or the teacher of his children;—and the planting by the hearthstone of every laborer, instead of the cross of Christ and the sweet belief in the Father of the Poor and the Orphan, the symbols and the creed of the new humanity and fraternity:—this, and much more than this, of hopeless misery and moral desolation, is to be the outlook of that Christendom which the Church of our fathers had created?

The Ancient Church the Sole Helper of Woman.

No,—please God! She is still living to speak to the minds and hearts of the toiling millions, to cheer and sanctify and guard their homes; to bless the union of the working-man with his chosen companion, to baptize their children, and protect their souls and bodies from the advance of these odious doctrines, and the hosts of impure and loathsome creatures that undertake to propagate them.

There is no authority, no living institution, no power on earth conscious of its ability to save woman, to save our homes, to save society and civilization from the joint destructive forces of an industry without a conscience and a socialism without a God, outside of that grand old Catholic Church, to whom alone have been made the promises of immortal life and unfailing love for the nations.

Would to God that a spark of the divine fire which ever burns in the heart of the great Mother, could glow in our words, as we now address ourselves to all enlightened readers in favor of these mighty armies of women toilers the whole world over!

Appeal against Heartless Industry.

We warn manufacturers and capitalists of every kind, who employ large numbers of persons, that they cannot persist in violating the laws of conscience, of humanity, of nature, without at length turning and banding against their heartless greed all the forces of the moral world,—nature, humanity, and conscience, marshaled against them by a revolted public opinion.

Spare little children, spare girls of tender years, spare women who are burdened with the cares of maternity. You need the labor of the poor man; you shall need, presently, the labor of his sons and daughters: pray tell us what sort of children can that overworked, bloodless, consumptive woman rear,—if you persist in thinking, or in acting as if you thought, that her nerves and muscles can outlast the iron and steel of your machinery? And how often have your looms broken down or got out of order, since she began her long labors by day and her vigils by night in the midst of their ceaseless clatter? You are careful, however, to repair your looms, or to renew a broken shaft, or wheel, or bolt;—but what care you for the restoration of that poor, pale woman's health when it gives way at length, or for its preservation by plentiful and wholesome food, by a warm and comfortable home, by refreshing sleep, and the simple, sweet delights of her own fireside?

It Cuts down the Tree to Gather the Fruit.

Foolish man! You do not cut down in your garden the peach-tree, the pear-tree, or the apple-tree to get at their delicious fruit,—for, you are mindful of the needs of another season;—you would not set fire to the cotton-field in spring because a late frost had impaired the prospects of the next harvest: are the homes of your workmen, and workwomen, less dear and less precious to you,—even in view of your industrial prospects, than the field in which the cotton they manipulate is grown? Is the peach, or the pear, or the apple, a fruit more rare or precious in your calculations than the children of your devoted toilers?

It Destroys the Child, the Woman, and the Home.

Your are careful to prune the tree, to manure it, to take every measure that the currents of life, each year, shall be renewed and reinvigorated in trunk and branches; and you exhaust the currents of life in the veins of your working men and women, and care not what may befall them, provided that your mills turn out so many bales of goods at a stated time. The child you employ is crippled even before she enters girlhood; the fresh and blooming girl before she reaches womanhood is like a half-opened flower, drooping, colorless, and wilted on its stem; while the once healthy and happy mother affords no nourishment, or only sickly nourishment to her puny offspring.

Is not this an outrage on the most sacred laws of nature? on what the moral world holds to be most dear?

Look on this Picture.

But there is worse than this. We hold up as a mirror the following description of maidenhood and womanhood in European factories, and leave it to our experienced readers to say if the features seen therein are those of any of the girls or women employed in our great American establishments.

Birth of the Factory Girl.

"Moralists show us the factory girl born amid want and corruption, almost entirely separated from her mother by the requirements of the workshop, forsaken rather than reared in one of those wretched burrows which are the only home of the working-man, and in which the only examples set before her childish eyes are scenes of drunkenness and dissipation: these examples follow her first footsteps as she begins her industrial career, while still a child. For even at that tender age she can sift the coke cinders and watch a few spindles, or perform some other light labor not above her strength.

Her Girlhood.

"It too frequently happens that by applying her to such untimely and barren labors as these, no time is left for religious instruction, for attendance at school,—nay, even for the outdoor exercise so necessary to physical development. Thus the child grows up to adult age, and becomes an apprentice.

"At this critical epoch begin for factory girls the terrible trials that so few of them pass through victoriously. Left alone and unprotected, without experience or instruction, in the midst of vast and crowded workshops, subjected to daily labor lasting eleven, twelve, or thirteen hours, obliged to be at work before dawn and to leave it after nightfall, obliged also, too often, to work side by side with men, and almost invariably underpaid for their labor,—these poor girls are exposed to ever-present temptations and allurements to sin.

Her Maidenhood and Its Dangers.

"Should it happen that the sexes are separated in the workshop the girls are still under the direction of the male superintendents, who, from their authority and influence, can do great mischief. In fine, during the long working hours in the unavoidable half-intimacy arising from proximity in the same occupation, conversations are carried on in half-whispers, and very unedifying confidences are made by one girl to another, which open up to an innocent soul an evil world unsuspected hitherto. Then, there are coarse jokes, indelicate allusions, raillery more fatal than outspoken obscenity,—and, above all, the contagious example of their associates,—all combining to destroy the very last remnants of native modesty preserved beneath the paternal roof...

Her Married Life.

"The industrial labor of women,—and this is its most serious result,—tends to the utter destruction of the working man's family, and the desertion of his home. Leaving the house before sunrise and returning to it after dark, and tied down to her post in the workshop during the daytime, the working-woman is only in name a wife and a mother; she is degraded down to the nature of a factory hand. There are no more meals in common, at least during the day; for she has no time to prepare them. There are no fireside joys for her: how can she tidy and brighten things in her poor little home when she comes back to it after twelve hours of hard labor, harassed, exhausted, and only yearning for rest and sleep? There are no sweet meetings at evening, after the day's toil, between husband, wife, and children. The husband knows that he will find no fire on his hearth, no warm food to cheer him, nothing but a dirty and untidy room, and a nervous and ill-tempered woman. So he will go, like his mates, to the tavern, to eat and drink with them there, and to go home at midnight, if he goes home at all.

Her Barren and Desolate Home: Baby-Farming.

"There are no children in these desolate homes. They are a nuisance to parents who have to work all day,—they take up too much time. Scarcely are they born, when they are sent to nurse in some of these well-known 'baby-farms,' where the deaths among these little innocents yearly amount to 25, 30, 40, 50, 60, and 70 per cent... All are thus deprived of this tender care so needed by infancy, of these first teachings given by a mother through her tears or her smiles; they lack that first education on a mother's knees (*l'éducation des langes*), which no after-training can supply."[90]

This then is the plague-spot, this the nature of the pestilence. Assuredly there is any thing but exaggeration in this statement. There are manufacturers, we gladly acknowledge it, in our great industrial districts, who are careful both of the health and comfort, and of the morality of their working men and women.

Americans Should Be an Agricultural and Seafaring People.

But ours is, or ought to be, by the very force of circumstances and from the splendid bounty of nature, an agricultural and pastoral country,—a country

---

[90] *La Question du Travail des Femmes en France et à l'étranger.*

of prosperous farmers and hardy seafaring men. Such avocations ought to secure the republic, for ages to come, happy, peaceful, virtuous homes, healthful and robust parents, with a robust and healthful and numerous progeny. Our industries, if carried on extensively, should be regulated by the same wise laws and the same spirit which prevail in the cantons of Switzerland.

Such Was the Ideal of the Puritans.

As things are, or threaten to be in the near future, the Eastern States, the proud cradle of American freedom and thrift, are threatened with the total and speedy extinction of the original population; and that which will fill their places for a brief time will be swept away in their turn by the pestilential blight which is now on the homes of the Puritans.

Industrial New England Realizing the Locust Plague.

Shall we point in vain to "the plague of locusts," and the pregnant lessons it teaches?

"The swarm to which Juba pointed grew and grew till it became a compact body, as much as a furlong square; yet it was but the vanguard of a series of similar hosts, formed one after another out of the hot mold or sand, rising into the air like clouds, enlarging into a dusky canopy, and then discharged against the fruitful plain. At length the huge innumerous mass was put into motion, and began its career, darkening the face of day...

"Heavily and thickly did the locusts fall; they were lavish of their lives; they choked the flame and the water, which destroyed them the while, and the vast living hostile armament still moved on...

"After they had done all the mischief they could by their living, when they had made their foul maws the grave of every living thing, then they died themselves and made the desolated land their own grave. They took from it its hundred forms and varieties of beautiful life, and left it their own fetid and poisonous carcasses in payment."[91]

---

[91] Newman's "Callista," ch. xv.

Assuredly the brave-hearted men and women who first landed in Massachusetts Bay, and who reclaimed from the forest and the inhospitable climate and the hostile forest-tribes the rugged soil on which they planted their own homesteads, contemplated the creation of a commonwealth and a race devoted principally to agriculture, and next to seafaring. It never entered their minds that, with a whole continent as their birthright, their descendants should cramp their souls, stunt their bodies, impoverish their blood, and make their homes barren and desolate, by turning the fair land into a vast workshop.

This Extension of Industry a Blunder.

Thank God, this plague-spot, which is a political, a social, and a moral blunder, is as yet confined within narrow limits;—and in the Middle States, in the South and the growing West, American homes are still sanctuaries of domestic virtue and happiness, woman is not degraded to a something little better than a machine, and man is not likely to become a socialist, "a working-man made drunk and poisoned with the wine of communism and unbelief," and becoming, living and dying, like the locust plague, the curse and blight of a continent which God has made so beautiful and so wealthy.

But, impossible as it is to reach or remedy this enormous evil in its effects on family life, on women, and young girls, we can, at least, try to make our instructions and exhortations reach the homes and hearts of these vast armies of poor toilers,—noble toilers, so many of them,—worthy of all the sympathy and zeal of true-hearted men and women throughout the country.

Remedial Measures from Religion.

Can we wonder that the Church, in her infinite tenderness for human souls tried by suffering and exposed to the most terrible temptations, feels so anxious to multiply her orders and communities of religious women, for the sole purpose of ministering to the bodily and spiritual wants of these hosts of their needy sisters? At this moment, our American women, remembering all that their own dear ones endured during our late civil war, are zealously employed in organizing relief associations for the sick and wounded of the two great armies contending on the battle-fields of Bulgaria and Armenia. That is laudable.

But let our charity, O American women, begin at home; and let us turn our eyes and hearts toward the bodily sufferings, the heart-aches, and the deep, deep misery of the five or six hundred thousand women, girls, little children, whose lives are poisoned, whose bodies and souls are destroyed, and whose homes are made desolate and utterly ruined, by the excessive abuses of industry!

How the Church Protected Women Toilers in the Middle Ages.

We have related above how the Church, in the ages of faith, freed the slave and the serf from their bondage; we might have told how she protected labor and industry of every description, encouraging both the freedmen farmers in the country, and artisans and laborers in the towns, to form associations for mutual aid and defense. She only interposed her authority to prevent such associations or guilds from becoming oppressive to their own members or aggressive toward others. She limited her care over them to the securing of obedience of the laws of God and the State by every one of their members, and to the practice of justice and brotherly charity toward each other. As early as the twelfth century the industry of the Low Countries (comprising the present kingdoms of Holland and Belgium) was very much developed, while, on account of the very narrow limits of arable land, agricultural occupations were confined in some parts to comparatively few. Hence there were many obstacles toward the settlement of poor girls or obtaining proper employment for them, and a large proportion of persons of the sex were thus forced to live in celibacy and left without any certain means of subsistence.

It was a sad state of things, for which the Church alone, the common parent, could find a remedy. Just when this multitude of homeless and unprotected women were at their worst, God sent a holy priest called Lambert-le-Bègue (or Lambert the Stammerer), who united these poor defenseless girls into communities half monastic and half industrial, where, living under a rule and obeying one common superior chosen by themselves, all could unite a life of retirement and prayer with a life of profitable labor,—all who chose making the ordinary vows of chastity and obedience during the time they chose to remain within the protection of the community, the others binding themselves to observe the rules while living there. Both the civil and the ecclesiastical authorities united to secure such a blessed retreat from danger or intrusion of any kind; and thus the women toilers who swarmed over the land found there either a sweet, safe, and permanent home, if they chose to abide there and accept the light yoke of the rule, or they found a secure and blissful home—as compared with the lot of their sisters outside—while they labored for a time in laying up provision for the future and practicing all the virtues they might bring with their savings to an independent home of their own.

Lambert-Le-Bègue and His Labor Communities.

From the holy founder, Lambert-le-Bègue, these women were called by the people Béguines,—a name which the virtues they practiced and the countless services they rendered to the public caused to be blessed all through the land. The chief cities of Holland and Belgium were but too glad to favor the establishment of branch communities, and thus down to the present day the dense and hardworking population of the Low Countries has found for its women toilers a most blessed refuge and protection in the creation of a poor priest.

At this moment the city of Ghent possesses two vast Béguinages, both founded in 1234, that of St. Elizabeth, containing some seven hundred inmates, and the other upward of three hundred. These resemble little towns in the midst of a great city, each being an aggregation of separate houses or convents under their own immediate superiors. They have a parish church of their own, and a cemetery; hospitals and infirmaries. From the very beginning they devoted themselves to sewing, weaving, embroidery, lace-work, and all other work congenial to the strength and habits of their sex. Of course they were bitterly assailed from age to age by the guilds or associations of weavers, etc.,—as well as by some of the religious orders, who disliked a mode of life which partook both of monastic discipline and secular liberty. Other establishments, founded in imitation of that of Lambert-le-Bègue, while copying some of the main features of his rule, added others less favorable to that union of religious fervor and application to labor which was his great aim. These spurious Béguines fell into various disorders, became infected with heretical opinions, and threw great discredit on the name throughout Germany. Nevertheless, the original establishments maintained their hold on the public esteem, and were protected by bishops and magistrates against foes of every kind.

And so the industrial centers of the Middle Ages were preserved from the double plague-spot of physical degeneracy and immorality. Surely, in our own dear country, the day may come when our hard-worked young men and women will be shielded in like manner beneath the folds of her mantle, who is alone upon earth the true mother of the children of God.

Advice to Young Women in Factories.

As things are in our midst,—we can only encourage, in our manufacturing towns, young women working there, far away from their families, to be most careful in choosing both their boarding-houses and their companions outside of labor hours. Would to God there existed in every great industrial center some religious order of women who would provide comfortable, airy, and secure homes for these unprotected girls, and take a motherly interest in finding them safe companions, rational and improving amusements,—all the means of sweet rest for mind and heart and body after their long hours of factory work! In such retreats, where the pure and pious atmosphere of home affection would surround them, the Sunday would be truly made for these weary ones a day of spiritual and bodily recreation,—heart and limbs would recover strength enough to face anew the labor and trials of the coming week; and from amid the fatigues and depression of the week, these poor young toilers could look forward to the repose of Sunday, and to the loving care of holy women who would combine for them the tenderness of a mother and the trustfulness of a sister.

How They Are to Refresh Heart and Mind.

The first need of a young girl, thrown a stranger into a large workshop, is to find a girl of her own age on whom she can lean, and to whom she may open her heart. This is an imperious necessity; and the danger is, that, in yielding to it, an untrustworthy companion may be chosen. There are many ways to avoid a choice so disastrous to the newcomer. It is impossible that there should not be in every large workshop, certainly in every factory, some one girl, or several, distinguished for goodness, prudence, and charity. These are well known to their companions, and a stranger anxious to find out one such who may be a guide and counselor to her, has only to look about her at first. Her own instincts, if she be truly good and God-fearing, will soon direct her safely,—in virtue of that rule by which like soon discovers like. Besides, if God places on your path a true priest, a man of God, who knows his flock well, he will easily and willingly direct you, a stranger, and desirous of saving your own soul, to some person who will prove a true and trusty friend to you. There are, too, in every village and town, in every manufacturing center, several families at least, whose goodness is as well known to all as the town hall or the parish church. Seek an acquaintance with these. If you be what we have supposed you to be, they will have no hesitation in showing you kindness and hospitality at first, and then, when they know you better, in admitting you to their intimacy. It will be a priceless blessing for you to find some such a household where your heart can be rested and refreshed once a week or more, by breathing the atmosphere of purity and peace that fills it, by letting the loving kindness of true hearts flow into your own just as the silent dew or the soft, warm summer rains sink into the thirsty and parched earth. And when you are privileged to be received into such a household, show how highly you value it by seeking no other so long as they are contented to allow you to find your needed rest and recreation there. Let your respect, your gratitude impel you to be more attentive, more kind, more devoted daily to every member of the family.

Value of a True Friend.

Should you not find a family of this description, God will send you a true friend,—and be both thankful and devoted to her. Two hearts drawn to each other by that love which has God for its principle, will find a thousand ways of pleasing each other, will be each a rest to the other from care and grief and discouragement. Two girls truly devoted to each other will not fail to devise from week to week new methods of recreation and amusement. Their good share of woman's wit will be good security against wearisomeness. But being, as we have said, God-fearing, they will both seek together in their exercises of piety and the frequent use of the sacraments the surest and sweetest heart-rest within reach of the lonely and the toil-worn.

Yes, for every one of you, poor children of toil, no matter on what part of the busy, noisy, wearisome factory world you happen to read this, be sure that there is no refreshment so great and strengthening as that which you will get in the heart of a friend full of God's love and grace, and in going frequently to his heart who is your Redeemer and your chiefest rest on earth and in heaven.

Reading and Music.

But the mind also needs repose and refreshment. If you have neither books nor other safe amusement, try to have the conversation of a friend, when you are freed from toil, and talk of pleasant things, forgetting the workshop, with its sights and sounds, and the whole world of labor and wretchedness connected with it. If there are libraries from which you can borrow, then try to have some work that can really rest your mind,—that can take you away into a better and brighter world than that in which you are condemned to toil on from day to day. If possible, read this book aloud with your friend; read in turns, and as well as you can, improving yourselves thereby. Should there be singing classes anywhere in which you can join, and should God have given you a good voice, then learn to sing, and sing with your whole soul. The exercise will develop your chest, and will give you for after-life a most delightful means of recreation for yourself and others.

Should you be employed on factory work demanding education and a certain culture,—if you have learned instrumental and vocal music,—then indeed will it be your own fault if your leisure hours do not afford you recreation that will be truly refreshing and elevating as well. Cultivate most assiduously both of these accomplishments, and make them useful in lightening the burden and refining the life of those of your sister-laborers who are less fortunate than yourself.

Beware of Extravagance in Dress.

The temptation to dress as well as the best, and then to outshine the most dressy, is one to which many girls weakly yield. They forget that this temptation leads to others far more fatal,—to the love of admiration, and to the road to ruin. Dress neatly always, never showily; and never be tempted to dress beyond your means, or even to go in dress to the full limit of your means. Neither men of sense nor women of sense admire showy girls; because they are not girls of well-balanced minds, or, but too frequently, of trustworthy virtue. Be anxious to cultivate both your mind and your heart: store the one with useful knowledge and the other with the fear and love of God. Showy hats and fine feathers often cover brains little better than a peacock's; and a showy silk dress is but a sorry covering for a fickle heart or a shaky reputation.

Be Saving of Your Wages.

No matter how scanty they may be, put by a part, though never so small, every week. Your generosity, while toiling so hard and rewarded so poorly, must be in denying yourself a good many little things which, if indulged in, would not add much to your happiness, and would take far too much from your little purse. Give moderately to such charities as deserve your support: it is not expected of you that you can have much to give. And piety does not demand that you should leave yourself unprovided against the day of need.

Be Pure-Hearted and Brave-Hearted.

You will find among your companions many who have never stained by deliberate venial sin their baptismal robe of innocence. If God has so shielded your soul, that you are thus privileged, then no words we could address to you could convey suitably our sense of the divine mercy in your behalf. You have read in the Old Testament history of the three Hebrew children cast into the flaming furnace by order of the impious Babylonian king. God's angel was with them in the flame, preventing it from harming them, while they sang a hymn of triumph to the glory of their Almighty benefactor.

You know that your soul is as dear to the God who created and redeemed it as these souls were to him before he became incarnate. You also know that his angel is ever with you, to save, befriend, and protect you in every danger.

It depends on you alone to put away that friendship and protection from you,—or to secure it more and more by your humility and fidelity.

Watchfulness over One's Outward Senses.

You must,—in the trials to which you are exposed, and which are as terrible as the ordeal of the flaming furnace,—have eyes and not see, ears and not hear, hands which never touch any thing that can defile. Never open your soul to any affection, never accept or give love, that you do not feel sure is blessed of God.

Do you wonder how God can preserve a soul stainless, sinless, holy and pure in his sight, in the midst of associations which tend continually to soil and pollute? Then listen, and judge for yourself, and learn to trust your heart to His keeping who made it.

How God Can Keep a Heart Pure Amid Corruption.

Travelers in the West India Islands, or among the vast forests of the adjoining continent, find swamps covering immense tracts of country, all covered with water made nauseous and poisonous by all kinds of decaying vegetable and animal matter. There are no springs, not one drop of wholesome water to be found for those who journey through these trackless wastes, with the terrible sun of the equator raging over their heads. But God has made a provision,—a most marvelous one, for the need even of the poor idolatrous Indian wandering there. The Indian guide will, when the traveler's thirst is most intolerable, lead him up to a gigantic tree all covered with the serpent-like forms of vines,—and with two blows of his light hatchet the savage will separate a length of two or three feet of a particular vine, first above and then beneath, stopping up with his hand the lower orifice, and bidding his civilized companion drink. The latter will find the piece of vine thus cut suddenly off, to be filled with a water most pure and delicious to the taste, and which in that extraordinary climate is pumped up from the swampy soil to the extremities of that vine far above in the sunlight.

Will you ask by what process nature enables the roots of that vine to filter the impure and poisonous water all around, separating and rejecting every thing that is unclean and unwholesome, and sending up the water thus purified to refresh and to feed the wild vines of the forest?[92]

God has never yet revealed to mortal man the secret of how life begins or is carried on in any one living thing, animal or vegetable. But to preserve your soul sinless, to watch over the source of life in your heart, is infinitely more of a care to your Heavenly Father than to send the life-current of sap—pure, cool, refreshing and vivifying— through the wild vine of the forest or the lordly tree that supports it.

"Well Kept Is What God Keepeth."

Put your heart in His hand;—"well-kept is what God keepeth;"—and be brave-hearted. Do not be cast down, because God is with you,—his child, and most dear to his heart. Accept your toil, every day that rises, in memory of him who toiled for you in the carpenter's shop; and when you stand in the midst of your companions, and the mighty machinery around you has begun to work and to clatter, love to remember that "the carpenter's Son," whose hand rules the motions of this vast and wondrous universe, is near you, that his love and protection surrounds like an atmosphere of peace and light. Lift your heart to him oftentimes through the day,—when you are weariest and faintest,—and think how your moments and heart-throbs are counted by him!

---

[92] In Kingsley's "At Last: A Christmas in the West Indies,"—we find the following passage: "In one of these palm-groves we landed, for we were right thirsty, and to drink lagoon-water would be to drink cholera or fever. But there was plenty of the pure water in the coco-trees, and we soon had our fill. A negro walked—not climbed—up a stem like a four-footed animal, his legs and arms straight, his feet pressed flat against it, his hand clinging round it—a feat impossible, as far as I have seen, to an European—tossed us down plenty of green nuts; and our feast began. Two or three blows with the cutlass, at the small end of the nut, cut off not only the pith-coat, but the point of the shell, and disclose—the nut being held carefully upright meanwhile—a cavity full of perfectly clear water, slightly sweet, and so cold (the pith-coat being a good non-conductor of heat) that you are advised, for fear of cholera, to flavor it with a little brandy. After draining this natural cup, you are presented with a natural spoon of rind, green outside and white within, and told to scoop out and eat the cream which lines the inside of the shell, a very delicious food in the opinion of Creoles."—Ch. xiii., pp. 336, 337. See, also, *ibidem*, p. 159.

So will the pure heart be the brave heart. And, thinking thus of him who counts your weary weeks and days, and keeps in store for you the repose and refreshment of the eternal years,—you can comfort yourself also with such thoughts as the following:

WORK.

What are we set on earth for? Say, to toil—
Nor seek to leave thy tending of the vines,
For all the heat o' the day, till it declines
And death's mild curfew shall from work assoil.
God did anoint thee with his odorous oil,
To wrestle, not to reign; and he assigns
All thy tears over, like pure crystallines,
For younger fellow-workers of the soil
To wear for amulets. So others shall
Take patience, labor, to their heart and hand
From thy hand, and thy heart, and thy brave cheer,
And God's grace fructify through thee to all.
The least flower, with a brimming cup, may stand
And share its dew-drop with another near.

CHAPTER XXI.

SERVANTS IN THE HOME.

Exhort servants to be obedient to their masters, in all things pleasing, not contradicting, not defrauding; but in all things showing good fidelity: that they may adorn the doctrine of God our Saviour in all things.

ST. PAUL, *Epistle to Titus*, ii. 9, 10.

Servants, be subject to your masters... Not only to the good and gentle, but also to the froward. For this is thankworthy, if, for conscience towards God, a man endure sorrows, suffering wrongfully. For what glory is it, if sinning and being buffeted, you suffer it? But if doing well, you suffer patiently, this is thankworthy before God. For unto this you have been called; because Christ also suffered for us, leaving you an example, that you should follow in his steps.

1 ST. PETER, ii. 18-21.

No servant is truly devout who is not laborious; a lazy piety in persons of their condition is a false piety.

ST. ZITA.

What instruction and encouragement must not servants themselves have received from reading the words inscribed over the chapel in Rome (dedicated to St. Zita), *Felixque potuit duobus dominis divino humanoque fideliter inservire.*[93]

The Patron Saint of Maid-Servants.

To very many of the readers of this book the mountainous and lovely region which gave birth to St. Zita,—a servant-maid from her twelfth to her

[93] "And happily could serve two masters—a divine and a human—with faithfulness."—DIGBY, *Compitum*.

sixtieth year,—will have a special interest in that it was the scene of the apostolic labors of one of St. Patrick's most glorious disciples. For to Lucca, about the year of grace 550, came St. Frediano (Frigidianus), a native of Ireland, who revived religion and piety in that part of ancient Etruria watered by the rapid and turbulent Serchio. His eminent virtues caused him to be chosen bishop of Lucca in 560, and he governed its see till his death in 580. No city in northern or central Italy is more deserving of a visit from the traveler,—the traveler, especially, who is seeking for health,—than this beautiful city, "Lucca the Thrifty," situated in a plain which seems a paradise in the lovely springtide and early summer, with its silk factories dating from the age of Dante and its woolen industries of still more remote origin. It was a liberty-loving country also; for Lucca was, it is thought, one of the cities which formed the ancient Etrurian confederacy, and for three hundred years (1055-1342) maintained its independence as a Christian republic.

One stupendous miracle is recorded of its Irish apostle-bishop. The terrible Serchio annually flooded the fertile surrounding plain, and not unfrequently devastated it. But the holy bishop, acting under an inspiration from on high, sallied forth one day when the waters were rising and spreading desolation on every side, and while his people were praying to heaven for relief,—and seizing a plowshare, he traced a new course for the devastating river. Into this channel the obedient waters rushed, and through it they have flowed ever since! In the next century two of the Lombard kings, Bertharic and Cunibert, erected a splendid basilica over the tomb of this great public benefactor,—and within that beautiful and venerable church is the tomb of her whom the gratitude of six hundred years has loved to call the patron saint,—the model and protectress of servants,—St. Zita.

What a Country Girl Could Do.

Look we one moment into the mirror of her heroic life. She was the daughter of a peasant family living in the mountains some eight miles from Lucca,—a family, whatever may have been its poverty in worldly goods, most rich in those of Christian virtue; for one of her uncles died in odor of sanctity in his hermitage on Mount Lupelia, among the Apuan Alps, and one of her sisters, Margarita, lived and died a saint in a Cistercian convent.

A Servant in Her Twelfth Year.

When Zita was in her twelfth year she accompanied her father to market, taking with her a basket of beautiful flowers, an offering, it may be, for the shrine of St. Frediano, which was the loved resort of pilgrims from all the country far and near. At any rate the father and his child were met by a nobleman of the name of Fatinelli, whose dwelling was next to the basilica, and with him the little maid was left as a servant by her parent. This happened in 1224. From that day till her death, on the 27th of April, 1272, Zita lived in that household, near the shrine of her revered St. Frediano, fulfilling, as the years went by, all the offices of a faithful and most pious servant, and embalming the whole of Etruria, the whole of Italy, with the sweet odor of her angelic virtues and heroic charities.

Her noble master, who little knew how much the fame of his own house was to depend on the sanctity of that lowly maiden, spared her neither hard labor nor harsh treatment. But his children testified, long after he had passed away, that unkind words and harsh deeds never called forth from the much-enduring maiden a word of remonstrance or a sign of anger or impatience.

She grew up to be a most beautiful girl, simple and sweet, like the bright, fragrant flowers that cover the hillsides and deep secluded valleys of her own native Alps. She had many suitors, but had early given her whole heart to the Crucified, and had to bear many a rude assault to preserve her treasure amid the lawless and armed violence of that troublous period. But more than once, in defense of it, her wonted lamblike meekness was changed into the courage and strength of the lion.

Where Zita Found Her Strength.

She drew this superhuman strength and all her other qualities from constant communion with the divine majesty in prayer, and that absorbing love of the hidden God, which would keep her soul entranced for hours, like that of Monica, near the mercy-seat. Nor did she employ the time set apart for her household work in these exercises of private devotion. Never was she known to leave any part of her domestic service unfulfilled; for she knew well that in serving her earthly masters with upright heart and scrupulous fidelity, she was doing His will to whom alone all right service is paid, and from whom all duty well performed has its assured reward.

In those ages, in free Lucca especially,—all classes, masters and servants alike, deemed it an indispensable act of piety to assist at the morning sacrifice, and much latitude was allowed, even in so industrious a beehive as Lucca, amid her teeming plain and flowering Alps,—to attend evening song. The practice of "Perpetual Praise," which St. Columbanus had brought from Ireland to Gaul, and from Gaul to the wild tracts around Lake Constance, he also established in Bobbio, where he died at the northern extremity of that same mountain range which Frediano had evangelized before him. And this heavenly practice of sending up at every hour of the night and day the sound of adoration and thanksgiving, was kept up by the great Benedictine family who supplanted the disciples of Columbanus, and by the Dominicans and Franciscans, who arose side by side with the Benedictines. The churches of Lucca thus resounded day and night with the voice of sacred song, and all laymen who were at leisure to do so loved to join in the psalmody. Zita, when her day's toil was over, found her delight in joining the worshipers in St. Frediano. She habitually rose at midnight and sang matins and lauds with the monks, or meditated and prayed before some favorite altar, or hidden in the gloom of some remote corner.

Nor did these vigils affect her health or impair her strength for the labors of the ensuing day. No strength is equal to such toil as that of a soul fired with the love of God and the neighbor. Zita came always away from the divine presence filled with a deeper reverence for her masters and a practical humility which showed itself in her unalterable patience and gentle bearing under ill treatment. It mattered little to her that they were in the wrong and she in the right:—whenever she saw them angry with herself or others, if meek and humble words did not suffice to turn away their wrath, she would ask forgiveness on bended knees.

This sweetness of disposition, this humility which was proof against the most unjust and degrading treatment, and which avoided praise or flattery as one would fly from the breath of the plague, produced a deep impression on the Fatinelli family, and inspired them at length with sincere veneration for this angel of their household.

Zita's Unbounded Charity.

An angel she assuredly was to all who were in need of bodily or spiritual assistance, this little serving-maid of the Fatinelli. The poor throughout the city and from the surrounding district soon learned to come to her, and where she found means to relieve their wants was the secret of him who blessed the charitable widow's cruse of oil and pot of meal. Her slender wages were all given to the needy, and so was every thing which the generosity of others bestowed on her. Besides, the sweet odor of sanctity cannot be concealed amid the obscurity in which God's humble servants hide themselves and their deeds, any more than the fragrance of the night-flowering cereus can be rendered insensible by the deepest darkness.

It took not very many years for the faithful citizens of Lucca to discover and appreciate the rare flower of holiness that bloomed beneath the shadow of San Frediano and at the very foot of their apostle's tomb. So, they were fain to make the little maid their almoner,—feeling that a special blessing went with whatever was given by her hand,—and they were fain as well to beg of her in return the precious alms of her prayers.

It was affirmed by those who watched her closely and were in the secret of her good works, that God wrought many miracles through his lowly servant,—miracles which tended, every one of them, to cure or relieve the soul much more than the body.

Her Charity Works a Miracle.

One day a pilgrim from among the crowds who continually flocked to the shrine of San Frediano, came for food and drink to the hospitable gate of the Fatinelli. It was in midsummer, and the poor man was faint with fasting and travel and the oppressive heat of the weather. But Zita had dispensed her store to the last morsel of bread and meat, and the last cupful of the native wine dealt out to wayfarers. In her unavailing compassion she was about to send him away, when, struck with a sudden inspiration, she asked him to wait, ran off for a vessel full of fresh water, and, making the sign of the cross over it, she bade him drink in God's name. The poor famished man tasted it, and drank a long, deep draught: the vessel was full, he said, of the most delicious wine he had ever tasted!

In the house she put away for the poor almost every thing given to herself for food; nay,—more than that,—she never slept in the neat and comfortable bed assigned to her,—but always managed to have it daintily prepared for the neediest of the poor or the sick who applied to her.

Her Charity Toward Souls.

Her charity toward the needy soul, however, far surpassed her care for the famished and the sick. It was then the custom,—one which has only been done away with by the impious revolutionary crew now controlling the government of Italy,—that whenever a culprit was condemned to death, the bells of all the churches rang to invite the entire population to beseech the divine goodness in behalf of the sinful soul. Zita, on such occasions, not satisfied with praying with the entire household, would spend whole nights in prayer, pleading with tears and pitiful moans for that obdurate soul.

And so, year after year, from childhood almost to her lovely womanhood, and to the most beautiful maturity of old age, did that glorious life of self-denial and devotion to the welfare of others unfold itself. Long before her bodily strength began to wane, her noble masters, who had learned to prize their pearl of inestimable worth, would have her cease from her labors in their service. They begged her to consider herself a member of the family, and made ample provision for her support. But, as our readers may well imagine, Zita held her service, her dependence, and poverty of too high a value before God, to accept these honorable conditions. Not for one day or hour did she cease to discharge, so far as she was permitted, all the offices she had so long performed so lovingly, so dutifully. No increase of age or infirmity could ever induce her to abate her labors in favor of the poor and the sick, to relax her austerities, or to abridge her long hours of ecstatic prayer.

The Servant-Maid the Glory of Her Master's Family.

The house in which she lived became almost a place of pilgrimage, during her lifetime; for prelates, princes, the illustrious and the learned, as well as the poor and afflicted, wished to look upon those angelic features all radiant like the face of Moses, with the light caught from long intercourse with the living God,—all were fain to hear sweet words of comfort or encouragement from that venerable woman, who had spent half a century in doing the work of a servant-maid;—princes and princesses, the highest and the best in the land, esteemed it a blessing to touch the hem of her garment; and the poor and sick would kiss her very footprints on the street.

The public voice affirmed that on that night of April the 27th, 1272,—when Zita's pure spirit quitted its earthly tenement, a star of surpassing brightness shone in the firmament above Lucca. The children, who worshiped her, as if by a common impulse, ran together toward San Frediano exclaiming: "Come, come, let us go to the basilica,—for Zita, the saint, is dead!" It was a wonderful event, and a most thrilling spectacle that which the glorious republic beheld during that night and the following days: the whole of central Italy seemed to be drawn as by some mighty magnetic force toward the spot on which lay exposed those venerable remains,—the virginal body of that lowly-born mountain maid,—one of the holiest and noblest of Italy's many noble and holy daughters!

St. Zita Still the Protectress of Her People.

No one will marvel that her native republic should have chosen St. Zita for special protectress; nor has the veneration which her name inspires, nor the faith in her unfailing interest in the welfare of her people been weakened either by the lapse of time or the sad changes which political passions and revolutionary impiety have made in manners and institutions and the very face of all things. The new Italian government has discrowned the beautiful city, swept away from her circle of lofty walls and ramparts the shady avenues of grand trees, which attracted and delighted natives and foreigners alike; the voice of "Perpetual Praise" has long ceased to resound over the waters of the Serchio, and church after church has been blotted out with the old convents and monasteries. But they have not, as yet, dared to touch the venerable Basilica of San Frediano,—not through respect for the memory or the work of the ancient Lombard kings, or through reverence for the Irish apostle of the Lucchese, but through a temporary deference to the popular will;—for the people still cling fondly to all that is connected with the name of their sainted benefactress. And so, even under Piedmontese rule, Lucca, each year, on the 27th of April, just when the spring has filled the land with beauty, fragrance, and song, renews the memory of her proud days of independence,—of the united reign of liberty and piety,—by celebrating with heartfelt enthusiasm the feast of her most glorious daughter.

St. Margaret of Louvain—A Servant in a Tavern.

A contemporary of St. Zita's was St. Margaret of Louvain, who lived and died a servant in a tavern. Do not weary if our Mirror should afford you a brief glimpse at one whom the Church reveres and glorifies as a virgin and martyr.

Perhaps some of our readers will exclaim, "What! a saint in a tavern?" Ay, truly, a saintly servant-maid leading a life of supernatural virtue in a tavern, and not only that, but a tavern which its master and mistress made the abode of the most devoted Christian hospitality, as well as the home sanctuary of every virtue which true servants of God could practice. It is a wonderful lesson, but a most pregnant one. So, we pray you, bestow a very attentive look on these three saintly Belgian personages in yonder tavern at Louvain.

Remember, dear reader, that when we speak of taverns we mean those of the thirteenth century—of the year 1275,—not of those of the nineteenth,—in the year 1878. The thirteenth century was the age of St. Dominic and St. Francis, of St. Louis, King of France, and of St. Ferdinand, King of Castile; and the nineteenth century is the age of democratic triumphs and humanitarian creeds, of godless empires and the most abject and hopeless human misery. A tavern in a Christian city in the thirteenth century meant a house kept to afford cheap or gratuitous hospitality to the pilgrim and the wayfarer, in which all his bodily wants were reverently attended to for the love of God much more than for lust of gain, and where his faith, his virtue, his life and his money were alike safe from every danger. A tavern in the nineteenth century,—in what was once a Christian country, or in one which boasts of its transcendent Christianity, is—... Well, we shall spare you a description of such as we know to abound in every thoroughfare of this vast metropolis. God forbid that the immense majority of our readers should ever be compelled to ask or to accept *the hospitality* of such abodes. For the weary pilgrim or penniless wayfarer there is no room in the luxurious palaces that modern progress has substituted to the taverns, *the hospitals, hostelries or hotels*, of our fathers;—and the poor traveler who can afford to put up at a modern tavern, in this land of liberty, at least,—will find but little that resembles Christian hospitality, and but few safeguards for his purse or his virtue. The scenes of reveling, riotousness, or debauchery which became the habitual characteristics of such places when the Church had lost the privilege of protecting the traveler and the pilgrim, and when these had ceased to be reverenced as sacred persons, were unknown in taverns or hostelries of the golden age of faith.

What a Tavern Ought to Be.

Would that all among our people who keep taverns would think a little of the great practical truth which we here hold up to them for meditation, and thus return to the Christian customs of their ancestors! It is because the multitude walk in that road of evil custom which leads to dishonor here and eternal misery hereafter, that we would urge upon the God-fearing the necessity and the merit of taking the right path,—the royal highway of the divine law.

The virtuous master and mistress of Margaret of Louvain followed faithfully that royal road, and their wonderful charity and heavenly life contributed much to confirm their humble maid-servant in the habits contracted in the poor home of her virtuous parents. All three had formed the resolution of forsaking a secular life and joining the Cistercian Order; Margaret had even made a vow of perpetual chastity as a preliminary to her future religious profession. The tavern and all their other property had been sold by these good people, and the money brought by the sale happened to be in the house, when some of the cutthroats who always thrive in the best communities disguised themselves as pilgrims and knocked for admission after nightfall. The master of the house, wishing to perform one more crowning act of hospitality, admitted them; and, as his store of provisions had not been replenished, he sent Margaret to a neighbor's for a vessel of wine. As soon as she was out of sight her masters were pitilessly murdered and the house was ransacked for plunder.

On her return Margaret was seized and borne away to a desert place. One of the murderers wished her to become his wife; for she was young and fair, and he knew her to be most virtuous. But no threats or persuasion availed to make her consent. She had vowed, she said, to be the bride of the Crucified, and could not without sacrilege accept any other love. The men, who knew not how to dispose of her, became enraged at her resistance, and her would-be husband plunged a knife into her heart. Thus died Margaret the martyr of chastity, crowning by this glorious witnessing the life of perfect faithfulness and humility she had led in her dear master's home. The body was thrown into the river Dyle, but it would not sink, and was borne upward against the stream to the city, where the multitude, and among them the sovereign of the country, Henry I., Duke of Lorraine, beheld the prodigy. The body was reverently taken from the river and solemnly buried in the church of St. Peter.

Great Number of Canonized Servants.

It must not be thought that these two saintly maidens, living at the same time, the one in the south of Europe and the other in the north, were rare moral phenomena in the history of the Church. It is far otherwise. That history places us in presence of a cloud of such heroic souls,—to whom the Great Mother paid the highest veneration, in order to show that she was the worthy bride of Him who said, "Blessed are the poor!"

St. Notburga was a kitchen-maid. "Saints Nereus and Achilleus, brothers, over whose tombs a splendid tomb was raised at half a league from Rome, were servants in the house of Domitilla, a niece of Domitian, and their remarks on the vanity of human pomp led to her conversion. St. Seraphia, martyr, was a servant at Rome in the house of Sabina, a widow lady, in the time of Adrian, who by the example of her maid's conduct was converted, all along with her other servants, and who, becoming herself a martyr, was interred by the side of her blessed maid. St. Maura the martyr was a nursery-maid at Ravenna in the time of Decius, who secretly converted her young mistress, Fusca, instructing her in the faith."[94] St. Genevieve, the patron saint of Paris, was but a poor shepherdess, tending the flocks of a master in the desert country around

[94] Digby, *Compitum*, b. i., c. vi.

the then inconsiderable city. Nor is the enumeration given above of the servant saints in any way complete. Many other revered names have been preserved by her who is the loving and immortal mother of humanity, among whom was the young slave Blandina, who bore such glorious witness to Christ at Lyons in Gaul. "I am a Christian," she would say in the midst of most horrible and repeated tortures, "I am a Christian: no evil is ever committed by any of us!" Among them also was Potamiana, most beautiful and most chaste, who, with her mother Marcella, was put to death in Egypt.

Advice to Servants.

In presence of this "cloud of witnesses" attesting how Christ and his Church delight to honor the highest virtue in the lowliest condition, we desire to utter solemn words of advice and exhortation to the women-servants whom our "Mirror" may reach. Already we have borne most willing testimony to the boundless generosity of our servants in both hemispheres: God alone can becomingly reward their unceasing and incredible sacrifices. But it is the life-long experience we have had of this exhaustless liberality, this living and large-hearted faith, ever ready to give its all for the cause of God and his Church,—which impels us to be more earnest than ever in showing how we would fain make the most generous return that is within the power of a single priestly heart, by pointing out a few of the virtues and qualities which would raise servants highest in the esteem of their masters and in the reverence of all mankind.

Humility.

Do not attach a false notion to this word, or the admirable and most necessary virtue which it designates. The world, which does not care to have a correct knowledge either of Christian doctrine or of Christian morality,—the world, which sneers at the terms "humble" and "humility,"—as if to be humble one must needs be a hypocrite, and as if humility was only a mask for villany and deceit,—this world must be enlightened by *your* lives,—by your actions much more than by your words,—as to the true sense of this great and fundamental virtue.

It does not consist in professions and protestations, or in mere interior desires and sentiments. It consists in our being ready to accept, and in accepting willingly, humiliations put on us by others,—especially when they are undeserved. There is no road to humility,—that virtue which prompts us to wish to be beneath the feet of others because we are sinners against God's tremendous majesty,—save by humiliation, by being brought down and humbled before men, put to shame and confusion in presence of those whose honor and esteem we covet.

Take the example of the Divine Master. He took upon himself the expiation of our sins; and as the beginning of sin is in that pride which sets up our own will against the will of the Most High, "He humbled himself, becoming obediant unto death, even the death of the cross." The terrible humiliations of this most shameful death he accepted before taking our flesh as the atonement for the guilt of pride. In taking our flesh, however, he took it with all its pure and hallowed affections, with every thing that could not mean guilt committed by himself, or any other condition incompatible with the infinite holiness of the Godhead. Among the sentiments and affections inherent in the human heart are a great horror of intense bodily pain and an insurmountable repugnance toward being put to public shame, or charged and branded with an infamy undeserved by one's own deeds.

This is the meaning of that agony of Christ's soul in the garden,—when he felt that Judas and his band were already on their way to seize his person, and foresaw the insults and outrages to be heaped on himself before dawn, as a prelude to the incomprehensible humiliations,—tortures of body, and tortures of soul,—of the morrow. Hence his agonized heart-cry, "If it be possible, let this chalice (this bitter cup of shame) pass from me!" The Divine Person incarnate was to bear in his human body and human soul the dreadful weight of our guilt and of its expiation. His chief merit, as perfect man, lay in the heroic willingness with which he accepted what was most abhorrent to flesh and to spirit,—the torture of his body and the humiliation put upon his soul. "Nevertheless not as I will, but as thou [wilt]." Now, see him rising up from his place of prayer, to face Judas and his band, to face Herod and his court, to face the hooting multitude in the street, to face the scourging and the crowning with thorns, to face the shameful cross, and to carry it so far as his strength permitted through the crowded city,—and to stretch himself on it a willing victim for every one of us! And all the while allowing himself to be led like a lamb to the slaughter, meekly, silently, uncomplainingly,—he the innocent and the most holy!

This is why the saints, who thirsted to be most like the Master, to follow him most closely, did not wait till humiliation and shame came to them, but went to meet it. St. Ignatius Martyr, condemned (at least so he believed and hoped when he wrote the words) to be devoured by wild beasts in the Roman amphitheater, could not contain his joy or restrain his impatience: "Would that I could enjoy the wild beasts! Would that I were ground between the lion's jaws, so that I become the wheat of Christ!" And his great namesake, long centuries afterward,—Ignatius de Loyola,—sallying forth in his matted hair and unwashed beard, and sordid raiment (he the proud, sensitive soldier of yesterday!) to court the jeers and jibes of the street rabble of Manresa, that he might learn to keep down his rebellious spirit and the resistance of a soul that yearned for praise and distinction.

There is no humility, then, save through humiliation! If you have caught our meaning, therefore,—you now understand the sense of the words which the Master was wont to address to all who wished to become his followers: "Take up thy cross, and follow me!" As you would take from the hand of a noble general a brilliant uniform to wear in the service under him, or a flag to carry and defend in the foremost ranks of battle,—as in entering a nobleman's service you would put on his livery;—so, in making the very first step in the road along which the Crucified leads you, *take, accept, love, embrace* shame, humiliation,—THE CROSS, in one word, as the glorious livery which distinguishes the sort of courage, of bravery, of heroism, which marks the Christian, the true child of God!

Hence the sublime lesson which St. Peter (to be soon crucified like his loved Master) teaches all servants:... "Unto this you have been called; because Christ also suffered for us, leaving you an example, that you should follow in his steps."

Oh! do not pass away lightly from this divine lesson. Look well into the mirror which the great disciple's words and example, and the greater Master's life and death hold up to you,—if you would understand aright how you are to make your own service a true following of Christ.

Humility,—subjection, heartfelt and loving obedience, and patience under wrong,—has to be the corner-stone of the edifice of your salvation,—of the salvation and sanctification of every Christian servant. This is the reason that St. Peter says, "Servants be subject to your masters;...not only to the good and gentle, but also to the froward. For this is thankworthy, if, for conscience toward God, a man endure sorrows, suffering wrongfully."

The Practice of Humility.

It consists in accepting with a true and heartfelt submission the service to which you bind yourself, knowing well that such service is not degrading in the eyes of men, but that you can yourselves make it most honorable by your gentleness, your truthfulness, and your fidelity. It cannot but be honorable in the eyes of God, if you only look up to him as the person whom you serve, obey, and study to please in your master and mistress. The very foundation of practical humility is in this supernatural view of your relation to your superiors. If you are guided by low views, human motives, and mere earthly feelings, you will look upon your service as a yoke which degrades you, and perform your duties only because you cannot help yourselves, or for the sake of the miserable wages you work for. God help the Christian servant that allows her mind to be darkened by these low views, or her heart to be narrowed by such false pride and such greed of gain!

Consider that whatever you do and suffer, you undergo and do for his sake who is Lord and Father over all, and in imitation of Him who spent thirty years under the roof of Joseph the carpenter, plying the same trade till he began his public missionary career, and all the while obeying his parents with unfeigned reverence and submission.

If you are a servant after Christ's own heart, you will be gentle,—invariably gentle,—gentle not only when treated with kindness and deference by your masters and fellow-servants, but more especially so when treated with unkindness, incivility and injustice. Let your chief aim be to please him, and obtain his praise, "Who when he was reviled, did not revile; when he suffered, he threatened not; but delivered himself to him that judged him unjustly."[95]

---

[95] 1 Peter ii. 23.

Be far more anxious to acquire and increase your store of merit with the Divine Master, by not only obeying faithfully and punctually when you are bidden to do what is pleasing, honorable, and of easy accomplishment, but more particularly by loving and prompt obedience when you are commanded to do what is distasteful, apparently degrading, or most difficult and laborious.

The willingness shown in obeying diligently and accomplishing most difficult things, when you are prompted to do so by kind words, by praise, or by your affection for your mistress,—may be very praiseworthy in itself,—but it is not humility. True humility consists in obeying a harsh order or in doing what is most irksome, and that for a person who evidently dislikes you or is disagreeable in many ways,—solely because you who are a sinner, and a lowly creature, are striving to imitate the obedience, the patience, the heroic perseverance of the Lord and Master.

Obedience Which Is Not Humility.

There are very many good servants, who are sincerely desirous of being humble and obedient, but who entirely misunderstand the way of being so. They will do any thing and work themselves beyond their strength to please a mistress or a master who have none but pleasant looks and kind words for them;—these good girls are also very punctual in receiving the sacrament, and fancy perhaps that they are truly pious and pleasing to God. But some of them cannot endure a single word of dispraise, a single unkind look, and will either fly into a towering passion, or become moody and surly, will brood for days over what they consider an injustice or an insult, and will only resume their cheerful looks and good temper when they are again fed with praise. This is any thing but humility.

Humility is self-denial as well as self-control. It denies and humbles this natural, proud, vain, praise-loving self of ours,—and is glad when pride and self-love have to suffer and to bleed. One of the first efforts of true humility, which makes us little and of no account in our own eyes,—is to make us patient, silent, self-controlled under reproof, insult and wrong. Let such moody, uncertain, and irascible persons look into the mirror of Christ's example and the examples of his saints, and set about examining their consciences. They have yet to know what humility is, and to make the first step on the road of that virtue which alone can render them followers of the Master.

Let humility, therefore, keep your soul in peace when the sound of harsh, unjust and cruel words is in your ears. But, this same sweet virtue will impel you to be a peace-maker among your fellow-servants. Learn to suffer from them with the same unalterable patience with which you endure the reproaches and ill-treatment of your masters. You are anxious to become more Christ-like every day; then make your profit of every opportunity sent you. It is a necessity for you to have that well-grounded humility which will enable you to amass daily and hourly great treasures of patience. Imitate, therefore, the thrift of the peddler on the street, or the shopkeeper behind his counter. What cares either of them for the quality or rank of the passers-by or the customers who come and go, provided these pay their money for what they buy, and thus increase the gains of the seller?

"A true lover of Jesus," wrote an English priest, dead in 1395, "when he suffereth harm from his neighbor is so strengthened through grace of the Holy Ghost, and is made so humble, so patient, so peaceable, and that so really, that what harm or wrong soever he suffereth from his neighbor, he still preserveth his humility, he despiseth him not, he judgeth him not, but he prayeth for him in his heart, and hath pity and compassion on him much more tenderly than of another man who never did him harm; and verily loveth him better, and more fervently desireth the salvation of his soul, because he seeth that he shall have so much spiritual profit out of that evil deed of that man though it be against his will. But this love and this meekness is wrought only by the Holy Ghost above the nature of man in them whom he maketh the true lovers of Jesus."[96]

True Fidelity Begotten of True Humility.

This uncomplaining subjection to your masters, founded on the love of the Crucified, and practiced in order to become in all things most like to our Model, cannot fail to inspire love as well as reverence for those to whom you

---

[96] Walter Hilton, "The Scale of Perfection."

owe obedience. "Whatsoever you do, do it from the heart, as to the Lord and not to men... Serve ye the Lord Christ." Such is the rule laid down by St. Paul.

Serve your masters, then, as you would Christ himself. Make all their interests your own. Be as saving of their substance as if it belonged to Christ, and you had a strict account to render to him, at the end of each day, of the employment of every moment of your time and the use made of every thing intrusted to you.

This conscientious fidelity, must always recall to your mind that you are not to lose or to waste; and, particularly that you are not to give away any thing whatsoever, without your master or mistress's knowledge and consent.

Stewards in great families are intrusted with purchasing and buying much;—they are in conscience bound to consult their master's interest in every outlay, and to do nothing through favor or human respect which would bring loss to those whom they serve.

And a cook or kitchen-maid has a like responsibility: she can only make such use of what is intrusted to her as her mistress wishes. But we are touching here on a point which most concerns the good name of all servant girls. We beseech them, therefore, as they love their own honor, to weigh well the advice here given.

Honesty One Characteristic of Fidelity.

It is a cardinal principle that we cannot dispose of what is not our own without injustice or wrong to the owner. No matter how praiseworthy a thing it may be to give to the poor, or to be generous to the Church or to charitable institutions, we must not presume to think that we have a right to feed or to clothe the poor with what is another person's, or that God will reward us for giving to religion or religious institutions what we cannot give without positive sin. I have no right to put my hand in another man's pocket, or in his purse, wherever I may find it, and make myself charitable or generous at his expense. What I thus take and give away I am bound in conscience to restore.

To be sure there may be poverty and want all around you, and your heart may be sorely touched by the misery you see, or think you see, in those who knock at your master's door for assistance. But you are not obliged to give alms for him; you can only dispense in charity at the door whatever your master or mistress places at your disposal. Like St. Zita, you can give your own food or a portion of it, but this is what many, very many can ill afford to do,—as their own pittance is barely sufficient for their sustenance. In no case can they go to the provision closet, and, against their master or mistress's will, take from it wherewith to help either the beggar at the door, or the needy among their own acquaintance. This would be simply stealing.

There is only one thing for you to do: have a perfectly clear and thorough understanding with your mistress about what you can or cannot give, as well as about the use to which all articles of food in your charge are to be put. A mistress may not be charitable or generous either to the poor or to her own servants. But, so long as you are in her household, you have only to be true to God, to your own conscience;—to be faithful to your trust, and never,—no, not in the most trifling matter,—to be dishonest under pretext of being charitable, or kind-hearted, or generous.

Faithfulness in Not Disclosing Family Secrets.

This is still more important than honesty. For the honor and good name of a family are of infinitely more importance than the gold and silver in their treasure chest, or the silks and jewels in their wardrobe. We can put back what we have wrongfully taken or given away,—and yet how hard do we find it to make this restitution? and how many fail in this obligation? But the wrong often done to a family's honor by rashly or criminally declaring what may turn to their disgrace in the public estimation, is a thing which can seldom if ever be repaired.

When you are admitted into a family as a servant, consider yourself, in the eyes of God, as a member of that family, and be as careful of its secrets—even in speaking to your fellow-servants,—as you would be of those of your own father and mother; guard its honor, and defend it as jealously as you would the honor of the mother who bore you. Nay,—that you may look higher than mere nature,—look upon the family as God's own household, in which you serve; and in promoting its interests, and protecting its good name, bethink you it is to the Divine Majesty you are doing service.

These were the rules and the sentiments familiar to those of your condition in the Ages of Faith; they are the sentiments and the rules of the Church.

Remember,—especially in a country which is not Catholic,—that your fidelity and honesty redound to the credit of your religion, just as surely as your untruthfulness and your dishonesty redound to its disgrace.

So is it with another virtue closely allied to fidelity,—

Truthfulness.

It is said of that "cloud of witnesses" into whose company we introduced you at the beginning of this chapter,—of St. Zita, and St. Margaret of Louvain, and that glorious virgin-band who attend the footsteps of the Lamb in heaven and on earth,—"In their mouth was found no lie; for they are without spot before the throne of God."[97] This was the beautiful description of the Christian maiden given us by the inspired pen of the virgin-apostle, so dear to the Master, and who had alone of all the Twelve followed Him to the very foot of the Cross: Their mouth never uttered a lie, their purity was as stainless as the new-fallen snow on the mountain-top,—unblemished chastity and unimpeachable truthfulness! What a mirror for the children of God through all time!

Hence it is that the other great apostle—"the Chosen Vessel"—Paul, wrote: "Walk ye as the children of the light: for the fruit of the light is in all goodness, and justice, and truth."[98]

Were this book to produce no other benefit to souls, than to inspire you, O daughters of the Great Mother,—"the Pillar and the Ground of Truth,"—with the firm determination to cultivate this one virtue as if your happiness here, and your salvation hereafter depended solely on your truthfulness,—it would be a most blessed result to our painstaking. Never, then,—we beseech you,—leave it in the power of man, woman, or child, or even of the angel who watches over your soul—to accuse you of telling a lie, or prevaricating in the slightest degree or the most trifling matter.

With the great St. Francis of Sales, you must be ever able to say that no earthly love, or hope, or fear could even make you carry a falsehood on your lips any more than a forged paper in your bosom. You, too, should ever say with this great Doctor of the Church:

---

[97] Apocalypse xiv. 5.

[98] Ephesians v. 8, 9.

"I belong to the blood of the ancient Gauls. What is on my tongue is precisely what comes from my heart. The prudence of the world, and the artifices of the flesh belong to the children of the world; but the children of God have no double meaning and no dissimulation."

As true religion would be only a living lie without true charity in our practice, so you must, as you hope for God's favorable judgment, make it a chief study to cultivate peace and charity among your fellow-servants.

It is always our interest, and should be our policy to be on good terms with all those in whose company we are obliged to live for any length of time. It is a poor excuse to say that they are disagreeable and distasteful to us. There never yet existed a family in which parents, children, and servants were exactly of the same amiable disposition. The practice of charity, of the home charities in particular,—is only so praiseworthy, so meritorious, and so richly rewarded by the Master, because it consists in bearing with each other's infirmities.

St. Paul addressed ta the Gauls of Asia Minor,—the first known converts from among the great Celtic race, the following brief admonitions: "By charity of the Spirit serve one another;"[99] and "Bear ye one another's burdens; and so shall you fulfil the law of Christ."[100]

Charity Toward Persons of Another Belief.

Living, as you are often forced to do, in families professing a creed different from your own, and, not unfrequently, bitterly hostile to it,—there are two things you must heed. Judge them kindly, and show them all the respect and fidelity which you would to masters of your own faith. In this respect, your duties toward them are absolutely the same. Be patient toward them when they assail or ridicule your religion: when this happens,—your only resource lies in making no answer whatever, and in not manifesting anger or resentment. Your edifying conduct will be the most effectual means of dispelling their prejudices,—prejudices which are those of birth and education.

The other precaution is,—never to permit yourself to excuse or extenuate what they blame or ridicule. You are not expected to know history or theology,

---

[99] Galatians v. 23.

[100] *Ibidem*, vi. 2.

or to give explanation about things far above the common intelligence. But be not ashamed of the truth which is in you, and never blush for that Great Church who is the only Mother of Christendom, and whose authority can alone restore the Christian religion to its old-time supremacy over the minds and hearts of men.

Thereby, you will be true to the Truth itself—the servants of God and his Truth.

Of the innumerable and inestimable services rendered to His cause,—the cause of that same Truth,—by servant girls in our day, more than one chapter and more than one book might be written. There is nothing so eloquent, so irresistible as such a life as that of Saint Zita, or Saint Margaret, or any one of the host of illustrious women who have sanctified themselves in the lowly position of servants, and have thus shown that it is not the place which makes the great-souled man or woman, but true greatness of soul that ennobles and hallows the place.

CHAPTER XXII.

SUPPLEMENTARY.

As we began this book by the description of the home and its sanctities, so do we now return to it before concluding, to point out two of the most precious and meritorious forms of motherly devotion,—in the person of the invalid mother, whom God keeps on her bed of sickness, for years, like a living lesson of heroism in suffering, and the stepmother who takes on herself the painful and difficult duties of motherhood toward the children of another. There are so many of both of these classes to be found in Christian homes,—women of angelic lives, models of perfect patience and long-suffering meekness! Let the lessons their examples teach us thus complete the entire circle of home-duties and home-virtues.

The Invalid Mother.

A young married woman of uncommon beauty and accomplishments, extensively known for her successful activity in every cause of public beneficence or usefulness, was paralyzed a few months after the birth of her sixth child. She was the idol of her household and her large circle of acquaintance. For she had the rare, rare felicity of creating neither envy nor jealousy by all her shining qualities, and by her untiring labors outside of her own home. She had, in the truest sense of the word, educated her husband, whose mind and heart, both very richly endowed, had been neglected in consequence of the early death of his mother; she had spurred him on to be foremost in his profession, and he was almost at its head, when this terrible affliction befell them; and she had made him a sincere and practical Christian. She would allow no one to teach her little children but herself,—and her training of them proved that she was just as admirable in imparting knowledge as she was in her facility for acquiring it. She had three sisters-in-law in the house, one her equal in years, and the two others her juniors; she had taught and trained them, making them adore her first, and then inspiring them with a keen appetite for knowledge. And she had made it a duty she never neglected, from the very first day she entered her husband's home, to catechize her numerous servants, teaching such of them as did not know their letters, reading, writing, and arithmetic.

And most touching it was to see the grief and consternation of these good servants, when it was first announced that their worshiped mistress was in imminent danger of death. The coachman who was sent in haste for the priest—a great, burly old cavalry-man, who had seen twenty battles—could scarcely tell his message intelligibly, and wept all the way back to the house. The rest of the servants were in the hall reciting, as best they could, the Litany of the Saints. The little patient herself and her noble husband were worthy of each other,—he holding her hand and whispering sweet words of comfort and resignation to the Divine Will. But God spared that precious life for ten years more. The use of her lower limbs, however, she never recovered.

But—as her husband afterward testified—never once in their most unreserved intimacy, did she express the faintest regret at being thus rendered inactive and helpless in the very prime of all her glorious utility. She would repeat continually, that this was God's crowning mercy to her, the pledge of her predestination, her being thus nailed to her cross with her dear Lord. All her prayers were said, all her daily actions performed during these ten years in thanksgiving for this most precious boon of suffering.

Nor did she, so far as her physician permitted, and when her recovered strength allowed her, give over to others the care of instructing her children, or of finishing the education of her younger sister-in-law. Nor did she discontinue her efforts to benefit the poor of the city and neighborhood, or to encourage every project in favor of religion. From her sick-bed she still directed all her former fellow-laborers who more than ever revered her and followed her counsels.

But who can speak worthily of the devoted care of every individual in that household for one so unselfish as was their beloved invalid? Her sisters, her children, her servants all vied with each other in their ardent desire to do her every service her condition required. They could scarcely endure to see any, even among her near relatives, allowed the privilege of waiting on her during her long nights of torture. For the last eighteen months of her life were one long agony. Life seemed to retreat slowly from one member to another, till she could move nothing but her head; but there the sweet soul dwelt serene to the end, like the mistress of an inundated house, as the destroying waters rise steadily around her, finds her last refuge on the rooftop,—there, with cheerful countenance and brave, loving words, consoling her dear ones while all is slowly undermined and swept away beneath her.

It was, indeed, a privilege to listen to the inspired words about God, and duty, and bearing the cross after Christ, and the glories of the everlasting kingdom, that she poured forth unceasingly to all who approached her; it was like a lesson from the "Imitation of Christ" to look for a few moments on that pale, sweet face all aglow with the light and love of the world into which she seemed to have entered... And when all was over, and the patient sufferer was at rest forever, the noble husband arose from his knees, and with uplifted arms, as if he too would follow his beloved companion, exclaimed, "I thank thee, O my God! the lessons of such a life and such a death are to me and mine the most precious of all thy favors!" And forthwith he made all present unite with him in singing the *Te Deum*.

How many such mothers are to be found in families of all classes, and what beautiful examples of filial piety, and unwearied devotedness on the part of families—even the poorest and most sadly burdened—could we not relate, were it not that we are warned to bring these teachings to a timely conclusion!

The Stepmother.

We must not part with this most worshipful embodiment of human goodness,—the true mother,—the queen and idol of the home, without doing reverence to another figure, often called by death and necessity to fill the mother's place in the household, and to discharge toward her orphans the sacred obligations attached to the place of parent.

If there is any thing on earth which can compensate a child for the loss of a mother at that age when the inspired love of a true motherly heart can read clearly the instincts of the childish soul, and when her firm and tender hand is so needed to unfold what is good and repress what is evil—that compensation can only be found in the womanly wisdom and devotion of a second mother—of her whom the world outside the family designate as stepmother.

Bad stepmothers are the exceptions to the generality of devoted, conscientious, and self-sacrificing women, who are selected by widowed fathers, with a fond parental solicitude, to be true mothers to their orphaned children. Need we speak here of the sore necessity which so often compels a father, in whose soul the dead still lives and is loved with an enduring love, to choose a second mother for his children, a mistress for his household? Even among the upper and wealthy classes, where so many means can be devised for obtaining persons to educate young orphans, there is often a peremptory reason for a second marriage. But among the laboring classes this necessity is far otherwise urgent and frequent. So, glancing merely at the reasons which justify the best of parents in contracting an alliance which is repugnant to their own finest sense, and without even naming such causes, we proceed to plead in favor of the stepmother, before describing her duties.

What Makes a Stepmother's Position Irksome.

In ninety-nine cases out of a hundred, the relatives of a deceased wife, even when they are good and virtuous people, look with coldness or aversion on the woman who takes the place of mother toward the children of their lost daughter and sister. And it is almost impossible, if the orphans are of an age to understand the difference between a mother and a stepmother, that they should not be made to show these unkindly feelings. The lot of a stepmother is, therefore, not an enviable one. And where she is a person who accepts the position and its responsibilities with the firm purpose of doing, to the very best of her power, a true mother's part, she is most deserving of sympathy, support, and unlimited Kindness.

It is most certainly the duty of the deceased wife's family, instead of putting an obstacle in the way of her successor, to aid her, on the contrary, toward the discharge of her difficult and delicate office. It is their duty, because the dearest interests of the orphans themselves are involved in the education their second mother will give them. It would seem, then, that every possible consideration of charity and self-interest ought to induce both the father's relatives and those of his deceased wife to join hands in making the new mistress of the home welcome, cordially welcome; and in aiding her by every demonstration of good will and affection to be, as she purposes, a loving mother to the children she takes to her heart to cherish and to rear.

Instead of doing what nature and common sense would point out, as the only judicious and beneficial course to follow, motives of sordid interest upset both the judgment and the conscience even among good Christian folk. Thus a serious responsibility is incurred through criminal and unwarrantable meddlesomeness, the education of the orphans and the happiness of their home are forever compromised.

This, however, is taking things at their worst. For the stepmother herself we have none but words of encouragement, if she be only bent on doing her duty thoroughly. She must make her husband feel that she has most truly adopted his children as her own. He soon discovers whether her love is a true one or not. Nor will his children be long in finding out whether or not the heart to which they are pressed beats with a genuine motherly tenderness for them. The eyes of children are very wise. They look into yours with a penetrating and steadfast gaze which is like the sounding-rod dropped down into the dark, deep waters and bringing up with it the secrets of the ocean-bed. You cannot conceal from these innocent but infallible eyes the secret of your inmost soul. They read you through and through in a marvelously brief space of time.

Begin by Loving Your Husband's Children as Your Own.

This is God's will in your regard; all His graces will aid you toward this most necessary and blissful result. Resolve, in your heart of hearts, that you will be obedient to Him in this, and devote henceforward your whole energy to its attainment. Shall we recommend one practice of piety to you, and beseech you to be earnest and faithful in its fulfillment? From the day you take possession of your new home make a league with its guardian angels, and take them as your helpers, your counselors, companions, and friends in the difficult task of discharging your motherly duties. This will be all the more necessary for you, if you find that there are evil influences at work to wean your children's hearts from you. Here is what we recommend in imitation of that wonderful man, the

Blessed Peter Favre, one of the lights of the 16th century, whom popes and saints revered during his lifetime as a man filled with the Holy Spirit.

Whenever he spent even a single night in a new house, it was his custom on crossing the threshold silently to invoke the assistance of the angels to whose care it was committed, and, on being shown into the apartment prepared for himself, he would close the door, and kneel successively in each corner, beseeching the Divine Majesty to grant him the special protection of the spirits of light and to drive away the spirits of darkness. Then, after reciting prayers to the guardian angels, he would sprinkle holy water over the room.

This is not superstition, but enlightened Catholic devotion. For the more we study divine things, the more light we obtain on the relations between this outward world we see and touch and the invisible and spiritual world, the more does the presence of these spirits, good and evil, become an ever-present reality to us. Like Elisæus and his servant, our eyes are opened to see the earth and the mountains round about covered with horsemen and chariots of fire, God's faithful host sent to protect those who do his work, and, though we may be appalled sometimes by the numbers and might of his enemies, we shall feel like the great Hebrew prophet that there are more with us than against us.

You are a Christian woman;—you must be a supernatural woman. You will have evil passions, earthly interests and feelings, and the malignant influences of the fallen angels to counteract; but you will have on your side God and his angels;—you will have the love, the veneration, the unbounded confidence of your husband. You will also have the pure and devoted love of his children; for true love cannot help being loved in return. But all this must be the result of your own supernatural devotion and piety.

Conclusion.

And so we are still before the CHRISTIAN HOME,—with the hosts of the guardian spirits camped round about, visible to the eye of our soul, like the lights of a great city seen through a mist from an overhanging mountain. Here are mothers, worthy of being on earth the living images of God's unsleeping watchfulness and unfathomable tenderness; daughters formed to their mother's perfect likeness, all innocence, self-denial, and unsparing devotion to the happiness of others; sons worthy to be the unselfish servants of such mothers and such sisters, trained to be the fearless and spotless knights of Truth and Justice in the evil days, and the promoters of all true liberty and progress in the peaceful days,—at all times the true sons of God; the vast armies of the daughters of toil, each bearing on her forehead the sign of Christ, each keeping her eyes fixed on Him whose whole life was labor, and crucifixion, and a martyrdom;—and above all this vast and glorious array,—the Heavens opened as in the vision of the great Patriarch, a pathway, like a far-stretching flight of shining steps ascending from earth to the City of God on high, the wide gates thrown open, angels of light ever moving along them in their brotherly ministration, and the Eternal God and Father of all amid the myriads of angels and saints, bending down to us with outstretched arms and radiant countenance,—while these words fall upon our ears and sink into our souls, like sounds of divinest music on the hushed waters:

"Blessed are the Poor!... Blessed are the meek!... Blessed are they that mourn!... Blessed are they that hunger and thirst after justice!... Blessed are the merciful!... Blessed are the clean of heart!... Blessed are the peace-makers!... Blessed are they that suffer persecution!... Be glad and rejoice, for your reward is very great in Heaven!"...

www.ingramcontent.com/pod-product-compliance
Lightning Source LLC
Chambersburg PA
CBHW031928110726
47902CB00001B/93

9781396318719